The World in Depression

The World in Depression
1929–1939

Charles P. Kindleberger

REVISED AND
ENLARGED EDITION

University of California Press
Berkeley   Los Angeles   London

History of the World Economy in the Twentieth Century
Volume 4

University of California Press
Berkeley and Los Angeles, California

University of California Press, Ltd.
London, England

Library of Congress Cataloging in Publication Data

Kindleberger, Charles Poor, 1910–
    The world in depression, 1929–1939.

    (History of the world economy in the twentieth
century; v. 4)
    Bibliography: p.
    Includes index.
    1. Depressions—1929.   2. Economic history—1918–1945.
I. Title.   II. Series.
HB3717 1929.K55   1986   338.5'42   85–8662
ISBN 0–520–05591–8 (alk. paper)
ISBN 0–520–05592–6 (pbk.: alk. paper)

Printed in the United States of America

 2 3 4 5 6 7 8 9

To the memory of E.C.K.

Contents

Text Figures

Tables

Preface to the
Revised Edition

Putting out a new edition of this book was my idea, not that of the publisher. Since it was first written thirteen years ago, the literature on the subject has grown substantially. I have learned a great deal from that literature, even though I resist changing most of my idiosyncratic views. I have also extended my knowledge in two principal directions by participating in two recent symposiums, one on the relationships between banks and industry in the 1930s, organized in 1981 by Gianni Toniolo, the second on the economic experience of Latin America in the 1930s, convened in 1982 by Rosemary Thorp.

Part of my interest in revision is to respond to those who doubt the merit of my thesis. Some are monetarists, whose most recent expression is by Roland Vaubel.[1] Others are Keynesians, such as Donald Moggridge, who believe that the Great Depression of the 1930s required much deeper therapy than my prescription offers—something more nearly on the order of the Marshall Plan.[2] I hope to be able to proceed in this discussion without polemics and without claiming to know more than is knowable.

1. Roland Vaubel, "International Debt, Bank Failures and the Money Supply: The Thirties and the Eighties," 1984.
2. D. E. Moggridge, "Policy in the Crises of 1920 and 1929," 1982.

My real purpose, related to the foregoing, is, I suppose, an evangelical one. I have failed to persuade large numbers of scholars that the depression was a worldwide phenomenon in origin and interaction rather than an American recession that, extended by policy errors on the part of the Federal Reserve System into a U.S. depression, spilled abroad. I apply to the 1930s the judgment of Robin Matthews on the world depression of a century earlier that "it is futile to try to draw any hard-and-fast line assigning to either [any] country causal primacy in the cycle as a whole or in its individual phases."[3] Monetarists, to be sure, have added one international aspect to their explanation of the depression: the Smoot-Hawley tariff, assumed to be contractionary when the usual macroeconomic models regard tariffs as expansionary, unless, of course, they give rise to retaliation through tariffs and import quotas abroad.[4]

Other themes of the original book have been ignored rather than refuted. These include the importance of the liquidity squeeze caused by the stock market collapse of October 1929 for commodity prices, which dropped worldwide by 12 to 20 percent in the year from August 1929 to August 1930; the importance of irreversible price declines for bank failures; the deflationary impact on the United States, Germany, and the gold bloc of the sharp depreciation of the pound sterling (causing appreciation of the dollar, the Reichsmark, and the gold currencies) by 30 percent from September to December 1931.

I hope to persuade that it is a grievous mistake to regard the depression as a single phenomenon or as an ordinary recession that escalated into a major depression mainly because of mistakes on the part of U.S. monetary authorities. One explanation is needed for 1929–30, which was much more than an ordinary recession, another for the years from 1931 to 1933. Most monetarists compare the monetary stock with real national income in the United States using 1929 to 1933 as a single period, but a very different impression is conveyed when it is noted that between 1929 and 1930 real income fell 10 percent, prices 12 percent, and money only 5 per-

3. R. C. O. Matthews, *A Study in Trade-Cycle History: Economic Fluctuations in Great Britain, 1832–1842*, 1954, p. 69.
4. See various authors in Karl Brunner, ed., *The Great Depression Revisited*, 1981, esp. Anna J. Schwartz, p. 22; Robert J. Gordon and James A. Wilcox, pp. 80–83; and Allan H. Meltzer, p. 158.

cent. Real money—the nominal amount divided by wholesale prices—actually rose in this period. All this does not mean, however, that one has to be a Keynesian for 1929 and 1930—one who believes that the setback in output and income came mainly from shifts in spending (for example, by consumers on housing and automobiles). I regard these explanations, like those of the monetarists, as too simple for a complex world. My explanation for 1929 and 1930 is financial but not monetarist, in the sense of being closely tied to the quantity of money.

It is healthy to confess that I have been unable to resolve completely a number of historical puzzles:

(1) My account of 1929-30 relies heavily on the liquidity squeeze coming from the stock market crash, which led to a sharp fall in the prices of commodities and most assets, with ultimate repercussions that led to bank failures. The question remains why a similar collapse of commodity prices in 1920–21 did not lead to bank failures and an extended depression. One can adduce a series of explanations. None is wholly persuasive.

(2) The Moggridge point that structural adjustment and not simply a lender of last resort was called for in the world economy, especially in the financial collapse of 1931, is impossible to prove either way. I believe that if the runs on Austria, Germany, and Britain had been halted by timely international help on a massive scale, the basic recuperative powers of competitive markets would have prevented the depression from going on so long and so deep. This is assertion, not demonstration, however, and Moggridge's alternative view merits respect.

(3) Sterling depreciation in September 1931, the book claims, failed to raise prices in Britain but drove them sharply lower in nonsterling areas, notably the United States and the gold bloc, less so in Germany, which was beginning to fence itself off by restrictions. In 1933, however, when the dollar was depreciated, prices rose in the United States and remained stable abroad. The difference was critical for world recovery. No obvious explanation for the difference between the episodes comes to mind.

In what follows, I retain the preface to the 1973 edition for what it may be worth, including the gist of an early paragraph that was cut out at the last minute on the basis of advice from a colleague that I now regard as misguided. The rest of the book is treated in the same way, with material and analysis added, little excised, except the numbers underlying some of the text figures that I now believe superfluous. The result is a fatter book. I hope it is a better one.

Preface to the
First Edition

"This is where I came in." When Dr. Wolfram Fischer asked me to write on the world economic history of the 1930s, I was delighted to comply. This was partly because of the surging intellectual interest in the world depression, which may be encountered among scholars everywhere. It was also partly to work out for myself the complex events of my youth and early professional life: events which brought me and many others into economics.

I start with March 1928 and the original four-million-share days in the New York stock market. I had left my suburb outside New York City to attend a secondary school in another state, but in late February 1928 the school was struck by an epidemic of pneumonia from which, in the days before antibiotics, three boys died. The rest of us were sent home for a period that lasted three weeks. There was nothing for me to do in Flushing: my friends were either away at other schools or locked up all day in the local high school. My father suggested that I get a job as a "runner," or office boy, in the Wall Street brokerage house with which he dealt. The recollection of my weekly pay has faded, perhaps $10 or $12, from which had to be subtracted daily 33 cents for the Long Island Railroad and 5 cents for the subway, each way. But the boom in the market and new highs in shares traded spilled over into higher take-home pay. When the office worked after 6 o'clock, as it did each day of my two-week stay to keep up with the back-office paperwork, we got $1 supper money. One could delay supper until one got home and have the money free and clear, or one could have a quite adequate supper for perhaps 40 cents and keep the rest.

Of those two weeks I vividly remember carrying daily a check for $1 million in my pocket to the National City Bank, as it then was known, to pay off the daily broker's loan. In the fifty-six years since then I have not handled a check for a similar amount.

The October 1929 crash of the stock market strikes no chords in my memory. With the rest of the world I was aware of it, but to a sophomore in college it meant little. The family's few stocks were owned outright rather than on margin. Despite the decline of business, and with the help of an uncle in shipping, I got a job the next summer working on a freighter delivering heavy equipment from Copenhagen to Leningrad and bringing back woodpulp from Kotka, Raumo, and Kemi in Finland. I don't think this was ordinary dumping, but I don't know. It was not the kind of exchange dumping that occurred after 1932 and is discussed in Chapter 8. It was memorable mainly for the fact that one could drink beer and spirits against one's pay after the ship reached Copenhagen. (My wages as a deck boy were $20 a month.) The trip cultivated an interest in international trade and a taste for Tuborg beer that have lasted all my life. (A friend of mine got a job working on ships in 1940 through his uncle. The uncle who helped me was a vice-president of a shipping company; his was vice-president of a seamen's union. Nepotism continued through the 1930s, but its locus shifted.)

Falling family income was still sufficient to pay both college expenses and my fare to Europe in the summer of 1931 to take advantage of a summer scholarship to the Students International Union. Salvador de Madariaga, who normally ran the seminar, had just been appointed ambassador to the United States from Spain, so we undergraduates from the United States and Europe were thrown in with older students at the Geneva School for International Studies, run by Professor (later Sir) Alfred Zimmern. It was an exciting experience, from the visiting lecturers to the farewells for Patrick Sloan at the end of the summer as he made his way, equipped with stacks of toilet paper and needles, to spend a year in the Soviet Union.

I cannot say, however, that I formed a very clear idea of the events described in Chapter 7. I have run across a notebook I kept that summer, which records lectures by Paul Douglas, E. M. Patterson from the United States, Maurice Bonn, Henri Hauser, Douglas Copland, and a host of others. There is even an outline of a seminar I myself gave in the economics group, entitled "Economic Conditions in the United States." None of these scribbles were helpful in what follows. I was aware of the Bank for International Settlements mainly because of a young employee who came down frequently from Basel to court one of the delightful Smith girls among the American colony in Geneva.

In February 1932, after graduating from college, I had the strengthening experience of being unemployed, but only for a limited period of eight or ten weeks. Again through influence I got a job as an office boy (complete with B.A. honors and a Phi Beta Kappa key) in what I am now, as a Keynesian, ashamed to reveal was the National Economy League, a pressure group founded by Archibald Roosevelt and other conservatives to insist on balancing the national budget. In July 1932, again through nepotism, I obtained another job as office boy with Johnson & Higgins, marine insurance brokers. The two memorable incidents of the next year in that capacity included the increase in first-class postage from 2 cents to 3 cents, which induced the firm to shift its downtown Manhattan communication system from the U.S. Post Office to its own staff (it was my first and painful acquaintance with an elastic demand schedule); and a slip of paper from the office manager stating that because of NRA (the National Recovery Administration)— and, I could read between the lines, "for no other reason"—my salary would be increased from $12 to $15 a week.

By February 1933 I had arranged to study graduate economics at Columbia University the following autumn. As an introduction, I took an evening course in money and banking from Ralph W. Robey, the financial editor of the *New York Evening Post*. In the early weeks of February and March 1933 he regaled the class with day-to-day accounts of the collapse of the American banking system, which made economics as exciting as *The Perils of Pauline*.

By some intellectual process that I cannot reconstruct, a term paper in the autumn term of 1933–34 in a class on international banking lit on the topic of competitive exchange depreciation between Denmark and New Zealand. Professor Benjamin H. Beckhart encouraged me to revise it for publication, and a reference to this, my professional baptism, may be found in Chapter 8. The early prejudice against flexible exchange rates remains.

After finishing class work and making a start on the dissertation in June 1936, I went to work in the International Research Division of the U.S. Treasury, under Harry D. White and Frank V. Coe, calculating purchasing power parities for various currencies, especially including those of the gold bloc. This was a temporary position; a permanent one opened up at the Federal Reserve Bank of New York on October 1, 1936. I was paid $200 a month in each job, or $2,400 a year. Mr. White asked me whether I would consider staying on at the Treasury. I allowed that I would be willing to consider an offer of a P-2 rating—professionals being rated on a scale from P-1 to P-6—which paid $2,600 a year. He regarded this as excessive, and I moved on, going to work in New York on October 1, 1936, four days after the formation of the Tripartite Monetary Agreement of September 26.

At the Federal Reserve Bank of New York I analyzed events in European economies and the New York exchange market, going through the gold scare of April 1937 and the dollar scare that followed in the autumn. In February 1939, before Hitler's march into Prague, I agreed to go the Bank for International Settlements in the summer. With the help of friends at the Board of Governors of the Federal Reserve System, I was called home after the fall of Paris in June 1940.

All this interests me far more than it will the reader, but it explains that this is where I came into economics and the extent to which this book is *recherche du temps perdu*. Perhaps more than the biases of youthful experience, however, the book reflects the intellectual idiosyncrasies developed during a score of years spent teaching after the war. The reader is duly warned against both sources of distortion.

Commissioned to be about the 1930s, the book concerns the world economy in depression. It is written from an American point of view, insofar as that is inescapable. I have used where I could materials from Europe, but there is not much about the Soviet Union and Asia. The picture is distorted on these accounts, but one should not pretend to know what one does not know.

I am also conscious that there is little of the social, political, and personal drama with which the depression is rife or fraught and which has been brought out in recent books by Studs Terkel, John Brooks, and Kenneth Galbraith. In reviewing a book in economic history using econometric methods, I once said I missed the sweat of the men handling the cotton and the sea chanties of the men aboard the ships. This book is short on colorful anecdotes on stockbrokers or applesellers beyond the autobiographical notes above. Neither is it econometric in the manner of the new economic history that tries to prove hypotheses rigorously with multiple regressions of lagged variables. It is history with a narrative, instead of tables of R squares, Durbin-Watson tests, and the like. So much the worse for it.

Finally, by way of apology, I find the key to why the depression was so wide, so deep, and so long in my speciality, the international monetary mechanism. This should surprise no one.

As a nonhistorian I have accumulated a series of debts to the profession and to those, like me, who are on its fringes. I am deeply impressed by the hospitality of the historical profession to outsiders, offering them help rather than protecting jurisdictional boundaries. First and foremost, I should like to thank D. E. Moggridge of Clare College, Cambridge, and Peter Temin, my colleague at MIT. Both read the manuscript with care and divided by specialization in improving it. Temin asked the big searching questions about proof and demonstration. Moggridge went way beyond the call of duty in calling attention to other evidence, questioning interpretations, and especially digging in the public records to provide additional material on a number of points on which the evidence was scanty.

If Moggridge and Temin belong in a noncompeting group, the list of my other intellectual creditors is given alphabetically to avoid invidious and impossible distinctions. Professor Lester V. Chandler of Princeton and Atlanta universities started me in business with a mountain of carbons of his notes from the Federal Reserve Bank of New York files and has been provocative and suggestive in a number of discussions. Stephen V. O. Clarke of the Federal Reserve Bank of New York read the manuscript and provided much useful comment and, additionally, has searched the bank's files on several points. Professor Heywood Fleisig of Cornell University, who is also working on the depression, shared with me his dissertation before publication and another important paper in draft and corrected an important error in my manuscript. George Garvy, vice-president of the Federal Reserve Bank of New York, drew my attention to the work of Woytinsky in seeking to promote public works in Germany in 1931 and 1932 and lent me the bank's copy of Grotkopp's *Die grosse Krise* before I obtained one of my own. Closely allied to the same subject, Professor Alexander Gerschenkron of Harvard University insisted on the importance of the expansionary ideas of Wilhelm Lautenbach, an Oberregierungsrat in the German Economics Ministry in 1930 and 1931.

Dr. Helen Hughes, now of the International Bank for Reconstruction and Development, was kind enough to lend me two draft chapters of her unpublished economic history of Australia. Professor Ryutaro Komiya at my request dug about in Japanese sources to try to find the answer to the riddle as to how Japan produced Keynesian policies as early as 1932 without a Keynes. Professor Peter H. Lindert of the University of Wisconsin commented on the first draft with incisiveness. James R. Moore, a graduate student at the State University of New York in Stony Brook, writing a dissertation on the World Economic Conference of 1933, was kind enough to furnish me with a bibliography of sources consulted by real historians. Professor Adolf Sturmthal of the University of Illinois provided fascinating material on the antipathy of Marxists in Germany to exchange devaluation.

The production process of a book of this sort also involves trying out various ideas in seminars and lectures. This I have done at the University of Alabama, the Cambridge Economic History group, Columbia University, and Cornell University and as a participant in discussion groups in the Council on Foreign Relations, the Institute of World Affairs at Salisbury, Connecticut (successor to the Students International Union of 1931), and the New York Metropolitan Economists group. The interchanges and discussions on these occasions, in which some of those named above took part, have been highly stimulating and suggestive.

Harvard University has hit on the generous courtesy of allowing neighboring scholars access to the bountiful stacks of the Widener Library free of charge for a month each year. I have availed myself twice of this valued privilege and am grateful to the university and to the librarian. If I occasionally consort with the rich library up the street, however, it does not mean that I am not devoted and faithful to the Dewey Library of MIT. Its friendliness and eagerness to help almost make up for the gaps in the collection, and I continue to be grateful to Barbara Klingenhagen, William Presson, and the others.

Mary Ann Reardon, now Mrs. Baily, assisted me in the early summer of 1970 by ferreting out piles of statistics, many more than I could use. Anne Pope distinguished herself in organizing all and undertaking much of the typing of the first draft. The final draft was produced by another old-timer, like Miss Klingenhagen and me, Mrs. Inez Crandall, now retired, who was a departmental secretary at MIT for some twenty years.

The book is dedicated to the memory of my father, E. Crosby Kindleberger, who struggled with great courage against a physical handicap and against the Great Depression.

1

Introduction

(It seems odd, fifty years after the event, that economists still do not understand, or at least cannot agree on, the world depression of the 1930s.)That disagreement has been registered often, but nowhere as succinctly as in the fall 1979 fiftieth anniversary issue of the *Journal of Portfolio Management*, entitled "The Great Crash: Causes, Consequences, Relevance."[1] The first three pieces on the crash, ordered, the editor states, by lot, are by Paul Samuelson, me, and Milton and Rose D. Friedman. These authors disagree fundamentally. Samuelson suggests in a witty piece that most of the work on the crash and depression deals with myth. He remains "eclectic" and holds that the Great Crash of 1929 was one of several important and somewhat "fortuitous" factors that reflected and intensified the Great Depression.[2] The Friedmans find nothing accidental in the depression, though they consider the Great Crash itself unimportant in what happened later. According to them, and to Milton Friedman in other writings, especially his and Anna Jacobson Schwartz's magisterial *A Monetary History of the United States, 1867–1960*,[3]

1. Vol. 6, no. 1.
2. Paul A. Samuelson, "Myths and Realities about the Crash and Depression," 1979.
3. Milton Friedman and Rose D. Friedman, "The Anatomy of Crisis . . . and the Failure of Policy," 1979.

(the depression was caused by U.S. monetary policy)[4] Only my essay suggested that (the depression was rooted in a complex systematic set of causes, international in scope and partly monetary or at least financial.[5])

Samuelson's emphasis on the fortuitous character of the depression is not entirely satisfactory. Financial crises have occurred with great regularity, or at least they did in the nineteenth century and prior to the end of the Second World War: 1816, 1825, 1836, 1847, 1857, 1866, 1873, 1890, 1907, 1921, 1929, 1937.[6] A number of these turned into great depressions. The great depression of 1873 to 1896, sometimes regarded by economic historians as *the* great depression, was perhaps different in origin, characteristics, and effects, so that on these scores one can regard the period from 1929 to 1939 as unique.[7] Going further back, however, produces the uniformities that the social scientist searches for. Like the First World War, the Napoleonic Wars were followed by a short, sharp deflation in 1816, comparable to that of 1920–21, and a period of monetary adjustment culminating in the restoration of the pound to par in 1819 and 1821. Then came a spurt of foreign lending from 1821 to 1825, followed by a stock market crash in 1826 and a depression. If one subtracts 100 plus three to five years from the major economic events of the 1920s and 1930s, interesting parallels emerge. The 1826 depression was not perhaps as deep or as widespread as that of 1929 or as those of 1837 and 1848 that followed it. But the timing is disconcertingly similar.[8]

Moreover, the European depression of the 1840s, not deeply shared in the rest of the world, presents the same issues as the 1930s as to origin and the role of accidental factors. British historians

4. 1963.

5. Charles P. Kindleberger, "The International Causes and Consequences of the Great Crash," 1979.

6. See my *Manias, Panics, and Crashes: A History of Financial Crises*, 1978, esp. pp. 253–59.

7. But note that J. T. W. Newbold found the origin of that depression in the "profound unsettlement of short-term money markets," arising from a withdrawal of £90 million from London in twelve months. These funds had been accumulated by Germany as part of its receipts of the Franco-Prussian indemnity of 1872 ("The Beginnings of the World Crisis, 1873–1896," 1932, pp. 437, 439). See also Walter Bagehot, *Lombard Street*, 1917, pp. 291ff.

8. Alexander Dana Noyes, *The Market Place: Reminiscences of a Financial Editor*, 1938, pp. 338–40.

think of the "commercial crisis of 1847–48" as largely the result of the railway mania, with an admixture of money panic associated with the failure of a series of grain dealers. On the Continent there was considerable difference of opinion. Cameron calls it "first and foremost a financial and banking crisis,"[9] whereas other economic historians direct attention to real causes, including the smallest wheat crop in fifty years in 1846, followed in 1847 by the largest crop in fifty years. Fohlen, more or less ignoring financial aspects, calls the "crisis of 1848 . . . in effect a series of economic and political accidents."[10] At a deeper level, it may be possible to detect a parallel between the crisis of 1848 on the European continent and the 1929 depression: both represented failures of the economic system at a transitional stage from one set of institutions and forms to another. But this is to anticipate.

Another form of "historical accident" might be the pure fortuitousness of regularly recurring cycles of three different periodicities reaching their depression phases simultaneously. The depression of a Kondratieff long cycle covering as much as fifty years arrived simultaneously with the depressions of a Juglar intermediate nine-year cycle and of a short-range Kitchin cycle in inventories. Vastly oversimplified, this is the Schumpeter view.[11] Sir Arthur Lewis identifies the 1929 depression with none of these but rather with the Kuznets cycle, resting on construction, with a twenty-year periodicity, like its famous predecessors of 1873 and 1893.[12]

Monetarists, such as Milton Friedman, think that the depression of 1929 was no accident. They find the origin was in the United States rather than in Europe or the periphery; in monetary rather than real factors; in policy rather than in the nature of institutions (or in the tasks required of them) in a national economy rather than in the operation of the international system. Within the limits of U.S. monetary policy, moreover, which excludes the villain of many another

9. Rondo E. Cameron, *France and the Economic Development of Europe, 1800–1914*, 1961, p. 125.

10. Claude Fohlen, *Une affaire de famille au XIXᵉ siècle: Méquillet Noblot*, 1955, p. 62.

11. Joseph A. Schumpeter, *Business Cycles: A Theoretical, Historical and Statistical Analysis of the Capitalist Process*, 1939. Schumpeter also makes allowance for "nonessential events which explain particular circumstances" (p. 908) and for "incidents, accidents and policy" (pp. 937ff).

12. See his review of the original edition of this book, *Journal of Interdisciplinary History*, 1975.

analysis—structural dislocation in Europe after the First World War or the failure of the United States to act like a creditor nation, particularly the imposition of the Smoot-Hawley Tariff Act of June 1930—they rule out stock market speculation and the delay in passing the Glass-Steagall Act of 1932, which overcame a domestic shortage of monetary gold by allowing the Federal Reserve System to substitute government securities instead of gold for the lacking eligible paper needed as backing for the central bank's liabilities. There would doubtless have been a recession or a depression with perfect monetary policy or with a money supply that grew in the United States at some optimal pace. But Friedman's explanation of the 1929 worldwide Great Depression is national, monetary, and related to a policy decision. It is unicausal. In my judgment it is wrong. Recently, starting with Allan Meltzer, monetarists have been admitting one international aspect to their analysis: the Smoot-Hawley Act.[13] The concession is slight, however, and the analysis remains almost wholly dependent on the quantity theory of money.

There is a host of similar explanations that rely mainly on a single root cause of the depression or a single origin. President Hoover was persuaded throughout his career in the White House and in writing his memoirs on the depression twenty years later that the origin of the trouble lay in Europe, starting with the difficulties of adjusting to the consequences of the First World War and accentuated by a financial crisis in 1931.[14] The widest-held European view is that the depression started in the United States: fundamentally in that country's unwillingness to write off war debts; more precisely in the stock market crash of 1929 or the frenzied lending of 1927 and 1928. More subtle analysts look to the failure to operate the gold standard properly, converting it to the gold exchange standard on some showings, lowering interest rates unduly in the United States in 1927 on others.

The usual debate is between two unicausal theories, Keynesianism and monetarism. The question is of the chicken-or-egg variety,

13. See Allan H. Meltzer, "Monetary and Other Explanations of the Start of the Great Depression," 1976, and the sources cited in note 4 in the Preface to the Revised Edition, above.

14. *The Memoirs of Herbert Hoover*, vol. 3: *The Great Depression, 1929–1941*, 1952. For a contemporary statement, see his Foreign Affairs Message to Congress, December 10, 1932, in U.S. Department of State, *Foreign Relations of the United States, 1931*, vol. 1, 1946, pp. xff.

(whether the failure of the money supply to grow led to a decline in spending, or whether an independent, autonomous decline in spending led to a decrease in the money supply.) Friedman and Schwartz opt for the first part of this (false, as I think) dichotomy; Peter Temin advocates the second.[15] In the Brunner return visit to the Great Depression, discussion runs almost entirely in terms of monetarism versus Keynesianism.[16] The Temin study argues that the test of whether spending (the *I-S*, or investment-saving, curve) moved first or whether the fault lay in a downward shift of the money supply (the *L-M* curve for liquidity and money) can best be resolved by the customary *IS-LM* analysis, plotting equilibrium curves for these variables against the interest rate and national income. If money decreases first, interest rates should rise, but if spending decreases first, interest rates decline. The analysis is limited to a single country, without the mechanism by which financial crisis in one country is propagated to others and without commodity prices, asset prices, capital flows, or exchange rates. It is usually silent on what causes autonomous shifts in spending—whether the exhaustion of a boom in automobiles or housing; a stock market collapse reducing wealth; or a fall in prices, cutting nominal incomes rapidly while symmetrical increases in real income elsewhere are realized and result in changed behavior, only slowly. For the most part, the debate has been conducted in terms of monetarism versus Keynesianism, money versus spending: two unicauses ranged against one another.

If along with any single or dominant cause we reject fortuitous or accidental events as the explanation of the Great Depression, we are left with a host of issues. In one perspective, we may ask how and where the depression originated, why it spread so widely, and why it went so deep and lasted so long. Questions about where and how it originated have an obvious interest apart from political recrimination, but in their turn they open up new conundrums about *causa proxima* and *causa remota* as well as *causa causans*. Assume that the answer to the question of where the depression originated is limited to the United States, Europe, and the periphery or to the relations among any two or three of them. We then need to know, first, what happened to produce the trouble, and second, why the eco-

15. Peter Temin, *Did Monetary Forces Cause the Great Depression?* 1976.
16. See Brunner, ed., *The Great Depression Revisited*.

nomic system failed to respond to deal with the trouble, either automatically, through the microeconomic mechanism of adjustments in supply and demand or through macroeconomic response through monetary and fiscal systems, or through policy reactions in which the automatic economic forces set in motion are reversed or supported in the interest of stability. Take, for example, the view that the depression originated in the recovery of European production in foodstuffs, raw materials, textiles, and so forth, the output of which had been expanded overseas during the First World War. This would be a real explanation instead of a monetary one, but it is not complete unless we can explain why overexpansion in one or more lines did not produce price declines that cut back output and redirected resources. Or, if the blame is laid on the halt in U.S. lending to Germany and the periphery in 1928, perhaps owing to the attraction of funds into the call money market supporting the rise in New York stock prices, it is necessary to explain not only how the halt in lending set the world economy into reverse gear but also why other forces did not move into action to offset the impact—either borrowing from a different source or in a different form through the automatic market mechanism—or why monetary or fiscal measures were not taken to offset the impact as a result of policy decision. The initial force may be contained in two ways—automatically or by policy decision—and to explain its consequences one has to account both for the failure of automatic forces in the economy to act and for the failure of decision-making machinery.

⸤The failure of economic policy is relatively easy. Throughout the chronological account of the depression that follows, we shall cite instance after instance of what, with hindsight, appears as economic illiteracy. There is no monopoly. Deflationists are found everywhere—Hoover, Brüning, Snowden, Laval. Examples abound of bad judgment—the British decision to return to the gold standard at par in 1925 and the similar Japanese decision taken in July 1929 and carried out in January 1930; of ill-conceived nostrums—the Roosevelt-Morgenthau-Warren attempt to raise commodity prices by changing the price at which the Reconstruction Finance Corporation bought newly mined gold in the United States and the Blum experiment with the forty-hour week in France in 1936; of too little and too late, such as the 50 million schilling ($7 million) loan for Austria on June 16, 1931, which the Bank of England made for a week (but was forced to renew many times). Often no one in authority had any positive idea of what to do and responded to disaster in the policy clichés of balancing budgets, restoring the gold standard, and reducing tariffs. Hobsbawm puts it too strongly perhaps: "Never did a ship founder with a captain and a crew more ignorant of the reasons for its misfortune or more impotent to do anything about it."[17] There were many economists and a few public figures in Britain (Keynes, H. D. Henderson, Mosley), in France (Reynaud), in Germany (Lautenbach, Woytinsky), and perhaps in the United States, though it is hard to dredge up names, who had domestic remedies that made sense in modern terms; and a number of suggestions put forward for the World Economic Conference of 1933 anticipated the decisions of Bretton Woods a calendar decade and intellectual light-years later. Roosevelt frequently confessed to his ignorance but had the virtues of not being doctrinaire and, more positively, of insisting on trying one thing after another until he found something that would help.[18]

(The emphasis on doctrine in policy formation may be too simple. In many instances, policy was constrained not by official understanding of economic principles but by public attitudes. The classic example was perhaps war debts, the American public being "more unanimous on this one question of foreign policy than on any other"[19] in wanting debts collected; even if Hoover and Roosevelt had wanted to cancel the debt—which they did not—they would have had no easy time doing it. (Hoover's failure to understand is

17. See E. J. Hobsbawm, *Industry and Empire: An Economic History of Britain Since 1750*, 1968, p. 179.

18. See Raymond Moley, *The First New Deal*, 1966, p. 6: "Roosevelt's knowledge of economics was limited"; and p. 244: "I doubt that Roosevelt or I could have passed an examination such as is required of college students in elementary economics. . . . We were rank amateurs in the very domain of knowledge that was of paramount importance." See also John Morton Blum, *From the Morgenthau Diaries*, vol. 1: *Years of Crisis, 1928–1938*, 1959, p. 141: "Roosevelt said [to Morgenthau]: 'You and I, of course, started with no knowledge of this subject, but the two of us have done well and have been able to more than hold up our end.'" Schlesinger quotes Roosevelt as likening himself to a quarterback who would try a variety of plays to find one that succeeded. See Arthur M. Schlesinger, Jr., *The Age of Roosevelt*, vol. 2: *The Coming of the New Deal*, 1959, p. 193. But Rexford G. Tugwell insists that Roosevelt had had courses in economics, "not only in such specialties as finance, transportation, taxation and insurance, [but] he was far from a beginner in economic theory" (*The Brains Trust*, 1968, p. 73).

19. See Robert H. Ferrell, *American Diplomacy in the Great Depression: Hoover-Stimson Foreign Policy, 1929–1933*, 1957, p. 33.

reflected in his insistence that, because the French had deposits in New York in excess of the amount due in, say, December 1932, they were able to pay, thus ignoring the distinction between capital and income or how the French Treasury was to gain command of the dollars or gold from the Bank of France without violating its statutes or the budgetary process.)[20] Equally adamant in its unwillingness to pay in December 1932 was the French Chamber, as was evidenced by Herriot's fall from power on December 14, 1932, when he proposed the payment of the installment due the next day.[21]

The failure of automatic forces to offset events that pushed the system in the direction of depression has received some attention with regard to the gold standard, but less in other respects.) The claim is widely made that it was not the gold standard that failed, but the way it was operated.[22] Countries that lost gold did not always deflate, and those that gained it, notably France and the United States, expanded too much or too little. The view that the United States had expanded too much in the 1920s, and to an inflationary degree, is held by Murray Rothbard and echoed by the English historian Paul Johnson, who relies on Rothbard for an interesting, but to my mind wrong-headed, chapter on the depression.[23]

20. *The Memoirs of Herbert Hoover*, vol. 3, p. 185. Hoover claims that the French would have paid in December 1932 had it not been for an unfortunate statement by Roosevelt at Warm Springs to the effect that he did not regard payment of the December 15 installment as a necessary condition for opening further negotiations. The amount due was $50 million, and French holdings in New York were $500 million.

21. See Henry L. Stimson and McGeorge Bundy, *On Active Service in Peace and War*, 1947, p. 217. Herriot was a real hero to Stimson for opposing his own people in the interests of international understanding—much bigger than anyone on the U.S. side of the Atlantic. Stimson was one of the few cancellationists in the U.S. government. See Elting E. Morison, *Turmoil and Tradition: A Study of the Life and Times of Henry L. Stimson*, 1960, p. 433, for an account of when Stimson and Mills went to the White House in January 1933 to ask President Hoover to take some bold step. "For a time the President was roused by the possibility of a 'great state paper,' but then he changed his mind. Stimson, he said, was 'ten million miles away from his position'—the 'debts were merely a chip on the current of ordinary prosperity.'"

22. See Lionel Robbins, *The Great Depression*, 1934, esp. pp. 97ff. Lord Robbins later revised his early views; see his *Autobiography of an Economist*, 1971, esp. pp. 154–55.

23. Murray Rothbard, *America's Great Depression*, 1975; Paul Johnson, *Modern Times: The World from the Twenties to the Eighties*, 1983, ch. 7. Note the parochialism of the Rothbard title.

The more usual view is that the United States failed to expand, as called for by its accumulation of gold during and immediately after the war, thus putting deflationary pressure on the world, especially on Great Britain.[24]

It is not so universally recognized that other aspects of the international monetary mechanism are supposed to work symmetrically; if the flow of capital stops, for example, it may be deflationary for the countries that cease to import capital, though it should be expansionary for those that no longer send savings abroad. Equally, the imposition of tariffs should be expansionary for the importing country, if contractive for the countries losing export markets. If prices of particular internationally traded commodities fall, the income and spending of countries specialized in these goods evidently also fall, but those of countries that regularly buy them should rise. Again, currency appreciation is deflationary, but the counterpart of depreciation in other countries pushes in the opposite direction. It is therefore inadequate to explain world depression by referring to losses of gold or markets, a fall of prices, or currency appreciation without specifying why the expansionary force, which is a counterpart to the depressive factor specified, did not function properly. There are a number of factors that can be pointed to, which will be explained as the occasions arise: accelerators, money illusion, elastic expectations, the dynamic spread of deflation to the banking system, and the like. Without some such asymmetry or positive feedback, however, no substantial depression is possible.

A symmetrical system with rules for counterbalancing, such as the gold standard is supposed to provide, may give way to a system with each participant seeking to maximize its short-run gain. This is the competitive system envisaged by Adam Smith where each man (or country) in advancing his own welfare advances that of the total, either because of an absence of interactions or because of external economies. But a world system of a few actors (countries) is not like this, and the fallacy of composition—that the total often differs from the sum of the parts—enters to affect the outcome. In advancing its own economic good by a tariff, currency depreciation, or foreign exchange control, a country may worsen the welfare of its partners by more than its own gain. Beggar-thy-neighbor tactics

24. A. J. Youngson, *The British Economy, 1920–57*, 1960, pp. 223–24.

may lead to retaliation, so that each country ends up in a worse position from having pursued its own gain.[25] National economic interests are sometimes complementary, sometimes opposed, with no one or two countries controlling the outcome, which rather depends upon the actions of them all.[26]

This is a typical nonzero sum game, in which any player undertaking to adopt a long-range solution by itself will find other countries taking advantage of it. Agreement that all should adopt a long-range strategy may be conceptually satisfactory, but it is likely to involve different degrees of sacrifice from different players at a given moment in time. Britain wants to stabilize currencies at $3.40 to the pound, while the United States lacks interest in the subject until the rate is nearer $4.86. Or postulate a network of reparations, war debts, and commercial loans in which Germany owes reparations to Britain and France and commercial debts to the United States; Britain owes to the United States about what it receives from Germany and is owed in war debts from France; France is to receive the lion's share of reparations, well in excess of its war debts to Britain and the United States. In this circumstance, Germany is more ready to cancel reparations than to default on commercial debts, since it owns some assets abroad and is interested in maintaining its credit. Britain is willing to cancel reparations, but only if war debts are excused. France insists on receiving reparations, wants war debts canceled, and is relatively indifferent to commercial loans. The United States can see no connection between war debts and reparations and is prepared in extremis to accept a mora-

25. See President Roosevelt's first inaugural speech: "Our international trade relations, though vastly important, are in point of time and necessity secondary to the establishment of a sound national economy. I favor as a practical policy the putting of first things first. I shall spare no effort to restore world trade by international economic adjustment; but the emergency at home cannot wait on that accomplishment" (*The Papers and Addresses of Franklin D. Roosevelt*, vol. 2: *The Years of Crisis*, 1938, p. 14). See also Blum, *From the Morgenthau Diaries*, vol. 1, p. 75: "European nations on the whole resented the gold-buying policy, but no nation had for several years shown much regard for the economic convenience of others, and in 1933 the pressure on the President was such that he had to do something"; and Hugh T. Patrick, "The Economic Muddle of the 1920s," 1971, p. 258: "There is some merit to criticism that Japan pursued a beggar-thy-neighbor policy; in the world economy at that time, though, neighbors had to look out for themselves."

26. See Oskar Morgenstern, *International Financial Transactions and Business Cycles*, 1959, p. 572.

torium on reparations and war debt, but it seeks to safeguard the sanctity of commercial debts and wants to revive war debt payments after the year's moratorium is over. No equitable solution is possible. Inevitably the system runs down to wipe the slate clean of reparations, debts, and service on commercial lending. In exactly the same way, the attempt of a system of countries with interlocking multilateral trade to achieve export surpluses tends to wipe out all trade as successive trading partners cut imports from the next country.

In these circumstances, the international economic and monetary system needs leadership, a country that is prepared, consciously or unconsciously, under some system of rules that it has internalized, to set standards of conduct for other countries and to seek to get others to follow them, to take on an undue share of the burdens of the system, and in particular to take on its support in adversity by accepting its redundant commodities, maintaining a flow of investment capital, and discounting its paper. Britain performed this role in the century to 1913; the United States in the period after the Second World War until, say, the Interest Equalization Tax in 1963 or perhaps the abandonment of the gold pool in 1968, the slamming down of the gold window in 1971, or the adoption of floating exchange rates in 1973. It is the theme of this book that part of the reason for the length and most of the explanation for the depth of the world depression was the inability of the British to continue their role of underwriter to the system and the reluctance of the United States to take it on until 1936.)

This game-theoretic interpretation of the international economic and monetary system, together with the insistence on an asymmetry in the operation of the system, also contributes to the general conclusion that the conventional wisdom of the period was not as wrong as most modern economists believe in its concern with the dangers of speculation, the necessity to raise prices, the desirability of lowering tariffs, and the need to stabilize exchange rates. It is true that stock market speculation was no longer a problem after 1929 and that no one knew how to raise world prices or even to raise national prices through exchange depreciation, which might only lower gold prices abroad. Programs for tariff truce or halting competitive exchange depreciation were purely negative, stopping forces that were making the world economy continue to run down without doing anything positive to reverse the positive-feedback mechanism. It is clear that the leading theorists and practitioners of the 1930s were wrong on a number of issues, such as budget balancing, and poor on therapy, but their diagnosis was not as weak as is widely believed today.

In the inescapable choice between chronological and functional organization, the book adopts mainly the former but associates each year or pair of years with a particular set of problems or occurrences. Chapter 2 sets the stage by discussing the recovery from the First World War to about 1926 and the position of war debts, reparations, stabilization of exchange rates, and foreign lending. Chapter 3 concentrates on 1927 and the approach of difficulties in central bank cooperation, the international capital market, and the rise in New York stock prices. Chapter 4 looks at the position in major foodstuffs and raw materials, which can be said to have turned between 1925 and 1928. And 1929 is, of course, the year of the stock market crash, the title of Chapter 5.

The years from 1930 to 1933 are each the subject of separate chapters dealing with "The Slide to the Abyss" (Chapter 6), "1931" (Chapter 7), "More Deflation" (Chapter 8), and "The World Economic Conference" (Chapter 9), respectively. Thereafter the chronological pace speeds up. Chapter 10 deals with 1934 and 1935 and is entitled "The Beginnings of Recovery." In 1936, and Chapter 11, "The Gold Bloc Yields." Chapter 12 deals with 1937 and the recession. "Rearmament in a Disintegrating World Economy" covers the final period of 1938 and 1939 and Chapter 13. A final chapter, "An Explanation of the 1929 Depression" (Chapter 14), brings the threads of the analysis together into conclusions.

To the extent that the organization is analytical rather than chronological, there are difficulties in following issues in the years before and after their holding of the center stage. Less developed countries are treated mainly in Chapter 4—on primary product prices, for example—but must not be lost sight of either at the depths of the depression in 1932 and 1934 or in the later stages of recovery.

In this chronological treatment a number of turning points deserve emphasis: 1929, 1930, 1931, and 1933—the stock market crash, the financial crisis, the failure of revival in the spring of 1930, and the missed opportunity of the World Economic Conference to organize recovery. Most analysis concentrates on October

1929 and May–June 1931.[27] The baffling second quarter of 1930 and June–July 1933, covering the World Economic Conference, are, however, important in explaining why the depression went so deep and lasted so long and why recovery was so incomplete.

27. See, for example, Herbert Hoover's division of the depression into five phases: (1) October 1929 to April 1931; (2) April 1931 to July 1931 (the quake from Europe); (3) August 1931 to December 1931 (the collapse of sterling); (4) December 1931 to July 1932 (reaching bottom); (5) the electoral campaign in the United States, leading to the bankers' panic of March 1933 (*The Memoirs of Herbert Hoover*, vol. 3, p. 38).

2

Recovery from the First World War

The year 1925 generally marks the transition from postwar recovery to the brief and limited boom which preceded the depression. This was the year of the stabilization of sterling and of the other currencies that followed it back to the gold standard. (In the United States it also marked the peak of the boom in a number of important respects: the collapse of Florida land speculation, the peak for postwar housing starts, and the highest price of wheat.) But 1924, with the stabilization of the mark and the Dawes Plan, would do as well, or 1926, when the last war debt settlements with the United States were reached and the French franc was stabilized de facto.

Recovery from the First World War was hindered in Europe by the loss of the cream of its youth and by the relative setback to its position owing to the stimulus to economic growth in the dominions, Japan, and the United States. By 1925 or 1926, however, Europe stopped looking back to 1914 and began to contemplate the future more confidently. The state of recovery achieved contained certain seeds of trouble, initial conditions from which the world depression of 1929 emerged. These concerned especially an increased reluctance by labor to accept wage decreases after about 1921, making for an irreversibility of wage and price increases;[1]

1. Peter Temin asserts that the First World War marks a watershed, before which entrepreneurs regarded wages as a fixed cost and after which as marginal. See his "Three Problems in Economic History," 1971, p. 67.

reparations and war debts, which, however much they appeared to have been settled by the Dawes Plan and the interallied debt settlements, were to prove destabilizing; the system of exchange rates, with the pound overvalued and the franc undervalued, resulting in the substantial accumulation of French claims on Britain; and the entry into world lending of the United States, substituting in part for Britain, with much enthusiasm, no experience, and little in the way of guiding principles.

The 1920–1921 boom and collapse

In 1919 and 1920 a short, sharp worldwide boom took place, reflecting mainly a scramble for goods to replace the inventories drawn down during five years of war. It was especially marked in Britain and the United States,[2] Pent-up financial accumulations were let loose on limited stocks, and prices soared. There were rumors that Bolshevik agents were spending counterfeit currencies in Western Europe to undermine the capitalist system by accelerating the inflation.[3] France, Germany, and much of the rest of continental Europe stood aside from the scramble, lacking the financial resources to participate, although an early attempt by the German iron and steel industry to pay off its wartime debt to Swedish ore producers in order to pave the way for future purchases led early to depreciation of the mark.[4] In addition to stock building, there was "rash speculation."[5] After a sharp rise in prices, however, there was a sharp fall as production started up and supplies emerged on the market. The swift rise and fall traced out a hairpin shape in the price indexes. In all cases, however, the fall, when it came in the summer of 1920 and especially in the spring of 1921, left prices well above 1914 levels.

2. Milton Friedman and Anna Jacobson Schwartz assert that the 1920 and 1929 contractions both originated in the United States, despite their worldwide character, and cite the evidence of leading U.S. gold movements (*A Monetary History of the United States, 1867–1960*, 1963, p. 360). Their opinion on both scores is not universally shared. For a somewhat different point of view which ascribes importance to monetary policy in the early 1920s and blames both the United States and Britain, see Jørgen Pedersen, *Essays in Monetary Theory and Related Subjects*, 1975, pp. 188ff.

3. See H. R. C. Wright, "Fears of Inflation in 1919: Wage Push and Conspiracy Theories," 1981.

4. Gerald D. Feldman, *Iron and Steel in the German Inflation, 1916–23*, 1977, pp. 93–94.

5. Erik Lundberg, *Business Cycles and Economic Policy*, 1957, pp. 15–16.

Conventional wisdom has it that this boomlet, or bubble, was entirely demand-induced, supported by speculation and the expansion of bank credit. A recent view holds that there were elements of cost-push in it, especially in the adoption of the eight-hour day in Europe after the war.[6] The demand for shorter working hours, which went back to the Second International of 1891, was led by socialist unions in such countries as France, Germany, and Italy. Among the Allies, all labor groups supported shorter working hours to allow enjoyment of the fruits of victory and to spread jobs among the demobilized troops. Hours declined 13 percent in Britain, largely in the first months of 1919.[7] The French government adopted the eight-hour day as early as April 1918.[8] In Italy the shorter day was won quickly "in one industry after another after the state had granted it in arsenals and the railways on June 8, 1919."[9]

The Socialist International had claimed that the eight-hour day would not cut production because of increased productivity from the better-rested workers. The argument was accentuated in Germany, where lack of food adversely affected output in 1917 and 1918, especially in heavy industries such as coalmining and metal working. When the Weimar Republic adopted the shorter workday after the war, an ancillary argument was that more labor time would increase German ability to pay reparations, which was not wanted.[10]

Whether entirely demand-led or containing a substantial element of cost-push, the bubble burst, and wages and prices fell. It was the last time, however, that wages could be depressed so far and so fast. In Britain average weekly wages fell 38 percent (and the cost of living 50 percent) between January 1921 and December 1922. Much of the compression was the consequence of sliding scale wage agreements.[11] These quickly fell into disfavor. When real wages in a few industries reached prewar levels, trade unions turned away from this device adopted during the wartime rise of prices. For the first time on any substantial scale, the economic system developed

6. J. A. Dowie, "1919–20 Is in Need of Attention," 1975, pp. 429–30.

7. Ibid., p. 439.

8. Alfred Sauvy, *Histoire économique de la France entre les deux guerres*, vol. 1: *1918–1931*, 1965, p. 535.

9. Shepard B. Clough, *The Economic History of Modern Italy*, 1964, p. 203.

10. This paragraph has benefited from a discussion at a conference on the German inflation after the First World War held in Berkeley, July 26–31, 1982.

11. D. E. Moggridge, *The Return to Gold, 1925: The Formulation of Economic Policy and Its Critics*, 1969, p. 78.

an asymmetry: with expansion from full employment, one encountered price and wage increases in the manufacturing sector; with contraction, there was stubborn resistance of prices and wages and unemployment.)The British example was the sharpest. But in Germany, too, it was noted that a new phenomenon—(unemployment—showed up after the war.[12])

It was not only wage rates that resisted compression. The boom of 1919–20 produced a rise in the price of capital assets, which in turn added to fixed charges. Houses, ships, and especially the equities of firms were sold at fancy prices, with a flurry of mergers, combines, and public flotations of private companies, with heavy burdens for the future in debt service to bond holders, especially banks, and in customary dividends.)In Britain the boom was fed by the prospect of the destruction of German competition in coal, steel, shipping, and textiles.(British dominance in these fields proved to be cruelly short-lived.)Hopes in coal were crushed by the disastrous strike of April–June 1921.(Shipbuilding was hit by technological advances elsewhere, especially Scandinavia, and by the later overvaluation of the pound. In cotton textiles, Japan's and India's invasion of profitable colonial markets occurred quickly.[13])

(In Germany, the inflation of 1922–23 induced a number of entrepreneurs) notably Hugo Stinnes,(to build up huge combines based on debt, which fell into difficulties once the mark was stabilized.[14]) The Stinnes empire collapsed. Other(firms that had managed to pay off indebtedness during the inflation lacked working capital and after stabilization had to borrow substantial accounts at high rates of interest. The major complaint of German enterprise was of "capital shortage."[15])

Reparations

Viewed from the 1980s,(the attempt by the Allies to exact reparations from Germany makes little sense.)The notion that(Germany

12. Wilhelm Grotkopp, *Die grosse Krise: Lehren aus der Überwindung der Wirtschaftskrise, 1929–32*, 1954, p. 14.

13. A. C. Pigou, *Aspects of British Economic History, 1918–1925*, 1948.

14. Gustav Stolper, *German Economy, 1870–1940: Issues and Trends*, 1940, p. 159.

15. Karl Erich Born, *Die deutsche Bankenkrise, 1931: Finanzen und Politik*, 1967, p. 15.

could be saddled at the same time with the costs of the war and reconstruction makes even less. At the time, however, there was ample precedent for taking this course. Germany had collected 5 billion marks in reparations in 1871 without involving France in any great difficulty.[16] Britain had led the victors at Waterloo in exacting 700 million francs from France after 1815. Now it was the turn of the French. Having paid twice, they were ready to receive.

The history of the unsuccessful attempt by the Allies, especially the French, to collect reparations from Germany is familiar and dolorous. It falls into three periods: the first, from Versailles in 1919 to the Dawes Plan in September 1924; the second, from the Dawes Plan to the Young Plan (1924 to 1930); the third, the little over fourteen months from the initiation of the Young Plan in April 1930 to the Hoover moratorium in June 1931. Unlike the war debts on which Britain paid installments to the United States in December 1932 and June 1933, reparations were moribund in June 1931, although they were not finally declared dead until the Lausanne Conference of July 1932. Certainly the depression finished reparations. Étienne Mantoux, the French economist who reacted belatedly but with sharp anger to Keynes's *Economic Consequences of the Peace*, insists that the reparations settlement of Versailles was in no way directly responsible for the depression. Perhaps this is so. But the history of reparations is bound up with the origins of the depression in so many indirect ways that its main outlines must be borne in mind.[17]

The Treaty of Versailles had been unable to fix an amount for German reparations. Any stated sum would have seemed too large to the Germans (and the Americans and possibly the British) and

16. A propos of the inflation caused in Germany by the receipt of reparations, Bismarck is reported to have said: "The next time we win a war against France, we'll demand that we pay her an indemnity." And in a contemporaneous dialogue between a German and a French diplomat, the former said: "It doesn't seem that we received those billions," to which the latter replied: "Nor that we paid them" (Sauvy, *Histoire économique de la France entre les deux guerres*, vol. 1, pp. 131–32). For an account of how the 1871 reparations were successfully transferred and why those after World War I were not, see my *Financial History of Western Europe*, 1984, pp. 239–50, 297–306. A description of the French payments to England after the Napoleonic wars is found in Cameron, *France and the Economic Development of Europe*, p. 76.

17. Étienne Mantoux, *The Carthaginian Peace, or the Economic Consequences of Mr. Keynes*, 1952, pp. 168–69; J. M. Keynes, *The Economic Consequences of the Peace*, 1920.

too small to the French. The treaty was content to deal with establishing general principles for paying in foreign securities, in payments in kind (that is, exports), and in foreign exchange, while setting up a Reparations Commission to work out detailed sums. This body produced a figure of 132 billion gold marks in April 1921. The Allied members of the commission calculated that 7.9 billion had thus far been paid in securities, ships, and deliveries, while the Germans claimed credit for having paid 20 billion. The difference at this stage was almost 12 billion marks, which the Germans claimed as the value of state works in ceded territories.[18] The French rejected a proposal for using German labor to reconstruct the Nord; proposed by Loucheur, the commissioner for the reconstruction of the devastated areas, and worked out with the cooperation of German foreign minister Walther Rathenau, it gave rise to objections from the French public, for reasons of sentiment, as well as from the construction industry, which wanted the orders.[19] The Germans, on the other hand, found it difficult to pay reparations in

---

18. Mantoux presents a table of reparation payments by periods, as calculated separately by the Reparations Commission and the German government (*The Carthaginian Peace*, p. 152):

PAYMENTS MADE	REPARATIONS COMMISSION	GERMAN GOVERNMENT
	(in billions of gold marks)	
November 11, 1918, to August 31, 1921	9.7	42.1
Under the Dawes Plan	7.6	8.0
Under the Young Plan	2.8	3.1
Other	0.8	14.6
Total	20.9	67.8

Differences between the two figures turn on particular interpretations; Mantoux states that the earliest German figure includes 8.5 billion for the German naval vessels scuttled at Scapa Flow.

To 29 billion for repayments made to the occupation of the Ruhr, Schacht adds 11 billion of seized foreign assets, 8 billion paid under the Dawes Plan as above, and 80 to 100 billion representing the value of German colonies lost at Versailles. See Hjalmar Schacht, *The End of Reparations*, 1931, p. 22. As we shall see below, when Schacht thought reparations, he thought colonies. A complete breakdown of payments made up to the end of 1924, prior to the Dawes and Young plans, is presented in Carl-Ludwig Holtfrerich, *Die deutsche Inflation, 1914–1923*, 1980, p. 145.

19. See P. J. Grigg, *Prejudice and Judgement*, 1948, p. 71; Lord Salter, *Memoirs of a Public Servant*, 1961, p. 164. For a similar German suggestion of July 1919, see Sauvy, *Histoire économique de la France entre les deux guerres*, vol. 1, p. 140.

kind, especially in coal, though when the British coal strike took place in 1926 their exports of coal rose briskly. Payments in foreign exchange and deliveries in kind to France dwindled in 1922 to such an extent that French and Belgian troops were sent into the Ruhr in January 1923.

Occupation of the Ruhr did not help. German employers and workers sabotaged output and distribution in a massive exhibition of passive resistance, or nonviolent warfare.) There was even violence: on March 31, 1924, Easter Saturday, a French squad of soldiers searching Krupps was "threatened" by a crowd of workers and, firing into them, killed thirteen, including five teenagers, and wounded fifty-two. The funeral was a highly emotional one. Throughout the occupation, the strain was said to be harder on French troops than on the German populace.[20]

The German government paid subventions to industry and discounted securities for banks to maintain payrolls. The inflation, already well under way in 1922, gave way to hyperinflation. There is some disagreement as to when the inflation shifted from rapid to hyper: possibly May 1921 after the Reparations Commission report; January 1923 with the Franco–Belgian occupation of the Ruhr; or intermediately, June 1922 with three strongly negative events—the French government's refusal to revise the reparation schedule of May 1921; the report of a bankers' committee,) headed by J. P. Morgan, (stating the impossibility of making a loan to Germany so long as reparations were not scaled down; and on June 22, the assassination of Foreign Minister Rathenau. The exchange rate went from 275 marks to the dollar in May to 370 in June. By October it was 485 and by June 1923, 16,667.)Grigg thought that the occupation of the Ruhr was "the most effective and direct cause of Hitler, and but for this there would have been no Second World War."[21] Most observers blame the inflation and the consequent pauperization of the middle class rather than the occupation of the Ruhr itself.[22] Whether one inevitably involved the other is perhaps an open question. But hyperinflation had one delayed result in making it difficult, after 1930, to fight deflation in the midst of depression. The collective memory of the devastation caused by inflation furnished those who believed in putting the economy through the purifying

20. Grigg, *Prejudice and Judgement*, p. 160.
21. Ibid., p. 172.
22. Mantoux, *The Carthaginian Peace*, p. 144.

fires of deflation with an inexhaustible supply of ammunition against programs of even moderate monetary or fiscal expansion.[23]

In their occupation of the Ruhr, the French collected $625,000 over costs in the first four months of 1923, compared with $50 million in the same period of 1922. A British attempt at mediation begun in May produced little immediate result. The hyperinflation raced on. Its effects suited almost no one.

Finally, in December the British, French, and Germans agreed to appoint two commissions. The first, of no importance save for French *amour propre*, was set up under Reginald McKenna to determine how much capital German citizens had managed to expatriate from under Allied noses (as well as the chances of getting it back). The second was organized under the chairmanship of Charles G. Dawes, the first director of the U.S. Bureau of the Budget, to consider means of balancing the German budget, stabilizing the currency, and fixing a new and viable level of annual reparations. While the United States had neither signed the Treaty of Versailles nor joined the League of Nations, having turned in revulsion from the intrigues of Europe after the war, the secretary of state, Charles E. Hughes, was willing to assist unofficially in the attempt to untangle reparations, albeit insisting that such reparations had no connection with war debts owed by the Allies to the United States. With Dawes, a Republican, was Owen D. Young, a Democrat lawyer and corporate executive, as well as several assistants from banking and academic life.[24] Banking observers and advisers in the background in London, especially Thomas Lamont of J. P. Morgan and Governor Montagu Norman of the Bank of England, had grave reservations as to the wisdom of the plan agreed to by the politicians and civil servants.[25]

The Dawes Plan involved a schedule of annual payments starting at 1 billion gold marks in the first year and rising to 2.5 billion in the fifth, varying thereafter somewhat according to changes in world prosperity (if gold prices changed upward or downward by more

23. Paul Einzig, *World Finance Since 1914*, 1935, p. 177.

24. For a discussion of the Dawes Plan by a working economist assistant, see Joseph S. Davis, *The World Between the Wars, 1919–1939: An Economist's View*, 1975, esp. pp. 55–69.

25. See Stephen A. Schuker, *The End of French Predominance in Europe: The Financial Crisis of 1924 and the Adoption of the Dawes Plan*, 1976, pp. 147ff., 272–83. The title of the book fails to convey its content.

than 10 percent).)There was to be a Reparations Agency in Berlin to oversee the raising of the necessary amounts in marks and to intervene to postpone payments in the event of serious transfer difficulties. A loan of 800 million marks was to be floated in various financial capitals against the collateral of German railroad securities.)This last provision was to satisfy Poincaré, who had continuously demanded *gages productifs* in the form of mines, forests, industrial plants, and the like.

(The Dawes loan played a fateful role. One hundred and ten million dollars of it were sold in New York,)underwritten by Morgan's. It was oversubscribed ten times. More than anything else,(this was the spark that ignited foreign lending from New York, first to Germany and shortly thereafter to Latin America and much of the rest of Europe.)[26] Some notion of the exuberance of U.S. lending to Latin America in these years is furnished by the expression that the borrowing countries used to characterize it: "the dance of the millions."[27]

(An initial success with a loan floated for political ends connected with reparations had on previous occasions been followed by a spurt of foreign lending.) In the settlement after Waterloo, French reparations were paid through discounting *rentes* with Baring Brothers of London. The success of that venture(stimulated British foreign lending in the 1820s.)(The French indemnity to Germany after the Franco-Prussian War was raised to the extent of 3.5 billion francs) by the famous Thiers *rente*, issued at a substantial discount.(This

26. See Herbert Feis, *The Diplomacy of the Dollar, 1919–1939,* 1950, p. 42. This may overstate the case somewhat, since J. P. Morgan & Co. had arranged a $150 million loan for Japan in February 1924 and one of $100 million to assist French stabilization in March 1924. But the Dawes loan was quickly followed up by similar bond issues for Krupp and Stahlverein, Thyssen, Krupp twice again, and subsequently for German municipalities.

Ilse Mintz makes it clear that the quality of foreign government bonds issued in New York deteriorated after 1924. Of those issued from 1920 to 1924, only 18 percent were in default on December 31, 1937, while of those issued from 1925 to 1929, the ratio of default on the same date was 50 percent. See Ilse Mintz, *Deterioration in the Quality of Foreign Bonds Issued in the United States, 1920–1930,* 1951, p. 6.

27. See Rosemary Thorp and Carlos Londoño, "The Effect of the Great Depression on the Economies of Peru and Colombia," 1984, p. 82: "'The dance of the millions' is at the center of our stereotype of the 1920s: a decade when North American salesmen pressed loans and American products upon unsuspecting governments, who, overwhelmed by this sudden access to credit and goods, borrowed with a recklessness only to be equaled in the 1970s."

made large profits for French commercial banks, *banques d'affaires*, and private individuals and diverted investment attention from industry to speculation in bonds, including foreign bonds, down to the outbreak of the First World War.)

Reparations may not have been directly responsible for the depression, as Mantoux claims they were not, but together with war debts they complicated and corrupted the international economy at every stage of the 1920s and during the depression through to June 15, 1933, three days after the opening of the World Economic Conference. Keynes's brilliant polemic, *The Economic Consequences of the Peace*, may have been distorting in many respects—self-confirming in its contention that if the Germans heard a reasonable argument to the effect that they could not pay, they would not, and devastatingly encouraging to American isolationists in its attacks on President Wilson as an incompetent invalid—but it was surely right in thinking it useful to cancel war debts, set a small figure for reparations such as $10 billion, and clear the issue off the international agenda.[28])

War debts

Reparations and war debts were joined in the minds of the British, French, Italians, and Belgians, but not in that of the United States, which disassociated them "with the obstinacy worthy of a better

28. See Keynes, *The Economic Consequences of the Peace*, pp. 135, 147, 200. For criticisms of Keynes's observations at the Paris conference, see Mantoux, *The Carthaginian Peace*, esp. p. 45, citing E. M. House and Charles Seymour, *What Really Happened in Paris: The Story of the Peace Conference, 1918–1919*, 1921; J.-B. Duroselle, *De Wilson à Roosevelt*, 1960, p. 115; and Sir Arthur Salter, *Slave of the Lamp*, 1967, pp. 85, 86. Salter thought the book mistaken in its main theme and fraught with disastrous consequences. He tried especially to persuade Keynes to omit the passage about "debamboozling the old Presbyterian." For a suggestion that Keynes did not always act in good faith in dealing with the reparations question, especially in 1922 when he worked secretly with the German reparations expert, Carl Melchior, see the review by Stephen A. Schuker of *The Collected Writings of John Maynard Keynes*, vols. 17–18, 1980.

Another suggestion that war debts be abolished and reparations cut to 53 billion marks—not far from Keynes's $10 billion—came from Loucheur, originally a commissioner for devastated areas, later a French negotiator on reparations, ultimately minister of finance. The same politician later grew very cynical and said, after a day in the Chamber of Deputies: "I am unable to tell the truth; they would kill me" (see Sauvy, *Histoire économique de la France entre les deux guerres*, vol. 1, pp. 144, 148).

Figure 1. Interallied debts at the end of the First World War (in billions of dollars).

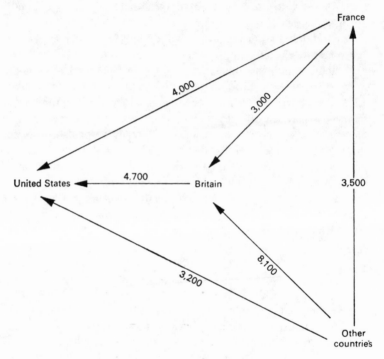

SOURCE: Alfred Sauvy, *Histoire économique de la France entre les deux guerres*, vol. 1: *1918–1931*, 1965, p. 169.

cause."[29] The United States refused to accept reparations from Germany. It wanted to be repaid for loans and advances to the Allies for wartime assistance prior to the Armistice, and for grain, cotton, and similar supplies—involving lesser sums—afterward. It was opposed to mixing political and economic questions but frowned on loans by Wall Street to countries that had not made and ratified their debt settlements with the United States. Smaller amounts were involved in the wartime obligations among the European Allies, with Britain being owed substantial debts by France, Italy, and (less usefully) Russia; France by Belgium, Yugoslavia, and so on. A schematic diagram is given by Sauvy, including the larger amounts owed

29. Sauvy, *Histoire économique de la France entre les deux guerres*, vol. 1, p. 167.

by Russia to Britain and France ($2.5 billion and $900 million, respectively).

(The British suggestion for cancellation of war debts,) originally advanced in Keynes's book, (was put forward in a series of formal exchanges of 1920 ending up in letters between Lloyd George and President Wilson and especially in the Balfour note of August 1, 1922, addressed to the other Allies. The last stated that, inasmuch as the United States insisted on collecting its war debts, the British had no choice but to collect debts owed to them but would do so only up to the limit of the British debt to the United States.

(French policy was to "commercialize" reparations, that is, to have Germany borrow in New York and use the money to pay off its obligations to France.)[30] This sort of "recycling" has been undertaken automatically by financial markets on various occasions: earlier in connection with the Thiers *rente* to raise the money to pay the French indemnity to Prussia after the war of 1870–71, and years later when the Organization of Petroleum Exporting Countries (OPEC), after raising the price of oil in 1973 and 1979, deposited its windfall profits in Eurocurrency banks to be loaned by the latter to oil importers. But no one in the United States was interested in substituting a commercial loan to a poor risk, Germany, for a government obligation owed by France, that was anticipated to be collectible.

(United States policy was set out time and again. It was prepared to negotiate but insisted on doing so with the debtors one at a time, with separate settlements taking into account ability to pay.) The executive branch of the government had no authority to cancel any obligations; this was a matter for Congress. Under legislation approved on February 9, 1922, though not conformed to strictly, U.S. settlements were made with thirteen countries in all, beginning with Finland and Great Britain in 1923 and ending with France and Yugoslavia in 1926.[31] A typical settlement, that of June 19, 1923, be-

30. Schuker, *The End of French Predominance*, p. 19. Lloyd George put forward a similar plan, originating with Keynes, at the Versailles peace conference that Assistant Secretary of the Treasury Rufus Leffingwell called "preposterous" (pp. 176–77).

31. For a detailed account, see Harold G. Moulton and Leo Pasvolsky, *War Debts and World Prosperity*, 1932. The lists of settlements are given on p. 82 for the United States and p. 115n. for Great Britain. For more recent accounts of the war debt issue between France and the United States, derived from archival sources, see Ellen Schrecker, *The Hired Money: The French Debt to the United States*, 1978; and Denise Artaud, *La question des dettes interalliées et la reconstruction de l'Europe (1917–1929)*, 1978.

tween the United States and Great Britain, provided for payments over sixty-two years with interest at 3 percent for the first ten years and 3.5 percent thereafter. The principal sum was made up of the monies actually advanced, plus interest at 4.5 percent to the date of settlement, plus and minus certain adjustments. In the French, Italian, and Yugoslav agreements, considerably lower interest rates were charged on the principle of lesser ability to pay. These averaged 1.6 percent, 0.4 percent, and 1 percent, respectively.

⟨ Like reparations, war debts exacerbated international economic relationships during the 1920s and the depression. The United States, for example, tried to use other economic considerations, such as access to the New York capital market, as a means of applying pressure to collect the debts, and to use the debts to accomplish other economic ends, such as the stabilization of the pound in 1932.[32] ⟩

⟨War debts, along with reparations, raised a transfer problem and hence became an issue of commercial policy. They had to be provided for in the budgets of debtors and were needed on occasion to balance the budgets of creditors. The United States contemplated paying a bonus to veterans out of its receipts. Like an aching tooth, war debts distracted attention. ⟩

32. After obtaining a loan from J. P. Morgan in March 1924, the French tried to borrow in New York again in November 1924 but were prevented from doing so by the informal ban maintained by the Department of State which responded to investment banker requests for its views on bond issues. Since no attempt had been made to settle war debts, it told the bankers and the French that it could not look on such a loan with favor. The ban was renewed in September 1925 when a French delegation in Washington failed to reach agreement with the United States, and once again in April 1926, after agreement had been reached but no French government dared to submit it to the Chamber for ratification. In this instance it was not needed, since stabilization was accomplished without the normal precaution of a foreign loan. See Feis, *The Diplomacy of the Dollar*, pp. 21–23. Poincaré told Moreau that the United States spent "enormous sums" on the French press to persuade French public opinion to ratify the accords. This would appear to be a case of the pot calling the kettle black (Emile Moreau, *Souvenirs d'un gouverneur de la Banque de France: Histoire de la stabilisation du franc*, 1954, p. 140).

For the continued insistence of Hoover that he would not cancel war debts without getting something for it, see Moley, *The First New Deal*, p. 50. Moley called the cancellation of war debts exchanging "a definite quid for an illusory quo—tariff concessions or the stabilization of the French and British currencies." This was in January 1933, after the Hoover moratorium, when the definite character of war debts was subject to some dispute.

Stabilization of currencies

(Stabilization waited on some settlement of war debts and reparations—or at least some start toward it. In Germany mortgages had been wiped out in the hyperinflation of 1922–23. A new currency, the Rentenmark, was introduced)on the basis of the security of German land and buildings in November 1923.(This was done slowly, alongside the old mark, but by restoring confidence it succeeded in halting and even reversing the inflation. Bankruptcies took place in increasing numbers after April 1924. Schacht, who became head of the Reichsbank in December 1923, negotiated British aid for the establishment of the Golddiskontobank to finance foreign trade in gold marks in early 1924.)

In August 1924,(with the acceptance of the Dawes Plan, the Rentenmark gave way to the Reichsmark, converted from the old mark at a trillion to one.)As part of the Dawes Plan, (the Reichsbank)became independent of the German government and(was strengthened with the Rm 800 million Dawes loan) It was required by Article 5 to maintain reserves, three-quarters gold, one-quarter foreign exchange—at a 40 percent ratio to note and deposit liabilities. Schacht maintained the(deflationary pressure.)(High interest rates) and the success of the Dawes loan(attracted more foreign loans.)The inflow of capital can hardly be thought of as a monetary phenomenon, responding to short-term interest rates and liquidity or associated with an overvalued exchange rate.(Germany still lacked real capital as a result of the war and inflation, despite some considerable capital formation during the inflation) In the first stages, the borrowing was largely for industry. Thereafter it spread to states and municipalities. Schacht conducted a campaign against unproductive borrowing. In November 1927, for example, he made a speech excoriating German cities for building "stadiums, swimming pools, public squares, dining halls, convention halls, hotels, offices, planetariums, airports, theatres, museums, etc., and the purchase of land."[33] This sort of inflow can hardly be described as the consequence of a shortage of capital.(The original shortage of capital,

---

33. Schacht, *The End of Reparations*, p. 33. However, in 1926 Schacht told Strong that if he could borrow $200 million to $400 million in long-term loans from the United States, for German industrial establishments and including possibly German municipalities in good credit standing, he could maintain stability of the mark (see Lester V. Chandler, *Benjamin Strong, Central Banker*, 1958, p. 335).

however, led to high interest rates, which stimulated the capital inflow. And in time this acquired a momentum of its own.)

(Stabilization of sterling) at par in the spring of 1925 was more debatable. It was debated at the time and is debated still. The issues in the discussion are to what extent it was accidental—the(result of destabilizing speculation in the pound,) which pushed it within shooting distance of parity in the autumn of 1924, or the result of deep-seated forces that were inexorably tending in this direction. Such forces were strong: the return to par has been characterized "as a question of prestige, a question of dogma, . . . almost a question of religion."[34] Another French view calls the return to gold an affair of wounded *amour propre* rather than of monetary policy.[35] A modern British opinion is less ironic but claims that the views involved were essentially moral and based on "deep faith in the mechanism of the prewar gold standard."[36]

 The City of London was, of course, interested in restoring its prewar position as a world financial center, and to a degree it succeeded. German reserves were increasingly held in sterling after stabilization, and after stabilization the Dutch returned balances to London from New York.[37])

British leading opinion was committed to a return to par if possible. The Cunliffe Committee on Currency and Foreign Exchanges) after the War, appointed in January 1918, accepted without argument the return to par as an objective.)The only open questions were whether it was possible, and if so, when.(From a low of $3.40 at the end of 1920, the pound recovered to $4.70 in the spring of 1923 as a result of capital inflows) from the Continent fleeing German inflation and French occupation of the Ruhr. Unemployment rose to 15 percent.)A suggestion that the government might take expansionary measures)to correct the unemployment and the election of the Labour government, which was committed to a capital levy, led to an outflow of funds in the second half of 1923 and depreciation to below $4.30. In February 1924 the Labour government

34. Sauvy, *Histoire économique de la France entre les deux guerres*, vol. 1, p. 121.

35. M. Perrot, *La monnaie et l'opinion en France et en Angleterre, 1924–36*, 1955.

36. Moggridge, *The Return to Gold, 1925*, p. 68.

37. See Stephen V. O. Clarke, *Central Bank Cooperation, 1924–31*, 1967, pp. 161–63; and Moreau, *Souvenirs d'un gouverneur de la Banque de France*, p. 136.

accepted the principles of the Cunliffe Report, and the movement was halted.[38] Expansion did take place, however, and unemployment was reduced without leading to or requiring much depreciation. The Bank of England took advantage of the improvement to press the government to appoint a committee of experts (under the chairmanship first of Sir Austen Chamberlain and, when he became foreign secretary in the Conservative government, of Lord Bradbury), including most of the members of the Cunliffe Committee, to make recommendations on two matters: (1) consolidation of the Treasury note issue that had come into existence during the war with the Bank of England fiduciary issue and (2) the course to be followed after the expiration of the Gold and Silver (Export Control) Act of 1920 at the end of 1925. The question of the note issue was postponable; some decision to renew or to abandon the gold embargo was not. Abandonment meant going back to gold at some figure, but presumably par.

The committee held hearings over the summer of 1924. All witnesses except Keynes and McKenna were optimistic about the ability of Britain to restore the pound to par. Calculations of purchasing power parities suggested that British prices were overvalued by about 10 percent, but most observers, including Keynes but not Montagu Norman, the governor of the Bank of England, thought that this discrepancy would be corrected by a rise in U.S. prices while British levels were held steady. The suggestion had even been advanced in 1923 that Britain should ship an extra $100 million in gold to the United States in payment of war debts to ensure this result, although Norman had countered that the United States could sterilize it. Moggridge characterizes Keynes's testimony as "ambiguous." Keynes was afraid that removing the gold embargo and appreciating the pound to par would result in Britain not in deflation but in inflation as American prices rose and the United States lost gold to England. Most observers thought that if U.S. prices did not go up it would not be impossible to squeeze British prices down another 10 percent. The committee prepared a draft report in September 1924 saying that there was no practical alternative policy to returning to gold but suggesting that it might be well to wait until American prices had risen.[39]

38. See Robert Z. Aliber, "Speculation in the Foreign Exchanges: The European Experience, 1919–1926," 1962, pp. 188–90.

39. See Moggridge, *The Return to Gold, 1925.*

At this point, after nine months in office, Britain's first Labour government fell. Snowden was replaced as chancellor of the Exchequer by Winston Churchill. The general expectation became accepted that sterling would be revalued. Speculation bid the currency up to $4.795, within pennies of the $4.86 parity. Norman decided that the time had come. There were a few more opportunities for reversing the course. The Bradbury Committee reported on February 5 and recommended in favor of resumption. On January 29 Churchill circulated a series of questions, largely in the Keynes-McKenna spirit, to Norman at the Bank of England, Lord Bradbury, Otto Niemeyer, and Ralph Hawtrey at the Treasury, questioning the desirability of going back to the gold standard, the timing of any return, and whether a better bargain might not be obtained from the United States as a price for a return. Moggridge regards this questioning as partly Churchill's way of coming to a decision and partly a reaction to worry over Beaverbrook's opposition. Whether this was merely papering the record, as Moggridge thinks,[40] or expressing a genuine doubt, as the most recent biography of Churchill maintains,[41] is impossible to settle definitively. Even after getting reassuring answers to his questions, Churchill asked for Niemeyer's reaction to an article by Keynes in the *Nation* on the return toward gold, commenting pointedly: "I do not know whether France with financial embarrassments is worse off than England with her unemployment." On March 17 Churchill gave a dinner party, attended by Niemeyer, Bradbury, Keynes, McKenna, and Grigg, at which Niemeyer and Bradbury argued for return and Keynes and McKenna against. In Grigg's view the "ayes" had it.[42] The decision was finally taken on March 20 and announced on April 28. The Gold Standard Act of 1925 became law on May 14, 1925, after operating de facto from the date of announcement.

No consideration was given to a return to gold at a different rate. The Bradbury Committee report states that such a policy need only be mentioned to be dismissed.[43] Moggridge quotes an ex-Labour

40. D. E. Moggridge, *British Monetary Policy, 1924–31: The Norman Conquest of $4.86*, 1972, pp. 66–67.

41. Martin Gilbert, *Winston S. Churchill*, vol. 5: *1922–1939: The Prophet of Truth*, 1977, ch. 5.

42. Grigg, *Prejudice and Judgement*, p. 182.

43. See W. B. Reddaway, "Was $4.86 Inevitable in 1925?" 1970, p. 23.

minister, Tom Johnson, who is said to have remarked after sterling left gold, "They never told us we could do that."[44] The perceived choice seems to have been "Go/No-go" at the prewar parity. Even Keynes accepted the rate. Reddaway blames the accident of the fall of the Labour government in October (over questions of a proposed treaty and loan with the Soviet Union and the dropping of the prosecution of a Communist journalist), which induced destabilization speculation. This may have affected timing. But the suggestion that a few more months or even years of $4.40 instead of $4.79 would have altered opinion substantially seems unlikely. Keynes and McKenna, who were close friends and saw alike on most issues, were heard out but failed to persuade. Keynes was brilliant but erratic, and his testimony on the issue was "ambiguous." Even ten years later at the World Economic Conference, as an American observed, "John Maynard Keynes was pretty generally regarded as an extremist."[45] All the small countries wanted stabilization (Sweden, tired of waiting, jumped the gun in March 1924; its central bank governor had been urging resumption). More important was the continuous pressure from the United States, including pressure for speed in returning to gold. Not only Benjamin Strong, the governor of the Federal Bank of New York, but Secretary Mellon and a host of other Federal Reserve officials were unhesitating in informing Norman in December 1924 and January 1925 that the time had come.[46] Strong's views were partly based on world considerations: the need to eliminate the malign effects of disturbed foreign exchange markets on world trade; and partly on two national grounds: the hope (1) of reversing the flow of gold to the United States and (2) of gaining international lending business for New York as a consequence of higher interest rates in London.[47] Under attack from Keynes, Churchill later believed he had made a mistake. At the time he felt he had little choice.

In retrospect, the return to gold at par must be marked up as an

44. Moggridge, *The Return to Gold, 1925*, p. 9.

45. James M. Cox, *Journey Through My Years*, 1946, p. 367.

46. Moggridge, *The Return to Gold, 1925*, p. 40.

47. Clarke, *Central Bank Cooperation, 1924–31*, p. 72. Strong was also concerned lest the pound deteriorate progressively against the dollar and provide incentive to the adoption of novel ideas, including especially a weakening of discipline against inflation (see Moggridge, *The Return to Gold, 1925*, p. 41).

inescapable error, although not all critics regard it so. As we have just seen, Reddaway suggests it was an unlucky accident. Youngson and a few other economic historians maintain that the trouble lay elsewhere: "What wrecked the gold standard was the self-regarding unwisdom of French and American monetary policies."[48] It was not that the pound was overvalued but that the French franc was valued too low. The difficulties in British export trades were the consequence not of too high a level for the pound but of structural changes from the war. This view seems, however, to ignore that contemporary purchasing-power-parity calculations, which suggested that the pound was 10 percent overvalued, overlooked the need for an adjustment in parity calculations because of the structural setbacks referred to and included the drastic mistake of thinking that prices and wages were continuously compressible downwards. Overvaluation of the pound was no doubt compounded by undervaluation of the franc as well as by an ultimate unwillingness to undertake expansive monetary policies in the United States after March 1929, when the stock market started its rise. It was, perhaps, inevitable as an attempt to restore the *status quo ante bellum*. It was nonetheless an important mistake.

Stabilization of the franc took place gradually over the summer and autumn of 1926 at an undervalued level, good perhaps for France but disastrous for the international monetary mechanism. But this dictum has also been challenged. Sauvy calls the stabilization an island of reason in a sea of errors and, while reluctant to rewrite history to contemplate what would have happened if Cleopatra's nose had been longer, is disposed to believe that at a higher rate France would have fallen into the world depression earlier.[49] His focus is on the history of France, however, not on that of the system.

At the time, the question was not where to stabilize but whether it was possible to do so at all. Monetary policy in France was in chaos. Reconstruction had been undertaken in the devastated regions with the slogan "Le Boche paiera." While waiting for reparations, expenditure had been financed with short-term borrowings. No finance minister was able to fund the debt at long term so as to

48. Youngson, *The British Economy, 1920–57*, pp. 233–34.

49. Sauvy, *Histoire économique de la France entre les deux guerres*, vol. 1, pp. 96–98.

lock creditors in. With most debt in short form, creditors could convert their assets into money in a brief space of time. Any political upset led to capital outflows and depreciation of the franc, inducing Aftalion to devise the "psychological theory of foreign exchange," which maintained that exchange rates fluctuated with national confidence in the government.

Such confidence was limited. A serious speculative attack on the franc took place in the last months of 1923 and in early 1924. It had been beaten back with the help of a $100 million loan from J. P. Morgan, with serious losses for the Austrian and German speculators involved.[50] But the gains from the successful defense were allowed to slip away. The loan was not renewed in September when the original six-month term was up because the bankers did not believe that France had mastered its finances.[51] Within France, moreover, there were deep political divisions as well as technical disagreement on financial policy.[52] Between the inception of the Dawes Plan in September 1924 and July 1926, there were ten different ministers of finance in almost as many governments. Ministers of finance, and governments generally, would fall when they were unable to get the budget approved by the Chamber of Deputies and then were refused credits at the Bank of France. From 18 to the dollar and 90 to the pound, the franc depreciated throughout 1925 and on into the spring of 1926. Raoul Péret, minister of finance under Briand in the spring of 1926, got his budget through Parliament in April, but the depreciation if anything accelerated. War debt settlements were made with the United States in April and with Britain, provisionally, in May. From the middle of April to the middle of May, the franc went from 145 to 170 to the pound. On June 1 Péret appointed a committee of experts to work out a means to

50. See Jean-Noël Jeanneney, "De la spéculation financière comme arme diplomatique: A propos de la première bataille du franc (novembre 1923–mars 1924)," 1982; Schuker, *The End of French Predominance*, pp. 96–97; and for the deleterious effect on Austrian banks, Edouard März, "Comment" on D. E. Moggridge, "Policy in the Crises of 1920 and 1929," 1982, pp. 190–91.

51. Schuker, *The End of French Predominance*, pp. 140ff. Jean-Claude Debeir takes a more cynical view, that J. P. Morgan was trying to extract better terms (see his "La crise du franc de 1924: Un exemple de spéculation 'internationale,'" 1978).

52. See esp. Jean-Noël Jeanneney, *François de Wendel en république: L'argent et le pouvoir, 1914–1940*, 1976, and his *Leçon d'histoire pour une gauche au pouvoir: La faillite du Cartel (1924–26)*, 1977.

halt the hemorrhage. Before the committee report had come out, the Briand cabinet changed finance ministers—from Péret to Caillaux—and changed the governor of the Bank of France from Robineau to Moreau. The franc reached 174. Confidence was still lacking. On July 17 the Briand government gave way to that of Herriot. The franc went to 220. On July 21 the Herriot government fell. The franc reached a low of 243 to the pound (49 + to the dollar, or virtually 2 cents). Citizens of Paris threatened tourists on the streets.

In Herriot's place returned Poincaré, the strong man, who served as his own minister of finance. Initially, he reversed the recommendations of the Committee of Experts, published on July 3, and lowered rather than raised taxes. This won the confidence of the propertied classes. The flow of capital reversed and the franc recovered to 199 to the pound on July 25 and to 190 on July 26. At this stage he adopted the policies of the committee in favor of raising taxes.

From the moment that Poincaré took charge of the government, the French franc was strong, and its quotation climbed in the exchange market. As early as August 7, the Bank of France was authorized to buy foreign exchange with French francs to slow down the rate of appreciation. It was unwilling to undertake such purchases, however, until it received assurance from the Ministry of Finance that any losses it might suffer from buying sterling at 150 francs to the pound and ultimately selling it at a higher franc rate such as 125 would be made good by the ministry. Such assurance was forthcoming only at the end of September.[53]

The Bank of France's entry into operations to hold down the value of the franc meant to Moreau abandonment of all notion of restoring the currency to its prewar par.[54] Such a hope was a vain one, no doubt, but it had been entertained by Poincaré, who regarded it as a moral question.[55] Even before this had been resolved in favor of a departure from the prewar rate—a long intellectual advance over the British, made possible, no doubt, by the much greater rate of inflation—the question of the eventual rate of stabilization was discussed. There were purchasing-power-parity calcu-

53. For the text of the law of authorization of August 7 and the agreement putting it into effect, see Moreau, *Souvenirs d'un gouverneur de la Banque de France*, pp. 62n., 105n.

54. Ibid., p. 108.

55. Ibid., p. vi.

lations. Some were made as early as August by Quesnay for the Bank of France,[56] others independently for Poincaré in November, when the franc was 130, by Rueff.[57] Quesnay's calculation, undertaken to show to Strong, gave a range between 131 and 196, with a preferred zone of 160 to 170 and a best figure of 163 to the pound. Rueff arrived at a range of 100 to 150, from which he deduced a figure of 120, close to the final rate of 124 francs to the pound and 3.92 cents and double the rate of July 21, but undervalued.

The rate was chosen, however, more by political than by intellectual means. At the end of October, the franc, then between 160 and 170 to the pound, began to rise. Poincaré could not make up his mind. Moreau was conscious of the importance of not too low a rate for the franc so as not to wipe out too much of the fixed-income securities of the middle classes through inflation; however, he was under pressure from businessmen, especially in the automobile industry, not to let the rate go so high as to put them under deflationary pressure. The Committee of Experts' report warned of too high a rate, which might produce a deflation like that in Britain, ruinous for industry, commerce, and agriculture. So far as one can tell from the memoirs, other central banks barely discussed the ultimate rate of stabilization and when they did, did not all speak with one voice. Strong and Norman were on holiday in France during the mounting of the crisis in the first three weeks of July. When Strong visited Moreau on July 20, and again on Norman's visit to Moreau on July 29, the talk was of the need for central banks to remain independent and of the possibility in due course of stabilization loans, but not of the rate. Adolph Miller, of the Board of Governors of the Federal Reserve System, did discuss the rate with Moreau in August, but the substance of his view was not recorded. Reginald McKenna suggested that the franc should be allowed to appreciate, Sir Arthur Salter that it should not rise too far.[58] In the end, Poincaré, who vacillated through October, came down on the side of stabilization

56. Ibid., p. 74; Chandler records Strong's mistaken belief that the study was by Charles Rist (*Benjamin Strong*, p. 374).

57. See Jacques Rueff, "Sur un point d'histoire: Le niveau de la stabilisation Poincaré," 1959, and his preface to Moreau, *Souvenirs d'un gouverneur de la Banque de France*, p. ix.

58. Moreau, *Souvenirs d'un gouverneur de la Banque de France*, pp. 34ff., 48ff., 160, 170.

at 120 francs to the pound when Léon Jouhaux, the head of the Confédération Générale de Travail, came to protest rising unemployment in export industries.[59]

(Most of the advice given to the French, from without and within, was focused on French problems, not on the impact of the French exchange rate choice on the system as a whole.)Whether one argues that the fault lay in British overvaluation or French undervaluation, or in some division of the blame between the two, there is hardly doubt that the relative overvaluation of the pound and undervaluation of the franc were dangerous for the system. From a national perspective, the French decision was made with care. From the viewpoint of the system as a whole, and with hindsight, it underrated the importance of the large amount of French capital abroad, which was unlikely to be reinvested in foreign securities after French losses on Russian bonds and therefore was likely to return to France. In this circumstance, a moderately undervalued rate to stimulate exports and import-competing industry would have been inappropriate, since it was desirable to have the capital return in part, as it went out of France, in real goods and services, that is, in the form of an import surplus. A French return flow of capital combined with an export surplus would strain the system, since it would have to be financed by increases in Bank of France reserves.

(It is a fair point that the British, more than the French, had an interest in underwriting the system and that the French had much less concern or responsibility. The decision about sterling was therefore more fraught with consequence for the system than that of the franc. The main French error, however, was in thinking only of the impact of the rate chosen on France and not at all of the system as a whole, given the fact that the British choice had already been made, albeit badly.)

(Italy also suffered monetary troubles in the 1920s. There was first the crisis of 1921, in which a number of banks got into trouble when the security bubble collapsed.)One—the Banca di Sconto— was allowed to go under. Mussolini's march on Rome took place in 1922. In 1926, following the return to gold of the pound and the

59. See Rueff, preface to ibid., and Charles Rist, "L'expérience de 1926 et la franc d'aujourd'hui," 1952, p. 66. Rist argues vigorously against Aron, who attributes the world depression in part to the French stabilization rate of 1926, stating that it had more profound causes, its origin was British not French, and that the role of the franc was not only negligible but nonexistent (pp. 70–71).

recovery of the French franc, he was ready to stabilize the lira. The lira had been, like the franc, 25 to the pound (19.3 cents to the dollar) in 1914, but it had sunk after the war to 150. Mussolini sought to restore it to 90—the so-called *quota novanta*. Governor Strong of the Federal Reserve Bank of New York was among those urging stabilization, at the behest of Secretary of the Treasury Andrew W. Mellon. In cooperation with Montagu Norman of the Bank of England, Strong helped to arrange a central bank loan of $75 million and a private one of $50 million to assist in stabilization.[60] The deflationary impact of the currency appreciation drove Italian security prices still lower and further weakened the Italian banks, which typically held industrial equities among their assets. Norman and Strong thought 90 to the pound and 5.263 cents to the dollar too high but allowed themselves to be persuaded by the governor of the Banca d'Italia, Bonaldo Stringher, who observed that these levels had already been reached in the market.[61]

Another country that tried to revalue its currency in the 1920s was Spain. Cut off from international markets by one of the highest levels of tariff protection in the world under the dictatorship of Primo de Rivera, it revalued the peseta between December 1924 and December 1926 from 72 percent of par to 79 percent, and then in March 1927 to 94 percent. At this level the speculators who had been buying pesetas turned bearish and sold them. In June 1928 the dictatorship tried to hold up the rate with an Exchange Intervention Committee armed with foreign exchange and gold worth 500 million pesetas, but the effort collapsed in October 1929 and foreign exchange reserves were left virtually exhausted.[62]

Other currencies in Europe were stabilized along with the pound, franc, lira, and peseta, but these were less important for the international monetary system than the major currencies, whatever importance they had for domestic macroeconomic conditions.[63] Of greater significance on an international scale was the fact that Nor-

60. See Chandler, *Benjamin Strong*, pp. 381–90; and Gian Giacomo Migone, *Gli Stati Uniti e il fascismo: Alle origine dell' egemonia Americana in Italia*, 1980, pp. 179–99.

61. Richard H. Meyer, *Banker's Diplomacy: Monetary Stabilization in the Twenties*, 1970, p. 52.

62. Joseph Harrison, "The Interwar Depression and the Spanish Economy," 1983, pp. 306–7.

63. Meyer, *Banker's Diplomacy*.

man and Moreau found themselves competing for influence among the separate central banks, concerned lest one or the other should take too long a lead in organizing a particular stabilization loan or should take too large a share in it. Strong became obliged to mediate between the two and, in the case of the Polish loan, to take the lead to avoid deadlock. Much of subsequent misunderstandings and antipathy grew out of these encounters: Moreau, suspicious, regarded Norman as an imperialist; Norman, impatient, accused Moreau of introducing politics into technical economic and financial matters.[64] It is hard to discern that the French had ambitions of their own beyond resisting British domination of all the central bank allies. Moreover, British designs for the system—the gold exchange standard, stabilization of exchange rates, restoration of the financial importance (hegemony) of London—could be said to be guided by national considerations rather than or as well as by those of the international monetary system. Norman believed in the dependence of the United Kingdom on the restoration of the world economy, as well as the obverse. For the leader it is often difficult to distinguish the public from the private good.

The last country to return its currency to par was Japan. It did so very late. Japan had participated in the inflationary price rise of 1919–21, with prices going from 200 to 320 before falling back to 190 (on the basis of 1913 as 100). It was beginning to stabilize the yen when its problem was compounded by the Tokyo-Yokohama earthquake of September 1, 1923. In March 1924 it let the rate go again under the pressure of easy finance from the circulation of "earthquake bills." The depreciation was not severe and was corrected in 1925 by gold sales. But after de jure stabilization of the franc in 1928, Japan was the only major country in the world off gold. Internal and external pressures to stabilize mounted. In particular, exporters and importers grew restive with the slight degree of

64. One of the most interesting passages in Moreau's memoirs records a report of a visit by Quesnay to London, where he saw not only Norman but also Niemeyer, Salter, Strakosch, and Kindersley. As reported by Moreau, Quesnay observed that the grand British design was not only to stabilize currencies, even without the support of the Bank of France, but to link up central banks into a cooperative network which could, independent of political considerations and even of governments, regulate the questions essential for prosperity, viz., monetary security, distribution of credit, and movement of prices. Moreau characterizes these views as "surely doctrinaire, no doubt somewhat utopian, even perhaps Machiavellian, but possible!" (*Souvenirs d'un gouverneur de la Banque de France*, pp. 136–37).

depreciation, and foreign bankers discussing Japanese financing urged a return to gold (but at a lower parity). Finally, in July 1929 the newly chosen Hamaguchi cabinet announced a policy of returning to par. Speculation bid up the rate from a monthly average of 43.88 U.S. cents in June 1929 to 48.96 in December. On January 11, 1930, the yen returned to par.[65]

U.S. lending

It is, of course, an exaggeration to claim that the Dawes loan set in motion foreign lending by the United States. Already during the war, foreign governments had borrowed in New York and Washington, typically using the facilities of J. P. Morgan & Co. until they were in a position to borrow from the United States government. There was a flurry of postwar lending through foreign dollar bonds, which reached sizable amounts in 1922. Operations in 1924, however, lifted the volume to a new high plateau of more than $900 million a year, from which it rose to above $1.25 billion in 1927 and 1928. The increases in loans to Canada and Asia and Oceania were not sensational. Those for Latin America and Europe were. Later, as we shall see, this lending stopped abruptly with awkward consequences.

A wide difference existed between the functioning of the New York market for foreign bonds and the London prewar market. This was not entirely for the reason given by Schumpeter, that U.S. lending offset such disturbances as reparations rather than undertaking new investment that would be transferred to the borrowing countries in real goods and services.[66] Nor was it mainly the high-pressure methods of New York bankers and the wasteful projects in Germany and in Latin America, contrasting with more experienced British bankers, of which so much has been made.[67] More interesting from an economic point of view is the fact that, in Britain, foreign lending and domestic investment were substitutes, except at business cycle turning points when they responded to interest rate changes and moved together. In the postwar United States, foreign and do-

65. This paragraph draws heavily on Patrick, "The Economic Muddle of the 1920s."

66. See Schumpeter, *Business Cycles*, vol. 2, p. 703.

67. See J. W. Beyen, *Money in a Maelstrom*, 1949, p. 45: "The United States had all the vigour of a newcomer . . . a sales department with a new article."

TABLE 1

U.S. AND BRITISH FOREIGN LENDING, ANNUALLY, BY REGIONS, 1924–29 (in millions of dollars)

United States	Europe	Asia and Oceania	Africa	Canada and Newfoundland	Latin America	Total[a]
1924	527	100	—	151	191	969
1925	629	147	—	137	163	1,076
1926	484	38	—	226	377	1,125
1927	577	164	—	237	359	1,337
1928	598	137	—	185	331	1,251
1929	142	58	—	295	176	671
Total	2,957	644	—	1,231	1,597	6,429
United Kingdom						
1924	159	314	66	20	31	590
1925	53	216	72	10	68	419
1926	120	226	32	29	129	536
1927	105	238	136	34	126	639
1928	164	232	80	98	96	670
1929	105	139	51	74	78	447
Total	706	1,365	437	265	528	3,301

SOURCE: League of Nations, *Balances of Payments, 1930*, 1932, p. 30.
[a]Including a small amount unspecified for the United Kingdom.

mestic lending were positively correlated in response to the cyclical movement of profits and interest rates, except at the turning points. The short-run divergences occurred particularly in the middle of 1928 and the first quarter of 1930.[68]

This profoundly contrasting behavior may have been linked to the exuberance of the American and the experience of the British investment communities, though it is difficult to see the connection. The difference is more that British lending followed a supply model in which a fixed supply of investment funds was allocated to domestic and foreign users according to the strength of their respective demands, whereas in the United States the supply of investible funds waxed and waned with the business cycle and was, after 1924, allocated in roughly constant proportions to the two outlets. What makes the economy behave in one way at one time and place and another at another is not, however, self-evident.

In the six years from 1924 to 1929, the United States loaned abroad some $6.4 billion and the United Kingdom $3.3 billion, as Table 1 shows. The patterns and volatility of lending differed. The dip in British security issues after 1924 was the result of the embargo applied from November 1924 through 1925 and most of 1926. Major declines to Europe and Latin America occurred in U.S. issues. For Asia and Oceania, particularly Australia, the decline from 1928 to 1929 occurred both in Britain and, to a greater extent, in the United States.

---

68. See Hal B. Lary, *The United States in the World Economy: The International Transactions of the United States During the Interwar Period*, 1943, pp. 92ff; and Alex K. Cairncross, *Home and Foreign Investment, 1800–1913*, 1953, pp. 187ff. Mintz (*Deterioration in the Quality of Foreign Bonds*, p. 11) asserts that U.S. foreign lending was negatively correlated with the cycle in the 1920s, but her work refers to short cycles, with recessions in 1924 and 1927, rather than to the eight-to-nine-year cycles of the 1920s and 1930s. She observes, of relevance to an accelerator model of foreign lending, that Australia, Germany, and Italy borrowed chiefly at times when they enjoyed high business activity, whereas Argentina, Brazil, and the Netherlands floated most of their loans when they were depressed, Austrian issues were about equal in the two periods, and the results for France were inconclusive (p. 17). For a general discussion of these pro- and countercyclical models in foreign lending, see C. P. Kindleberger, "The Cyclical Pattern of Long-Term Lending," 1982.

3

The Boom

After recovery to 1925 or 1926 came the boom. It was not general, uninterrupted, or extensive. Moreover, it contained increasing signs of tension: in the accumulation of inventories of primary products (discussed in Chapter 4); in the rise of security prices to dizzying heights (discussed in Chapter 5); and in the exacerbation of financial and political difficulties. But it was a boom

The major exceptions were Britain, Italy, and Japan. Britain shared but little in the expansion, spending virtually all the 1920s in the doldrums. Unemployment was severe throughout the decade, both before and especially after the General Strike of 1926, which had resulted from the coal strike that followed the attempt to squeeze prices and wages down further after the stabilization of the pound. Coal, steel, shipbuilding, textiles, and housing were depressed. Unemployment was heavily concentrated in Wales, Manchester, and the northeast. It is important not to exaggerate. New industries, London, and the southeast did well. There was expanding employment and technological progress in automobiles, chemicals, and electrical equipment. The year 1929 showed a sharp spurt in industrial production over 1928. On the whole, however, the 1920s were, except for 1929, a lost decade for the United Kingdom.[1]

---

1. This is something of an exaggeration. R. S. Sayers makes the point that while coal, steel, textiles, and shipbuilding were deeply depressed, chemicals, automobiles, and electricity flourished as Britain applied German and American innova-

Italy, as we saw in the last chapter, suffered a stock market decline in 1926 as a consequence of the deliberate attempt to appreciate the lira. On top of the bank crisis of 1921, the finance of industry went badly throughout the decade.

On the other side of the world, Japan suffered relative depression, growing at only half the speed it achieved in the preceding and following decades, as government and financial authorities held credit tight in an effort to improve the value of the yen. A major cause was the Tokyo-Yokohama earthquake of September 1, 1923, which required a large program of reconstruction and credit expansion and depreciated the yen. A banking crisis in 1927 cut short a threatened new expansion of credit. A three-week moratorium was necessary in April and May; many small banks failed, and some large ones were merged. But the Japanese economy was not tightly bound to the rest of the world; its troubles had no repercussions.

In addition to exceptions, there were interruptions. The United States experienced a "recession" in 1927, when the industrial production index based on 1923–25 fell from 111 in May to 99 in November. In retrospect, this episode is thought to lack the characteristics of a normal business cycle and to reflect primarily the decision of Henry Ford to close down automobile production for six months to permit the changeover from the Model T, on which production had been concentrated since before the war, to the Model A in an effort to compete more effectively with Chevrolet. This recession was not without importance in contributing to the decision to lower interest rates in the United States to help to resolve a European financial impasse.

The other interruptions occurred in Germany in 1926 and again in 1928. The 1926 recession was clearly domestic in origin. That of 1928 is frequently thought to have been caused by the cutoff in U.S. lending to Germany in the second half of 1928.[2] However, a more

tions. The result was an impressive rise in real productivity ("The Springs of Technical Progress in Britain, 1919–1939," 1950). Ingvar Svennilson calculates that real income rose from 82 in 1921 to 105 in 1929, or 28 percent in eight years; but 1929 was lower in real income per head than 1919, and 1921 was particularly depressed (*Growth and Stagnation in the European Economy*, 1954, table A.1, p. 233). Sean Glynn and Alan Booth have argued recently that the unemployment in Britain between the wars was structural, not Keynesian (see their "Unemployment in Interwar Britain: A Case for Relearning the Lessons of the 1930s?" 1983).

2. See M. E. Falkus, "The German Business Cycle in the 1920s," 1975, replying to Peter Temin's "The Beginning of the Depression in Germany," 1971, which

profound analysis of the case produces the opposite conclusion, that the recession in Germany in 1928, of domestic origin, halted the capital inflow.[3] The issue is complex. In December 1926 Schacht withdrew exemption from capital gains tax from foreign subscribers to German bonds. This produced a collapse of foreign borrowing in the first half of 1927. When the exemption was restored because of this collapse, the movement of capital to Germany in the second half of 1927 and the first half of 1928 reached the highest level of any twelve-month period to work off the backlog of deferred borrowing. According to Balderston, the decline that followed in the second half of 1928 was due not to the rise in the New York stock market but to the weakening of internal conditions in Germany that contributed to a deterioration of German credit abroad.[4] Some portion of the decline may be attributable to a diversion of attention from foreign bonds to American equities, however, as judged by the sharp declines in foreign lending to other parts of the world beginning in the third quarter of 1928, as shown in Table 2 below.

The boom was pronounced in the United States, in Australia and Canada, and in France. In the less developed countries there were signs of trouble in the accumulation of stocks and the beginnings of weakness in raw material prices. Even in the United States there were the problems already referred to: a collapse of the Florida land boom in 1925, with bank failures set in train, and a decline in housing starts, which reached 950,000 in 1925 and then declined until May 1927 before recovering briefly between then and April 1928.

In the United States the boom was built around the automobile, not only the manufacture of vehicles, but tires and other components, roads, gasoline stations, oil refineries, garages, and suburbs. The combustion engine spread into transport with the use of trucks and to the farm, where tractors replaced horses.[5] Electrical appliances—radios, refrigerators, vacuum cleaners—unknown at the start of the decade, were commonplace by 1929. Another innovation was in motion pictures, with talkies introduced in 1926. The

---

claimed that the causes of the decline in the capital flow to Germany were domestic, not foreign, i.e., not the beginnings of the boom in the New York stock market.

3. T. Balderston, "The Beginnings of the Depression in Germany, 1927–30: Investment and the Capital Market," 1983.

4. Ibid., table 7, panel h, p. 407.

5. For a view that emphasizes the role of the automobile and its associated industries—for both the boom of the 1920s and the decline of the 1930s—see W. W. Rostow, *The World Economy: Theory and Prospect*, 1978, pp. 210–13, 335–37.

sale of more expensive items was assisted by the introduction during this period of installment credit: by 1925 the volume of installment paper outstanding was $1.375 billion and by 1929, $3 billion. While impressive, the boom was not frenzied, except perhaps in stock market speculation. Pressure on real resources was moderate. Unemployment was 3.1 percent in 1929. In January 1929 wages were only 5 percent above January 1925. Commodity prices fell almost 5 percent from 1926 to 1929, rising 5 percent in farm products and falling almost 8 percent in other commodities. Unless one concentrated on the stock market—and even there there are questions, as will appear—the boom was not spectacular.

The relevance of these remarks is that there is an important school of thought that believes that whatever goes up must come down and that it cannot come down unless it has gone up. "It is agreed that to prevent the depression, the only effective method is to prevent a boom."[6] "A condition of recovery is the gold standard to preserve interlocal equilibrium and avoid the development of booms."[7] "A satisfactory theory of the boom explains the depression. In the crisis what has been sown during the boom has to be reaped."[8]

Murray Rothbard insists that the boom from 1921 to 1929 was highly inflationary in character, caused by lax monetary policies of the Federal Reserve System, and that even if prices did not go up there was still inflation because they should have gone down given the substantial increases in productivity taking place.[9] One chapter in his book, in fact, has the subtitle, "The Lure of a Stable Price Level." Contemporary opinion in Europe, on the other hand, considered that the United States had not expanded enough to raise prices, as it should have after acquiring large amounts of gold during and after the war.

Friedman and Schwartz are explicit in separating out the stock market in the United States from business expansion. "Far from being an inflationary decade, the twenties were the reverse." "Federal reserve policy was not restrictive enough to halt the bull market

6. Robbins, *The Great Depression*, p. 171.
7. Ibid., p. 172.
8. Wilhelm Röpke, *Crises and Cycles*, n.d. (but the preface to this book, translated from the German, is dated 1936), p. 119.
9. Rothbard, *America's Great Depression*, esp. part 2, entitled "The Inflationary Boom, 1921–29." A conservative general historian who follows Rothbard's lead is Paul Johnson. See his *Modern Times*, ch. 7.

yet too restrictive to foster vigorous business expansion." They are particularly concerned to dismiss the 1920s as a period of marked inflation and expansion because the stock of money failed to rise— "a phenomenon not matched by any previous or subsequent expansion."[10] This goes too far in the other direction to deny the reality of the boom. Industrial production in 1929 reached a level of 75 percent above 1913 in the United States, contrasted with 10 percent for Germany and 9 percent for Britain, 52 percent for Belgium and 39.5 percent for France. If comparison is made with 1924 rather than 1913, however, Germany does better than any of the other industrial countries.

Fed by the undervaluation of the franc, the French boom not only did well compared with 1913 or 1924, but it endured. In the first place, industrial production reached its peak in the first half of 1930 rather than in 1929, and it did not slow down until the latter half of 1931. Second, the records reached in 1929 lasted until well after the Second World War. This tells more about the depression in France than about the boom. But there is no gainsaying an increase in output which took the annual index of production up from 110 in 1927 (down from 126 in 1926) to 139.5 in 1929. The French budget ran large surpluses, the government debt to the Bank of France was paid off, and security prices doubled after currency stabilization. Late in 1929 the French minister of finance, Henri Chéron, announced that he had accumulated a surplus of 17 billion francs in the Treasury, compared to only one million in July 1926. This had contributed to the surplus in the balance of payments of the previous years. Its rapid expenditure upon publication of its existence helped to maintain French domestic prosperity into 1930, but this also turned the balance of payments around.[11]

The gold exchange standard

The League of Nations called a conference that met in Brussels in 1920 to discuss various issues of international finance: the purchas-

10. Friedman and Schwartz, *A Monetary History of the United States, 1867–1960*, pp. 298–99.

11. Sauvy, *Histoire économique de la France entre les deux guerres*, vol. 1, pp. 105–6. Note the similarity to the Juliusturm, accumulated by the Germans from the French indemnity in 1871, and the Schäffer surplus in the same country after 1951; see Frederick G. Reuss, *Fiscal Policy for Growth Without Inflation: The German Experiment*, 1963, pp. 157–58.

ing-power-parity theory of the foreign exchanges; the possible establishment of an international bank to mediate between potential lenders and borrowers; and how to revive the international capital market. Nothing, it was thought, could be decided so long as the question of German reparations remained unresolved.

In 1922 France and Britain called another conference on international monetary reconstruction to meet at Genoa.[12] The British, under the inspiration of Montagu Norman, worried about the adequacy of the world's gold supply. The prewar gold price remained fixed, but mining costs had risen because of wartime inflation. Moreover, the higher price level increased the demand for gold reserves by central banks. The experts recommended that national monetary authorities should explicitly adopt the substitution of foreign exchange for gold in reserve holdings. Many central banks had, in fact, held reserves in claims on London, Paris, and Berlin.[13] The recommendation was that this practice be institutionalized.

But the experts did not recommend that any particular central bank should hold foreign exchange, or which foreign exchange should be held. Since foreign exchange is both an asset and a liability, where there are alternative assets, such as gold or other currencies, it is a sensitive liability, possibly subject to the instability of Gresham's law. In domestic monetary theory a distinction is made between outside money as an asset that is no one's liability, such as gold, and as a liability that is not expected to be paid off, such as locally held government debt. In the international economy gold was the only outside money, and it was relatively scarce. In addition, gold was joined by the dollar as an alternative to sterling.

Sterling in the hands of the British Commonwealth was perhaps outside money: like domestic government debt, no one expected it to be paid off. But sterling in other hands, especially those of continental bankers who contemplated moving out of sterling into dollars or gold, was clearly inside money—an unstable component of the total.

Part of the problem for a central bank with liabilities to foreign holders arose from market conditions. There were various reasons why an asset holder would want to hold foreign assets rather than

12. Stephen V. O. Clarke, "The Reconstruction of the International Monetary System: The Attempts of 1922 and 1933," part 2: "The Negotiations of 1922," 1973, pp. 4–18.

13. Peter H. Lindert, "Key Currencies and Gold, 1900–1913," 1969.

gold and one foreign exchange rather than another. These reasons include safety, trading requirements, convenience, tradition, loyalty, and hope of speculative gain. In addition to these reasons, however, there is also the return. Other things being equal, asset holders kept their funds where they could earn the highest yield. This meant that a country that wanted to discourage foreigners from withdrawing their funds and converting them to domestic currency or gold had to maintain competitive interest rates.

Foreign central banks are moved by most of the considerations that affect private asset holders, plus several more. A central bank is presumably not a profit-making institution and can disregard fine calculations to maximize earnings, even though it needs income to operate. Its responsibility for the safety of its assets is a grave one, since it acts for the country as a whole. But the central bank may choose to move from gold to foreign exchange or vice versa, or from one currency to another, as a matter of economic policy, affecting the interest differential between its market and foreign markets or a particular foreign market. Or it may do so for the purely political reasons of assisting a foreign country in its policies or bringing pressure to bear on it.

Germany had originally acquired sterling as the counterpart of the British share of the Dawes loan. Schacht and Norman worked together closely in the issuance of the loan and in getting the Gold-diskontobank established, and Schacht had every interest in assisting in the stabilization of the pound at par, to the limited extent the Reichsbank then counted, since a rise in the pound increased the value of the bank's reserve holdings. When toward the end of 1926 there was an excessive inflow of foreign capital into Germany, however, he faced a dilemma. He was unwilling to see the inflow of capital continue, but he was equally reluctant to repel it by lowering domestic interest rates, which would have contributed to domestic expansion. Accordingly, he chose to convert sterling to gold to tighten interest rates abroad. This would keep the capital in London.

The Bank of England was as unwilling to raise the interest rate as the Reichsbank was unwilling to lower it. British unemployment was widespread; still tighter money would have produced resistance from the Treasury and political unrest. Accordingly, the Bank of England allowed the gold to leave without responding in the traditional manner. German power over the London market was not substantial. But the episode suggested that the period of effective functioning of the gold standard was coming to an end.

French accumulation of sterling

The stabilization of the franc at 124 + to the pound and 25 + to the dollar (3.92 cents) raised a more serious problem. The undervalued rate both stimulated the current account in the balance of payments, subsidizing exports and import-competing production in France, and encouraged inward capital movements. Much of the capital inflow was the repatriation of French capital that had been exported in 1925 and early 1926 when the franc depreciated. Some was doubtless foreign capital buying francs in hopes of a further appreciation in the future. The Bank of France bought foreign exchange to hold down the rate of exchange, carrying it on its balance sheet under "Miscellaneous Assets" since the regulations made no provisions for holding foreign exchange. Purchases started off slowly in November 1926 and proceeded steadily in the early months of 1927. At the end of April the Bank of France paid back a loan from the Bank of England, which convinced the market that the only direction the franc could go was up. There was no longer use in keeping French funds abroad, and foreign capitalists who thought the rate might appreciate placed their bets. The Bank of France's holdings of foreign exchange went from £5.3 million in November 1926 to £20 million at the end of February, £60 million at the end of April, and £160 million at the end of May.[14]

This accumulation of sterling put Moreau in a strong position and Norman in a weak one. As an opening gambit, the Bank of France began to convert sterling into gold. A conference in Paris at the end of May brought a confrontation between the two viewpoints, Norman asking the French to declare the franc legally stabilized in order to discourage those speculating on a rise in its value, and the French, like Schacht earlier, asking the British to raise interest rates as a means of slowing down the capital inflow into France. The French were unwilling to stabilize—there were banking interests like Rothschild who hoped for a still higher rate, based not on con-

14. See Chandler, *Benjamin Strong*, p. 371; and Clarke, *Central Bank Cooperation, 1924–31*, p. 111.

siderations of international stability but on domestic interests. By the same token, Norman was unable to raise interest rates—a storm would break out if he tried it, he said, with its center presumably Churchill at the Exchequer.

There were threats of further conversions of sterling into gold, although the French were unwilling to push so hard as to force Britain back off gold. On the other side, the British threatened to present for collection the whole war debt since the French had not ratified the Churchill-Caillaux war debt agreement of 1926, even though they were paying on schedule.

A compromise was reached, involving New York. The French agreed to hold a certain amount of sterling representing what it was estimated would be needed to pay off foreign bull speculators in francs when they at last became discouraged and unwound their positions. This amount was given as £70 million to £80 million. Of this, £30 million would be converted immediately to gold, with the Federal Reserve Bank of New York furnishing £12 million in gold from its London stock against sterling. To complete the deal, the Bank of France altered its support prices in the exchange market to discriminate in buying against sterling and in favor of dollars.[15]

This agreement relieved the immediate situation. An attempt to build wider and stronger means of cooperation was sought at a conference held among Norman, Strong, and Schacht, with Rist representing Moreau, in early July 1927 at the home of U.S. Secretary of the Treasury Ogden Mills on Long Island. The purpose was to see whether the pressure on Germany and Britain could be relieved by lowering rates in the United States rather than by raising them in Europe; to explore the relationship, if any, that existed between monetary policies in general and slipping commodity prices worldwide; and to deal with the Bank of France's large and growing accumulation of sterling and dollars. There is no complete account of this conference, which lasted, or at least was intended to last, for eight days, but only a short paragraph in Moreau's diary. This summarized the decisions of the Federal Reserve Bank of New York to lower its interest rate to help London and Berlin (but not Paris, Moreau records); to make gold available to continental Europe from New York at the same price as gold in London in an effort to spare

15. See Clarke, *Central Bank Cooperation, 1924–31*, pp. 119–20, 167.

London's stock; and to buy the Bank of France's sterling with dollars.[16]

The gold standard was supposed to work automatically, with countries gaining gold undertaking further expansion and those losing it contracting. By the 1920s, however, this automaticity had begun to unravel, and central bank coordination was needed to assist or replace it. It was of course not the first example, but it was one of the most striking and might be said to be a precedent for consultation among monetary authorities with a view to coordinating macroeconomic policies after the Second World War—at Chequers in 1966, at the Organization for Economic Cooperation and Development (OECD) and the Bank for International Settlements (BIS), and ultimately at summit meetings of heads of state in the late 1970s and the 1980s.

The famous 1927 action of the Federal Reserve System in lowering interest rates can wait briefly. First, it is worth noticing the device that was hit upon by the Bank of France to undertake domestic open market operations in a contracting direction without inducing a flow of foreign capital to Paris. From a domestic viewpoint, gold was as awkward as sterling. Forward contracts to buy sterling, however, were not. Accordingly, from August 1927, after the inflow of capital into France had subsided, the Bank of France operated in its money market by selling sterling to the market against forward cover rather than by selling franc securities. The forward purchase of sterling (sale of francs) could be adjusted to make it attractive for the Paris money market to hold sterling spot against a forward sale. Private funds were thus subtracted from the Paris market and added to the British. The policy was initiated not just before de jure stabilization in June 1928, as Ragnar Nurkse states,[17] but in August 1927. In May 1928 these forward purchase contracts of the Bank of France amounted to $440 million and by June 1928 almost $600 million.[18]

•

16. Moreau, *Souvenirs d'un gouverneur de la Banque de France*, p. 372. In the last item, Moreau was probably referring to a decision by the Bank of England to buy French sterling with dollars to the amount of $25 million.

17. League of Nations (Ragnar Nurkse), *International Currency Experience: Lessons of the Interwar Period*, 1944, p. 36.

18. Chandler, *Benjamin Strong*, p. 417; and Clark, *Central Bank Cooperation, 1924–31*, pp. 121–22.

Total claims of the Bank of France on the gold of the rest of the world, represented by its total exchange, spot and forward, amounted to $1.45 billion in May 1928 and somewhat less a month later at the time of stabilization. This gave it tremendous power over the markets where it held claims. The fact that, as in June 1928, a third to half of this amount consisted of forward claims, unbeknownst to the British authorities, lent still greater instability to the system. The British were aware of the likelihood that Bank of France official claims might be converted into gold—an eventuality it was important to guard against. Privately held sterling was doubtless regarded as different. To the extent that such sterling is held against a forward sale to an official body, however, it presents an identical risk of conversion as official sterling.[19] There is no indication that the British knew the size of the problem they labored under as a result of awareness of the French forward operations. Nervous as they were, they were not nervous enough.

All this time the Bank of France and the Bank of England quarreled with each other about the unimportant issue of which would take leadership in the stabilization program of the lesser currencies of Europe. Governor Strong of the Federal Reserve Bank of New York was called in to blunt the dispute. He sympathized with Moreau to the extent that he thought Norman's intrigues and interest in financial leadership petty. But he found Moreau threatening.[20] Moreau was Strong's friend, but Norman was his intimate. He would have preferred not to take sides. More and more, together with Schacht and Moreau but not Norman, he regarded the gold exchange standard rationalized at Genoa as an uncertain basis for the

19. For a modern distinction between private and official foreign exchange holdings, which similarly fails to distinguish between outright private dollars and those held under official forward contracts, see Review Committee for Balance of Payments Statistics, Report to the Budget Bureau, *The Balance of Payments Statistics of the United States: A Review and Appraisal* (E. M. Bernstein Report), 1965.

20. See Chandler, *Benjamin Strong*, p. 421. Some years later, Moreau wrote an article in the *Revue des Deux Mondes* revealing that he had been conscious of his capacity to push Britain off the gold standard as early as May 1927. This is extensively quoted in Sir Henry Clay, *Lord Norman*, 1957, pp. 228–32. For an explicit statement in Moreau's diary, see the entry for February 6, 1928, recording Moreau's discussion of the imperialism of the Bank of England with Poincaré: "We have powerful means of pressure on the Bank of England. Would it not be useful to have a serious conversation with M. Norman, with a view to dividing Europe into two zones of financial influence which would be attributed respectively to France and to Britain?" (*Souvenirs d'un gouverneur de la Banque de France*, p. 489).

world economy. A particularly shaky element in the picture, for those who believe that individual actors are important to history, was the fact that Norman was pro-German and pro-Schacht, anti-French and anti-Moreau. The last feeling was heartily reciprocated by the Frenchman.

Easy money in the United States and the stock market

The Long Island conference of early July 1927 set in motion a decision of the Federal Reserve System to reduce its interest rates. This was not done solely for the purpose of assisting the British in attracting capital and halting the loss of gold. It was not a "dilemma situation" in which domestic considerations pushed in one direction, international in another. The 1927 recession was in the minds of the Federal Reserve authorities, as were slipping world commodity prices. Beginning in July 1927 and stretching to September, the Federal Reserve System bought $200 million in open market purchases and lowered its discount rate over the system by half a percentage point, with 3.5 percent as the rate for the Federal Reserve Bank of New York.

How significant this action was in stimulating the rise in the stock market that began in the spring of 1928 is debatable. Galbraith dismisses it out of hand.[21] Friedman and Schwartz are inclined to think it may have contributed to the rise of the stock market but that the Federal Reserve System's real error occurred later when it directed policy partly to the stock market and partly to the level of business, so that conflict was bound to arise between the two objectives of monetary policy. They believe that the authorities should have ignored the stock market, as they had ignored the Florida land boom, and concentrated on the level of business, which would have supported a more expansionary policy from 1927 through to 1929. But either objective would have been better than both. The trouble came from stalking two targets with one weapon.[22]

21. J. K. Galbraith, *The Great Crash, 1929*, 1955, p. 16.

22. Friedman and Schwartz, *A Monetary History of the United States, 1867–1960*, pp. 291ff. Pedersen agrees with the Friedman and Schwartz position, but for a different reason. He believes the market was not unduly high. Unlike them, moreover, he blames the Federal Reserve System for the crash and believes that the crash was important for the subsequent depression. See *Essays in Monetary Theory and Related Subjects*, pp. 197ff.

To lay all the blame for the 1928–29 stock market rise and the subsequent crash at the door of the 1927 action is excessive, but to dismiss the easier monetary policy as irrelevant also goes too far. That monetary policy was reversed in the spring of 1928 without restraining the market does not settle the issue in favor of there being no connection. A touch of the whip may be enough to cause nervous and excitable horses to run away and later to resist powerful hauling on the reins. Nervousness and excitability in this case are more important than the character or extent of the stimulus. The market had been working up to a speculative climax since 1924. Three-million-share days had been reached twice in 1925 and three times in the spring of 1926. Four million shares were traded on March 1, 1928. Brokers' loans rose 24 percent in the second half of 1927, to $4.4 billion. New issues boomed.

Nor is it reasonable to ask that the Federal Reserve should have ignored security markets, which have an effect on business conditions, albeit an indirect one. If there was no dilemma as between the international monetary economy and domestic business, that between business and domestic financial markets was painful. Herbert Hoover warned against stock market speculation from his position as secretary of commerce, just as Schacht preached against German borrowing. But President Coolidge was not stirred.[23] And there was no way to forecast in mid-1927 how nervous and excitable the stock market would become.

The halt in foreign lending

Foreign long-term lending kept pace with the New York stock market through the first half of 1928. Domestic corporate bonds had turned down in mid-1927 in favor of corporate stocks, but foreign bonds reached new peaks in the fourth quarter of 1927 and the first half of 1928. The collapse occurred after June 1928, especially for German, other European, and Asian and Oceanian issues, as Table 2 shows. Canadian borrowing dropped sharply in the third quarter of 1928 but recovered. New issues for Latin America held up for a

---

23. *The Memoirs of Herbert Hoover*, vol. 3, pp. 5–13. Hoover was supported by Adolph Miller of the Board of Governors of the Federal Reserve System in opposing Strong's help for the international position. He called Strong "a mental annex to Europe" (p. 8).

year until the third quarter of 1929. But the change after June 1928 is unmistakable.

A somewhat parallel change took place in trade in outstanding securities, especially U.S. securities representing mainly equities traded on the New York Stock Exchange. Instead, however, of an outflow that halted, there was a small outflow in 1927 that gave way to a sizable inflow in 1928 and 1929. The figures are shown in Table 3, together with the annual data for 1927–29 on U.S. trade in outstanding foreign securities, as opposed to the new issues of Table 2. These last show a somewhat, but not wholly, different pattern.[24]

In a thesis at Yale, Heywood Fleisig has attempted to break down these data on trade in outstanding securities within calendar years so as to form an estimate of the total change in capital flow from the eighteen months before June 30, 1928, to the fifteen months that followed to the end of September 1929. The object of this exercise, of course, is to form an impression of the size of the convulsive change in the long-term capital flow that occurred at the end of June 1928.

The movement in new issues can be estimated directly, and the change in direct investment is small and readily gauged. The problem comes in estimating the change in the flow through outstanding securities. The breakdown of trade in outstanding securities within the calendar years 1928 and 1929 is undertaken on a variety of assumptions. The first is a straight proportion of the annual figures within quarters. The second assumes that American and European investors sell each other's securities when the New York stock market is steady or declining but buy when prices in that market are rising. The third assumes that when the New York stock market is steady or declining, Europeans sell U.S. securities while Americans buy European securities, with capital flowing out on both accounts, whereas when New York stock prices are rising, there is an opposite combined capital inflow. Fleisig also makes assumptions about the

24. Beyen points out that the Netherlands floated a number of loans in New York because of the low rates of interest, but was not interested in the foreign exchange. When New York rates rose and the bonds cheapened, they were repatriated rapidly, within a year of issue (*Money in a Maelstrom*, 1949, p. 13). For a demonstration that new issues of securities for foreigners were often bought back by foreigners very quickly, with the result that figures for new issues, uncorrected for trade in outstanding securities, may be misleading, see D. C. M. Platt, *Foreign Finance in Continental Europe and the United States, 1815–1870: Quantities, Origins, Functions, and Distribution*, 1984.

TABLE 2

NEW CAPITAL ISSUES FOR FOREIGN ACCOUNT IN THE UNITED STATES, QUARTERLY, 1928–30: NOMINAL VALUES, EXCLUDING REFUNDING (in millions of dollars)

	Capital exporting countries[a]	Germany	Other Europe	Total Europe	North America	Latin America	Asia and Oceania	Total
1928								
I	13.2	46.7	109.5	179.4	40.5	86.4	15.6	312.1
II	32.0	153.8	94.2	280.0	74.8	74.3	100.6	529.7
III	16.1	14.2	19.5	49.8	6.8	81.9	0.4	118.9
IV	11.7	62.4	24.6	93.7	63.4	88.4	19.9	270.4
1929								
I	42.9	21.0	16.4	80.4	56.8	73.4	53.7	264.3
II	3.9	—	3.3	7.2	114.1	70.3	2.0	193.6
III	14.0	—	8.7	21.7	28.8	29.8	0.4	79.7
IV	24.2	8.5	—	32.7	96.1	2.5	2.3	133.7
1930								
I	—	43.3	26.6	69.9	42.9	39.3	11.5	269.3[b]
II	—	113.5	14.5	128.0	83.7	143.0	50.3	429.6[b]
III	—	10.0	25.0	35.0	49.0	16.1	—	100.1
IV	—	—	—	—	105.7	0.6	—	106.3

SOURCE: League of Nations (Bertil Ohlin), *The Course and Phases of the World Economic Depression*, 1931, pp. 320–21.

[a]Belgium, Czechoslovakia, France, the Netherlands, Sweden, Switzerland, and the United Kingdom.

[b]Including "international issues," not specified in the preceding columns, amounting to $105.7 million and $24.6 million, respectively, during the first and second quarters.

TABLE 3
TRANSACTIONS IN OUTSTANDING SECURITIES BETWEEN THE UNITED STATES AND FOREIGN COUNTRIES, 1927–29 (in million of dollars)

	Domestic Securities			Foreign Securities		
	U.S. purchases from foreigners	U.S. Sales to foreigners	Net U.S. purchases (−) or sales (+)	U.S. Purchases from foreigners	U.S. Sales to foreigners	Net U.S. purchases (−) or sales (+)
1927	624	594	−30	143	336	+193
1928	490	973	+483	483	389	−94
1929	917	1,295	+378	307	412	+105

SOURCE: Hal B. Lary, *The United States and the World Economy*, 1943, p. 107.

TABLE 4

CHANGE IN CAPITAL FLOWS FROM THE UNITED STATES IN OUTSTANDING SECURITIES, BY PARTICULAR PERIODS, 1927–29, UNDER VARIOUS ASSUMPTIONS (*in millions of dollars; U.S. purchases* − *; sales* +)

	Assumption 1 (proration)	Assumption 2 (opposing flows)	Assumption 3 (parallel flows)
January 1, 1927, to June 30, 1928	+ 350	− 50	− 800
July 1, 1928, to September 30, 1929	+ 500	+ 1350	+ 3050
(Change)	(+ 150)	(+ 1400)	(+ 3850)
Implicit October 1, 1929, to December 31, 1929	+ 200	− 250	− 1200
Three-year total	+ 1050	+ 1050	+ 1050

SOURCE: Heywood W. Fleisig, "Long-Term Capital Flows and the Great Depression: The Role of the United States, 1927–1933," 1970, table 1, p. 33 (figures rounded).

size of the response to these price changes as well as about the direction. The total net movement for the three years is unchanged. Varying the assumptions about what happens in the first two and three quarters thereafter gives one not only the swing figure between the eighteen months to June 1928 and the fifteen months thereafter, but an implicit capital movement for the last three months of 1929, as shown in Table 4.

No one of the assumptions has evident validity as a dominant rationalization of actual behavior. They are good mainly to churn out numbers. A comparison of the figures in Table 4 and gross purchases and sales in Table 3, however, makes the results produced by the third assumption impossible. The implicit outflow of capital for the last three months of 1929 is equal to total gross purchases of U.S. and foreign securities from foreigners for the whole year of 1929. Moreover, in the nature of security transactions, the normal practice, even in rapidly moving markets, is for foreigners to buy and sell, with net sales or purchases as a rule less than 20 percent of the gross movement in the same direction. The straight proration of the first assumption understates the change in the capital inflow after June 1928, but the second assumption probably overstates it by a considerable amount. As an educated guess, I am inclined to suggest inflows of $200 million in the first eighteen months, $900 in the next fifteen, for a swing of $700 million, and an implicit outflow of $50 million in the last three months of 1929.

On this showing, there was a swing of something on the order of $2 billion in lending by the United States in the eighteen months from January 1, 1927, to June 30, 1928, and from July 1, 1928, to September 30, 1929, $1.275 billion in new foreign securities, minus $100 million in direct investment, plus, perhaps, $700 million in outstanding securities. This was a substantial amount.

What was it that hit U.S. foreign lending in June 1928? The short answer is the stock market. Investors were diverted into stocks; financial intermediaries, who were not permitted to buy stocks, loaned funds on the call market. Interest rates rose sharply beginning in the spring of 1928 as the Federal Reserve System sold off the additions to its open market portfolio of the summer of 1927 and more and raised the rediscount rate three times. Turnover rose on the New York Stock Exchange. Call money loans went from $4 billion at the end of 1927 to $5.275 billion at mid-1928 and $6.4 billion at the end of the year. Banks withdrew to an extent from the market, but nonbanks took their place and more. Railroads and industrial companies as well as financial houses turned from real investment to call loans, which were safe, liquid (it was thought), and high-yielding.

An ancient dispute going back to the 1920s concerns whether the stock market boom absorbs money.[25] We shall encounter later the question whether the stock market crash hurt business. The question here is whether the boom also hurt it by diverting money from normal business transactions. It is evident that the stock market boom can stimulate business by making investment financing easier—as appears to have been the case in foreign direct investment—by raising dividends and wealth to increase household spending and by lifting business and household expectations. The possible negative impact is mainly on monetary policy, as evidenced in the pressure of the Federal Reserve System in the first half of 1928 to tighten

25. Samuelson calls it a "Talmudic quandary" ("Myths and Realities about the Crash and Depression," p. 9) and lists it as number 5 among his "Fossils from Old Debates." For a sophisticated econometric study that concludes that the stock market did increase the transactions demand for money, independently of real output and interest rates, see Alexander J. Field, "Asset Exchanges and the Transactions Demand for Money, 1919–29," 1984.

credit and in the diversion of money from business and household spending to stock market speculation. The last two factors work together to tighten credit conditions in the industrial and commercial sectors.

An a priori objection to the view that the stock market absorbs credit is that for each individual or company that buys a security and uses money for the purpose there is another who sells it and acquires money. The stock market therefore leaves the volume of money unchanged. Like so many a priori arguments, this is irrefutable on its own terms but of doubtful empirical relevance. If the money supply is divided between the financial circulation on the one hand and the transaction circulation on the other (to use an expression of Keynes denoting money used for expenditure against goods and services), a stock market boom can draw funds from the transactions to the financial circulation. New security issues, of course, produce a movement in the opposite direction. Intense interest in the stock market, however, is likely to enlarge the amount of funds held ready for opportunities to speculate and to shrink those that normally turn over in the production, distribution, and consumption of goods. The boom may not reduce the supply of money in general and hence may escape detection, but does it reduce that available to sustain income flows?

The debate is generally put in the context of a closed economy. In an open economy with financial connections with other markets there is little doubt that a stock market boom can absorb funds from abroad. This may be positive, as when foreigners buy U.S. securities on balance: money is reduced abroad in the financial or transactions circulation and increased in the United States in the financial circulation. The symmetry found in the a priori argument does not apply here. If the stock market boom cuts off foreign lending, the analysis is slightly more complex. A foreign economy has presumably counted on a flow of monies from the U.S. financial circulation to the transaction circulation abroad. This is now stopped, so that there is a relative shrinkage of the foreign transactions circulation with expansion of the U.S. financial circulation.

What applies to international transactions, moreover, equally fits interregional movements in the United States. A stock market boom may, as the a priori reasoning insists, leave the total money supply unchanged but divert funds from the country to the city.

While expectations, increases in wealth, and easy credit in the boom stimulate spending and prosperity, the absorption of funds from abroad, from the country, and from the transactions circulation locally applies contractive pressure to the system.

The increase in the demand for money can be seen in the rise of various interest rates in New York while the amount of money in the system, M_2, moved sideways, as shown in Table 5. Money held more or less steady from 1927 to the middle of 1930, whereas the more volatile interest rates more than doubled and the rate on prime commercial paper went from 4 to 6.25 percent.

The significance of all this is that the rise of the stock market led to a rise of interest rates, which produced a cutoff of capital lending to Germany and the periphery (the views of Balderston and Temin above notwithstanding).[26] And rising capital exports from a leading financial center, suddenly turned off, produce dramatic declines in income abroad that are likely to have repercussions on the unstable center. It happened in 1825, 1857, 1866, 1873, and with special violence in an episode that resembles both 1929 and 1982, the Baring crisis of 1890.[27] It is rather like the childhood game of "snap the whip," in which a line of children holding hands starts running until one end-child halts; the children at the other end find themselves going faster and faster with centrifugal force until they are catapulted off into space.

The World Economic Conference of 1927

The 1920s saw both an increase in tariffs throughout the world and pressures, largely unsuccessful, to reduce them. The tariffs had been applied after the war to protect the new industries that had grown up when trade was cut off, to protect new countries carved out of the Austro-Hungarian Empire, and especially to protect domestic industry against so-called exchange dumping, the surge of exports from countries with seriously depreciated currencies. International conferences at Brussels in 1920, Portorose in 1921, and Genoa in 1922 strongly recommended against the imposition of higher tariffs, but to little avail. There was no escape from the Fordney-McCumber tariff in the United States in 1922 or the McKenna duties in Britain in 1916, rationalized in the Safeguarding of Indus-

26. For references, see notes 2 and 3, this chapter, and associated text.
27. See my "International Propagation of Financial Crises: The Experience of 1888–93," 1984.

TABLE 5

U.S. MONEY SUPPLY AND INTEREST RATES, 1927–JUNE 1930; ANNUAL AVERAGE 1927, MONTHLY AVERAGES 1928 THROUGH JUNE 1930

(money supply in billions of dollars; interest rates in percent per annum)

	Money Supply M_2[a]	Prime Commercial Paper (4–6 Months)	Stock Exchange Time Loans (90 Days)	New Stock Exchange Call Loans	U.S. Govt's	Bond Yields Corporate Aaa	Baa
1927	44.4	4.11	4.35	4.52	3.34	4.51	5.48
1928							
January	45.7	4.00	4.38	4.15	3.18	4.46	5.35
February	45.8	4.00	4.56	4.33	3.19	4.46	5.33
March	46.1	4.13	4.63	4.48	3.17	4.46	5.32
April	46.5	4.38	4.94	5.06	3.20	4.46	5.33
May	46.5	4.50	5.25	5.69	3.24	4.49	5.42
June	45.9	4.75	5.69	6.32	3.29	4.57	5.55
July	46.0	5.13	6.00	6.06	3.42	4.61	5.58
August	45.8	5.30	6.25	6.91	3.48	4.64	5.61
September	46.0	5.63	7.00	7.40	3.46	4.61	5.59
October	46.3	5.50	7.13	7.12	3.47	4.61	5.58
November	46.4	5.38	6.94	6.86	3.38	4.58	5.55
December	46.6	5.38	7.50	8.86	3.45	4.61	5.60

1929						
January	46.2	5.38	7.15	6.94	3.52	4.62	5.63
February	46.3	5.50	7.63	7.47	3.62	4.66	5.66
March	46.2	5.88	7.88	9.80	3.74	4.70	5.79
April	46.1	6.00	8.75	9.46	3.64	4.69	5.80
May	45.8	6.00	8.75	8.79	3.64	4.70	5.80
June	45.9	6.00	8.25	7.83	3.69	4.77	5.94
July	46.4	6.00	7.75	9.41	3.64	4.77	5.95
August	46.3	6.13	8.88	8.15	3.71	4.79	6.04
September	46.3	6.25	8.88	8.62	3.70	4.80	6.12
October	48.2	6.25	8.13	6.10	3.61	4.77	6.11
November	45.0	5.75	5.50	5.40	3.35	4.76	6.03
December	45.9	5.00	4.88	4.88	3.36	4.67	5.95
1930						
January	45.3	4.88	4.75	4.31	3.42	4.66	5.92
February	45.5	4.75	4.75	4.25	3.41	4.69	5.89
March	46.2	4.25	4.25	3.56	3.29	4.62	5.73
April	45.6	3.88	4.13	3.79	3.37	4.60	5.70
May	45.2	3.75	3.50	3.05	3.31	4.60	5.72
June	45.3	3.50	2.88	2.60	3.25	4.57	5.78

SOURCES: Money Supply: Milton Friedman and Anna Jacobson Schwartz, *A Monetary History of the United States, 1867–1960*, 1963, table A-1, pp. 712–13.

Interest Rates: Federal Reserve System, *Banking and Monetary Statistics*, 1943, pp. 448–51, 468–70.

[a]M_2 is equivalent to currency held by the public and by commercial banks in demand and time deposits.

tries Act of 1921. Tariff increases were particularly substantial in the outlying portions of the British Commonwealth, which at the Imperial Conferences of 1923 and 1926 urged Britain to consider preferential duties favoring dominion goods. The fall of the Baldwin government, which led to Britain's first Labour administration in December 1923, had been brought about by a Conservative attempt to abandon the tradition of free trade.

The League of Nations was disturbed by this upward trend in tariffs and undertook to hold a World Economic Conference in Geneva in 1927 to negotiate a tariff truce. The effort was largely a European one, and the issue was not critical. Foreign lending lubricated international trade more than tariffs restricted it. But tariffs were a potentially disturbing element in the system, especially the prospect of abandonment of most-favored-nation treatment and the spread of preferences. One achievement of the conference was a convention to abolish prohibitions of imports, but this was covered with reservations by one and another country and failed to secure enough ratifications to come into force. The other was a tariff truce, looking to ultimate reductions. This succeeded. In his presidential campaign in the summer of 1928, however, Herbert Hoover promised to raise tariffs in the United States to assist farmers struggling with falling prices. Following his inauguration in March 1929, he called a special session of Congress to make good his promise. Hearings before the House Ways and Means Committee began in the last days of the Coolidge regime, starting on January 7, 1929. Notice of the hearings did not restrict the contemplated tariff increases to agricultural products. The process thus started was to result, fifteen months later, in the Smoot-Hawley Tariff Act, which became law in June 1930.

There was little force behind the 1927 movement to reduce tariffs. Britain was of two minds on the subject: Labour supported lower tariffs, but the Conservative government was tempted by Empire preference while the Liberals were ineffectual. Its high-tariff tradition left the Continent uninterested. Indeed, as wheat prices went off after 1926, Germany reimposed the duties it had been forbidden to levy prior to the Dawes Plan; Mussolini opened war in the Battle for Wheat in July 1925; and the French imposed tariffs and milling quotas, requiring large admixtures of domestic with imported wheat by millers. The subject of wheat arose in the World Economic Conference of 1927, but nothing was done about it. Not only was the United States not a member of the League of Nations, it was governed by Republicans with a high-tariff tradition. There was no leadership. There was no action.

The Young Plan

In June 1928, the agent-general for reparations, S. Parker Gilbert, suggested in his regular report that the time had come to replace the Dawes Plan with a settlement of the reparations question. No single reason underlay this proposal. Gilbert was worried that reparations had been paid largely by borrowing, though it is doubtful whether he foresaw any imminent decline in loans. Germany was discontented with an arrangement that imposed restrictions on its sovereignty, such as the occupation of the Rhineland and the surveillance of its budget by the Reparations Agency. There was still no total sum fixed. The French wanted the Dawes obligation to be commercialized. It was generally recognized that the annuity of 2.5 billion gold marks was too onerous for the German economy, despite its recovery. A decision was reached in September 1928 to convoke a new committee of experts to meet in Paris in February 1929 and to prepare a "final and definitive settlement" for recommendation to governments.

The neutral chairman was Owen D. Young from the United States, which took no part in the conference but kept in touch with Young and instructed him to keep war debts out of the discussion. In this he failed, and reparation payments were made subject to reduction by eight-twelfths of any net relief on war debts obtained by the creditors. Schacht represented Germany. His negotiating offer on April 16, 1929, was regarded as an ultimatum. In it he seemed to demand the return of German colonies and the Polish corridor—although he later claimed that he had merely stated that without the colonies and the corridor Germany would be unable to pay reparations.[28]

The French were furious, and the conference was in crisis. In

---

28. See Schacht, *The End of Reparations*, pp. 66, 73–75, 139, and ch. 17 (pp. 231ff.); and Hjalmar Schacht, *Confessions of "The Old Wizard,"* 1956, p. 224. For Schacht's fixation on lost colonies, see also Hjalmar Schacht, *The Stabilization of the Mark*, 1927, p. 245 and esp. p. 246, where he notes, "Colonial activities have an educative and moral significance . . . a moral effort for any people. They imply self-training and discipline." Ten years later, he was still harping on the same theme: see Hjalmar Schacht, "Germany's Colonial Demands," 1937, pp. 223–34.

subsequent accounts, Schacht accused the French of deliberately at-
tacking the German currency by statements to the press and in-
structing French banks to withdraw their deposits from Germany,
and he drew a somber conclusion: "This French attack . . . upon
German currency . . . was the seed of that ever-growing lack of
confidence which today [1931] hangs over the entire world."[29] The
statement that the French deliberately attacked the mark by withdrawals of French private funds is repeated in the Reichsbank annual report for 1929 and receives apparent confirmation by Pierre
Quesnay from two disparate sources. The files of Owen D. Young
record a remark of Quesnay to Fred Bate, secretary to the Young
Committee, on April 18 that $200 million would be withdrawn from
Germany by noon the next day.[30] Shepherd Morgan, of the Reparations Agency staff, another American, reports that when he asked
Quesnay what the French withdrawals from Germany meant, he received the reply, "C'est la guerre."[31]

Simpson, who is very favorable toward Schacht in a recent biography, does not mention it, nor do other persons who were present,
such as Leith-Ross.[32] The *Economist* notes the rumor of a "deliberate attack" but states that it "is doubted for there is no evidence
of any large withdrawal of short-term money by either Paris or London banks."[33] The figure alleged to have come from Quesnay is
likewise unbelievable. The $200 million is roughly the total amount
of gold lost by the Reichsbank from the beginning of the year to
April 23, 1929: Rm 745 million. It lost another Rm 251 million in
the following week, which included the near-panic day of April 26.
But the French made no long-term loans to Germany.[34] The with-

29. Schacht, *The End of Reparations*, p. 91.
30. Clarke, *Central Bank Cooperation*, p. 165.
31. Rolf E. Lüke, *Von der Stabilisierung zur Krise*, 1958, pp. 171–72.
32. Amos E. Simpson, *Hjalmar Schacht in Perspective*, 1969, ch. 2, "The
Young Plan and After," pp. 28ff.; Sir Frederick Leith-Ross, *Money Talks: Fifty Years
of International Finance*, 1968, ch. 10, "The General Strike and the Revision of
Reparations," esp. p. 119. Leith-Ross mentions the "tantrums and exhibitionism of
Dr. Schacht." Another participant who makes no reference to the episode in his
memoirs is Dr. Paul Schmidt, later Hitler's interpreter, who was present as second
German interpreter, ranked by a man from the ministry of finance. Schmidt claims
that Moreau received exact instructions from Poincaré and states that the only man
who lost his temper ("Choleriker") was Emile Francqui, the Belgian delegate. See
Paul Schmidt, *Statist auf diplomatischen Bühne, 1923–45*, 1949, pp. 166–67.
33. *The Economist*, May 4, 1929, p. 966.
34. League of Nations, *Balance of Payments, 1930*, 1932, p. 92.

drawals brought the Reichsbank gold reserves down to 41 percent of its demand liabilities, perilously close to the limit of 40 percent established in the Dawes Plan.[35] The only figure for the short-term loans is Rm 700 million for June 1931—much later, and consistent with a short-term claim of $200 million in 1929. Schacht asserts that he stopped the withdrawal by threatening Parker Gilbert that if the French withdrew their balances, Germany would cease paying reparations, and that Gilbert succeeded in inducing the French to halt the action.[36] That there were withdrawals from Germany was clear, but this may have been as a result only of concern that the reparations conference was breaking down. What actually happened is in some doubt. That central bank cooperation between France and Germany had broken down is not.

The excitement subsided, and the Reichsmark gained strength in the exchange market, though it did not recover its gold. Schacht signed the experts' report in June, though he confessed to some misgivings. If he signed because of German financial weakness, as is alleged, the French threat, if there were one, would have been successful in the short run but at a cost to the system.[37]

The details of the settlement are of limited relevance to the depression. Politically, it differed sharply from the Dawes Plan in that it was not to be imposed on Germany but to be freely accepted. The Reparations Agency would be withdrawn from surveillance of German finances and French occupation troops from the Ruhr. In economic terms, compromise was reached between a German offer of 1.65 billion gold marks a year for thirty-seven years and an Allied demand for 2.3 billion gold marks for fifty-nine. It was agreed that the reparations would start at the lower figure and rise toward the higher. The annual payment was divided into an unconditional and a conditional amount, the latter of which could be postponed in the event of transfer difficulties. A bank was established to monitor

35. Heinz Pentzlin, *Hjalmar Schacht: Leben und Wirken einer umstrittenen Persönlichkeit*, 1980, p. 118.
36. Schacht, *Confessions of "The Old Wizard,"* p. 222. Pentzlin notes that a good part of Schacht's frustration came from the fact that the agent-general for reparations, S. Parker Gilbert, had reached agreement on the Young Plan with Chancellor Gustav Stresemann but that the latter had failed to inform Schacht (*Hjalmar Schacht*, p. 115). Schacht characterized the French action as "clumsy and stupid" (*ebenso plump wie dumm*) (ibid., p. 119).
37. Edward W. Bennett, *Germany and the Diplomacy of the Financial Crisis, 1931*, 1962, p. 7.

the payments from the outside and assist in effecting transfer. A $300 million Young Plan loan, divided two-thirds among the creditors and one-third available to Germany, started the system off. The Young Plan is possibly connected with a run on another currency, the pound. The experts' report was debated by the Allied powers at a conference at The Hague in August 1929 and was finally agreed on in January 1930 at a second Hague conference after expert committees had resolved some loose ends. It took effect from April 7, 1930. The central issue at the first Hague conference had been the unwillingness of Philip Snowden, the Labour chancellor of the Exchequer, to accept the experts' recommendation on the division of reparations. The British policy of collecting in reparations and war debts what it paid out in war debt service had not been fully carried out; striking an attitude he thought would be popular in Britain, Snowden insisted on a new division that would raise the British share. The prime minister, Ramsay MacDonald, and the Foreign Office thought it absurd to raise an international conflict and threaten to break up the conference over 80 percent of £2.5 million.[38] In the course of the debates, Snowden called an argument by Chéron, the French minister of finance, "ridiculous and grotesque," an expression strong in English but still stronger in French.[39] This led to difficulty. Shortly thereafter, Quesnay, in the company of two other experts, Pirelli from Italy and Francqui from Belgium, waited on Leith-Ross and stated that the French government viewed Snowden's attempt to change the division of the Young Plan as inadmissible. If he did not change his demand, he went on, the French government would convert its sterling into gold and transfer it to Paris. As he tells the story, Leith-Ross rang for a messenger and had the

38. Grigg, *Prejudice and Judgement*, p. 228.

39. Schmidt, who was present at The Hague as a German interpreter, claims that *ridicule et grotesque* is an inexact translation of "ridiculous and grotesque." The latter expression could be used in the House of Commons; the former would not be accepted in the Chamber of Deputies. See Schmidt, *Statist auf diplomatischen Bühne, 1923–45*, p. 178. When I happened to recount this story to René David, a French professor of international law, he extended it. He had been in London at the time, and he said that the French interpreter, realizing his mistake, apologized the next day and offered the press a correction. "Ridiculous," he explained, meant "laughable," "funny," or "amusing," while "grotesque" meant "bizarre," "curious," or "original." He should therefore have translated "ridiculous and grotesque" as *amusant et original*.

men shown out without a reply.[40] But there are those who think that the French, with £240 million, as Leith-Ross put the figure, actually did withdraw some in gold in September. Most opinion holds that the serious British gold losses of August and September, which amounted to $45 million, were the result of capital flows to New York after the Federal Reserve discount rate was finally raised. On the other showing, the words "ridiculous and grotesque" led to French conversions in London and forced the Bank of England to put up its discount rate. This, rather than the failure of the Hatry companies, triggered off the rise in the Bank of England discount rate and the collapse of the New York stock market. But we are getting ahead of our story. We must now look away from Europe and the United States to world commodity markets.

40. Leith-Ross, *Money Talks*, p. 124.

4

The Agricultural
Depression

An independent depression in agriculture?

After the New York stock market crash in October 1929, the collapse in industrial production and the financial crisis of 1931 led to a deep depression in agriculture and more generally in industrial production. The loss of real income in agriculture was broadly as acute as in industry, although output was sustained and prices declined rather than the other way around. Before the crash, however, it is an open question whether an independent depression in agriculture helped to cause the stock market crash, the decline in industrial output, and the banking collapse. Observers such as Sir Arthur Salter have claimed that there was a business cycle, an agricultural depression, and a financial crisis—each largely independent of one another.[1] This follows the school that ascribed the Great Depression to a series of historical accidents. In his State of the Union message of December 2, 1930, President Hoover attributed the origin of the depression to some extent to factors within the borders of the United States, particularly speculation, but also pointed to other deep-seated causes, chiefly worldwide, especially overproduction in "wheat, rubber, coffee, sugar, silver, zinc and to some extent cot-

1. Sir Arthur Salter, *Recovery: The Second Effort*, 1932, pp. 32, 37.

ton."[2] Later he narrowed the blame to Europe and overproduction by cartels that artificially increased prices: "European statesmen did not have the courage to meet these issues."[3] A somewhat parochial view by an expert on Asia and Africa runs to the effect that serious overproduction of rice, especially after the bumper crop of 1928, on top of the surplus of wheat, drove down prices in agricultural countries and reduced their purchasing power, producing the world depression.[4] But a usual view is that the depression in agriculture was a consequence, not a cause, of the worldwide depression, which was generally held to have started in speculation in the United States or in structural changes arising from the First World War.

The extent of the depression in agriculture before October 1929 raises awkward questions of timing. A loss of farm income worldwide may have occurred, but without implications for industrial production or financial conditions, and have been on its way to being overcome when it encountered an industrial depression or a financial bind. Or, conversely, agriculture may seem to have been bearing up, with income and output sustained, but only by making commitments to fortune so as to render it extraordinarily vulnerable to a mild setback outside the sector. As in every aspect of the story of the depression, moreover, one must make clear why certain difficulties of, say, overproduction do not correct themselves through the pricing mechanism, rather than lead to cumulative reductions in prices, value of sales, and income for primary producers.

In the account that follows, considerable importance is given to interconnections among the agricultural, industrial, and financial sectors, both in originating and spreading the depression and in making it so difficult to overcome. In particular, it rejects the view of modern Keynesian thought that price changes of one set of pro-

2. U.S. Department of State, *Foreign Relations of the United States, 1930*, vol. 1, 1945, p. vii.

3. *The Memoirs of Herbert Hoover*, vol. 3, pp. 61–62.

4. A.J.H. Latham, *The Depression and the Developing World, 1914–1939*, 1981, pp. 184–85. The problem in rice was that the importing countries were becoming more nearly self-sufficient, while the exporters increased their specialization and output. The *coup de grâce*, according to Latham, was a bumper crop in 1928–29 in both wheat and rice. Together they amounted to 160 million metric tons, as compared with 144 million two years earlier and 128 million in 1920–21 (appendix table 13, p. 204).

ducers are unimportant to macroeconomic behavior since losses of this group are offset by gains to its customers. The conventional wisdom was, in this judgment, correct in the importance it attached to raising primary-product prices, though wrong in the way it went about it. The attempt by individual countries to raise agricultural prices by quotas and tariffs for imported goods or by subsidies and exchange depreciation for exports could not help being mutually frustrating and making matters worse. Any good that might arise from the efforts of one country to cut back supply to the level of existing demand (at existing prices) was likely to be reaped by other producers. International agreement to raise prices in concert eluded success because of the difficulty, without strong leadership (and sacrifices by the leader), to arrive at a workable solution that would not reward violators. It was to prove impossible to raise agricultural prices by themselves. The answer was to increase world spending to provide enough lubrication for the system and make resource reallocation possible.

Agriculture and the business cycle

Up until the business cycle of 1857, or perhaps 1866, the harvest was the measure of business conditions. A bumper crop lowered the price of bread, and hence industrial wages, and simultaneously provided an outlet for industrial produce by enlarging farm income. Crop failure, on the other hand, led to depression. Differences existed from situation to situation, depending on particular conditions in land tenure and whether the economy was open for foreign trade. The system of land tenure, by its effect on the distribution of income between landlord and farmer, influenced the character of farm spending. More rather than less foreign trade dampened the movement of prices resulting from changes in yield, thereby stabilizing wages but destabilizing farm income.

Some time after the middle of the nineteenth century, however, business cycles appeared to come to exist largely independent of farm income and to be related to financial conditions or the state of industrial inventories, expenditure for plant and equipment, or population movements. There was a tendency to forget agriculture altogether. When an economist laid stress on structural dislocation, as Ingvar Svennilson did, for example, it had to do not with farm output and income but with excessive investment or failure to readapt in industry.[5]

Outside Western Europe, however, agriculture was of continued importance. Farming accounted for a quarter of total employment in the United States in 1929 and farm exports for 28 percent of farm income. Regions of recent settlement, including the Dominions, Argentina, and Uruguay, had higher percentages on both scores. Almost two-fifths of world trade was in agricultural products and another fifth in mineral raw materials.

The failure of the price system in farm products is readily explained. It resulted in part from the restoration of production in Europe under circumstances where production elsewhere had expanded to fill wartime gaps. It was also the usual failure of the price system in products with a long period of gestation between new investment, in response to price increases, and ultimate output, as in tree crops.

Once overproduction gets under way, government policy in producing areas enters the picture. As prices slip, exports may be subsidized, stockpiles accumulated, or, in a few cases, exports (and occasionally production) restricted. For agricultural production as a whole, Timoshenko suggests that stocks are a better index of oversupply than prices, because of government attempts to maintain price by purchases.[6] An index of world agricultural prices and stocks based on 1923–25 as 100 shows prices declining gradually from the end of 1925 to a level of about 70 from July to October 1929, while stockpiles increased by about 75 percent.[7] Thereafter, as finance for holding stocks became scarce, the pace of price declines increased. For the months from November 1929 through Jan-

5. See his *Growth and Stagnation in the European Economy.* Erik Lundberg, his fellow countryman, dismisses structural factors in coal mining, shipbuilding, and textiles after the First World War on the grounds that they existed again after the Second World War but proved unimportant under the impact of sustained demand. See his *Instability and Economic Growth,* 1968, p. 33. For a contrary view, see Moggridge, "Policy in the Crises of 1920 and 1929," which holds that maintenance of liquidity and demand in 1929 would have been insufficient. What was needed in his opinion was structural adjustment, such as, for example, that undertaken by Europe with U.S. assistance after the Second World War.

6. Vladimir P. Timoshenko, *World Agriculture and the Depression,* 1953, p. 25.

7. Ibid., table 10, pp. 122–23. The indexes cover (with weights) cotton (9), wheat (6), sugar (6), rubber (3), silk (2), coffee (2), and tea (1). The figures for stocks exclude those on the farm and in consequence represent an understatement.

uary 1930 the index averaged 64, a decline of almost 9 percent from the July-to-October level. And then the deluge: 58 in March 1930, 51.4 in June, 45.5 by August, and in December 1930, 38.9, a 50 percent drop from the first half of 1928. By December 1932 the index had fallen almost another 50 percent, to 24.4 percent of the 1923–25 base, while stocks had risen to 260 on the same base. The annual price declines for 1930, 1931, and 1932 were 40, 28, and 12 percent. The comparable declines in the money supply, using M_2 and measuring from December averages, were 4, 14.8, and 8.8 percent.

Commodity problems

The leading agricultural commodities in 1929 world trade are set forth in Table 6, which covers all items of more than $250 million. The list is arbitrary, since the total array from which it is drawn separates some items—for example, wheat and wheat flour, or corn and lard, or raw wool and carded and combed wool—and combines others. It is evident at a glance that the commodity problems are by no means all European. Of the enumerated list, only wheat, sugar, silk, and butter are produced in any quantity in Europe. As will be seen, moreover, while all primary commodities declined during the depression, they declined at different times and by different amounts. Carlos Díaz Alejandro, referring to Latin America, regards the separate behavior of individual countries as the outcome of a "commodity lottery."[8]

Figure 2 shows world production, prices, and stocks for cotton, wheat, sugar, silk, and rubber from the list in Table 6, plus tea and tin, and a general index of all commodities, taken from the League of Nations study of instability. Note that 1929 = 100, which means that the curves all intersect then without any implication that this is an equilibrium year. From the fact that stocks are rapidly rising and prices rapidly falling, it will be evident that 1929 was not stable.

Figure 3 groups three commodities from Timoshenko for a shorter period, ending in 1932, and with a different base, 1923–25: coffee and wool, not covered in the League chart, and rubber, which is repeated to assist comparison.

8. "Latin America in Depression, 1929–39," 1982, p. 336. He uses the same expression in a later paper, "Latin America in the 1930s," 1984, p. 20.

TABLE 6

VALUE OF WORLD AGRICULTURAL EXPORTS, 1929,
AND PERCENTAGE EACH IS OF TOTAL

	Value (in millions of dollars)	Percent of total
Raw cotton and linters	1,400	11.3
Wheat	825	6.6
Sugar, including glucose	725	5.8
Wool	700	5.5
Coffee	575	4.5
Silk	550	4.4
Rubber	425	3.4
Butter	400	3.3
Rice	400	3.3
Tobacco, raw and waste	350	2.8
Corn	250	2.0
Enumerated items	6,600	49.9
Total	12,500	100.0

SOURCE: Henry C. Taylor and Anne Dewess Taylor, *World Trade in Agricultural Products*, 1943, table 2, pp.10–12.

The most important commodity by value—cotton—shows no particular increase in stocks or fall in price until 1929. An attack of boll weevil in the southeastern United States in the early part of the decade raised the price and gave impetus to the expansion of cotton production by new methods of machine cultivation in Texas and Oklahoma and by more traditional means in new countries, such as Brazil, India, Peru, and Egypt. Production in Alabama, Georgia, and South Carolina was, however, greatly reduced. This contributed to bank failures in the Atlanta Federal Reserve district in 1929, prior to the stock market crash, but cotton as a whole was not in great trouble. The pressure was local.

Nonetheless, the position of cotton was important to the United States. Testifying to the House Committee on Banking and Currency in the spring of 1926, Governor Benjamin Strong of the Federal Reserve Bank of New York said: "Our chief exports are agricultural products, and the chief of them is cotton, which goes mostly to England." And then, in a remark that was ostensibly directed to the stabilization of sterling in 1925 but that carried the hint of a 1927 Federal Reserve easy-money policy and prescience for the

Figure 2. World production, prices, and stocks of primary commodities, 1920–38 (1929 = 100).

SOURCE: League of Nations, *Economic Instability in the Postwar World: Report of the Delegation on Economic Depression*, 1945, p. 85.

Figure 3. World production, prices, and stocks of coffee, wool, and rubber, 1923–32.

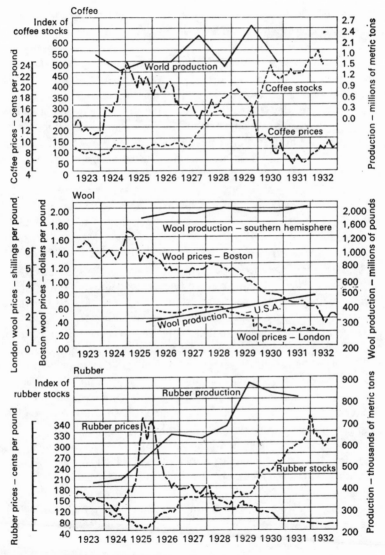

SOURCE: Vladimir P. Timoshenko, *World Agriculture and the Depression*, 1953, pp. 20, 21.

events of 1931, he went on: "It should not be overlooked that one of the greatest menaces to the trade of this country is depreciating foreign exchange."[9]

The position in wheat was very different. The price declined and world stocks rose from 1925, with some leveling of stocks after 1929 though a precipitous fall in price. Production showed only a limited rise. Acreage outside Europe had expanded greatly during the First World War, as Table 7 shows. It was aided by immigration into Australia and Canada and by the reduced need for fodder for horses. Within the United States total, moreover, there was a shift from the small farms of the east to the Great Plains, where mechanization, including tractors for seeding and combines for the harvest, could produce wheat at 60 cents a bushel as against $1 in the east.[10] In Europe acreage came back, but not all the way.

In the United States and Canada attempts were made to support the price of wheat on a national basis. The United States had the Federal Farm Board, which bought and stockpiled. The comparable organization in Canada was the Wheat Pool, operating out of Winnipeg. The McNary-Haugen Farm Relief Bill, which would have subsidized U.S. exports to maintain the domestic price, was vetoed. Australia and Argentina lacked the financial capacity to hold up the price for their farmers, and even if they had been able to borrow abroad could hardly have held wheat for long through the lack of storage facilities. They were thus obliged to export. As the Continental markets outside Britain closed down one by one, they sold where they could and drove prices downward. (The same position held in rice, where the exporting countries—Burma, Siam, and French Indochina, the trade of which was largely in the hands of Chinese expatriates—lacked storage facilities so that each year's crop had to be consumed before the following harvest.)[11]

The capacity to finance wheat in storage was not an unmixed blessing. It led to the temptation to speculate, which was not always rewarded. In the autumn of 1928 Canada already had a large amount of wheat in storage, but with a record crop and a world shortage of hard wheat, which usually commanded a premium over the ordinary wheats of other major exporters, it decided to hold

9. Chandler, *Benjamin Strong*, p. 267.
10. Schumpeter, *Business Cycles*, p. 739.
11. Latham, *The Depression and the Developing World, 1914–1939*, p. 178.

TABLE 7

WHEAT ACREAGE, SELECTED COUNTRIES AND WORLD, 1909–14, COMPARED WITH 1924–29 (*in millions of acres*)

	1909–14	1924–29
Overseas exporters	87.51	117.37
Argentina	16.05	19.94
Australia	7.60	11.97
Canada	9.95	22.57
United States	53.91	62.99
Europe	187.13	183.13
European exporters	95.31	89.42
ex-European exporters	37.27	41.70
European importers	50.48	47.39
ex-European importers	4.07	4.62
Total	274.64	300.50

SOURCE: Wilfred Malenbaum, *The World Wheat Economy, 1885–1939*, 1953, pp. 236–37.

back exports. This was expensive for the economy and for the balance of payments. It was necessary to dump some securities on the New York market and to withdraw funds from the call money market. In January 1929 the gold drain led to an informal embargo on gold exports, but short-term capital inflows prevented the Canadian dollar from depreciating. Also in January, the prospect of damage to winter wheat from storms in the Soviet Union and the United States led to more holding back of exports. But European buyers went on strike against the high premiums of hard over other wheats and switched sources of supply. Black Tuesday on the Winnipeg Wheat Exchange in early May drove the price down. Lower prices failed to repair the decline in exports. Compounding their mistake and relying on mediocre 1928–29 crops in Argentina and Australia, the Wheat Pool and private grain interests continued restraint in selling the 1929 wheat crop. This policy proved disastrous, leading to loss of wheat exports, weakness in the Canadian dollar, tight money, and widespread losses. The shortage of hard wheat produced a spread of 42 percent in July 1929, compared to a normal one of 10 cents on a bushel of wheat priced at $1.25. When Canada was forced to sell for lack of storage space toward the end of the year, however, the spread returned to normal in a matter of months.[12]

At this time, there was little to be said for the Australian response of a "Grow More Wheat Campaign" undertaken after the collapse of prices of wheat and wool in mid-1929. A Labour government headed by Scullin replaced the Nationalist–Country party coalition in the autumn of 1929 and raised wheat acreage by 22 percent in 1930. With little or no capacity to store, it had to be exported and contributed further to the reduction of the world price.

Various attempts were made to tackle the wheat problem on an international basis but with no results until much later. Wheat came in for discussion at the World Economic Conference in 1927, but no resolutions were reached. Following the precipitous fall in price in 1929, twenty international conferences seriously addressed themselves to the question between 1930 and 1933, two being devoted to imperial preference, seven being limited to the producers of Eastern Europe, and eleven being general. Only in 1933, and then aided by a drought in North America, did it prove possible to reach agreement in principle among the major overseas producers. This was embodied in the International Wheat Agreement, but it did not extend to detailed acreage reductions.[13]

A further element in the world wheat market was the Soviet Union. Grain exports had made up 36 percent of Russian exports in 1913 and somewhat less in the mid-1920s. Soviet policy was directed at changing from grain to industrial exports. Difficulties in breaking into markets for finished goods and in obtaining credit for needed imports of capital equipment led to a decision in 1927 and 1928 to force wheat exports. The first year was hurt by poor crops, the second by difficulties in getting peasants to deliver their surpluses to the foreign trade organization. In 1930 a bumper crop made it possible to expand exports from 100,000 metric tons in 1929 by twenty-three times to 2,290,000 tons in 1930. But prices were falling, and the value of exports increased only ten times from $15 million to $150 million. As prices continued to fall in 1931, compulsory and widespread collectivization was combined with ra-

12. See Edward Marcus, *Canada and the International Business Cycle, 1927–39*, 1954, pp. 12, 53–56; Vernon W. Malach, *International Cycles and Canada's Balance of Payments, 1921–33*, 1954, p. 29.

13. Wilfred Malenbaum, *The World Wheat Economy, 1885–1939*, 1953, ch. 11, "Solution by International Agreement."

tioning in cities and areas that normally had grain deficits. Exports doubled to 5,220,000 metric tons, but the value of exports failed to rise. Untold millions of peasants starved to death as exports were forced on the world in the face of surpluses elsewhere. Campaigns were launched against Soviet imports in many countries—the United States, Canada, France, Belgium, the Netherlands, and Eastern Europe—but not in Germany or the United Kingdom. The Soviet Union has many times been accused of seeking to undermine the capitalistic system by dumping goods on it at low prices.[14] In this case, as in practically all others, the country was acting in what it regarded as its own best interests, but clumsily and at great sacrifice to its people.[15]

The pattern in sugar was broadly similar to that in wheat, though applying to a different set of countries. Rapid expansion after the war, especially in Cuba and Java, was followed by a comeback in European production. To the expected recovery of Continental Europe were added new policies in Britain: imperial preference for cane beginning in 1919 and subsidy to domestic beet sugar producers after October 1, 1924. So rapid was the European recovery that by the mid-1920s Czechoslovakia was unable to find markets for its traditional exports.[16] Hardest hit in the depression was Java. During the 1920s it had benefited from the development by Dutch agronomists of new seeds that increased production. But it lacked a sheltered market. Protection cut off its market in India, where a white-sugar process, which did not use bone char and was therefore not offensive to Hindu sensitivities, was put into production in 1930. This forced Javanese exports down from three million tons in 1928–29 to one-sixth of that amount three years later. The fall in prices produced trouble everywhere. Riots broke out in Cuba as early as 1928, not waiting for the actual depression, which was to stimulate fifty revolutions in Latin America.[17] Attempts at international agreement were undertaken consistently after 1927, but none was reached

14. In his State of the Union message of December 2, 1930, President Hoover blamed the "methods" by which Russia sold her "increasing agricultural exports to European markets" for contributing to the prolonging and deepening of the depression. But this was still 1930, and the worst was yet to come.

15. See Michael R. Dohan, "Soviet Foreign Trade: The NEP Economy and Soviet Industrialization Strategy," 1969, esp. pp. 560ff.

16. Vladimir P. Timoshenko and Boris C. Swerling, *The World's Sugar: Progress and Policy*, 1957, p. 19.

17. Ferrell, *American Diplomacy in the Great Depression*, p. 222.

until the "Chadbourne" International Sugar Agreement of May 1931, which halted the rise in stocks and ultimately cut them back, but without stabilizing or raising the price.

Rubber and coffee follow a broadly similar pattern of rising stocks and falling prices starting before 1929, except for the addition of two factors: (1) very high prices early in the decade, which, because of the period of gestation, stimulated output with long delays, and (2) valorization schemes. That in coffee was formal. In rubber, the Stevenson Plan of 1923–24 in British Malaya and Ceylon raised the price of rubber to the highest level of the commodities charted, from which it fell to the lowest. The Netherlands East Indies, which did not restrict output, earned vast profits and expanded planting.

Rubber and coffee are alike in that new plantings take a long time to yield output, and this gives rise to a cobweb cycle in which today's rise in price stays high for an extended period. This is moderated somewhat in rubber by native production, produced from existing trees, in which tapping varies with price. Bumper crops in coffee in 1927 and 1929 would have driven the price down much sooner had it not been for the valorization program. Undertaken by the Brazilian government in 1917 and 1921, it was partly responsible for the rapid extension of planting in the mid-1920s. In 1924 the federal government abandoned the attempt to maintain the price, but the provincial government of São Paulo took over. This managed to hold the price until September 1929, through one bumper crop when stocks climbed from three million bags to thirteen million and a short crop when they fell to 10.3 million. The second bumper crop of 1929–30 added another ten million bags to stocks, financed with difficulty by a São Paulo loan in London of £100 million. By the end of 1929, the price had fallen in half.

Wool showed the same pattern as wheat, with a few changes in the countries concerned. Sheep numbers grew everywhere during the 1920s, and the average fleece rose 16 percent in weight in Australia, which had by far the largest flock. Prices declined gently after 1924–25, and then, after a sharp break in August 1929, much more precipitously. From the behavior of an index of woolen-using industrial activity in six major countries, Ronald Walker argues that the fall in the wool price was the consequence not of expanded supply, nor of substitution for wool by other fibers, but primarily of demand for textiles as a whole. This is put forward only as a "fair conclusion" as opposed to a self-evident one.[18] But it is notable that when Germany stopped borrowing, the volume of its wool imports between 1928 and 1929 dropped 19 percent.[19] Seventy-seven percent of Australian production was exported and accounted for more than 42 percent of total exports and 14 percent of national income. With the break in wheat and wool prices coming in June and August 1929, prior to the stock market crash, Australia was well into the depression before most of the rest of the world.

One of the worst-hit commodities, though it is not included in the list, was lard. Corn is used to fatten hogs on the farm more than it is sold as feed, and hogs are slaughtered for pork and lard. Denmark, Canada, and New Zealand slaughter their pigs at an early age and at a light weight to obtain lean bacon. American farmers, with excellent land for growing corn, at that time fed animals to much greater weights so as to produce fat pork and lard. The United States produced some 2.5 billion pounds of lard in 1929, and exported one third of it. The two largest markets were Germany and Cuba, with 26 percent and 10 percent of exports, respectively. Income in both was affected early in the depression: Germany by the halt in foreign lending, Cuba by the decline in the price of sugar. American farmers believed that the decline in the price of hogs was intimately bound up with the collapse of the U.S. export market for lard and pork (a much smaller proportion of total output). Tariff increases abroad were attributed in turn to retaliation against the Smoot-Hawley Tariff Act of June 1930, although balance-of-payments difficulties and the desire to protect their own farmers are sufficient explanation for the German and Cuban actions. After the droughts of 1934 and 1936, the United States found it necessary to import corn from Argentina, and the export market in lard was never regained. In the early days of the depression, however, the decline in the prices of corn, hogs, and lard spread bank failures from the wheat country of the Minnesota, Kansas City, and St. Louis Federal Reserve districts to the Chicago district covering rural Iowa and Illinois.

---

18. E. Ronald Walker, *Australia in the World Depression*, 1933, p. 92.

19. Ibid., p. 91. With 23 percent of its wool exports, Germany was the leading Argentine market in 1929, even after the decline. See Carlos F. Díaz Alejandro, *Essays on the Economic History of the Argentine Republic*, 1970, p. 21.

Falling farm prices and tight money

Falling farm prices, the halt to foreign loans, and protective tariffs all interacted. To begin with, farm debt was serious. Total farm mortgages in the United States had risen from $3.3 billion in 1910 to $6.7 billion in 1920 and $9.4 billion in 1925. In some states as much as 85 percent of farms were mortgaged. In Canada in 1931, more than one-third of wholly owned farms had mortgages averaging 40 percent of their value. In Germany, landowners had paid off their debt in the inflation but had contracted new ones, with the largest farms mortgaged for half their value.

What was true of the farm sector within industrial countries applied equally to agricultural countries. The gross debt service of six major agricultural exporters—Argentina, Australia, Canada, India, New Zealand, and the Union of South Africa—rose from $725 million in 1923 to $900 million in 1928. Brazil and the Netherlands East Indies accounted for debt service of $300 million annually in 1928–29, and Poland, Romania, Hungary, and Yugoslavia for $200 million more. For all twelve countries, the total of interest and principal due was $1.4 billion with only small gross receipts, and $100 million for Canada, as an offset.[20] A halt in lending to Germany cut down the market for their primary products. A halt in lending to the countries themselves put them under pressure that led to drawing on overseas balances, sales of gold, and in a number of cases to exchange depreciation, pushing the burden of adjustment on other countries. When the international economy works well, declines in exports are matched by increased borrowing. When borrowing halts at the same time that exports fall, adjustment in national economies labors under a double handicap.

The position can be illustrated with the well-documented case of Australia.[21] From 1923 to 1928 the external debt of Australia rose from £420 million to £570 million, or an average increase of £30 million annually. This was regarded by some as an "orgy of foreign borrowing." Others considered it merely "excessive." Debt service rose from 16.2 percent of exports to 19.2 percent. Part of the diffi-

20. Timoshenko, *World Agriculture and the Depression*, pp. 55–56.
21. In these paragraphs, I have benefited not only from Walker, *Australia in the World Depression*, and Sir Douglas Copland, *Australia in the World Crisis, 1929–1933*, 1934, but also from two draft chapters of an Australian economic history, not completed, by Helen Hughes.

culty lay in the method of borrowing. Commonwealth and Provincial governments would run overdrafts with London banks and pay them off by floating bond issues when either the sums became large enough to warrant it or the banks extending the overdrafts became restless. In 1927 a shortage of London funds led briefly to financial stringency in Australia, partly attributed to the rapid development at home of installment credit. A British economic mission visited the dominion and attributed the difficulties to departures from traditional English laissez-faire, especially to government ownership of the railways and the central bank, the arbitration system for setting wages, and the tariff, which had laid "an excessive and possibly even a dangerous load upon the unsheltered primary industries." Shortly thereafter the Australians appointed their own commission, headed by J. B. Brigden and including the economists Copland and Giblin. This defended the tariff as enabling Australia to support a higher population than it could otherwise, but expressed concern over the rising burden of overseas debt, referring both to its amount and higher interest cost.

In 1929 the situation became more difficult. In January a London loan was subscribed to the extent of only 16 percent and had to be taken up by the underwriters. In April the London market refused to issue a loan. London banks pressed for payments on overdrafts. Slowly and reluctantly the Australian banks were obliged to restrict advances, putting pressure on the local economy. By May unemployment was rising rapidly. By November it affected 13 percent of trade union members. (This was to rise to 30 percent in the second quarter of 1932.) From £24 million in 1928, London funds of the Commonwealth Bank sank to £16 million by June 1929 and to under £8 million by September. The trading banks were asked to exchange their gold for notes in November; in December 1929 the exchange of gold against notes became compulsory for banks and public. Australian currency began to depreciate, a process euphemistically termed developing a premium on sterling. The Commonwealth Bank rationed sterling to the trading banks, and the trading banks in turn rationed their customers. Outside the trading banks, a market developed in which sterling was traded at a premium. The premium started at 1 percent in December 1929, went to 2 percent in January 1930, and officially to 6.25 percent (higher in many dealings) in March 1930. The rate further rose to a 9 percent premium in November 1930 and then broke wide open. The Bank of New

Figure 4. Australian export prices in Australian currency, sterling, and gold, 1929–33 (1928 = 100).

Australian currency ——————
Sterling — —— —— —
Gold ------------

SOURCE: Douglas Copland, *Australia in the World Crisis, 1929–1933*, 1934, p. 30.

South Wales withdrew from the bank cartel in January 1931 to trade at the market. The premium rose to 18 percent, then 25 percent, and finally reached 30.25 percent in March 1931, when it was frozen by the Commonwealth Bank. When the pound sterling went off gold in September 1931, however, the Australians held sterling at the 30.25 percent premium (28 percent depreciation of the Australian pound) to obtain the additional benefit of the decline in the pound. While Australian export prices in gold went to the 30 percent range of 1928, and sterling prices to the 40s, prices in Australian currency were in the 50 percent range, and sometimes the 60s, as Figure 4 shows.

There was almost no support for exchange depreciation. Bankers felt that sterling exchange parity "had almost a mystical force."

Scullin, the new Labour prime minister in Australia, sought help in London early in 1930 but received only a new British economic mission, headed by Sir Otto Niemeyer, which advised deflation and clinging to sterling parity. The Labour treasurer, G. G. Theodore, was practically the only heretic who wanted a policy of expansionary central bank credit for government spending, with exchange depreciation to hold the balance of payments in check. A group of Australian economists, however, including Giblin, Dyason, and Copland, in June 1930 drew up a program for deflation and equal sacrifice. This provided for the exchange rate to find its own level, but largely as a substitute for tariffs, which distorted efficiency. This was ultimately accepted as government policy, and early in 1931 it resulted in a 10 percent wage cut as a part of the equality of sacrifice.

The combination of reduced exports and the impossibility of borrowing led to losses of reserves and exchange depreciation, shifting the burden of adjustment to others. This was the case not only in Argentina and Australia, but also in the two countries closely associated with them—Uruguay and New Zealand, respectively—and beyond these pairs, and prior to 1931, in Brazil, Bolivia, Venezuela, and Spain. Canada, Chile, and the Eastern European countries, not to mention the grain-producing areas of the United States and the Soviet Union, bore the strain without submitting to exchange depreciation. The first group shifted rather than avoided its losses, and the gold standard began its disintegration on the periphery of the world economy.[22]

Gold losses

It is difficult to form a view from the statistics for this period of what happens to gold and foreign exchange reserves together. The gold figures have been compiled by the Federal Reserve Board for

22. William Adams Brown, Jr., *The International Gold Standard Reinterpreted, 1914–1934*, vol. 2, p. 902. The League of Nations, *Review of World Trade, 1934*, 1934, pp. 14–15, records declines in average gold prices for a number of commodities, mostly primary and semimanufactures, from 1929 to 1934, which is after the start, in March 1933, of a rising trend in gold prices. The largest decline, in raw silk, was 84 percent, followed by copper at 75 percent, butter at 73 percent, wheat at 71 percent, and Japanese cotton gray-goods, gasoline in the United States, and Brazilian coffee at 68. Among those that had fallen the least were mowing machines at 10 percent, tin at 32 percent, steel girders at 36 percent, and coal at 39 percent. For depreciating countries, of course, the declines in price were reduced.

TABLE 8

GOLD MOVEMENTS OF LATIN AMERICA
AND THE FAR EAST, 1929–32 (*in
millions of dollars, net exports*[−])

	Latin America	Far East
1929	− 178.5	− 28
1930	− 183	− 12
1931	− 190	− 179
1932	− 13	− 28

SOURCE: *Federal Reserve Bulletin*, July 1931,
p. 394, for original data, and subsequent issues.

year-ends through 1927, and monthly since June 30, 1928, when
the Bank of France's new statement was issued. Data on gold holdings do not tell unambiguously what the state of a country's balance
of payments is, since it may have been gaining or losing foreign
exchange. Typically, however, a primary-producing country will allow its foreign exchange holdings to rise and fall, calling on gold
only when its foreign exchange is dangerously low. To the extent
that this is the case, gold losses are a signal of considerable distress.

Latin America and the Far East lost gold throughout the whole
depression, as the Federal Reserve data on movements indicate.
These are shown in Table 8.

It is notable, however, that the wheat countries lost gold well before those specializing in other commodities. The Australian example, not covered in the table, has already been cited. Canadian gold
movements are affected by complex financial relations with the
United States and so perhaps do not signify. Its gold losses were
heavy in the six months to June 1928, and again in the first nine
months of 1929, before the stock market crash. The substantial
Latin American loss in the table is attributable almost entirely to
Argentina. That country had gained gold during the course of borrowing through June 1928 but lost it precipitously thereafter. During
1929 it lost a total of $173.3 million—64 percent of it before the
crash, that is, by the end of September. Hungary, the largest of the
European wheat exporters, lost one-fifth of its small gold stock—$7
million—also in 1929 before the crash. Australian gold losses were
recorded in the last three months of the year; their independence of
the stock market crash is attested by the earlier decline in London
funds of the Commonwealth Bank, referred to above.

Java, the sugar country, lost gold prior to September. (Cuba at that time had no central bank, and the U.S. dollar circulated in the country side by side with the peso.) The coffee countries held on to their gold until the first six months of 1930, and so did Japan with its silk.

Something of the same pattern may be detected in the redistribution of reserves among the several Federal Reserve districts within the United States, although the data are by no means unambiguous. Between the end of 1928 and the last week in September 1929, New York gained reserves together with a number of other districts, and the western agricultural districts—St. Louis, Minneapolis, and Dallas—all lost. After the effects of the crash had subsided, moreover, and pressure was again on the agricultural regions, New York once more gained, while the heavy losers were Chicago, St. Louis, Minneapolis, Dallas, and, irrelevant for this view, Boston.

Like Australia, Argentina was finally unable to prevent exchange depreciation. The rate slipped slightly from 97 U.S. cents to the peso in the first half of 1928 to 95.5 cents at the end of the year, where it held through November 1929; in December 1929, together with Uruguay, it abandoned the gold standard, the first of a long line of abandonments. The average exchange rate for the month came to 93 cents, then 85 cents by March 1930 and 75 cents by December 1930. Pressure on the price of corn in the United States was substantial through third markets in which the two countries competed for exports, even though the Smoot-Hawley tariff of 25 cents kept Argentine corn out of American markets.

Theory suggests that exchange depreciation raises the price of exports in local currency or lowers the price in foreign currency, or a little of both. What happens depends on the elasticities. For a small country that has no impact on world prices, so that the demand for its products is infinitely elastic at the going price, the total impact will be felt in rising prices in local currency. For the major exporter of a commodity in inelastic demand, prices abroad will fall. Typically, it makes a considerable difference whether the world is prosperous and able to take additional exports readily, or depressed, with any one price decline matched by others.

In the 1930s the depreciation of the peso failed to raise prices in Argentina but depressed them in gold, that is, in dollars and sterling. A 6 percent depreciation of the Australian pound and a 20 percent depreciation of the Argentine peso were not responsible for the total fall in the price of wheat by 50 percent and more between December 1929 and a year later. The Australian pound especially can be exonerated, for it held steady at a 6 percent premium on sterling from April 1930 to October, while the price of Australian wheat in London was falling from 40 shillings a quarter to less than 30. Moreover, in 1930 gold prices of other commodities fell as fast as or faster than the Australian–Argentine commodities of wheat, wool, and hides. It is even possible that the strong correlation between depreciation of the peso and weakness of wheat prices in Winnipeg, Chicago, and Liverpool runs from the price of wheat to the peso rather than the other way. And yet the depreciations created real difficulty. A detailed study of the relation suggested to Marcus that the causation ran from depreciation to decline in the world wheat price, rather than the other way around.[23] In 1930 the Argentine peso made the pace; from December 1930 to March 1931, when the price of wheat fell from 57 U.S. cents to 41 cents, it was the Australian pound.

Copland insists that Australia did not indulge in competitive currency depreciation, since gold export prices fell 50 percent in 1930, when the depreciation was limited, and suggests that gold prices were being deflated independently. For 1931 and 1932, when Australian gold export prices fell another 35 percent, he concedes that the case is more serious but is unwilling to accept the conclusion that depreciation caused the decline in gold prices, which were, again, the result of international deflation.[24] But this is the essence. Begin with deflation, and then let one country depreciate—Argentina. This drives the deflation further. Then another—Australia—and there is more international deflation. With inelastic demands, a small surplus added to currency depreciation by successive countries drives the deflationary pressure on.

Agricultural prices and the depression

There is no doubt that the primary-producing countries were having difficulties prior to October 1929, with falling prices, rising stocks,

23. Marcus, *Canada and the International Business Cycle, 1927–39*, p. 91.

24. Copland, *Australia in the World Crisis, 1929–1933*, pp. 103ff., esp. p. 107. Díaz Alejandro states that Argentine policies—depreciation *cum* import duties—were "to some extent of the beggar-thy-neighbor type" (*Essays on the Economic History of the Argentine Republic*, p. 102n.). Note, however, that Argentina did not default on its foreign debt in the 1930s, whereas most other countries in Latin America did.

inability to sustain borrowing, and the necessity to maintain debt service. For the world, however, the question is why these lower prices, for example, did not lead to higher real incomes in the industrial sector, and hence to more spending and prosperity; or why the halt in lending to this sector did not lead to more loans and higher investment in other areas. Many economists argue that deflation in one sector cannot spread, because the losses of primary producers are offset by the gains of the rest of the world: "as a matter of principle, an amount of purchasing power exactly equal to the loss in agricultural countries would be devoted by consumers in industrial countries to purchasing industrial goods previously exported to agricultural countries."[25]

The question is in the same class as those that ask whether the stock market boom can cut spending or whether the effects of depreciation are not symmetrical, with deflation in the appreciating country matched by expansion in the country whose currency depreciates. The view taken here is that symmetry may obtain in the scholar's study but that it is hard to find in the real world. The reason is partly money illusion, which hides the fact of the gain in purchasing power from the consumer countries facing lower prices, and partly the dynamics of deflation, which produce an immediate response in the country of falling prices and a slow one, often overtaken by spreading deflation, in the country with improved terms of trade, that is, lower import prices. The consuming countries might ultimately have realized that their real incomes had increased, permitting them to expand spending. But the process is time-consuming. Meanwhile, the primary producers cannot wait. They spring into action with tariffs, quotas, and exchange depreciation.

Even the consuming countries do not find the improved terms of trade welcome in all respects. To defend the import-competing sector—typically the farmer, who in addition to serving as a romantic and idealized type often has political power—the consuming countries impose quotas and tariffs and resist cheap imports. Deflation gets the edge over expansion through increased real income owing to lower prices at a constant money income.

Exchange depreciation compounds the difficulty. In most cases it was an involuntary rather than a positive act of expansion. That fact did not make the world impact symmetrical. Some theorists claim

25. Hans Neisser, *Some International Aspects of the Business Cycle*, 1936, p. 31.

that using depreciation to correct overvaluation is inflationary for the world, whereas depreciation that achieves undervaluation is deflationary.[26] The distinction is less interesting than differences in the setting, as between a world of inflation and a world poised on the edge of deflation. In the 1970s and 1980s, when goods were in relatively short supply and the world was inflating, exchange depreciation left world prices unchanged and raised those at home. In the 1930s, however, it was a buyer's, not a seller's, market. Stocks were heavy. Exchange depreciation failed to raise prices at home— though it might lead them to level off—and pushed them down abroad. In these circumstances, successive exchange depreciations were deflationary for the world. And as pressure on agricultural prices weakened the position of banks and insurance companies loaded with mortgages, the deflation spread.

Structural deflation

In the period following the Second World War, a model of structural inflation was developed to explain persistent inflation in less developed countries. Starting with a small excess of demand over productive capacity, a country can find itself on a course of continuous inflation as the various sectors try to pass on to the others the burden of the shortfall. Workers raise wages, industrialists raise prices, farmers hold back supplies. Rising prices turn the balance of payments adverse, leading to exchange depreciation, a rise in the cost of living as the prices of foreign goods mount, and a new attempt by workers to raise wages. Monetarists maintain that the process would be halted once monetary authorities refused to permit expansion of the money supply so that, say, industrialists could not obtain the credit to pay higher wages or consumers the credit to pay higher industrial prices. The structuralist answer is that the alternative to a small credit expansion at each point where the issue arises is a large collapse, possibly economic, possibly political, and there is no firm ground on which the monetary authorities can take their stand.

From 1925 to 1929 a process of what might by analogy be called structural deflation occurred in the world primary-product economy.

---

26. Milton Gilbert, *Currency Depreciation*, 1939, p. 157; see also Gottfried Haberler, *Prosperity and Depression*, 1937, p. 334.

Instead of excess demand, there was excess supply. A few countries tried to meet the situation by absorbing the excess supply in stockpiles. Without an adjustment in production, this only stored up trouble. Other countries, one by one, found it necessary to evade the consequences of the excess supply by keeping it out of the domestic market or selling the crop for what it could bring, thereby perhaps cushioning the consequences at home by depreciation, which forced prices down abroad. The excess supply imposed a kind of structural deflation on the system.

Deflation spreads from commodity to commodity, on the farm and from the farm to the city. T. W. Schultz was quoted in 1934 as stating:

> When foreign markets for cotton, wheat, lard and tobacco disappear, it is only a matter of time until the prices of butter, beef, mutton and eggs are dragged down. American farming is still dominated by the export group. . . . Nor is the city outside of its influence.[27]

No mechanism is specified for the spread of deflation from export to domestic crops, though presumably what Schultz had in mind was supply shifts out of one line into the other. For the impact of farm depression on urban unemployment, Schultz set out the familiar purchasing-power argument, without specifying why the city did not gain from improvements in its terms of trade.

The monetarists will argue that this deflation is monetary in character and that had the countries of the world prevented shrinkage in their money supplies the deflationary spiral could have been halted. Albert Hahn wrote in 1931: "Just as in inflation, it first seems that individual prices are going up, so in deflation one speaks of separate price declines of copper, rubber, agricultural products, automobiles, instead of a rise in the value of money."[28] We may agree that this was so after the stock market crash. The rise in agricultural stocks and the slippage of prices after 1925 make it clear, however, that there were structural factors at work. The structural cracks in the world economy were there, as was some world overproduction

27. Commission of Inquiry into National Policy in International Economic Relations, *International Economic Relations*, 1934, p. 215 (quoted by C. E. Hearts, President, Iowa Farm Bureau Federation).

28. Quoted in L. Albert Hahn, *Fünfzig Jahre zwischen Inflation und Deflation*, 1963, p. 84.

of commodities. But the situation was not so desperate that it could not have been rectified if prices had not collapsed in 1929, followed by the collapse of the banks and the money supply. Surpluses, the liquidity crisis, exchange depreciation, and finally bank failure and money collapse produced the fateful mixture.

5

The 1929
Stock Market Crash

The market

To the extent that the depression was ushered in by the stock market crash, it was the crash in New York that was of consequence. Canadian prices went higher from 1926 and declined further from their peaks, compared to New York. They were the tail of the dog. European security markets had for the most part turned down earlier: Germany as far back as 1927, the United Kingdom in mid-1928, France in February 1929. The Vienna stock market, which had led the parade in the crisis of 1873, was quiet, waiting for 1931. The action was in New York. It had its effect worldwide, but not through tightly parallel movements in security prices.

At the time, the rise of the New York stock market seemed spectacular. The Dow-Jones industrial average went from a low of 191 in early 1928 to a high of 300 in December and a peak of 381 in September 1929, or double in two years. Two sharp setbacks occurred, in December 1929 and March 1929, which in October 1929 tended to lull speculators into thinking that the market was merely undergoing another adjustment. Daily turnover increased at the peaks from 4 million shares in March 1928 and 6.9 million in November 1928 to 8.2 million in March 1929. The average number of shares traded daily in 1929 was 4,277,000: with only 1.1 billion shares listed, this was an annual turnover of 119 percent for outstanding shares, as contrasted with 13 percent in 1962.[1] Profits were substantial, and while price–earnings ratios rose from a conservative 10 or 12 to 20, and higher for the market's favorites, this was in anticipation of continued increases in earnings and dividends. The market has been described as an "orgy of speculation," a "mania," a "bubble," and other terms denoting a loss of contact with reality. There was, to be sure, the normal quota of frauds, such as Insull; speculators in high places, like Charles Mitchell and Albert Wiggins at the head of the two largest New York banks, the National City and the Chase; foolish predictions of continued price increases, prosperity, new eras, and the like, about which it is easy to be ironic. The fact is that the Dow-Jones industrial peak of 381 for 1929 is not out of line, after allowance for the change in the value of money, with the same index in the 1,100–1,400 range in 1983–84 and not much ahead of 750 in 1970. The danger posed by the market was not inherent in the level of prices and turnover so much as in the precarious credit mechanism that supported it and the pressure it exerted on credit throughout the United States and the world.

If, with the advantage of hindsight, the market no longer looks as if it was at dizzying heights, it seemed so to contemporary observers. Hoover had been warning against the use of credit in the market since 1925, although he was unable to persuade Calvin Coolidge to speak out against stock market speculation. Coolidge in fact insisted in March 1929, as he left office, that U.S. prosperity was absolutely sound and that stocks were cheap at current prices. Hoover claimed that Adolph Miller, an idiosyncratic member of the Board of Governors of the Federal Reserve System, supported his views of the danger inherent in the market and that the board took action when Hoover became president.[2] This is not entirely accurate. Roy Young, chairman of the Federal Reserve Board, spoke out against excessive speculation in February 1929 and stated that unless the banks curbed their brokers' loans, which were feeding the speculation, the Federal Reserve would take action. But in March the Board of Governors turned down a recommendation by George

1. Robert Sobel, *The Great Bull Market: Wall Street in the 1920s*, 1968, p. 123. Sobel comments that turnover reached 160 percent in 1907 and a record 319 percent in 1901.

2. *The Memoirs of Herbert Hoover*, vol. 3, p. 13.

Harrison, governor of the Federal Reserve Bank of New York (in Benjamin Strong's place after his death in October 1928), for an increase in the discount rate from 5 to 6 percent. It was too soon after the completion of the Treasury's financing at 4.5 percent. The New York bank was concerned that market rates had risen above the rediscount rate and that the banks were only too comfortable with $1 billion of borrowed Federal funds. On the other hand, it hesitated to raise interest rates for fear of the pressure this would place on the gold reserves of European central banks.

The agony of the dilemma is apparent in the exchange between Harrison in New York and his chairman of the board, Owen D. Young, at the Young Plan talks in Paris. Young insisted on the need for the Federal Reserve Bank to take prompt and effective control of the market, not only for prestige but also to curb the call money rate, which dominated the world's monetary position and menaced the reserves of central banks recently returned to the gold standard.[3] In a separate telegram he suggested that Harrison should go over the head of the board in Washington and take the case to President Hoover or to the secretary of the Treasury, Andrew Mellon. In reply, C. M. Woolley, secretary of the New York bank, informed Young that the board had rejected a rate increase and that the bank would possibly tackle Hoover and Mellon, but that if this did not help it might consider lowering the discount rate to repel foreign funds attracted to the call money market.[4] The present position was exquisitely painful. A higher rate to break the stock market or a lower rate to repulse the attraction of call money—one or the other might furnish relief.

Roy Young was followed in public utterance to talk down the stock market by Paul M. Warburg, one of the fathers of the Federal Reserve System and the leader of Kuhn, Loeb & Co. The signals reminded Warburg of the panic of 1907. Stock prices were too high, forced up by a colossal volume of loans and an orgy of speculation to a level unrelated to prospective increases in plant, property, or earning power. The market paused, regrouped, and moved higher. Bankers, barbers, bootblacks, and professors talked the market up. The Federal Reserve Bank of New York was finally permitted to raise its discount rate to 6 percent on August 9. The market paid no

---

3. Federal Reserve Bank of New York files, Owen D. Young (Paris) to Harrison, March 12, 1929.
4. Ibid., C. M. Woolley to Young (Paris), March 15, 1929.

Figure 5. New York stock prices (Standard Statistics index) (1926 = 100), 1926–38.

	1926	1927	1928	1929	1930	1931	1932	1933	1934	1935	1936	1937	1938
Jan.	102	106	137	193	149	103	54	46	84	81	114	148	100
Feb.	102	108	135	192	156	110	53	43	88	80	120	154	99
Mar.	96	109	141	196	167	112	54	42	85	75	124	154	96
Apr.	93	110	150	193	171	100	42	49	88	79	124	144	86
May	93	113	155	193	160	81	38	65	80	86	118	138	86
Jun.	97	114	148	191	143	87	34	77	81	88	119	134	92
Jul.	100	117	148	203	140	90	36	84	80	92	128	142	106
Aug.	103	112	153	210	139	89	52	79	77	95	131	144	103
Sep.	104	129	162	216	139	76	56	81	76	98	133	124	104
Oct.	102	128	166	194	118	65	48	76	76	100	141	105	114
Nov.	103	131	179	145	109	68	45	77	80	110	146	96	114
Dec.	105	136	178	147	102	54	45	79	80	110	144	95	112

SOURCE: League of Nations, *Statistical Yearbooks*, various years to 1934; 1935–38, Standard Statistics index based on 1934–36 as 100, converted to 1926 base.

TABLE 9
BROKERS' LOANS BY SOURCE, 1927–29 (*in millions of dollars*)

Date	New York banks	Banks outside New York	Others	Total
Dec. 31, 1927	1,550	1,050	1,830	4,430
June 30, 1928	1,080	960	2,860	4,900
Dec. 31, 1928	1,640	915	3,885	6,440
June 30, 1929	1,360	665	5,045	7,070
Oct. 4, 1929	1,095	790	6,640	8,525
Dec. 31, 1929	1,200	460	2,450	4,110

SOURCE: Federal Reserve System, *Banking and Monetary Statistics*, 1943, p. 494.

attention. On September 1 the stock exchange added more seats, awarding a quarter seat to each member in its own stock split. The price of a seat hit an all-time high of $625,000, up more than fourfold over the $150,000 level of 1926. With the help of a sizable expansion in brokers' loans at 10 percent, the market inched up another notch. As shown in Figure 5, the Standard Statistics index of industrial shares hit 216 for a peak monthly average above the 1926 base of 100.

The credit squeeze

As the market rose, the pressure on the international financial system mounted. If the New York Federal Reserve Bank had not been allowed to raise the discount rate since July 1928 or sell off its open market portfolio, it could still apply pressure on commercial banks in the city to restrain both their own loans and those for their banking correspondents to the call loan market after the end of the year, as Table 9 shows. Their place was taken by others.The vast bulk of brokers' loans by others came from U.S. firms. A considerable amount came from abroad, together with foreign purchases of U.S. stocks. The data are inadequately detailed to trace the extent of the movement. Breakdowns are available only for year-ends that are not turning points, and these fail to give adequate coverage.[5] But there

5. Lary notes that foreign monies loaned to brokers via overseas banks through their American agencies are recorded as a deposit inflow and a brokers' loan of a New York bank (see Lary, *The United States in the World Economy*, p. 114, n. 31). Three such agencies were responsible for $115 million of such loans at the end of 1928 and $53 million at the end of 1929.

is universal agreement that the New York stock market, nervousness over the Young Plan in April and May 1929, and French gold conversions put great pressure on the system. How much was owing to each one of the three forces is impossible to say. Italy raised its discount rate first in January, Britain a full percentage point in February, then Italy again and the Netherlands in March. Tension in Paris over the Young Plan in April and May led to discount rate increases in Central Europe, especially in Germany, Austria, and Hungary. In July the rate was increased at the National Bank of Belgium. The pressure from New York was persistent and continuous. In the first half of 1929 the United States gained $210 million in gold and France $182 million.

The pressure was particularly acute on London. With New York rates high, various borrowers—from Germany, Hungary, Denmark, and Italy—were seeking sterling loans when they really wanted dollars.[6] Norman expressed concern about the scramble for gold. Bank of England reserves reached a high for the year of $791 million at the end of May, following the Young Plan crisis, but declined steadily thereafter, and precipitously in July. Norman raised with Harrison the possibility of long-term financing by European central banks in New York, either with the Federal Reserve system or in the market. Discussions were undertaken and carried some distance but finally abandoned, apparently when the new Labour government in Britain decided to deal with the gold losses by raising the fiduciary issue and releasing gold behind the Bank of England's note liabilities.[7] Norman recorded in his diary that "Nearly half the time was taken up by bank rate and international interest rates." The Labour chancellor, Snowden, was opposed to an increase in the discount rate on the grounds that this would hurt business and not help the balance of payments, but rather would merely lead to still higher rates elsewhere. The governor promised he would not raise bank rates for fun, but only if it were essential.[8] It proved to be.

On August 9 the Federal Reserve Bank of New York moved again. The booming stock market called for higher interest rates; faint signs of weakness in the economy suggested the opposite course. In a telegram sent to the principal European central banks, Governor Harrison explained that the rediscount rate was being

6. Clay, *Lord Norman*, p. 251.
7. Clarke, *Central Bank Cooperation, 1924–31*, pp. 162–64.
8. Clay, *Lord Norman*, pp. 297–98.

raised from 5 to 6 percent but that the bank hoped to buy bills later to ease the market, presumably after the stock market rise had been halted. "While our domestic situation calls for such a policy, we of course have in mind the need of the European economy also for lower interest rates in New York."[9]

The New York stock market took no notice of the instruction. The pressure on London continued. Norman was looking for an excuse to raise the Bank of England rediscount rate. On September 20, one day after a new high in the New York market—one which proved to be the interwar peak on the *New York Times* index—the occasion presented itself. The Hatry empire collapsed in London. This was a series of companies, investment trusts, and operating units with interests in photographic supplies, cameras, slot machines, and small-loan companies, controlled by one Clarence Hatry. Caught up in the speculative fever, Hatry was having difficulty borrowing £8 million to buy United Steel and use it as a base for a wider coup in British steel. He tried to use fraudulent collateral from his various companies, was caught out, and went into bankruptcy. Stock exchange dealings in the Hatry securities were suspended, and the financier and several of his associates arrested. In the unsettlement, the Bank of England rate was raised from 5.5 to 6.5 percent on September 26.

Apart from the Frankfurt Insurance Company in August, and unlike other crashes, it was the only warning.[10]

The pressure spread to Scandinavia, and Sweden, Denmark, and Norway put up their rates. By the end of September, Bank of England gold stock was down to $640 million, a decline of almost 20 percent in four months. On August 5 Norman had told the Commit-

9. Federal Reserve Bank of New York files, Harrison cable to principal European central banks, August 10, 1929.

10. Noyes, *The Market Place*, p. 326. Signs of bank weakness in Europe were not altogether absent. The Bodenkreditanstalt had been rescued in 1929 through merger with the Creditanstalt, as discussed in Chapter 7, below, and the Lancashire cotton banks were so sick that the Bank of England had to rescue William Deacons of Manchester when the auditors refused to sign the balance sheet on January 8, 1929. This was done secretly, however, and caused no anxiety. In April 1929 it proved further necessary for the Bank of England and a consortium of its joint-stock bank owners to rescue the Banca Italo-Britannica, the troubles of which developed well before the world slump. Some help was sought and obtained from Mussolini, whose *quota novanta* contributed to the losses. See Richard S. Sayers, *The Bank of England, 1891–1944*, 1976, vol. 1, ch. 10, esp. pp. 253ff., 259ff.

tee of the Treasury that unless there was a change, especially in France and the United States, some part of Europe, including the United Kingdom, might be forced off the gold standard.[11] In these circumstances the New York stock market crash came as great relief, and Norman expressed surprise that they had not been forced off gold.[12]

Business decline

All this time, business was slipping. The National Bureau of Economic Research puts the reference cycle peaks as April for Germany, June for the United States, and July for Britain. Production in Belgium hit a peak in March and declined by 7 percent to the end of the year. In Canada various depressing influences took over after the spring of 1929 and produced a decline in business activity.[13] In South Africa the downturn came in the second quarter.[14] Everywhere except France money was tight, consumption had leveled off, new capacity was coming on the market for which there was no evident demand, and inventories were piling up. Only in France was production rising.

Conditions were at their worst in Germany. There had been a lockout in the Rhenish–Westphalian steel industry in November and the early days of December 1928, which depressed output and the indexes. Next followed a period of intense cold from December to March 1929, with the average temperature in Berlin the lowest since the start of record keeping early in the nineteenth century. Much tighter money, owing to the withdrawals of April–May, had eased somewhat with the return flow after the settlement of the Young Plan, but by the summer of 1929 the existence of depression was unmistakable.[15] Inventories rose prior to the stock market crash. Unemployment at 1.9 million persons was larger than the 1.6 million unemployed in the United States, although the population was, at 64 million, only half of the American 122 million.[16] The Frank-

11. Clay, *Lord Norman*, p. 252.

12. Ibid., p. 254.

13. Marcus, *Canada and the International Business Cycle, 1927–39*, p. 13.

14. J. C. DuPlessis, *Economic Fluctuations in South Africa, 1910–1949*, n.d. (1950 or 1951), p. 50.

15. Carl T. Schmidt, *German Business Cycles, 1924–1933*, 1934, p. 50.

16. Born, *Die deutsche Bankenkrise, 1931*, pp. 33, 38.

furt Insurance Company provided a spectacular failure in August. By the autumn, the numbers of business failures and protested bills were rising sharply.

The slowdowns in the United States have been ascribed to a variety of causes, which to some extent converge but show wide variation in emphasis and some contradiction. The decline in housing was attributable partly to reduced family formation, which in turn resulted from the stoppage of immigration in the early 1920s and a variety of cultural consequences of the war.[17] In part it was the result of a scarcity of financing. The overexpansion of fixed investment was a function of the stock market boom and of easy credit for business investment, or of the too-high profits relative to wages that raised the demand for new plant. Underconsumption is the counterpart of overinvestment, arising from diversion of income into the stock market or from a lag of wages behind profits. The result was a temporary exhaustion of investment opportunities, the piling up of inventories, and uncertainty.

Business was in trouble long before the crash. In March a Federal Reserve official noted that building contracts awarded were decreasing rapidly, "always a precursor of a general decline."[18] March was also the peak of automobile production, which fell from 622,000 in that month to 416,000 in September, at the height of the stock market, perhaps as a result of the tightening of interest rates and the rationing of credit outside of brokers' loans. The industrial production index fell after June, and the decline in industrial production, prices, and personal income from August to October was at annual rates of 20, 7.5, and 5 percent.[19] These last indications of malaise were not apparent before the market collapse. On this showing, the stock market rise may have contributed to a weakening of the business position, but the crash was less a cause of the depression than a signal of the need to pause and regroup.[20]

The stock market crash

September 1929 marked the peak of the market, on average, as well as the daily peak that was reached on September 19 (on the *New*

17. Clarence L. Barber, "On the Origins of the Great Depression," 1978.
18. Federal Reserve Bank of New York files, C. M. Woolley to Young (Paris), March 15, 1929.
19. Friedman and Schwartz, *A Monetary History of the United States, 1867–1960*, p. 306.
20. Sir William Arthur Lewis, *Economic Survey, 1919–1939*, 1949, pp. 53–55.

York Times index). After moving sideways, it started slipping on October 3, declined throughout the week of October 14, and gave way to panic on "Black Thursday," October 24. An attempt was made by the leading bankers to organize a pool to stop the collapse; Richard Whitney went from post to post on the floor of the exchange, placing bids for a syndicate.[21] But the following week saw a further slipping on Monday and a new panic on Tuesday, October 29, "Black Tuesday," with 16.4 million shares traded—a record that stood for almost forty years. Some recovery took place to the end of the month, and then lows for the year were reached on November 13. The Dow-Jones industrial average had fallen to 198 from 381 on September 3. It ended the year at 250.

Two weeks before the October 24 drop, brokers' loans for "others" declined by $120 million, largely because of withdrawals by foreigners.[22] If this was the trigger, was it the last link in a chain that led from Snowden's characterization of Chéron's argument as "grotesque and ridiculous" via Bank of France gold conversions and the Bank of England increase in the discount rate or, in a less political and more commercial linkage, that ran from the August increase in the bank rate in New York to pressure on London, which resulted in the Hatry bankruptcy, which in turn raised interest rates there and drew funds back from New York?[23] Whichever it was, once the panic had set in "others" contributed to it by withdrawing their brokers' loans. Some companies became worried that the fall

21. A similar consortium of German banks was organized "in the second half of 1929," to support share prices, but it was unable to do so and ended up accumulating millions of Reichsmarks' worth of securities that fell in value below cost. See Manfred Pohl, *Hermann J. Abs: A Biography in Text and Pictures*, 1983, p. 26. The peak of the German stock market had been 175 in April 1927 (based on 1924–26 as 100). By June 1928 it was down to 148, by September 1929 to 125, and by December, in sympathy with the New York stock market, to 107.

22. Friedman and Schwartz, *A Monetary History of the United States, 1867–1960*, p. 305n.

23. Jude Wanniski has another explanation based on rational expectations, i.e., that markets respond to unanticipated events and adjust values appropriately to the outcome of some relevant economic model. (*The Way the World Works*, 1977, p. 130). His view is that the stock market crash of October 24, 1929, was a response to the action of a Senate subcommittee, reported on an interior page of the *New York Times*, in rejecting an attempt of some members to hold down a proposed increase in a tariff on carbide. This would anticipate by nine months the completion of the Smoot-Hawley tariff and its signing into law by President Hoover, along with foreign tariff retaliation. Most economists are skeptical of such prescience and of such a violent and immediate reaction to a future hypothetical event.

in prices might lead to closing of the stock exchange and freezing their assets, which had seemed so liquid, as had happened during the 1873 stock market debacle.[24]

New York financiers tried to support stock market prices, not only by direct purchase but by holding back on margin calls and taking over loans called by outsiders. In October alone the New York banks took over $1 billion of these loans.[25] In their efforts to stop the panic New York banks were assisted by the Federal Reserve Bank of New York, which violated its standing orders from the Open Market Committee, which limited operations to $25 million a week and bought $160 million worth of securities in the week ending October 30 and $370 million in all to the end of November. These actions were later ratified by the board of governors, but Harrison's action in exceeding his authority was the basis for later recrimination and dispute between the New York and Washington authorities. Together with the open market expansion, the rediscount rate was lowered to 5 percent on November 1 and to 4.5 percent on November 15. Liquidation of foreign balances and loans in New York continued: $450 million was withdrawn from October 31, 1929 (after the crash, but the nearest reporting date), to the end of the first quarter of 1930, and another $100 million was bought from private hands by foreign central banks.[26] Half the withdrawals were for the account of the United Kingdom.

Did the stock market crash produce effects of its own? On October 29, Hamlin and James of the Federal Reserve Board feared it would bring on a real business depression, although the other members of the board did not think it would.[27] More than forty years later, the majority opinion receives strong analytical support:

> The stock market crash in 1929 was a momentous event, but it did not produce the Great Depression and it was not a major factor in the Depression's severity. A sharp but not unprecedented contraction was converted into a catastrophe by bad monetary policy. . . .
> Whatever happens in a stock market, it cannot lead to a great depression unless it produces or is accompanied by a monetary collapse.[28]

24. Noyes, *The Market Place*, p. 333.
25. Sobel, *The Great Bull Market*, p. 149.
26. Lary, *The United States in the World Economy*, pp. 117, 119.
27. Elmus R. Wicker, *Federal Reserve Monetary Policy, 1917–1933*, 1966, p. 147.
28. Milton Friedman in *Newsweek*, May 25, 1970, p. 78.

Friedman does not have in mind Harrison's effort to soften the tension in the New York money market during the autumn of 1929. In his view, such discounting in a period of panic is unimportant. What is important is to maintain the money supply over time. This is an issue which must be postponed until later, however. There was no decline in the U.S. money supply until October or December 1930, during which time the depression may or may not have been great, but it was certainly deepening rapidly.

The first impact of the crash on the international monetary scene was to relieve it. The Bank of England lowered its discount rates three times between October 29 and the end of the year; the Netherlands and Norway twice; Austria, Belgium, Denmark, Germany, Hungary, and Sweden once. An exception to this easing tendency was Canada, where the U.S. dollar went to a sharp premium. Margin calls from Canadian speculators in the New York market produced a higher demand for U.S. dollars than the supply emanating from money withdrawn from the brokers' loan market.[29]

The propagation of financial crisis from one country to another can work through a number of channels: (1) the marking down of internationally traded securities and commodities in physically separate markets connected by arbitrage; (2) such marking down without actual trading taking place as participants in one national market are affected by the psychology of those in another; (3) changes in income from spending that affect other countries through the foreign trade multiplier, that is, declines in income spilling over into other countries through reduced imports; and (4) an impact on the monetary side of the balance of payments, for example when a deflationary shock in one country draws gold from abroad and enforces monetary contraction there. The first two avenues work with great rapidity, the last two with lags. Table 10 and Figure 6 show that the collapse of the New York stock market was quickly communicated abroad, to the same extent in Canada and Belgium, in dampened degree elsewhere.

That a rising stock market can hurt business by tightening credit was suggested in Chapter 3, even though firms selling equities may

29. Marcus, *Canada and the International Business Cycle, 1927–39*, pp. 64, 69. Canada had in fact been forced off the gold standard in 1929 by an outflow of capital invested in the rise in the New York stock market. See Ronald A. Shearer and Carolyn Clark, "Canada and the Interwar Gold Standard, 1920–35: Monetary Policy without a Central Bank," 1984, esp. pp. 293ff. and fig. 6.7.

TABLE 10
SHARE PRICES IN SELECTED MARKETS, MONTHLY, SEPTEMBER–DECEMBER 1929 (index numbers on various bases)

1929	Belgium	Canada	France	Germany	Nether-lands	Sweden	Switzerland	United Kingdom	United States
September	112	316	526	125	118	167	239	144	216
October	98	255	496	116	113	162	221	135	194
November	92	209	465	112	98	155	212	121	145
December	79	210	469	107	100	154	215	121	147

SOURCE: League of Nations, *Statistical Yearbook*, various issues.

Figure 6. Share prices in selected markets, monthly, 1926–35.

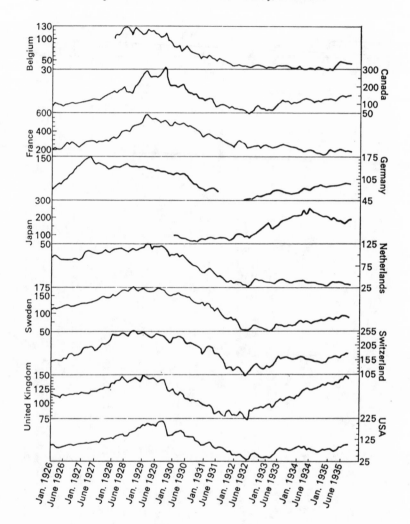

	Belgium	Canada	France	Germany	Japan	Nether-lands	Sweden	Switz-erland	United Kingdom	United States
	Jan. 1928	1924	1913	1924–6	Jan. 1930	1921–5	Dec. 31 1924	nominal	1924	1926
Base	=100	=100	=100	=100	=100	=100	=100	=100	=100	=100
1926										
Jan.		92	205	72		95	111	154	116	102
Feb.		99	210	79		97	113	158	114	102
Mar.		94	200	83		96	112	160	113	96
Apr.		93	200	92		93	114	158	111	93
May		91	205	91		91	117	158	113	93
Jun.		93	223	97		91	121	169	115	97
Jul.		96	259	106		91	124	169	113	100
Aug.		101	246	117		91	124	176	114	103
Sep.		106	263	120		91	122	177	116	104
Oct.		104	253	132		92	123	173	116	102
Nov.		106	234	140		92	124	175	117	103
Dec.		107	222	139		91	125	175	116	105
1927										
Jan.		109	244	158		94	127	185	120	106
Feb.		114	249	169		104	127	197	119	108
Mar.		117	270	163		105	127	198	119	109
Apr.		121	288	175		104	130	198	119	110
May		125	279	168		103	134	200	122	113
Jun.		122	269	152		102	136	190	122	114
Jul.		121	279	158		102	139	193	122	117
Aug.		131	275	155		103	146	198	124	112
Sep.		146	281	148		107	149	211	126	129
Oct.		155	283	143		112	146	210	131	128
Nov.		158	271	128		110	146	213	131	131
Dec.		162	305	136		109	146	223	131	136
1928										
Jan.	100	173	333	143		111	155	243	137	137
Feb.	110	168	320	138		115	150	242	136	135
Mar.	108	172	362	136		116	154	242	141	141
Apr.	121	177	408	143		118	158	247	143	150
May	127	184	413	147		117	163	249	148	155
Jun.	129	170	414	148		111	163	244	143	148
Jul.	121	170	396	144		109	161	240	139	148
Aug.	108	167	444	143		113	170	250	140	153
Sep.	126	185	458	143		115	176	256	143	162
Oct.	120	201	459	141		112	170	255	146	166
Nov.	115	229	476	140		113	168	251	143	179
Dec.	111	237	498	142		115	170	253	139	178
1929										
Jan.	112	286	579	139		120	172	254	149	193
Feb.	121	293	585	134		125	167	249	148	192
Mar.	118	266	564	133		125	165	239	143	196
Apr.	119	269	541	133		116	164	231	143	193
May	111	269	546	128		121	165	236	144	193
Jun.	109	264	524	131		121	169	246	141	191
Jul.	104	271	500	129		121	173	243	138	203
Aug.	107	294	506	127		122	171	242	142	210
Sep.	112	316	526	125		118	167	239	144	216
Oct.	98	255	496	116		113	162	221	135	194
Nov.	92	209	465	112		98	155	212	121	145
Dec.	79	210	469	107		100	154	215	121	147
1930										
Jan.	79	209	501	113	100	100	157	232	124	149
Feb.	80	206	487	113	99	101	157	233	119	156
Mar.	70	210	485	111	90	98	160	236	116	167
Apr.	77	221	495	114	79	100	155	234	120	171
May	80	196	474	114	79	94	153	223	119	160
Jun.	75	165	448	109	68	85	148	209	112	143
Jul.	70	162	454	102	65	82	147	211	112	140
Aug.	66	153	436	95	66	76	137	212	106	134
Sep.	64	160	428	93	60	75	134	209	110	139
Oct.	62	129	395	87	57	73	129	202	103	118

	Belgium	Canada	France	Germany	Japan	Nether-lands	Sweden	Switz-erland	United Kingdom	United States
Base	Jan. 1928 =100	1924 =100	1913 =100	1924-6 ·100	Jan. 1930 =100	1921-5 =100	Dec. 31 1924 =100	nominal =100	1924 =100	1926 =100
Nov.	53	129	378	83	65	67	129	195	105	109
Dec.	57	120	349	78	69	60	132	178	99	102
1931										
Jan.	55	125	366	72	69	60	123	188	96	103
Feb.	61	129	369	77	74	67	130	204	94	110
Mar.	56	128	359	83	80	69	129	207	96	112
Apr.	53	107	343	84	79	64	120	200	94	100
May	46	89	318	74	77	56	110	180	80	89
Jun.	54	91	326	67	82	50	120	181	82	87
Jul.	49	95	309		86	51	108	169	86	90
Aug.	45	94	300		81	45	99	157	82	89
Sep.	40	79	264		78	37	85	123	78	76
Oct.	39	74	245		65	37	82	129	87	65
Nov.	35	87	239		68	39	86	132	92	68
Dec.	36	74	217		78	35	79	117	81	54
1932										
Jan.	38	74	253		97	37	83	124	82	54
Feb.	39	71	294		99	37	78	131	81	53
Mar.	37	72	272		97	36	56	129	86	54
Apr.	34	58	253	45	89	28	52	116	83	42
May	31	51	225	46	90	27	51	103	77	38
Jun.	32	49	229	46	86	25	51	106	73	34
Jul.	34	57	235	46	92	28	58	121	88	36
Aug.	41	70	243	49	96	35	66	131	86	52
Sep.	41	74	245	56	106	39	66	138	90	56
Oct.	38	63	231	54	109	37	63	131	90	48
Nov.	34	63	235	55	126	37	61	127	92	45
Dec.	37	58	247	59	157	35	57	126	91	45
1933										
Jan.	35	61	239	61	169	35	54	135	95	46
Feb.	33	58	229	61	152	33	50	129	96	43
Mar.	31	59	215	67	149	32	52	133	92	42
Apr.	34	70	218	71	157	31	59	140	93	49
May	37	89	238	72	160	35	66	155	96	65
Jun.	38	107	251	70	166	39	65	166	101	77
Jul.	38	122	253	69	174	40	65	158	108	84
Aug.	38	117	251	65	174	39	63	160	108	79
Sep.	35	119	241	61	193	36	64	160	110	81
Oct.	33	104	233	60	206	34	65	158	115	76
Nov.	33	113	225	62	211	34	64	156	114	77
Dec.	32	111	224	65	210	37	65	156	113	79
1934										
Jan.	37	119	212	68	215	39	72	160	118	84
Feb.	32	124	210	72	215	39	76	162	116	88
Mar.	30	129	194	75	237	39	71	162	122	85
Apr.	30	133	200	73	223	38	76	159	124	88
May	32	128	201	72	229	36	74	157	127	80
Jun.	32	126	194	75	253	34	71	157	124	81
Jul.	30	117	185	77	236	34	73	155	124	80
Aug.	34	120	179	79	232	33	74	153	125	77
Sep.	33	119	170	82	220	33	76	152	127	76
Oct.	31	122	164	81	214	32	82	148	128	76
Nov.	30	125	158	78	197	29	80	148	132	80
Dec.	29	126	163	78	202	28	83	152	131	80
1935										
Jan.	31	130	198	81	192	30	86	160	137	81
Feb.	29	129	188	83	186	34	84	160	133	80
Mar.	38	126	185	85	193	34	80	164	130	75
Apr.	44	131	190	87	178	34	83	167	138	79
May	48	144	215	88	178	34	86	160	137	86
Jun.	46	145	207	91	163	33	90	170	141	88
Jul.	44	144	188	92	162	32	90	171	141	92
Aug.	42	146	191	93	172	32	87	174	148	95
Sep.	43	147	185	90	187	30	85	172	141	98

SOURCE: League of Nations, *Statistical Yearbook*, various issues.

raise capital more easily, and it should follow that a falling stock market can help it by financial ease. The effect through reducing the incentive to issue securities is likely to outweigh the gain through lower interest rates. But the economy does not always behave symmetrically, and a difference may be made if the stock market decline takes place in a shorter compass than the rise. There may well be no aid for business in lower interest rates overtaken by faster and more powerful forces of deflation.

The liquidity panic

The foreign capitalists and U.S. out-of-town banks and corporations who withdrew call money from the New York market caused large losses to individual investors, who in turn cut their spending. Firms that had counted on ready access to the New York stock and bond markets joined in the race for liquidity and cut their spending. Production fell sharply, and inventories were run off. The liquidity panic extended to mortgages, which were normally financed at that time in the United States on unamortized three-year obligations so that a third came due annually. House owners seldom had the cash to pay them off. Where a mortgage holder wanted the money and a house owner had difficulty in getting a new loan elsewhere—which was frequently the case—foreclosure was undertaken. The price of housing and new building dropped sharply, far faster than can be explained by wealth effects from the loss of stock market value, the decline in population growth, or the Kuznets cycle.[30]

The speed of the drop was impressive. Industrial production fell from 110 in October (on a seasonally adjusted basis) to 105 in November and 100 in December—the fastest drop in the index since 1920. Much of this was the result of the behavior of automobiles, which fell from 440,000 units in August to 319,000 in October, 169,500 in November, and 92,500 in December. Model changes came at the end of the year in the 1920s, but the low point was normally November, not December.

More impressive than industrial production was the decline in commodity prices and in imports. Hoover claims that the decline in farm prices did not come until January 1930, as a result of the support operations of the Federal Farm Board.[31] It is true that the aver-

30. See William F. Butler, "Is Another Great Depression Possible?" 1969, p. 5.
31. *Memoirs of Herbert Hoover*, vol. 3, p. 50.

TABLE 11
CHANGES IN U.S. PRICES OF SELECTED
COMMODITIES (*September–December 1929, in
percent*)

Imported Commodities		Exported Commodities	
Cocoa	− 15.4	Corn	− 14.1
Coffee	− 13.1	Cotton	− 5.6
Copper	− 9.3	Wheat	− 3.6
Hides	− 18.4		
Lead	− 8.8		
Rubber	− 25.7		
Silk	− 10.0		
Sugar	− 6.9		
Tin	− 10.1		
Zinc	− 16.7		

SOURCE: Calculated from Table 14.

ages show a fall of only 3 to 5 cents on wheat from September to December, following a decline of 14 cents in the first half of November, and on cotton only 5 percent. But corn was off 14 cents from October to December from 92 cents in September, and foreign products like coffee, cocoa, rubber, silk, hides, and tin were badly hit.

The Farm Board may have played a part, as may the breakdown of such price-fixing devices as the coffee valorization scheme in Brazil, but a crucial part of the rapid decline turned on finance. Most imports at that time were shipped to New York and other ports on consignment and sold on arrival in commodity markets. Buyers financed their purchases at banks. However, New York banks, bemused by the necessity to take on brokers' loans abandoned precipitously by out-of-town banks and "all others," cut credit lines to commodity buyers. Bear speculation by individuals may have played a part. It is significant, however, that prices of exports, financed within the United States, fell less than import prices and that among imports only one commodity, sugar, financed mainly by the refining importers concentrated in such ports as Boston, Baltimore, and New York, fell less than the consignment commodities. The figures are given in Table 11.

The fall in commodity prices in New York communicated itself abroad in the marking down of export commodities, arbitrage, and

TABLE 12
PERCENTAGE CHANGE IN WHOLESALE PRICES AT
ANNUAL RATES FOR SELECTED COUNTRIES,
AUGUST 1929–SEPTEMBER 1930

United States	France	Japan	Canada
− 12.2	− 6.7	− 22.3	− 16.0

United Kingdom	Germany	Italy
− 14.9	− 10.8	− 14.3

SOURCE: Anna J. Schwartz, "Understanding 1929–
1933," 1981, table 5, p. 24.

psychological infection. Prices fell abroad as much or more than
those in the United States, as indicated in Table 12. The decline in
commodity prices in turn affected trade. U.S. imports fell with sur-
prising speed: from $396 million in September 1929, somewhat
above the $360 million average of the three previous months, they
fell to $307 million in December, a decline of 20 percent. The de-
cline in German imports, shown in Figure 7 with those of the
United States, did not take place until the first quarter of 1930. This
is the sort of lag one would expect where imports are purchased
abroad and then shipped, rather than bought on arrival. The result
of the rapid decline in imports into the United States was an export
surplus of more than $100 million in each of the four months from
October 1929 through January 1930, when the decline in exports
caught up.

Deflation, then, moved from the decline in stock markets to production cuts and inventory runoffs in one sequence, and from stock
prices to commodity prices to the reduced value of imports in another. Both were fast. The connection between the stock market and
commodity markets was partly psychological and undoubtedly at
the outset partly through the credit machinery as banks and firms
struggled to become liquid. By the end of the year, credit markets
were easing rapidly and this source of pressure was over. It was too
late. The positive-feedback mechanism—cutting imports from less
developed countries, which cut imports from the developed—was
well under way and gathering force. On the rise, the stock market
cut off capital movements to the developing countries; in decline, it
produced a liquidity crisis that led to rapid reduction in these coun-

Figure 7. U.S. and German merchandise imports, monthly, 1928–30 (in millions of dollars).

	United States			Germany		
	1928	1929	1930	1928	1929	1930
January	341	359	317	321	312	311
February	342	364	283	298	243	236
March	379	371	304	295	244	199
April	327	396	306	281	299	212
May	348	381	282	260	271	198
June	317	350	320	266	258	195
July	323	347	218	283	305	217
August	353	373	217	260	257	190
September	325	357	227	261	248	176
October	368	396	245	290	364	236
November	328	332	197	271	277	175
December	334	307	201	264	240	163

SOURCES: League of Nations, *Statistical Yearbook*, various issues; League of Nations, *Monthly Bulletin of Statistics*.

tries' exports. The process fed back to the United States. By the turn of the year, U.S. exports had turned sharply downward.

The other connections between the stock market and business conditions through credit availability for business and through wealth and income effects on owners of securities doubtless came into operation in 1930.[32] None of them can have had time to work in 1929, except perhaps in the anticipations of businessmen. Such of them that were expansive were overwhelmed by the cumulative forces of deflation already under way.

In the light of the sudden collapse of business, commodity prices, and imports at the end of 1929, it is difficult to maintain that the stock market was a superficial phenomenon, a signal, or a triggering, rather than part of the deflationary mechanism. One should not be dogmatic about it, but it is hard to avoid the conclusion that there is something to the conventional wisdom that characterized the crash as the start of a process. The crash led to a scramble for liquidity on the part of both lenders to the call market and owners of stocks. In the process, orders were canceled and loans called. The action of the Federal Reserve in buying securities in the open market and lowering the rediscount rate in New York brought credit markets quickly into good order. By this time, however, the deflation had been communicated to fragile commodity markets and durable goods industries. The stock market crash is less interesting for the irony it permits the historian, bemused by the foibles of greedy men, than for starting a process that took on a dynamic of its own.

32. See Frederic S. Mishkin, "The Household Balance Sheet and the Great Depression," 1978.

The Slide to
the Abyss

Revival in early 1930

The New York stock market leveled off in the first few months of 1930, as Figure 5 indicates, and so did a variety of other indicators, including industrial production, imports, and employment. Employment actually picked up from the December level. Prices continued to decline in a number of commodities—cocoa, coffee, rubber, hides, silks, copper, tin—during the first quarter, but less precipitously than in the closing three months of 1929. On May 1 President Hoover stated that the United States was not through its difficulties but that he was convinced that the country had passed the worst. Correct on the first score, he could hardly have been more wrong on the second.

International lending revived, both for the less developed countries and for Europe, particularly Germany. Total U.S., British, Dutch, and Swiss foreign issues amounted to $1.7 billion for the year 1930 as a whole, compared with $1.3 billion in 1929 and $2.1 billion in 1928. The largest amount was issued in the second quarter, when loans totaled $727 million, compared to the record figure of $750 million in the second quarter of 1928.[1] Of this, $300 million represented the Young loan, issued in June; £100 million was

1. Robbins, *The Great Depression*, p. 72.

borrowed by São Paulo in London to finance the coffee surplus, swollen by the 1929 bumper crop. In March, faced with budgetary difficulties over aid to agriculture and unemployment relief, the German government borrowed $125 million from Kreuger and Toll, the Swedish match monopoly, which the latter discounted with Lee, Higginson & Co. in the United States. Other borrowers in New York were from Latin America, Australia, and Japan; in Britain, from the Dominions. For a time it looked as though the international capital market were functioning again after its diversion of a year and a half. It was needed. The halt during the stock market boom had postponed many security offerings, some of which were still wanted despite a lower level of capacity utilization. Writing in October 1929 of Germany's recovery, James W. Angell expected that a large part of the foreign issues held up by the Paris conference on the Young Plan in April–May 1929 would be offered in the United States in the autumn and winter of 1929. He went on to conclude that though it sometimes reflects weakness, borrowing in the case of Germany represented the building up of the country's strength from which were flowing rich returns.[2]

The Young loan provided a sharp contrast to the Dawes loan of 1924. Rather than being oversubscribed ten times and leading to a wave of foreign lending, the U.S. tranche, $100 million of the total, went to a discount shortly after issuance. Moreover, while the United States was reducing interest rates, capital was leaving for France. The French capital market showed interest in the capital issue for the Bank for International Settlements in May and for the Young loan. Tranches of both were oversubscribed. The momentum could not be sustained. Mobilizing the Young monies strained the market, diverting it from foreign lending and attracting short-term funds to Paris from New York and London. At the end of July, Harrison of the New York bank cabled to Moreau that he was concerned about losses of gold to France, not for the United States but in the broad aspects of the whole problem. In particular, he hoped for more foreign loans from France. The Bank of France replied through Moret, who was to be Moreau's successor upon the latter's resignation in September. Moret asserted that France did not want the gold inflow, which he believed to be largely seasonal. There

2. James W. Angell, *The Recovery of Germany*, 1932, p. 359.

were difficulties in the way of expanding foreign lending, especially the depression, which discouraged demand, and the need to dispose of certain prior issues, such as the failure of Vienna to settle its prewar debts.[3]

On one view of the depression, the continued revival of international long-term lending was vital. Those who blamed the depression on the preceding boom or inflation were typically not moved to make lending easy. They thought it necessary to put the system through the wringer, to liquidate the mistakes of the past and eliminate dead wood. Their ranks included such economists as Robbins and Hayek and, in the U.S. government, the secretary of the Treasury, Andrew Mellon.[4] Opposing them were many differing schools of thought, ranging from monetarists, market stabilizers, and interventionists to planners, all of whom thought it useful, however, to bolster rather than liquidate markets. The issue is fundamental. In a stabilized world, a recession in one part of the world economy is balanced by expanded lending by the depressed country. This finances balance-of-payments deficits of other countries and enables investment to be maintained. Britain operated such a mechanism in the years before 1914; it was unable to do so after 1929. The United States cut its spending on the products of the rest of the world. But neither it nor France proved able or willing to maintain the system with loans.[5]

It is not entirely clear why this was so. The 1924 and 1927 minidepressions in the United States had been cushioned by U.S. and British lending. A start was made in the first months of 1930. Neisser and Modigliani suggest that no other country than Britain had

3. Federal Reserve Bank of New York files, Harrison cable to Moreau, July 31, 1930; Moret cable to Harrison, August 2, 1930.

4. "The 'leave-it-alone liquidationists,' headed by Secretary of the Treasury Mellon . . . felt that government must keep its hands off and let the slump liquidate itself. Mr. Mellon had only one formula: 'Liquidate labor, liquidate stocks, liquidate the farmers, liquidate real estate.' He insisted that when people get an inflationary brainstorm, the only way to get it out of their blood is to let it collapse. He said: 'It will purge the rottenness out of the system. High costs of living and high living will come down. People will work harder, live a more moral life. Values will be adjusted, and enterprising people will pick up the wrecks from less competent people'" (*The Memoirs of Herbert Hoover*, vol. 3, p. 30). Paul Johnson states that this was the only sensible advice Hoover received throughout his presidency (*Modern Times*, p. 244).

5. Hans Neisser and Franco Modigliani, *National Incomes and International Trade: A Quantitative Analysis*, 1953, pp. 131–34.

Figure 8. Common stock prices, interest yields, and discount rate of the Federal Reserve Bank of New York, monthly, 1929–March 1933.

SOURCE: Milton Friedman and Anna Jacobson Schwartz, *A Monetary History of the United States, 1867–1960*, 1963, p. 304.

Figure 9. Yields on foreign bonds by ratings compared with high-grade U.S. domestic issues.

SOURCE: *Moody's Manual of Investments: Government Securities* (New York: Moody's Investor Service, 1931), p. 12. Reprinted in Jeffrey Sachs, "LDC Debt in the 1980s," 1982, p. 227.

NOTE: Each curve is based on average yields to maturity for forty bonds. The list of forty foreign bonds includes twenty government, fifteen municipal, and five corporate issues.

the apparatus to undertake compensatory lending. The explanation may fit France. In the United States, the market mechanism existed, though it may have suffered from the decline in foreign lending in the year-and-a-half layoff and to some extent had been discredited by excesses. But the machinery started up well enough. Why did it come to a stop?

One reason was that many potential borrowers had lost their creditworthiness. Bankruptcy, default, currency depreciation, political coups, and especially falling commodity and asset prices made many domestic businesses and foreign countries unattractive risks for loans. Interest rates declined on relatively safe commercial paper in the United States and held steady for government bonds. From August 1930 the yield on second-rate corporate bonds (*Baa*) started upward. The same phenomenon had earlier occurred in foreign bonds, where the good issues held steady and the riskier ones went down in price and up in yield. The message is conveyed in Figures 8 and 9, borrowed from Friedman and Schwartz for U.S. issues[6] and from Jeffrey Sachs for foreign bonds.[7] The divergence between high- and low-quality issues reflects a drastic change in expectations and loss of confidence. It is especially marked in foreign *A* and *Baa* bonds (but not *Aaa* or *Aa*), which declined during all of 1929, recovered sharply until April 1930, and then started down again, ending in collapse in November and December. As Schumpeter put it, "People felt the ground give way beneath their feet."[8]

The same loss of confidence was registered in direct investment. While United States portfolio lending to the "periphery" rose between 1929 and 1930 (from $71 million to $225 million for Latin America, and from $17 million to $77 million for Asia, Oceania, and Africa), direct investment declined. In 1929 U.S. firms invested $205 million in businesses in Latin America, in 1930 only $41 million; the comparable figures for Asia, Oceania, and Africa are $65 million and $14 million, respectively.[9] In 1930 the London market was closed to issues for foreign governments. Sometime after March 1930 prices started down again. The timing differed

6. Friedman and Schwartz, *A Monetary History of the United States, 1867–1960*, p. 304.

7. Jeffrey Sachs, "LDC Debt in the 1980s, Risk and Reforms," 1982, p. 227.

8. Schumpeter, *Business Cycles*, vol. 2, p. 911.

9. Heywood W. Fleisig, "The United States and the World Periphery During the Early Years of the Great Depression," 1972.

from commodity to commodity, but there was by June no mistaking the direction and extent of the movement. Profit opportunities were shrinking rapidly. The depression had passed a point of no return from which it was impossible to recover by loans for ordinary business purposes.

Tariffs

The conference to settle the details of the tariff truce, proposed in 1929 as a holding action while the tariff reductions agreed to in principle at the World Economic Conference of 1927 were worked out, finally convened in February 1930. The time was not propitious. The Smoot-Hawley Tariff Act had passed the House of Representatives in May 1929 and was under intensive study in the Senate. Neither the United States nor the Dominions, which were planning tariff increases, attended the "Preliminary Conference with a View to Concerted Economic Action"; of the twenty-seven countries that did attend, only eleven signed the final convention not to raise tariffs before April 1931. The limit for ratification, November 1, 1930, saw the list reduced to seven: Britain, the four Scandinavian countries, Belgium, and Switzerland.

While other countries had raised tariffs before the Smoot-Hawley Act became law, the course of the legislation through Congress had been followed with close attention, and the chances of a presidential veto carefully weighed. There were more than thirty formal foreign governmental protests. Some of the retaliation is said by Jones to have anticipated the enactment of the legislation, but it is difficult to disengage reason from excuse.[10] France and Italy raised tariffs on automobiles in March 1929. India put up its tariff on piece goods in February 1929. A new and general tariff increase took place in Australia in April 1930, on top of a series of special increases in November and December 1929. But the passage of the Smoot-Hawley tariff through the Senate in March 1930, its emergence from Committee in April, final passage, and signing into law on June 17, 1930, let loose a wave of retaliation. Jones discusses in detail the reactions of Spain, concerned about the tariffs on grapes, oranges, cork, and onions, which passed the Wais tariff of July 22, 1930; of

10. Joseph M. Jones, Jr., *Tariff Retaliation: Repercussions of the Smoot-Hawley Bill*, 1934.

Switzerland, which objected to increased duties on watches, embroideries, and shoes and undertook a boycott of U.S. exports; of Canada, reacting to tariffs on many food products and logs and timber, which changed governments in August 1930 and then raised tariffs three times through the Ottawa Agreement of August 1932; and of Italy, which objected to tariffs on hats and bonnets of straw, wool felt hats, and olive oil and took reprisals against U.S. (and French) automobiles on June 30, 1930. New tariffs were also enacted by Cuba, Mexico, France, Australia, and New Zealand.

In his 1932 presidential election campaign, Roosevelt attacked the tariff as a cause of the depression in a speech at Sioux City, Iowa, on September 29, 1932, accusing the "Grundy tariff," as he called it after the senator from Pennsylvania who had played a leading role in its passage, of having forced other countries off gold by preventing them from paying their debts in goods. This was the standard accusation that the United States had failed to act like a creditor nation. Roosevelt went on to claim that when they ran out of gold, foreign countries sent more goods, which meant that tariffs had the effect of lowering prices rather than the usual one of raising them. Hoover's reply to these charges was evasive. He accused the Democrats of threatening to lower tariffs and thereby weaken the position of American agriculture. As he signed the bill, he remarked that no tariff act was perfect. In his memoirs he emphasizes that the tariff had nothing to do with the depression, having been enacted nine months after the stock market crash—a thin argument in the light of the year and a half it had been in the process of passage.[11] In general, he dismisses the issue as unimportant.

The importance of the 1930 tariff to war debts and reparations is clearly overrated. Unlike the 1,028 American economists who urged President Hoover to veto the bill, most economists are not disposed today to use balance-of-payments arguments for or against tariffs. While tariffs have macroeconomic effects on income and payments, which will cumulate if tariffs pile up through mutual retaliation, the main impact of a single tariff increase is felt in resource allocation and income distribution. Moreover, while the macroeconomic effect on trade abroad is adverse, it is offset to some degree by the favorable domestic macroeconomic effect on income. The decline in imports at the old level of income is partly undone

11. *The Memoirs of Herbert Hoover*, vol. 3, p. 291.

by the increase in income from the spending diverted from abroad to home products. Lewis asserts that it was not a mistake to raise tariffs in 1930, though they should have been lowered in 1933.[12]

This is not the way it is viewed now by monetarists. Starting with Allan Meltzer, more and more monetary economists are inclined to lay stress on the Smoot-Hawley Tariff Act, ignoring the Keynesian, foreign trade multiplier of Sir Arthur Lewis and for the most part failing to mention retaliation explicitly.[13] The Wanniski notion that a small, critical vote in a Senate subcommittee on a tariff question produced the stock market crash of Black Thursday and Black Tuesday, October 24 and 29, respectively, was noted earlier and deemed farfetched. The monetarists do not go so far.[14] Sachs makes the point that the tariff cut off foreign exports, worsened the terms of trade abroad (though this presupposes no retaliation), and was a contributing cause to foreign defaults.[15] The fact that the second decline in *Baa* foreign bonds (see Figure 9) preceded Hoover's signing of the Smoot-Hawley Act by three months does not necessarily mean that the tariff did not cause the bonds to drop and yields to rise: anticipation at this interval may have been a contributing disturbing factor.

Let us agree that the Smoot-Hawley Tariff Act, after taking retaliation into account, was a deflationary force. The real failure, then, was in leadership. Hoover can perhaps be forgiven for thinking of agricultural tariffs in the 1928 presidential campaign. Tariffs were, as Schumpeter put it, "the household remedy" of the Republican party. The error was in treating it as a sovereign remedy, given to all who asked.[16] Democrats had to share the blame with Republicans since the latter, together with the White House, lost control of the bill. Schattschneider concludes his classic study of the passage of the legislation with the words: "To manage pressure is to govern;

12. Lewis, *Economic Survey, 1919–1939*, pp. 60–61.

13. Meltzer, "Monetary and Other Explanations of the Start of the Great Depression."

14. See, among others, passages in the papers in Brunner, ed., *The Great Depression Revisited*: Anna J. Schwartz (p. 22); Robert J. Gordon and James A. Wilcox (pp. 82ff.); somewhat ambiguously, Allan H. Meltzer (p. 150); Karl Brunner (pp. 331–32).

15. See Sachs, "LDC Debt in the 1980s," p. 226.

16. E. E. Schattschneider, *Politics, Pressures and Tariffs: A Study of Free Private Enterprise in Pressure Politics as Shown by the 1929–30 Revision of the Tariff*, 1935, pp. 283–84.

to let pressures run wild is to abdicate."[17] Hoover and the United States abdicated. The signing of the bill was "a turning point in world history,"[18] not for technical economic reasons but because it made clear that in the world economy no one was in charge.

If cultural identification of an economic instrument and a political party led to higher tariffs in the United States, it held them back in Britain. Unemployment had risen from 1,204,000 in March 1929 to 1,700,000 a year later. The Labour government, in office since July 1929, was committed to free trade. An economic advisory council appointed by MacDonald in January 1930 set up a task force under Keynes's direction to provide a diagnosis of the underlying economic position and to recommend remedies. The secretary, Hubert Henderson, wrote progress reports on the depression and thought its cause was high interest rates and that it could be cured by cheap money. Keynes and G. D. H. Cole, the intellectuals on the subcommittee, favored stimulation of home investment, tariffs and controls on imports, and subsidies for exports, in contrast to the business view of their colleagues that the difficulties were the result of high taxation and wages, social services, trade union restriction, and the prospect of more to follow under the Labour government.[19] The Conservative opposition greeted Keynes's espousal of tariffs with pleasure. For a number of years, leading Conservatives had wanted Britain to impose tariffs all around so that they could remove or reduce them on empire (later Commonwealth) goods in a move for empire preference. Their slogan was "Men, money, and markets," meaning emigration to the dominions and preferences in lending and trade for the empire.[20]

17. Ibid., p. 293.

18. Salter, *Recovery: The Second Effort*, pp. 172–73.

19. Keynes was a free-trader, opposed to the restoration of the pound to par in 1923 and an advocate of tariffs and export subsidies, without advocating depreciation of the exchange rate in 1930–31. After depreciation of sterling he was less forceful in his advocacy of tariffs, but he never reversed his position entirely. Barry Eichengreen finds an intelligible, consistent trail through these changes. See his "Sterling and the Tariff, 1929–32," 1981, and "Keynes and Protection," 1984. The latter paper is discussed by Mark Thomas ("Discussion," 1984) who, however, finds that the general assertion that Keynes exhibited radical shifts in his attitude toward free trade is not overdrawn. See also Alec Cairncross and Barry Eichengreen, *Sterling in Decline*, 1983, pp. 53ff.

20. Ian M. Drummond, *Imperial Economic Policy, 1917–39: Studies in Expansion and Protection*, 1974.

MacDonald and Snowden were not persuaded by any of the nostrums proposed by the economists, however. When the House of Commons met in October 1930, the King's Speech voiced the grave concern of the government but offered no program. Labour backbenchers complained that it offered no socialism; the leading Liberal, Lloyd George, no public works; the Tories, no protection.[21]

At the Imperial Conference of October 1930, Bennett, the Canadian prime minister, whose country had enacted an emergency tariff against 125 classes of American products the month before, came down hard in favor of a Canada- and empire-first policy. The British government was unwilling to cooperate. Together with the Dutch, the British proposed to the second International Conference with a View to Concerted Economic Action in November that other members of the conference should reduce their tariffs by 25 percent, especially on textiles and iron and steel, as a quid pro quo for the British and the Dutch remaining committed to free trade. The answers received the following spring were noncommittal. British leadership in commercial policy was undermined intellectually at home and in practice in the empire and was ineffective in Europe.

When Great Britain ceased to provide world leadership in the field of trade restraints, it did so with a vengeance. When the Netherlands, Belgium, and Luxemburg initialed an agreement at Ouchy for mutual tariff concessions of 5 percent a year for ten years, in violation of their most-favored-nation commitments, but defended their exchange parities against the pressure exerted by external depreciation, the United States, a bitter opponent of trade discrimination, reserved its rights. Britain demanded reciprocity, even though her negotiators were on their way to Ottawa to work out the scheme for empire preference. This torpedoed the Ouchy convention.

U.S. monetary policy

In November 1929 President Hoover decided to lower taxes and to ask firms not to reduce wages but to maintain investment. Niveau comments: "Keynes could not have done better."[22] No element in

21. Grigg, *Prejudice and Judgement*, pp. 243–45.

22. Maurice Niveau, *Histoire des faits économiques contemporains*, 1969, p. 231. For an opinion highly critical of Hoover, see Rothbard, *America's Great Depression*, ch. 7. He states that the program was inflationary and that Hoover "must be considered the founder of the New Deal in America" (p. 168).

the implied policies was developed far or for long. The major tool of anticyclical policy was cheap money. Elsewhere, and especially in Germany, the authorities embraced budget balancing to maintain business confidence.

The New York rediscount rate, which had been reduced twice in November, was lowered four more times, in 0.5 percent steps, in February, March, May, and June. This brought the rate on June 20 to 2.5 percent, compared with 6 percent in August 1929. It was to fall to 1.5 percent in May 1931. Bank indebtedness to the Federal Reserve System declined from $1 billion in June 1929 to slightly under $200 million a year later as a consequence of the open market operations following the crash, the return of currency from circulation, and gold inflows from the Far East and Latin America, particularly Brazil. The New York bank asked the board to reduce the rate from 3.5 to 3 percent in April rather than in May. This was unanimously disapproved. In June Harrison asked the Open Market Committee to undertake more vigorous purchases of government securities. He was voted down four to one. Later in the summer he was urged by other officials in the Federal Reserve Bank of New York to go back and push for more open market operations. He was skeptical. On the whole, the Federal Reserve Bank of New York and the board in Washington expected to accomplish through rate reductions what should have been done by open market operations.[23] In July 1930 Harrison, in a long letter favoring expansion, argued in terms of credit conditions and made no reference to the stock of money.[24]

Friedman and Schwartz argue that between January and October 1930 the Federal Reserve System should have undertaken massive open market operations.[25] This conclusion is based on an analysis that states that credit conditions are unimportant compared to the stock of money. The interest rate may be low in historic perspective but high relative to investment opportunities so that it fails to encourage loans. What counts is money supply. But by this criterion and their interpretation of the statistics, there was no occasion for a different monetary policy until November 1930, when under the im-

23. Wicker, *Federal Reserve Monetary Policy, 1917–1933*, pp. 150–53.
24. Friedman and Schwartz, *A Monetary History of the United States, 1867–1960*, p. 370.
25. Ibid., p. 392.

pact of bank failures the money supply began to decline.[26] The declines were small, however, until March 1931, and in nominal terms only.[27] Real money, that is, nominal money deflated by the decline in the price level, actually rose continuously from August 1929 to the first half of 1931. This fact is ignored by most monetarists, although Roland Vaubel states that it can be easily explained by an increase in the demand for real dollar balances.[28] But the source of this increased demand is unclear.

Bank failures had been continuous from 1925, especially in the Middle West where prices of commodities and farm land had started down in 1925 after an enormous rise during and following the First World War. White blames these failures on the system of unit banking, with thousands of small independent banks forbidden to organize across county or state lines.[29] The rate of failure of these banks picked up after October 1929 and in turn put increased pressure on

---

26. Ibid., p. 309.

27. Friedman and Schwartz state that the stock of money started to decline in October 1930, after having gone sideways. This is difficult to accept on their own figures:

	CURRENCY HELD BY PUBLIC AND DEMAND DEPOSITS	CURRENCY AND COMMERCIAL BANK DEPOSITS	CURRENCY, COMMERCIAL BANK DEPOSITS, AND MUTUAL AND POST SAVINGS DEPOSITS
		(in billions of dollars)	
August 1929	26.471	46.278	55.303
September 1930	25.042	45.080	54.502
March 1931	24.758	43.882	53.839
December 1931	21.894	37.339	47.913

SOURCE: Ibid., basic tables, pp. 712–13.

28. Vaubel, "International Debt, Bank Failures and the Money Supply," p. 253. Vaubel concedes that there could have been a dramatic shift from private long-term securities and real assets to riskless short-term securities eligible for discounting. "Note that if this was the case, it would have been more appropriate to issue money *and* [his emphasis] government securities (to finance a budget deficit) than to issue money in exchange for government securities [expansionary open-market operations or rediscounting]." Ibid., p. 253, n. 4. That such a dramatic shift occurred in 1930 seems clear from figs. 8 and 9 and detracts from the simple-minded case that the quantity of money alone counted.

29. See Eugene Nelson White, "A Reinterpretation of the Banking Crisis of 1930," 1984.

commodity prices. The money supply, however, remained largely unaffected.

Friedman and Schwartz date the first banking panic from the failure of the Bank of the United States in New York City in December 1930, a failure they ascribe to the nervousness of depositors affected by the bank failures in the Middle West. There had, however, been another failure of importance a month earlier, that of Caldwell and Company of Nashville, Tennessee, which brought down a series of associated banks, insurance companies, and industrial companies in Tennessee, Arkansas, Kentucky, South Carolina, and Illinois. Caldwell had invested aggressively in low-grade municipal bonds on pyramided credit provided by his chain of banks and insurance companies. The collapse of the stock market and the spread between high- and low-grade risks in the bond market had kept him scrambling for cash to stay afloat from October 1929.[30] Wicker claims that his failure was not the result of the stock market crash, but the McFerrin monograph on which his article is based makes the opposite conclusion almost inescapable.[31] It was a case of an aggressive bank trying to grow rapidly by taking on risky loans, and the same trouble—this time in real estate—accounted for the December 1930 failure of the Bank of the United States. Caldwell and the Bank of the United States, like farm banks, lacked both eligible paper for discounting and government bonds to sell for cash. Some deus ex machina was needed to shore up the prices of commodities and of risky financial assets. It was not enough to make money abundant and cheap; credit worthiness had to be improved by reversing the outlook.

German political difficulties

When Germany restricted long-term borrowing abroad in the late 1920s, it failed to limit short-term. It is not clear why. Beyen suggests that the dangers were not faced inside Germany, even by Schacht, adding, "It would not have been the first nor the last time . . . that consciousness was being 'repressed.'"[32] By the end of

---

30. See John Berry McFerrin, *Caldwell and Company: A Southern Financial Empire*, 1939; 1969.

31. Elmus R. Wicker, "A Reconsideration of the Causes of the Banking Panic of 1930," 1980.

32. Beyen, *Money in a Maelstrom*, 1949, p. 45.

1930 short-term credits to Germany had reached Rm 14.5 billion to Rm 15 billion, compared with Rm 10.8 billion of longterm loans.[33] The consequence was that Germany was sensitive to political developments, not only in the international situation, as recounted in connection with the Paris meeting on the Young Plan in April 1929, but to domestic events. It lacked only an Aftalion to develop a psychological theory of foreign exchange; the major difference with France in 1924 to 1926 was that Germany was subject to the outflow of foreign funds, France to domestic.[34]

A crisis occurred in March 1930 because of unemployment. When provision for unemployment insurance had been made in 1927, it was contemplated that it might be necessary to support as many as 800,000 unemployed at one time. By early 1930 the number was 1.9 million. The Unemployment Insurance Fund, being in deficit, had to be made up by the German government, which thereby suffered a budget deficit. The Socialist party proposed raising contributions to the fund by a 4 percent levy, largely on government officials whose contracts provided protection from unemployment. In the clash within the governmental coalition between the Socialists and the German People's party representing the government workers, Brüning sought to mediate. When the Müller government fell, Brüning took over in a new coalition that included no Socialists and proceeded to deflate. Deflation was called for by German obligations under the Young Plan, by the fear of inflation, which persisted from 1923, and by the notion that profits could be restored by pushing wages down as far as prices had fallen. The budget had to be balanced: old taxes were raised on incomes, turnover, and beer, and new ones imposed on unmarried persons, warehouses, and mineral water. Expenditures were reduced.[35]

The deflationary policy was followed for two fateful years,

33. Rudolf Stucken, *Deutsche Geld- und Kreditpolitik, 1914 bis 1963*, 1964, p. 71n. These figures are from an investigation of 1933, which produced a higher result for the end of July than the Layton-Wiggins figures usually cited, i.e., Rm 13 billion instead of Rm 8 billion.

34. Dietmar Keese argues from balance-of-payments data that the outflow of domestic capital was more important than foreign withdrawals. The case relies on associating the substantial "Errors and Omissions" item with domestic capital flight, whereas Keese acknowledges that much of it reflects the failure of foreigners to renew trade credits ("Die volkswirtschaftlichen Gesamtgrössen für das Deutsche Reich in den Jahren 1925–36," 1967, pp. 70ff.).

35. These paragraphs rely heavily on Born, *Die deutsche Bankenkrise, 1931*.

though its inadequacy should have been immediately clear. In March 1930, 537,000 fewer were employed than in March 1929, compared with a December-to-December difference, 1928 to 1929, of 176,000. With Brüning's taking of office, the number rose to 1,432,000 in April, and in August, after his first decrees, to two million. After Brüning's further deflationary steps of December 1930, the difference between March 1931 and March 1929 employment reached 2.8 million.[36]

One group in Germany did not share in the sacrifices: agriculture, especially the large-scale agriculture of eastern Germany. This class received protection, cheap credit, and special consideration in the form of *Osthilfe*, "help for the East." Under the Dawes Plan, certain taxes had been levied on German industry to pay reparations. When the Young Plan superseded the Dawes arrangements, the tax was not abandoned but was diverted to Osthilfe as interest and tax reductions for 13,000 large landowners. In the depth of the depression it amounted to Rm 170 million. It was perhaps inconsequential in comparison with import restrictions, which raised German agricultural prices Rm 2 billion above the level of world prices in 1932, but the incidence was clearer.

The process of raising revenue and cutting expenditure was political, and while Brüning governed by decree, under Article 48 of the Weimar Constitution he had to submit the program to the Reichstag. On June 18, 1930, the Reichstag voted to abrogate his decrees. Brüning's reply was to dissolve the Reichstag and call for new elections on September 14, two years before they were required. This proved disastrous.

The September elections showed marked gains, from twelve to 107 seats for the National Socialists, but also gains on the opposite wing for the Communists from 54 to 77 seats. Brüning's Center party recorded a small advance, but the other members of the coalition lost heavily. The Socialists remained the largest party, with 145 seats; the coalition had only 171. Two immediate consequences followed, both serious: first, a withdrawal of foreign funds, and second, a decision by Brüning, who chose to continue in office, to develop a more nationalistic policy as a means of governing.[37] This

36. Keese, "Die volkswirtschaftlichen Gesamtgrössen," p. 39.
37. See Heinrich Brüning, *Memoiren, 1918–1934*, 1970, p. 199, where veiled suggestions regarding the necessity for a revision of reparations calmed the cooperating parties and were clearly understood in the United States and the United Kingdom without arousing a negative reaction at the moment (October 1930).

consisted primarily of opposition to reparations but later came to include naval rearmament and a proposed Austro-German customs union. The attack on reparations was muted briefly during the loan negotiations. It was raised by Schacht, out of office, who undertook a tour of the United States to speak against the Young Plan. But it aroused strenuous opposition in France, whose newspapers threatened withdrawal of French credits to Germany, and a milder reaction from Britain in the form of a note, dated December 10, 1930, which challenged Germany's interpretation of its obligations.[38] The withdrawal of foreign funds forced the Germans to organize a new credit of $125 million from a syndicate headed by Lee, Higginson & Co. This was completed on October 11.

German commercial banks had about Rm 18 billion in deposits in June 1930, up from a monthly average of less than half that amount in 1926. By 1929, 38 percent was of foreign origin. The ratio of own capital to deposits was 1:10, as opposed to the earlier level of 1:7 and British practice of 1:3. Liquidity ratios had fallen from a prewar level of 7.3 percent to 3.8 percent in 1929; secondary reserves had also shrunk from 49 to 37 percent.[39] Certain assets short-term in form were long-term in fact, whereas a considerable but unknown portion of the bankers' acceptances, ostensibly owed abroad on the basis of bills of lading for goods moving in international trade, were actually finance bills with nothing behind them but the credit of the drawing banks.[40]

Deposits in German commercial banks declined by Rm 330 million in August, by 225 million in September, and by 720 million in October, a total of Rm 1.28 billion. The Reichsbank lost Rm 1 billion in gold. The position was stabilized by the loan at the end of the year, but it remained weak, and the banks did not aid it by buying up their own shares, which were falling on the securities market. The banks were to be obliged to write off large security losses at the end of the year. Meanwhile the Darmstädter u. Nationalbank (Danatbank) bought up 28 million of its outstanding Rm 60 million

38. Bennett, *Germany and the Diplomacy of the Financial Crisis, 1931*, pp. 22, 26.

39. Born, *Die deutsche Bankenkrise, 1931*, pp. 19–22.

40. Beyen, *Money in a Maelstrom*, 1949, p. 82. Beyen notes that one German company claimed that the foreign banks knew the collateral was nonexistent. In a class in money and banking that I took at Columbia in 1933, Ralph W. Robey recounted the story of a New York banker adding up the amounts of a number of bills drawn on his bank by a German correspondent, with the result that a series of odd sums added to a round amount in the millions.

of capital (to the summer of 1931); the Commerz u. Privatbank, 37 million out of Rm 75 million; and the Deutschebank u. Diskonto-gesellschaft, 35 million out of Rm 285 million. This reduced their liquidity and lowered their capital to deposit ratios.[41] Money rates, which had eased with the relaxation of credit in the United States in the first half of the year, tightened in the second. One-month money, for example, which had declined from 8.78 percent in December 1929 to 4.43 percent in August, was back to 7.24 percent at the end of the year. The strain was mounting, politically, financially, and economically.

Other European banks

The banks of other European countries faced problems in 1930. The rescues of the William Deacons Bank in England and of the Boden-kreditanstalt in Austria, both in 1929, were mentioned earlier. William Deacons was the only British bank in real trouble. Although joint-stock banks had experienced a difficult decade from their frozen industrial credits of 1919–20, on the whole British and French banks escaped the troubles of the rest of the Continent, especially marked in Germany and Italy.[42] There were one or two problems among private French banks, and one substantial commercial bank was allowed to fail. For the most part, however, French banks gained enormous liquidity from the return flow of capital after 1926 and, with the help of a tradition that opposed industrial lending, retained it well into the 1930s.[43]

It was the so-called mixed or industrial banks of Germany, Italy, Austria, Hungary, and Spain that had difficulties. These loaned heavily to industry at long term and bought industrial equities, a practice that was quite at variance with the English banking tradition, occasionally honored in the breach, of confining lending to short-term credits. The problem was not acute in Spain, which

41. Born, *Die deutsche Bankenkrise, 1931*, pp. 60–61.
42. See Gianni Toniolo, "Per un' analisi comparata delle cause delle crisi bancarie nell' Europa dei primi anni Trenta," 1982, esp. pp. 226–28, 231–34. This paper is contained in one of several volumes on Banks and Industry between the Wars, the proceedings of a conference held by the Banco di Roma to celebrate its centennial. An English version of some of the specialist papers is published in the *Journal of European Economic History* in a special issue: *Banks and Industry in the Interwar Period*, 1984.
43. Jean Bouvier, "Le banche francesi, l'inflazione e la crisi economica, 1919–1939," 1982, esp. fig. 3, p. 18, and fig. 4, p. 19.

stood to one side, both in the expansion of the 1920s and the contraction of the 1930s.[44] The Italian experience, however, was particularly severe, and it throws light on major banking troubles in Europe well before those of the United States.

The proximate difficulties of the Italian banks went back to the *quota novanta*, the sharp appreciation of the lira in 1926 from 150 to the pound to 90. This caused serious deflation, knocked down the Italian securities market, jeopardized the Banca Italo-Britannica, and led the four major commercial banks at the request of the monetary authorities to attempt a stabilization of security prices. In the course of this effort they lost 200 million lire.[45] The troubles went deeper still, to the weaknesses of the Italian capital market, which had called for similar direct intervention by the authorities at the outbreak of war in 1914 and again in the crisis of 1921. With accumulated losses from 1926 and falling prices, the Italian banks were in a debilitated position in 1929. As early as March 1930 various steps were taken to segregate bad assets. While the chiefs of the leading banks spoke confidently at annual meetings of their ability to avoid a crisis in spite of everything, they also spoke of moving carefully and prudently so as not to embarrass or brusquely cut off their clients.[46] In the summer of 1930 a number of small and medium provincial banks began failing and were either taken over by other banks under the guidance of the Bank of Italy or furnished with state guarantees provided by the Istituto di Liquidazione, created in 1926.[47]

By the end of the year there was still no public discussion of the mounting troubles. On December 31, 1930, the Bank of Venice was liquidated and the Provincial Agricultural Bank of Rovigo was "salvaged," to use the Italian word; 330 million lire were made available to the Credito Italiano and its subsidiary, the Banca Nazionale di Credito, which the Credito Italiano had been pushed into creating in the spring. These actions doubled the amount of assistance provided in eight previous rescue operations.[48] Continued distress extended to the Banca Commerciale Italiana in the spring of 1931, but

44. Gabriel Tortella Casares and Jordi Palafox, "Banche e industria in Spagna, 1918–1936," 1982.

45. Gianni Toniolo, *L'economia dell' Italia fascista*, 1980, pp. 215–16.

46. Ibid., pp. 206–7.

47. Gianni Toniolo, "Crisi economica e smobilizzo pubblico delle banche miste (1930–1934)," 1978, pp. 300–301.

48. Ibid., p. 301, n. 64.

this was kept secret so as not to cause a panic, and the bank was granted further extensions of government credit. Government intervention, directly and through the Bank of Italy, took over increasing amounts of industrial assets, which were ultimately used in 1933 to create the Istituto per la Ricostruzione Italiano (IRI), the Italian counterpart of the U.S. Reconstruction Finance Corporation.

The fact that acute banking distress in Europe was in advance of or contemporaneous with the U.S. bank panic of November and December 1930 should throw additional doubt on the widespread belief in the United States of a U.S. origin of the depression.

Commodity prices

Lewis states that the failure of the recovery of the first half of 1930 to hold up was the result of the continued decline in commodity prices.[49] The point is at variance with Lewis's other remark about prices, which is that they do not matter because one sector's loss is another's gain.[50] Fleisig offers the suggestion that if the transfer is from poor to rich, total spending will contract as the gainers save a larger portion of the transfer than the losers dissave.[51] This is a small and academic point. The essential truth is found in the conventional wisdom that price declines are deflationary insofar as they "check confidence, provoke bank failures, encourage hoarding and in various ways discourage investment."[52] Lewis's first opinion amounts to a disbelief in money illusion that is widely shared today, especially by monetarists. Price changes should be ignored because the gains and losses cancel out—to believe otherwise is to believe in money illusion, which is unacceptable. But there is much to be said for the conventional wisdom of the period: when prices are falling, gains, or at least the realization of gains, lag behind losses; the banks of the losers fail; gainers do not establish new banks. The law of symmetry does not hold up.

Accepting this, however, we still have to address a puzzle. If the fall in prices was an important factor causing the depression of the 1930s, why did not the fall of prices in 1920–21 initiate a compa-

49. Lewis, *Economic Survey, 1919–1939*, p. 55.

50. Ibid., p. 46.

51. Fleisig, "The United States and the World Periphery in the Early Years of the Great Depression," p. 35.

52. Lewis, *Economic Survey, 1919–1939*, p. 56.

rable depression? Exclude Britain from the discussion, because its markets were indeed hurt by the price decline following the giddy expansion of bank credit in the 1919–20 boom. In the United States the stock market collapse of 1920–21 was communicated to commodity prices in the same way as in 1929, but the collapse of commodity prices was shrugged off in 1922 and thereafter, as it was not, I would claim, in the second half of 1930. For background, compare the prices of the two periods in a variety of price indexes, as shown in Table 13.

The 1920–21 price behavior is much more sharply peaked than that of 1929–30. There are three explanations for this. First, in 1920–21 underlying resources and income had little time to adjust to either the rise or the fall. Second, the earlier boom and collapse centered in inventories, first acutely short, then overstocked, and the strong demand for long-term investment. In 1930 the demand for long-term investment was weak. Third, the 1920–21 price decline took place in a seller's market in housing, capital investment, and durable consumer goods, which remained in effect throughout the early 1920s. After 1925, however, prices began a slow decline in a long-term buyer's market, leading ultimately to the 1929 crash. In December 1930 Keynes addressed the difference between the two episodes and found that the 1921 price decline had taken place from a boom level of abnormally high profits, whereas in 1929 and 1930 prices dropped below costs that had fallen very little.[53] All this, however, runs great risk of implicit theorizing, and the task of distinguishing between the episodes analytically remains unfinished.

Table 14 shows the pattern of price decline for a number of significant commodities by monthly averages for the end of each quarter from June 1929 to the end of 1930. There is no single profile, although in most cases the drop from September to December 1929 was sharp, as was that from March to June 1930 or June to September. Coffee, cotton, rubber, and wheat fell more than 50 percent between September 1929 and December 1930, with disastrous consequences for the exports, income, and central bank reserves of Brazil, Colombia, the Netherlands East Indies, Argentina, and Australia. While declines in copper and silk were not as dramatic, their impact on Chile and Japan was severe. Fleisig notes that where foreign investors contribute heavily to export production, as in Chilean

53. John Maynard Keynes, "The Great Slump of 1930," 1930, p. 136.

TABLE 13

U.S. PRICE INDEXES, 1919–21 AND 1925–32: ANNUAL AVERAGES, SELECTED YEARS AND SELECTED COMMODITY GROUPS (*in index numbers*)

	1919	1920	1921	1925	1929	1930	1932
General price index (Snyder-Tucker) (1913 = 100)	175	193	163	170	179	168	132
Wholesale prices (Warren and Pearson) (1910–14 = 100)							
All commodities	202	226	143	151	126	107	97
30 basic commodities	217	231	126	157	141	118	74
Farm products	221	211	124	154	147	124	68
Textile products	240	293	168	192	161	143	130
Building materials	209	272	177	184	173	163	130
Fuel and lighting	198	311	184	183	158	159	133

SOURCE: U.S. Bureau of the Census, *Historical Statistics of the United States, 1789–1945,* 1949, table L-1-14, p. 231.

TABLE 14
PRICES OF SPECIFIED COMMODITIES (selected months, 1929–30)

	cocoa	coffee	copper	corn	cotton	hides	lead	rubber	silk	sugar	tin	wheat	wool	zinc
	¢ per lb	¢ per lb	£ per long ton	¢ per bushel	¢ per lb	¢ per lb	¢ per lb	¢ per lb	$ per lb	¢ per lb	¢ per lb	$ per bushel	¢ per lb	¢ per lb
1929														
June	10.51	23.5	74.3		18.04	16.8	6.80	20.56	4.96	3.52	44.26	1.50	—	6.64
September	10.79	22.5	75.3	91.9	17.62	19.6	6.69	20.19	5.20	3.98	45.38	1.37	—	6.78
December	9.13	15.5	68.3	78.0	16.64	16.0	6.10	16.06	4.68	3.71	39.79	1.32	—	5.65
1930														
March	8.67	14.0	69.2	74.5	14.74	14.2	5.56	15.25	4.68	3.43	36.81	1.15	98	4.94
June	8.31	13.4	50.0	79.0	13.21	15.2	5.31	12.38	3.56	3.28	30.30	1.05	92	4.45
September	6.26	12.0	46.3	91.7	10.15	14.6	5.35	8.19	2.93	3.14	29.64	.87	91	4.27
December	6.16	10.5	46.8	64.9	9.16	10.7	4.95	8.94	2.69	3.29	25.27	.77	86	4.09

SOURCE: *Commodity Yearbook, 1939, 1939,* for all but copper. For copper, see *Yearbook of the American Bureau of Metal Statistics, 1930, 1931.*

copper, the local economy has the protection of the impact of the fall in price on foreign profits.[54] On this showing, the price declines in cocoa, coffee, and silk were harder on peasant producers than those in copper, rubber, and tin, where much of the decline was deflected back to Europe and the United States through lower returns on investments. In Chile this was small comfort, as the country was simultaneously affected by a 70 percent decline in exports of nitrate of soda, which made up 45 percent of its exports in 1928–29, as a consequence of the depression and the development of synthetic nitrates in Germany.[55] The fall in raw silk was particularly painful for Japan, which had just returned the yen to parity in January 1930. Silk made up 36 percent of exports in value in 1929 and contributed 19 percent by value of total farm production. Two out of five families depended on it for cash income. The fall in value of silk exports from 781 million yen in 1929 to 417 million in 1930 led to gold losses of $135 million by November 1930.

The question remains why prices kept declining. Interest rates fell in the first half of 1930, but not fast enough to stimulate sufficient investment to enable primary producers to hold goods off the market. The weight of old inventories was heavy and made the position altogether different from that of 1920–21, in which prices had been bid way up and then allowed to fall as expectations were belied, but without the burden of stocks accumulated over several years. Exchange depreciation in the first half of 1930 exerted deflationary pressure on world prices in coffee, hides, wheat, and wool, and tariff increases and quota restrictions in copper, corn, cotton, hides, lead, wheat, and zinc forced an unchanged export supply on a restricted world market.

New lending stopped because of falling prices, and prices kept falling because of no new lending. As the less-developed countries lost access to loans and spent their gold and foreign exchange reserves, they were forced to sell old quantities of primary products for what the market would bring. Deflation spiraled.

But the process remains puzzling. Did the decline in lending emanate from the demand or the supply side? The rapid reduction in interest rates suggests the former, but the New York capital market

54. Fleisig, "The United States and the World Periphery in the Early Years of the Great Depression," p. 42.

55. Stephen Triantis, *Cyclical Changes in Trade Balances of Countries Exporting Primary Products, 1927–33*, 1967, p. 32.

may well have been rationed, as London was unwilling to lend at lower rates because of the dubious prospects for debt service in a world of falling prices. Would a more experienced capital market have carried through a sustained revival of lending in recession, whereas New York, having overdone it in one direction, now overdid it in the other? The decline in prices and the halt of the precarious revival of long-term lending in the spring of 1930 are critical to the length and depth of the depression, as they led to the financial crisis of 1931. Their explication is still unclear, although they had nothing to do with the money supply.

7

1931

Price declines continued into 1931 from the end of 1930. Some contribution to the trend came from the continued depreciation of the Argentine peso and the new break in the Australian and the New Zealand pounds. A determined optimist could find some hope for an upturn in prices. Norddeutsche Wollkämmerei, a German wool-combing undertaking known as Nordwolle, bought a year's supply of wool on funds borrowed from the Darmstädter u. Nationalbank (Danatbank) in early 1931, anticipating higher prices.[1] But deflation was widespread and spreading wider. As commodity prices fell, business profits declined, and with them security prices. As security and commodity prices fell, many bank loans became uncollectable. Pressure mounted against all banking systems, but in the beginning especially against those systems and banks that had over-borrowed, overlent, or lent to dubious risks. In Europe the number was legion.

The Banque Adam closed its doors in Paris in November 1930, and the Banque Oustric failed, unleashing a scandal that implicated three government officials and led to a short-lived new cabinet.[2] It was followed in January 1931 by the Laval government, which was committed to deflation. The weight of foreign short-term indebted-

1. Born, *Die deutsche Bankenkrise, 1931*, p. 75.
2. Sauvy, *Histoire économique de la France entre les deux guerres*, vol. 1, pp. 413ff.

ness was heavy throughout Europe. In November, at the time of the first Paris bank troubles, market tightness drew French funds from London in such volume that gold could not be shipped fast enough to keep the exchange within the gold points.[3] The Bank of France came to the market's assistance, but Quesnay, now of the Bank for International Settlements, suggested that the British should float a loan in France to fund a portion of the French sterling holdings. Norman explored the matter with Moret in December 1930, but without success.[4] A month later, the President of the Reichsbank, Luther, wrote to the U.S. ambassador in Berlin to suggest the funding of perhaps $350 million to $475 million of American short-term claims on Germany. This proposal evoked no response in Washington.[5] Still another suggestion was the so-called Norman Plan, originated by Sir Robert Kindersley, that the Bank for International Settlements should create a subsidiary to raise money in Paris and New York, to be used to assist "those borrowers whose relief and rehabilitation are an agreed object of policy." It was envisaged that the body might have some £25 million to £50 million of capital and perhaps £100 million of debt, which would be used, according to Skidelsky, to assist Germany and Eastern Europe, Australia and South America—Britain's traditional markets.[6] It aroused enthusiasm in neither France nor the United States. The French were willing to contemplate a long-term loan to Britain in French francs, though not an indirect one. If French funds were going to be lent, it would be the French who did it. The British were unwilling to borrow francs rather than sterling, although it is not entirely clear why the creditor should take any exchange risk. In New York, Jay Crane, in charge of foreign operations for the Federal Reserve Bank, wrote that international control raised serious difficulties and would not overcome the reluctance of New York to purchase foreign securities. J. P. Morgan & Co. cabled the Bank for International Settlements

3. The exact position of the gold points in 1930 was subject to change as the Bank of France refused to accept standard gold instead of fine gold. The gold points then depended on the costs of refining and delays in getting standard gold refined when refinery capacity was fully utilized or on the possibility of exchanging standard gold for fine in a third country such as Germany, with its extra costs of transport. See Paul Einzig, *International Gold Movements*, 1932, ch. 12, esp. pp. 101ff. This point, among many others, has been brought to my attention by D. E. Moggridge.

4. Clarke, *Central Bank Cooperation, 1924–31*, p. 178.

5. Ibid., p. 177.

6. Robert Skidelsky, *Politicians and the Slump: The Labour Government of 1929–1931*, 1967, pp. 285–86.

that, like the French, it was unwilling to surrender its judgment to an institution open to political influence.[7]

The Creditanstalt

Just as in May 1873 and July 1914, with tension growing among Germany, France, and Britain, the crack, when it came, appeared in Austria. In the early spring of 1931, a Dutch bank wrote a polite letter to the Creditanstalt in Vienna saying that it was obliged to raise the charge on its acceptance credits from 0.25 percent a month to 0.375 percent. It was a timorous letter, says Beyen, not a prescient one, and the bank was somewhat surprised when the Creditanstalt chose to pay off the loan rather than renew at the higher rate.[8] Three months later the Creditanstalt could have used the money.

The Austrian economy had been in disarray since the Treaty of St. Germain of 1920. Its finances had required League of Nations loan assistance, which entailed international supervision between 1922 and 1926. An Austrian economic historian observes that the conditions laid down by the league commission were purely financial, with the loan handed out piecemeal, in marked contradistinction to the assistance under the Marshall Plan after the Second World War.[9] Austrian tradition involved close ties of industry with banks, which provided fixed as well as circulating capital, but the Austrian banks had lost their most profitable areas of operations in the Sudetenland and Trieste. Industrial capital was consumed in the postwar inflation, and financial capital in the unsuccessful bear speculation against the French franc in 1924 that produced failures of the Allgemeine Industriebank, the Austro-Polnische Bank, and the Austro-Orientbank, as well as the private Union Bank owned by one Bosel, with grave difficulties for Kolmar & Co., Kettner, and the Brothers Nowak.[10] März calls this episode "the opening shot of a series of bank failures culminating in the breakdown of the Creditanstalt seven years later."[11]

There was no real recovery after 1924. Unemployment remained high in 1925 and 1926, decreased slightly in 1927 and 1928, but

7. Clarke, *Central Bank Cooperation, 1924–31*, p. 180.
8. Beyen, *Money in a Maelstrom*, 1949, p. 52.
9. März, "Comment," p. 190.
10. Jeanneney, "De la spéculation financière comme arme diplomatique," p. 25.
11. März, "Comment."

then rose again in 1929. For the period as a whole it averaged 10 to 15 percent. The Austrian government had no economic policy.[12] Wages rose 24 percent from 1925 to 1929, contributing to the unemployment. The annual cost of social benefits rose from 258 million schillings to 383 million. This in turn led to high taxes. The banking system, hurt by both the breakup of the Austro-Hungarian Empire and inflation, had adjusted haphazardly, placing heavy reliance on short-term credits from abroad. The Creditanstalt in particular was said to have been demoralized by the easy availability of credit from British and American lenders to its customers.[13] Domestic capital markets functioned badly in both Austria and Hungary, with banks providing credit to industry in short-term form, which often proved to be long-term in reality. As outstanding credits became frozen, banks typically converted the debt into shares in the borrowing firm. After the Creditanstalt merged with the Bodenkreditanstalt, the former owned about 60 percent of Austrian industry and was called the "monarch of Austrian industry."[14]

Banking weakness showed up well before the fall of world prices. After 1924, one by one, small weak banks were taken over by larger, sometimes stronger banks. At the beginning of 1927, the Bodenkreditanstalt took over the Union Bank and the Verkehrbank. In 1929, the Bodenkreditanstalt was itself fused overnight with the Creditanstalt. The Bodenkreditanstalt brought to the Creditanstalt large loans to industrial concerns which could be maintained only by the device of ignoring market values. Like the German banks, the Bodenkreditanstalt had bought in its own shares to maintain their price and depositors' confidence. When the Creditanstalt took over the Bodenkreditanstalt, it acquired 80 million schillings of capital. But it also acquired 140 million of accumulated losses, as it learned later when a British chartered accountant revealed the truth. In May 1931 losses were still at 140 million schillings, and capital at 125 million plus disclosed reserves of 40 million for a total of 165 million. Under Austrian law, if a bank lost half its capital it had to "turn in its balance sheet," or close down.[15] In an effort to rescue

12. K. W. Rothschild, *Austria's Economic Development Between the Two Wars*, 1947, p. 47.

13. Vera Micheles Dean, "Austria: The Paralysis of a Nation," 1933, p. 259.

14. Rudolf Nötel, "Money, Banking, and Industry in Interwar Austria and Hungary," 1984, p. 162.

15. Fritz Georg Pressburger, "Die Krise der Österreichischen Creditanstalt," 1969, p. 83.

the Creditanstalt, the government, the National Bank, and the House of Rothschild, the last with help of the Amsterdam branch, furnished 100 million, 30 million, and 22.5 million schillings, respectively. But the announcement of the support operation on May 11, 1931, started a run, partly foreign, partly Austrian.[16]

It is widely maintained that the Austrian Creditanstalt closed its doors as a consequence of French withdrawals of credits provoked by the proposed Austrian-German customs union. This proposal went back to a German working paper for the World Economic Conference of 1927. It had been discussed between Curtius, the German foreign minister, and Chancellor Schober of Austria at the first Hague conference on the Young Plan in August 1929 and again on the occasion of Schober's visit to Berlin the following month.[17] Initially seen as a device to improve German-Austrian relations, it was taken up by Brüning as an item of positive foreign policy to divert the electorate from National Socialist gains in September 1930. Official German circles appeared to be painfully surprised that France objected to a customs union as being contrary to the Treaty of Versailles, which forbade only the much more far-reaching step of *Anschluss*. There is some doubt whether this surprise was genuine.[18] Whether Germany was naive or disingenuous, however, the French foreign office objected, but French banks on instructions did not pull out French credits.[19] There were probably few such credits to begin with, and total foreign deposits declined only from 466 million schillings ($67 million) at the end of 1930 to 442 million ($63 million) at the end of April 1931.[20]

The run started as the news of the Creditanstalt's difficulties became known. The country needed foreign exchange to help with the run and sought a loan of 150 million schillings ($21 million). It went to the League of Nations Financial Committee, which in turn

16. Walter Federn, "Der Zusammenbruch der Österreichischen Kreditanstalt," 1932.

17. Julius Curtius, *Sechs Jahre Minister der Deutschen Republik*, 1948, pp. 118–19.

18. See Ambassador Sackett's dispatch to the secretary of state of March 24, 1931: "A portion of the German press evidently considers the agreement as a first step toward evading treaty rights" (Department of State, *Foreign Relations of the United States, 1931*, vol. 1, 1946, p. 570).

19. Born, *Die deutsche Bankenkrise, 1931*, p. 56.

20. Federn, "Der Zusammenbruch der Österreichischen Kreditanstalt," p. 421.

referred it to the Bank for International Settlements (BIS). Under the leadership of its president, Gates W. McGarrah, the BIS arranged a loan of 100 million schillings ($14 million) from the ten largest central banks. The process took from about May 14 to 31. On May 14, when McGarrah approached the Federal Reserve Bank of New York, he had already lined up the Reichsbank, the Bank of England, and the National Bank of Belgium. Whether the further delay was the result of a French request for the renunciation of the customs union, as most observers think, or merely the time required to arrange for a standstill among the Creditanstalt's creditors and to obtain the Austrian government's guarantee of Creditanstalt's borrowing, as Clarke asserts,[21] is not self-evident. The niggardliness of the sum and the delay together proved disastrous.

By June 5 the credit was exhausted and the Austrian National Bank requested another. Still under pressure, the bank raised its discount rate to 6 percent on June 8 and 7.5 percent on June 16. The new credit was arranged by the BIS, by June 14 this time, but subject to the condition that the Austrian government should obtain a two-to-three-year loan abroad for 150 million schillings. At this point the French interposed the condition that the Austrian government should abandon the customs union with Germany. The Austrian government refused, and it fell. A new government took office. But meanwhile, on June 16 Governor Norman of the Bank of England took on unilaterally a 50 million schilling ($7 million) credit to the Austrian National Bank for one week.[22] The gesture was a rebuke to the French for mixing politics and finance. It is widely thought to have deepened the Bank of France's antagonism toward Norman and to have inspired the conversion of its sterling into gold. Regardless of the consequences in this direction, the vital point is that it marks the end of Britain as a lender of last resort: $7 million for one week! Shades of the advice of Walter Bagehot: "In a crisis, discount and discount freely." The loan was renewed each week through June and July until in August, the pound coming under pressure and the League of Nations arranging a 250 million schilling loan from seven governments, the Bank of England requested repayment.

21. Clarke, *Central Bank Cooperation, 1924–31*, p. 189.
22. Born mistakenly believes that Norman lent the whole 150 million schillings (*Die deutsche Bankenkrise, 1931*, p. 66).

The Hoover moratorium

During the course of his speaking tour of the United States denouncing reparations in October 1930, Schacht paid a visit to Mellon, the secretary of the Treasury, who asked whether Germany could pay reparations better after a two- or three-year moratorium. The idea of a temporary postponement was widely discussed at the time.[23] Hoover's proposal nine months later was not original.

At the end of May 1931 Austrian financial difficulties ramified widely and led to runs on the banks of Hungary, Czechoslovakia, Romania, Poland, and Germany. Some wondered whether American creditors knew the difference between Austria and Germany.[24] But President Hoover was aware and, if his account is to be believed, prescient. Ambassador Sackett arrived from Berlin on May 7 with news from Brüning of a disastrously developing financial situation, with credits drying up, currency difficulties, pressures for repayment of debts, and refusal to renew accounts. This was before the Creditanstalt. On May 11, still before he had heard of the Creditanstalt difficulties, Hoover asked Stimson and Mellon for suggestions. They had none to offer. He called in the Federal Reserve Board. They thought he was seeing ghosts. On June 5 he suggested a moratorium to Mellon. The secretary objected that it was Europe's mess. The European press kept insisting that U.S. policies sucked up gold and undermined European financial systems. Hoover "knew this to be untrue, and another example of Europe blaming the United States for its own failures."[25] But he was prepared to concede, in a phrase he used twice in his memoirs, that gold and short-term credit behaved like "a loose cannon on the deck of the world in a tempest-tossed era."[26]

The pressure on Germany began in May. Deposits at the banks fell in that month from Rm 15.448 billion to 15.07 billion. The Reichsbank lost no gold, partly because of the placement of 120 million marks of the newly founded Berlin Power and Light Company with a foreign syndicate, the last commercial loan. The major difficulties were at the larger banks, with withdrawals in May of Rm

23. Bennett, *Germany and the Diplomacy of the Financial Crisis, 1931*, p. 23.

24. Ibid., p. 117, quoting the *Deutsche Allgemeine Zeitung* of May 27 and June 10, 1931.

25. *The Memoirs of Herbert Hoover*, vol. 3, pp. 64–67.

26. Ibid., p. 67; see also p. 189.

97 million at the Danatbank, Rm 70 million at the Dresdner, Rm 59 million at the Deutsche. At the time of the Creditanstalt, the Karstedt company, a department store chain that had been expanding rapidly with bank credit, was reported to be in trouble; at the end of May the Nordstern insurance company began to founder.[27]

June was the difficult month. In the first six days the Reichsbank lost Rm 164 million in gold, and then matters worsened. The trouble was partly self-induced. On June 5 the Brüning government published a decree lowering the salaries of civil servants, decreasing unemployment assistance, and levying a new crisis tax. To sugar the pill it remarked that Germany had reached the limit of its capacity to deal with reparations—a statement intended for internal consumption. Visiting London with Luther, president of the Reichsbank, and Foreign Minister Curtius in search of help, Brüning said that the German government had no intention of taking any steps on reparations before November 1931 at the earliest, provided foreign credits were not withdrawn. He spoke of the German need for new foreign loans. Norman stated that the real problem was presented by Austria and that Germany would get by.

Norman had not, however, taken into account the internal political position in Germany. On June 10–11 the Socialist, Communist, and Center parties asked for a convening of the Reichstag to lift Brüning's power to govern by decree. This *Aufruf*, or "summons," produced a heavy drain of funds. Within four days the Reichsbank had lost Rm 400 million in gold. On June 13 it raised its discount rate from 5 to 7 percent; this slowed down the movement. On June 17 the withdrawal died away, having cost Germany Rm 1.4 billion in gold losses—more than half its total at the end of May—and reduced its reserve ratio from 60 to 48 percent. Then came the announcement of the failure of Nordwolle, the wool concern that had earlier in the year gambled on a rise in the price of wool. The company had borrowed heavily from the Danatbank and sought to hide its losses by transferring its inventories, at cost, to its Dutch subsidiary, Ultramarine, and expanded its gross assets on the books by creating extensive claims between its branches in Argentina and Bremen. The extent of the eventual losses was not known on June 17, when the company announced merely that it had a loss of Rm

27. For accounts of the difficulties of Karstadt and Nordwolle, in which Hermann J. Abs, then a partner of Delbruck, Schickler & Co. and later head of the Deutsche Bank, played a part, see Pohl, *Hermann J. Abs*, pp. 27–30.

24 million covered by a reserve of 22.5 million.[28] The withdrawals picked up again, and the Reichsbank lost Rm 90 million on June 19. On June 20 the picture was again reversed, but briefly. As early as June 5 President Hoover laid before Mellon, Mills, and Stimson a "bold, emphatic proposal" to assume leadership himself and to place a moratorium on all intergovernmental debts. The Treasury was apathetic. Mills said he needed the debt payment to balance the budget. Hoover went ahead. Adding Governor Eugene Meyer, Chairman of the Board of Governors of the Federal Reserve System, President Harrison of the New York Federal Reserve Bank, and Dwight Morrow, ambassador to Mexico and former J. P. Morgan partner, to his group, he got advice from June 6 to 16. The group wanted a two-year moratorium but chose one of one year in deference to the anticipated attitude of Senator Borah, who was strongly anti-Europe and isolationist. Stimson states that Hoover was beset by fears and very difficult to work with. One of his fears was that the moratorium might connect war debts and reparations. Dwight Morrow strongly urged that France be consulted beforehand, but the decision not to do so was taken so as to evoke the maximum shock effect. It was arranged that President Hindenburg would write to Hoover to ask for the moratorium. Ambassador Claudel was informed on June 19. The moratorium was announced on June 20.[29]

The Hoover moratorium hit France like a bombshell. The response would have been even more bitter, Stimson believed, had it not been for the skill and force with which Laval managed the extremists. But the French refused a direct acceptance. They insisted on different treatment for the conditional and unconditional payments in the reparation schedules under the Young Plan, asking for discussions that would take "a day or two." Secretary Mellon was in Europe and visited Paris to negotiate the details. The talks stretched out and the favorable response in international financial markets flagged. On June 25 a credit of $100 million was arranged, with $25 million each from the Bank for International Settlements, the Bank of England, the Bank of France, and the Federal Reserve Bank of New York until July 16. It was not in time to help the Reichsbank statement of June 23, which would have shown a re-

28. Born, *Die deutsche Bankenkrise, 1931*, p. 75.
29. See Morison, *Turmoil and Tradition*, pp. 347–50; and Stimson and Bundy, *On Active Service in Peace and War*, pp. 202–6.

serve ratio below 40 percent had it not been for an overnight deposit of $5 million from the Bank of England.[30] By June 30 $70 million of the loan had been used up. By July 5 it was gone. Hoover threatened to isolate France by dealing separately with each country over the moratorium. On July 6 the French agreed, and the moratorium took effect.

The French had a real point. In urging the French to cooperate, the U.S. government had stated that the French stood to lose only $100 million in reparations from the moratorium, while the United States lost $250 million.[31] In reply, the French noted that one principle of reparations was that the unconditional annuities should be on a par with commercial obligations, whereas the moratorium made them inferior. The French had 52 percent of reparation payments, which were lost, but only a miniscule proportion of the commercial debts, which were preserved.[32]

The run on Germany

Neither the credit nor French agreement to the moratorium was able to stop the run on Germany. The June 30 statements revealed how heavily foreigners had drawn down their claims on German banks. On July 1 the extent of Nordwolle's losses were made known. On July 5 a newspaper in Basel, the home of the Bank for International Settlements, reported that a German bank was in trouble. A few days later the Danatbank was named. The German banking crisis exploded. On July 9 Luther flew to London, Paris, and Basel seeking assistance.[33]

30. Clarke, *Central Bank Cooperation, 1924–31*, p. 193. Clarke notes that the Federal Reserve Bank of New York had been authorized by the board to lend $50 million to the Reichsbank. Luther had asked for much more, and when only $100 million was provided, asked for the announcement of the amount to be withheld so as not to reveal its inadequacy. Through inadvertence, however, the amount was made known. Foreign credit calls were resumed on June 27. See Born, *Die deutsche Bankenkrise, 1931*, pp. 82–83.

31. Department of State, *Foreign Relations of the United States, 1931*, vol. 1, p. 46.

32. For a contemporary account, highly sympathetic to the French viewpoint but ignoring the wider impact, see H. F. Armstrong, "France and the Hoover Plan," 1931.

33. This is the first use of air travel by government officials, only a month after President Hoover spoke from Washington with secretaries Stimson and Mellon in Europe, the first official use of the transatlantic telephone.

The Bank of England was unable to help; the French were prepared to do so, provided they received some indications of German intentions that inspired trust—specifically, the abandonment of the Austro-German customs union, cancellation of the Panzer cruiser under construction, and the forbidding of military demonstrations, including those of the National Socialists. Brüning returned to Berlin for two days. On July 13 the banks closed briefly. When they reopened on July 16, foreign credits were blocked and the discount rate was raised from 7 to 10 percent. On July 18 all banks except the Danatbank, which was thoroughly disliked by the other banks for its aggressive tactics and was finally allowed to fail, joined in a *Haftungsgemeinschaft* (guarantee corporation) under the leadership of the Golddiskontobank. A new Akzept- u. Garantiebank (acceptance and guarantee bank) was started to provide a third name on paper so as to make it eligible for discount at the Reichsbank and to replace foreign credits that had been withdrawn. This opened for business on August 1 with a discount rate of 15 percent and quickly discounted Rm 1.205 million for the commercial and savings banks.[34]

French and German opinion agreed that the German banking crisis should be resolved by a fresh loan. On the terms of the loan, however, there was a wide difference. The French clung to the idea of a private loan guaranteed by the governments of France, Britain, and the United States, with political guarantees given by Germany. The Germans were persuaded of the necessity for a guaranteed extension of the stabilization of existing short-term credits to the German economy and, in addition, for a new loan, but one free of political conditions. The French had in mind $500 million; the Germans preferred to think in terms of $1 billion.[35]

Secretary of State Stimson left Washington for a vacation in Europe on June 27 and was visiting European capitals when he en-

34. Pohl, *Hermann J. Abs*, p. 33.

35. For an account of one rescue loan from the Warburg bank in New York to the Warburg bank in Hamburg, which cost Paul M. Warburg half his fortune, see James P. Warburg, *The Long Road Home: The Autobiography of a Maverick*, 1964, pp. 92, 98. Warburg states that the New York banks accumulated a fund of Rm 50 million to be used to shore up the weakest German bank, which proved to be the Danatbank, but that Brüning turned down the offer of this rescue loan, with tears in his eyes but without explanation. This was later revealed to have been because the Danatbank had a mysterious Rm 10 million bad loan to President Hindenburg's son, Oskar, which the government did not want to come to light.

countered the issue. He favored the idea of a new loan to Germany and opposed political conditions. But he was unable to win Hoover's support. Hoover noted the U.S. prospective budget deficit of $1.6 billion and thought it preposterous to expect Congress to lend more money to Germany in such circumstances. Moreover, he thought a private loan was impossible. He recommended instead the stabilization of existing credits. In Britain, Arthur Henderson, the foreign minister in the Labour government, was attracted to the idea of a loan, but Governor Norman maintained that the Bank of England had "already lent quite as much as is entirely convenient in Austria, Hungary and Germany to avoid financial collapse."[36] He was also fearful that if Germany obtained a government-guaranteed loan, these would be sought by Australia, India, and many other countries.[37] A meeting of ministers was called on July 20 in London. During the course of it, the idea of a loan of new money gradually died as neither the British nor the Americans were willing to agree. The meeting produced an extension for three months of the $100 million central banks' loan of June 25 and a standstill agreement on withdrawals of foreign credits. To ascertain what these amounted to, a special committee was appointed under Albert Wiggins to work with the Bank for International Settlements. Walter Layton drew up the report for the Wiggins committee, stating that there were Rm 23 billion in foreign funds remaining in Germany at the end of July 1931, of which Rm 8 billion were in short-term form. German claims on foreigners amounted to Rm 8.5 billion, of which one-fifth were short-term. The standstill agreement freezing foreign claims on Germany was initially concluded for a six-month period but thereafter was continuously renewed on an almost automatic basis.

Stimson liked the "excitement of the moratorium"[38] and thought the standstill agreement "the neatest and most successful [negotiation] of his career."[39] In his view, the moratorium was "one of the best things Mr. Hoover ever did."[40] It is difficult to approve the superlatives, unless Stimson is trying to say something about other negotiations and other things.

36. Federal Reserve Bank of New York files, cable Norman to Harrison, July 3, 1931.
37. Clarke, *Central Bank Cooperation, 1924–31*, p. 199.
38. Morison, *Turmoil and Tradition*, p. 353.
39. Stimson and Bundy, *On Active Service in Peace and War*, p. 209.
40. Ibid., p. 208.

The attack shifts to sterling

In mid-July sterling weakened. The usual explanation is that the publication of the Macmillan Report on July 13 worried sterling holders as it revealed to the world the extent of foreign sterling balances.[41] This interpretation suffers from the fact that the press failed to note the figures.[42] Several sources suggest that the French were taking revenge on the British for failing to support French views over exacting political conditions from Austria and Germany.[43] This is probably incorrect. The pressure seems to have come from the commercial banks in the smaller countries of Europe—Belgium, the Netherlands, Sweden, and Switzerland—which, having lost liquidity through the blocking of German credits, sold sterling to increase their gold reserves.[44] The Macmillan Report tended, if anything, to underestimate Britain's sterling liabilities; its contribution to policy was confused. Keynes and McKenna came out for expansionist policies, with maintenance of existing exchange rates but the imposition of tariffs and import restrictions. The majority supported the maintenance of the exchange rate, but Ernest Bevin advocated devaluation. The central recommendation was that all three countries—Britain, France, and the United States—should expand spending simultaneously, but the emphasis on tariffs and/or devaluation of the minority conveyed a more nationalistic flavor.

A more profoundly discouraging impact on the foreign exchange market for sterling was conveyed by the May Report, the work of a committee set up in March 1931 under the chairmanship of Sir George May to make recommendations on the Labour government's budget proposals. The draft was communicated to Snowden on July 24 and published a week later. Both majority and minority on the committee agreed that there would be a budget deficit of £120 million, though neither took account of the fact that this included provision for sinking funds. The majority blamed it on government extravagance and proposed cutting unemployment insurance (to the

41. Great Britain, Committee on Finance and Industry, *Report*, Cmd. 3897, 1931.

42. Skidelsky, *Politicians and the Slump*, p. 340.

43. Born, *Die deutsche Bankenkrise, 1931*, p. 66; see also Bennett, *Germany and the Diplomacy of the Financial Crisis, 1931*, p. 152.

44. Willard Hurst, "Holland, Switzerland, and Belgium and the English Gold Crisis of 1931," 1932.

extent of two-thirds of the total saving of £100 million), while the Labour minority blamed it on deflation and suggested taxing the rich. The report called for foreign loans. Efforts in this direction had begun earlier with a loan of £50 million arranged with the Federal Reserve System as early as July 24, Sir Robert Kindersley going to Paris for a loan of similar amount from the Bank of France on July 26. These two loans were announced on August 1. The Bank of England raised its discount rate from 2.5 to 3.5 percent on July 23, and to 4.5 percent on July 30. In all, it lost $200 million in reserves during the second half of July. David Williams comments that the Bank ceased to use discount policy as a means to combat the crisis because of large-scale unemployment.[45] With liquidity tight abroad and confidence in sterling shaky, it is doubtful whether the crisis could have been corrected by a 10 percent bank rate, which, according to tradition, would draw gold from the moon.

The crisis proceeded to its climax without Governor Norman, who became ill on July 29 and was sent away to convalesce after he had recovered. The last entry in his diary on July 27 was: "Danger of suspension of gold payments."[46]

The £100 million were not used when the foreign exchange market reopened on August 4 after the bank holiday. The French share had been divided between the Bank of France and the commercial banks, and the French wanted the two to be drawn simultaneously in equal amounts. This would have informed the French money market of the state of British exchange support, so the bank postponed using the credit until the matter could be straightened out. The process took several days. The bank was also slow to support sterling as a means of putting pressure on the government, with which it strongly disagreed. During the resulting interval, the psychological benefit of the credit was lost and pressure on sterling was maintained.[47]

The May Report provided encouragement to deflationists in Britain and abroad and set the stage for a classic political struggle. MacDonald and Snowden became convinced that Britain could not maintain the gold standard without further loans. The Bank of England and private bankers in New York and Paris were persuaded

45. David Williams, "London and the 1931 Financial Crisis," 1963, pp. 524, 527ff.

46. Andrew Boyle, *Montagu Norman*, 1967, p. 266.

47. Clarke, *Central Bank Cooperation, 1924–31*, pp. 207–9.

that, to be creditworthy, Britain had to correct its deficit by the methods outlined by the majority in the May Report, that is, by a cut in unemployment compensation. Henderson strongly opposed this policy and proposed instead a 10 percent tariff for revenue. The Bank of England reported that a serious cut in unemployment compensation was necessary before foreign loans could be obtained. The trade unions, led by Ernest Bevin who favored devaluation and a turning inward from the world economy to the empire, withdrew their support from the Labour government, which fell on August 24. The loans, amounting to $200 million each from Paris and New York, were provided on August 28, after the formation of the National government with MacDonald still prime minister and Snowden still chancellor.[48] The division within the Labour party was deep, as the left wing accused the right of submitting to "a bankers' ramp." The bankers replied that they had merely found out from abroad whether certain actions would be sufficient to restore confidence in the currency.[49] The dispute is typical. The lenders think they impose conditions to achieve desirable economic results and to protect the loan; the borrowers, however, view the conditions as doctrinaire, ideological, and politically intrusive.[50]

On September 10 the National government introduced a new budget designed to levy increased taxation of £80 million a year and to provide economies of £70 million. Within a few days, though, there were new bankruptcies in Germany, which communicated tension to Amsterdam, which in turn drew funds from London. On September 16 there was unrest among naval personnel at Invergordon over the prospect of pay reductions. This was exaggerated by the press into a mutiny in the Royal Navy.[51] If the Royal Navy were to go, how long would that other mainstay of nineteenth-century liberalism last—the gold standard run by the City of London? The pace of withdrawals accelerated. On September 21 Great Britain left the

---

48. For a detailed account of the formation of the National government, see R. Bassett, *Nineteen Thirty-One: Political Crisis*, 1958.

49. Grigg, *Prejudice and Judgement*, p. 257.

50. See John Williamson, ed., *IMF Conditionality*, 1983.

51. According to David Divine (*Indictment of Incompetence: Mutiny at Invergordon*, 1970), it was more a strike than a mutiny. Vansittart called it a "demonstration" in *The Mist Procession: The Autobiography of Lord Vansittart*, 1958, but notes that "Europe thought that revolution had started, that troops were unpaid, and mobs starving" (p. 425).

gold standard.[52] The initial intention was that this would be for a matter of six months.

The Bank of France was in no way implicated in the September withdrawals, as it probably was not in July. Leith-Ross states how cooperative the Bank of France was in the provision of the August 28 loan. The Bank of France was left with £65 million on September 21 when sterling went off gold, and Clément Moret, the governor of the Bank of France, was decorated as a Knight of the British Empire in October.[53]

The role of the small central banks has been criticized by Born, Bennett, Hurst, Einzig, and others. Einzig tells the story of Vissering of the Netherlands Bank, who asked the Bank of England for a gold guarantee, was scornfully invited to take his total balance of £11 million in gold, and decided against it. Later the Netherlands Bank briefly contemplated a suit against the Bank of England for the implicit guarantee contained in a telegram from Sir Ernest Harvey to Vissering:

> Confidential—With reference to our conversation on Wednesday last [August 26] you will no doubt have seen the official announcement today of the conclusion by our government of large credits in New York and Paris. I trust this announcement will serve to abolish all doubts as to the safety of foreign funds in London.[54]

The Swiss National Bank sold all but £300 thousand by September 20.[55] A folktale has it that the National Bank of Belgium, asking a week ahead of the event whether sterling would be devalued, was told "no." Complaining later, it was informed that if it asked ille-

52. For a table of daily losses of gold and foreign exchange, see Cairncross and Eichengreen, *Sterling in Decline*, p. 68.

53. Leith-Ross, *Money Talks*, p. 139n. The author adds that central bank cooperation was much closer than with some of his predecessors. This dictum stands in some contradiction to the thesis of Clarke (*Central Bank Cooperation, 1924–31*, esp. p. 220) that central bank cooperation was effective up to mid-1928 and a failure thereafter.

54. Public Record Office, Treasury File T 160/439/F12712 Dutch Sterling Balances at Bank of England, Aide-mémoire left by M. R. Van Swinderen at Foreign Office, January 21, 1932. Paul Einzig, *The Comedy of the Pound*, 1933, p. 44, has an almost literal rendering of this telegram. The exact reference has been furnished by D. E. Moggridge.

55. See Clarke, *Central Bank Cooperation, 1924–31*, p. 214, n. 104; and the annual report of the Swiss National Bank, *Federal Reserve Bulletin*, April 1932, p. 252.

gitimate questions it would get illegitimate answers. While this story is undoubtedly apocryphal, the record does contain revealing comment. The National Bank of Belgium had had £25 million on deposit in London at the end of 1930, constituting 62 percent of its total holdings of foreign exchange. The bank was worried about sterling. From September 1930 to September 1931 it bought a small amount of gold—2 billion Belgian francs, or roughly $20 million— and switched some sterling into dollars and French francs, cutting its balances in London almost in half from the 1930 year-end figure.[56] As Baudhuin puts it, the National Bank "had always applied itself to reduce this figure [the balance] to the point where the Bank of England would have been willing to complain." When sterling went off gold, the Belgian authorities, meeting on September 21, decided that they could not liquidate their remaining sterling since this would have been an unfriendly act. "They thus held back before this act which would have appeared remiss in the light of the duties imposed by international solidarity."[57] In addition, the minister of finance thought that Britain would quickly reestablish the gold standard at a not very different parity, and he agreed to underwrite any losses on sterling that the National Bank might incur.[58] Solidarity with the Bank of England, calibrated to what would lead to complaint, did not extend to the dollar, as will shortly appear.

The depreciation of sterling

The pound fell from $4.86 with remarkable speed. Within a few days it was off 25 percent, to $3.75, before recovering slightly to $3.90. The authorities made no attempt to intervene in the market or even to maintain orderly conditions. Many people anticipated a decline comparable to the postwar falls of the French franc or the Italian lira and were anxious to liquidate their holdings. The Bank of France participated in this liquidation. According to Einzig, it offered to forbear from selling sterling against an exchange guarantee, but the British government was not prepared to take on com-

56. Herman van der Wee and K. Tavernier, *La Banque Nationale de Belgique et l'histoire monétaire entre les deux guerres mondiales*, 1975, ch. 5, esp. pp. 437–40.
57. Fernand Baudhuin, *Histoire économique de la Belgique, 1914–1938*, 1946, vol. 1, pp. 249–50.
58. Van der Wee and Tavernier, *La Banque Nationale de Belgique*, p. 241.

mitments in foreign exchange.[59] By December the rate had reached a low of $3.25, 30 percent below par, averaging $3.47 for the month. This involved a 40 percent appreciation in those currencies that had not immediately followed sterling off gold. Grigg later commented: "Britain had gone off gold, not in a genteel way, but with a catastrophic fall of 30 percent or more, which destroyed whatever basis of coherence and stability the world had at that time."[60]

By December 1931 the chancellor of the Exchequer adopted a policy with respect to sterling, proposed by Governor Norman of the Bank of England, which provided for the authorities to refrain from dealing unnecessarily; to ignore the question of profit and loss; to avoid deliberate depreciation, even at the risk of allowing reserves to fall dangerously low; to allow sterling to find its own long-run level; and to avoid an attempt to fix the rate prematurely.[61] Omitted from the list, which Clay states was maintained up to the outbreak of war in 1939, is a consideration of the impact of depreciation on other countries.

Twenty-five countries in all followed Britain off gold, largely in the empire, Scandinavia, and Eastern Europe, as well as such trading partners as Argentina, Egypt, and Portugal. Canada split the difference between the U.S. dollar and sterling, experiencing some depreciation against the U.S. dollar but appreciation against sterling and, especially painful, against the Swedish krona (newsprint) and the Argentine and Australian currencies (wheat). The Union of South Africa resisted depreciation, together with the U.S. dollar, the gold bloc, and the German mark.

Germany struggled at the time, and has struggled in the historical literature ever since, over what the appropriate policy should be (and should have been) and what considerations should enter into it. Germany was committed in the Young Plan to maintain its exchange fixed in terms of gold. The French regarded this as legally binding; the British did not. The United States opposed devaluation of the Reichsmark, but the Bank of England, its American adviser, Oliver M. W. Sprague, and J. M. Keynes, in a speech at Hamburg in Jan-

---

59. Einzig, *The Comedy of the Pound*, pp. 32–33, 43–44. Treasury records on French balances do not confirm this plausible account.

60. Grigg, *Prejudice and Judgement*, p. 184.

61. Clay, *Lord Norman*, p. 405.

uary 1932, urged depreciation.[62] The German representative at the Bank for International Settlements, Edgar Salin, was an advocate of depreciation and made a trip to Berlin to urge it. He had perhaps been influenced by the British view expressed at the BIS. A large number of individual Germans also advocated relieving the deflationary pressure of the Reichsmark's appreciation caused by the depreciation of sterling. These included Carl Krämer, Walter Grävell, Rudolf Dahlberg, Werner Sombart, Wilhelm Grotkopp, Heinrich Dräger, Wilhelm Röpke, and Albrecht Forstmann—but they were outsiders.[63] The establishment was opposed, and for many reasons: it was contrary to the Young Plan; it would increase the local currency cost of foreign debt service; the Americans and the French were opposed, and the French might call German credits.[64] But the major reasons were the desire of Brüning to show that paying reparations was impossible—any help to the balance of payments worked against that—and fear of inflation. All portions of the political spectrum associated exchange depreciation with inflation because of their close connection in the early 1920s. Anyone who recommended devaluation "was almost in danger of his life." The

62. Jürgen Schliemann, Die deutsche Währung in der Weltwirtschaftskrise, 1929–33: Wärungspolitik und Abwertungskontroverse unter den Bedingungen der Reparationen, 1980, pp. 183–90. Schumpeter quotes the opinion of "a man who ought to know" that Britain opposed devaluation of the Reichsmark, though Schumpeter was skeptical (Business Cycles, p. 943). Twenty years later, Brüning told Grotkopp in an interview that Britain had regarded devaluation by Germany as a violation of the Young Plan. There was, however, sufficient opinion on the other side of the question to have provided a defense, if Germany had sought one.

63. Schliemann, Die deutsche Währung in der Weltwirtschaftskrise, 1929–33, pp. 236–48, esp. p. 236, n. 2. Schliemann observes that Dahlberg and Grävell explicitly proposed in December 1930 a 20 percent devaluation—considerably less than the 30 percent depreciation of sterling at the time (p. 241). Brüning's memoirs almost forty years after the event record a secret understanding with Luther that the Reichsmark would be devalued 20 percent after reparations had been halted (my emphasis). See Heinrich Irmler, "Bankenkrise und Vollbeschäftigungspolitik (1931–1936)," 1976, p. 307. Schliemann calculates that a 20 percent depreciation would have contributed little to bringing the balance of payments into surplus and would not have been worth the political and economic drawbacks (p. 358).

64. Born, Die deutsche Bankenkrise, 1931, p. 45. It is not clear that American official circles would have objected, but Benjamin M. Anderson, the conservative economist of the Chase National Bank, gave an interview to Deutsche Volkswirt in which he said that devaluation would be greeted in the United States as a signal for a new inflation of bank notes (ibid.).

slogan generally was "Hands off the exchange rate."[65] Luther returned from a holiday on September 21 to find that the cabinet had already agreed not to attach the mark to the pound on the grounds that, eight years after the inflation, the public would react strongly against devaluation. He expressed his complete agreement with the decision.[66] In a speech in November, Brüning admitted that many people "have the opinion that now that the pound has fallen we ought to make a dash for it and devalue. I shall defend to the end against taking any inflationary measure of any kind."[67] The leading Marxist theorist and former Social Democrat minister of finance, Rudolf Hilferding, asserted in a debate with Woytinsky that it was

insanity that London had abdicated its role as the economic center of the world. . . . Germany's main task continued to be to protect its currency. He predicted increased unemployment in England as a result of depreciation.

To Woytinsky, who counterargued that Britain's credit would be stronger and that others would devalue, increase their exports, and

65. Hahn, *Fünfzig Jahre zwischen Inflation und Deflation*, pp. 103, 106–7. The debate over whether Brüning and Luther had ample room for decision making or were constrained by external circumstances and public opinion continues virtually to this day. A notable defender of Brüning who argues that his room for maneuver was limited is Knut Borchardt in "Zwangslagen und Handlungsspielräume in der grossen Wirtschaftskrise der frühen dreissiger Jahre: Zur Revision des überlieferten Geschichtsbildes," 1979. Borchardt has returned to the subject in "Could and Should Germany Have Followed Great Britain in Leaving the Gold Standard?" 1984. In opposition, see, for example, Carl-Ludwig Holtfrerich, "Alternativen zu Brünings Wirtschaftspolitik in der Weltwirtschaftskrise," 1982. Irmler notes that the answer to the question whether Germany had an alternative in 1931 would be taken today as self-evident. It was nonetheless strongly debated at the time. Of all the reasons against following sterling off gold, in his estimation fear of inflation was the strongest ("Bankenkrise und Vollbeschäftigungspolitik [1931–1936]," pp. 305–6). Gerhard Kroll insists that in posing the question as one between stable exchanges or inflation, the Brüning cabinet was fighting ghosts ("Die deutsche Wirtschaftspolitik in der Weltwirtschaftskrise," 1966, p. 401).

66. Hans Luther, *Vor dem Abgrund, 1930–1933: Reichsbankpräsident in Krisenzeiten*, 1964, 53–55.

67. Heinrich Brüning, "Keine Reparationen mehr," a speech before the Reichsparteiausschuss of the German Center party on November 5, 1933, in Wilhelm Vernekohl, ed., *Reden und Aufsätze eines deutschen Staatsmannes*, 1968, p. 75. Note Brüning's view (*Memoiren, 1918–1934*, p. 431) that the October conversions of gold were a device by which the Quai d'Orsay put pressure on the United States to support the French view on German reparations.

reduce their unemployment, Hilferding shouted "Nonsense."[68] The error was expensive for Germany. Following the exchange appreciation of the Deutschmark in 1961, Hahn said that if a 5 percent upward valuation aroused such opposition in industry, what must the deflationary pressure of a 40 percent revaluation have felt like?[69] The German government pursued a policy of deflation, and so did the British. The gold bloc and the United States had serious balance-of-payments problems; in neither the British nor the German case was this true, thanks respectively to depreciation and the Standstill Agreement. Both fought an inflation that did not exist. The necessary wedge between British and world prices created by depreciation developed through the reduction of world or gold prices, not the rise of those denominated in sterling or the countries that devalued with sterling.

The contrast is with the gold bloc and Japan. Within the gold bloc, Italy, having appreciated the lira from 150 to the pound to 90—the *quota novanta* discussed earlier—now found itself with an exchange rate of 70 to the pound, a *quota sessanta*. Ernesto Cianci finds it striking that the failure to devalue the lira along with sterling is passed over in relative silence, whereas the *quota novanta* of 1926 is still under vigorous discussion. He attributes the failure to depreciate in 1931 not to any of the reasons adduced in the German academic and political debate but above all to prestige, and to false prestige at that.[70] In December 1934 Italy followed Germany into foreign exchange control.

After the fall of the pound, speculators began selling yen. Within

68. W. S. Woytinsky, *Stormy Passage: A Personal History Through Two Russian Revolutions to Democracy and Freedom, 1905–1960*, 1961, p. 467. For an account of the conservative character of Marxist ideas on depression remedies, see Adolf Sturmthal, *The Tragedy of European Labor, 1918–1939*, 1943, part 3, "Labor in the Great Depression," and ch. 7. Sturmthal quotes Fritz Naphtali, a leading Socialist expert, who had written a book on *Wirtschaftskrise und Arbeitslosigkeit* (Berlin: 1930) to the effect that it was necessary for the crisis to run its course (pp. 86–87). "No tampering with the currency" was the almost unanimous slogan of the left, partly because of laissez-faire principles and partly because of the memory of the 1923 inflation when wages failed to keep up with prices and when trade union funds lost all value overnight (pp. 87–88).

69. Hahn, *Fünfzig Jahre zwischen Inflation und Deflation*, p. 80.

70. Ernesto Cianci, in the "Debate," in Banco di Roma, *Banca e Industrie fra le due guerre*, vol. 1, 1981, p. 163.

three months the Bank of Japan had lost 675 million yen in gold, prohibiting the export of gold on December 14 and suspending the gold standard on December 17, 1931. What followed, Patrick says, could not have been anticipated from the record of Japanese behavior or economic analysis, one of the most brilliant and highly successful combinations of fiscal, monetary, and foreign exchange rate policies the world has ever seen.[71]

During the 1920s a small minority opposition had campaigned against the restoration of the yen to par, holding out for a lower rate. Led by Tanzan Ishibashi and Kemekiki Takahashi, a distinguished journalist, it had fed on the views of Gustav Cassel and later of Keynes, whose *Tract on Monetary Reform* was translated into Japanese in 1924 and *Treatise on Money* in 1932. These works did not anticipate the theory of public spending, but they impressed Ishibashi and Takahashi with their advocacy of a managed currency.

With the failure of the return of the yen to par, the view of the heretics came to the fore. The journalist Takahashi was initially critical of the theories of Korekiyo Takahashi, the former prime minister (1921–22) and minister of finance (1918–22) and minister of finance in the new cabinet that took power after the depreciation of the yen. But the politician Takahashi intuitively understood the potentiality of deficit financing with a flexible exchange rate, and his writing of the period showed that he already understood the mechanism of the Keynesian multiplier, without any indication of contact with the R. F. Kahn 1931 *Economic Journal* article. The balance of payments was protected not only by the flexible exchange rate, but also by the foreign exchange control laws of July 1932 and March 1933. The Bank of Japan lowered discount rates from 6.57 percent in March 1932 to 2.29 percent in April 1936. The fiduciary issue of the Bank of Japan was raised from 120 million yen to 1 billion.[72] But the primary reflationary mechanism was government spending. Under Takahashi's finance ministry, central government expenditures rose 20 percent in each year of 1932, 1933, and 1934 and, in all, from 31 to 38 percent of net domestic product. Sufficient to produce recovery, this expansion failed to satisfy the militarists,

71. Patrick, "The Economic Muddle of the 1920s," p. 256.

72. Eigo Fukai, "The Recent Monetary Policy of Japan," in A. D. Gayer, ed., *The Lessons of Monetary Experience, Essays in Honour of Irving Fisher*, 1937, p. 391.

who wanted unlimited military expenditures. In consequence, they assassinated Takahashi, aged eighty-two, in 1936.[73] The Japanese share in imports of such an area as the Netherlands East Indies, as a consequence of exchange depreciation, rose from 12 percent in 1930 to 31 percent in 1933 when the Indies government took protective measures.[74]

Liquidation of dollars

On September 21, 1931, the day sterling was devalued, Governor Moret of the Bank of France asked the Federal Reserve Bank of New York whether it minded the conversion of dollars into gold. Harrison assured him it did not. On September 22 the Bank of France converted $50 million to gold, and the National Bank of Belgium $106.6 million. The Bank of France explained to Crane, in charge of foreign operations, that it had sold forward a certain amount of gold to Belgium and Switzerland and wanted to replace it before delivery so as not to show a loss in its statement.[75] Gold losses in the statement of the Federal Reserve System were unavoidable, and when they were reported they disturbed the foreign exchange market. On October 1 the Bank of France earmarked another $25 million, on October 8 another $25 million, and on

73. The gist of the foregoing paragraph was communicated to me by Ryutaro Komiya, who observed that there is no standard historical work on the reflationary policies of the Takahashi finance ministry. *Who's Who in Japan, 1930–1931* notes that Takahashi was born in July 1854, studied English at Yokohama, was "sent to America to study, in 1867, and was for several months treated as a slave through the treachery American [sic] of his knavish guardian; returned home the following year. Principal of Osaka English School, 1875. President of the Patent Bureau which he resigned in 1890; went to Peru to exploit the silver mine being defrauded by a German swindler." His banking career in Japan started in 1891, and his public career in 1904 when he was "Financial Agent for raising loans in England and America, and dispatched there twice on that Important Mission [sic]." For an overview of Takahashi's career and views, see Dick K. Nanto and Shinji Takagi, "Korekiyo Takahashi and Japan's Recovery from the Great Depression," *American Economic Review*, 1985.

74. A. Neytzell de Wilde and J. Th. Moll, *The Netherlands Indies During the Depression: A Brief Economic Survey*, 1936, pp. 57, 58. The expansion had started before depreciation, but after the loss of half the outlet for its silk in the United States. In cotton textiles, Japan had 30 percent of the Netherlands East Indies market in 1928, 48 percent in 1931, and 76 percent in 1933 (p. 54).

75. Federal Reserve Bank of New York files.

October 13 $20 million. Moret explained to Harrison on October 7 that the "considerable losses sustained by the Bank of France on balances it maintained in London by solidarity and politeness induce me to consider a priori the matter [of converting dollar balances] in a special light."[76] A memorandum from Governor Hamlin to Eugene Meyer at the Board of Governors of the Federal Reserve System quotes reports from Paris, based on discussions with the Bank of France and newspaper articles, to the effect that the Bank of France would maintain its holdings of dollars "provided that the [Federal Reserve] follow a conservative policy likely to uphold and maintain the dollar at its present value, and not resort to inflation."[77] This produced a reaction by letter from Harrison to Meyer on December 18 to the effect that the New York bank would make no commitments. The Bank of France was free to take gold, and the Federal Reserve Bank was free to adopt any credit policy it chose. Bank of France acceptances and deposits held with the bank, which had been $190 million, were down to $86 million. Harrison had been told that the French had decided not to take any more gold, as the directors were worried about the loss of earnings.[78] The loss of gold from the Federal Reserve System from mid-September to the end of October amounted to $755 million. A memorandum of December 17, 1931, from W. R. Gardner of the board staff to Governor Meyer noted that the National Bank of Belgium had acquired $131 million in gold, the Netherlands Bank $77 million, and the Swiss National Bank $188 million, and referred to panic among the central banks.[79] The bulk of the rest went to France. It is hard to see what was meant by the statement in the annual report of the Bank of France for 1932: "The Bank abstained from disposing of its dollar assets in the autumn of 1931 when the United States was faced with important withdrawals."

The monetary authorities in the United States responded to the gold loss in the classic way by raising the discount rate. A rise of a full percentage point on October 9 followed by another a week later brought the New York bank rate only to 3.5 percent.[80] Even this

76. Ibid.
77. Ibid., memorandum of November 24, 1931.
78. Ibid., letter of December 18, 1931.
79. Ibid.
80. Emile Despres recounted in the preface to his collected papers that a telegram he drafted for W. Randolph Burgess's signature from shipboard in October 1931 to

bothered Harrison, who pressed to have the effects offset by open market operations. But the system was hesitant about disturbing European confidence, which might lead to more gold withdrawals and more currency hoarding.[81] At their meeting at the end of November the Open Market Committee authorized purchases of $200 million, but only $75 million were bought in December. Banks outside the main financial centers rediscounted heavily. Bank failures spread.

Friedman and Schwartz maintain that the pressure on the U.S. gold supply following British suspension of the gold standard was not critical in U.S. economic life, which continued to decline consistently from March 1931 to mid-1932.[82] It is difficult to accept this verdict. Not only the money supply, but commodity prices, security prices, imports, and, to a lesser extent, industrial production declined faster after devaluation than before.[83] European and especially French pressure on the U.S. gold stock was to be resumed in the early months of 1932, although it would then be offset. The

---

the Federal Reserve Bank of New York strongly opposing the rate increase was considered by the board and delayed the decision by one day. "This initiation into policy formation always seemed to me like the story of my life." See *International Economic Reform: The Collected Papers of Emile Despres*, 1973, p. xii.

81. Wicker, *Federal Reserve Monetary Policy, 1917–33*, p. 169.

82. Friedman and Schwartz, *A Monetary History of the United States, 1867–1960*, p. 322.

83. See the following:

U.S. ECONOMIC INDICATORS, MARCH 1931 TO JUNE 1933
(seasonally adjusted, 1923 − 25 = 100)

	Industrial production	Construction contracts	Factory employment	Factory payrolls
March 1931	87	77	78	75
August 1931	78	59	74	64
September 1931	76	59	73	62
June 1932	59	27	60	43

	Freight car loadings	Prices	Currency in circulation and demand deposits (adjusted) (in billions of dollars)	Imports (unadjusted) (in millions of dollars)
March 1931	80	76	24.8	205.7
August 1931	72	72	23.4	168.7
September 1931	69	71	23.4	174.7
June 1932	52	64	20.4	112.5

SOURCE: *Federal Reserve Bulletin*, various issues.

double-barreled impact of the appreciation of the dollar and capital outflow maintained and accelerated the deflationary pressure.

Moreover, it is worth penetrating some distance below the total quantity of money. Just as interest rates on second-grade bonds, domestic and foreign, rose when interest rates on governments and high-grade bonds fell to low levels, so the money supplies of all producers and consumers did not move evenly together. One study shows that large firms in the United States became more rather than less liquid,[84] another that the contraction of bank credit caused a greater reduction in output than can be explained by the smaller quantity of available money alone.[85] Still other recent interpretations recur to the old theme that a system that forbade branch banking made for thousands of small, inefficient banks making poor loans.[86] But of course most generalizations that hold good in the aggregate lose force when one disaggregates.

84. Helen Manning Hunter, "The Role of Business Liquidity During the Great Depression and Afterwards: Differences Between Small and Large Firms," 1980.

85. Ben S. Bernanke, "Non-monetary Effects of the Financial Crisis in the Propagation of the Great Depression," 1983. This article does not deal explicitly with the prices of commodities and financial assets as they may affect debt deflation—for example, no price series are shown—but it states that a useful way to think of the 1930–33 debt crisis is as the progressive erosion of borrowers' collateral relative to debt burdens (p. 265). It is further at variance with the themes of this chapter in holding that Britain's going off gold, among other events, was "connected very indirectly (if at all) with the path of industrial production in the United States."

86. Eugene Nelson White, "A Reinterpretation of the Banking Crisis of 1930," 1984. A counterexample to this interpretation, though perhaps not a very cogent one, is the November 1930 collapse of the Caldwell *chain* (my emphasis) of 120 banks and other financial companies.

8

More Deflation

Contemporary conventional wisdom in the early 1930s thought falling commodity and asset prices important. One expression of this viewpoint came from Keynes as he was beginning work on *The General Theory*, which tends on the whole to ignore prices:

> All this nervousness and hysteria and panic, which is [*sic*] making a farce of our currency arrangements, and bringing the world's financial machinery to a standstill . . . has its roots in the slow and steady sapping of the real resources of the banks as a result of the progressive collapse of money values over the past two years. . . .
>
> There is a degree of deflation which no bank can stand. And over a great part of the world, and not least in the United States, the position of the banks, though partly concealed from the public eye, may be in fact the weakest element in the whole situation. It is obvious that present events cannot go much further without something breaking. If nothing is done, it will be amongst the world's banks that the really critical breakages will occur.
>
> Modern capitalism is faced, in my belief, with the choice between finding some way to improve money values toward their former figure, or seeing widespread insolvencies and defaults and the collapse of a large part of the financial structure.[1]

1. John Maynard Keynes, "The Consequences to the Banks of the Collapse of Money Values," 1931, pp. 151, 157, quoted by Richard F. (Lord) Kahn, *The Making of Keynes' General Theory*, 1984, pp. 132–33.

Keynes had little appreciation of the process by which the seizing up of bank liquidity in the United States after the stock market crash drove down commodity and other asset prices. Writing in the summer of 1931, moreover, prior to sterling going off gold, it was too early to consider the impact of currency appreciation on gold prices in the United States, the gold bloc, and Germany. Further deflation came from the quotas imposed by France, reducing outlets for inelastic supplies of primary products, and from tariffs imposed by all countries. Britain not only depreciated sterling in 1931 but raised tariffs in 1932 as well, to provide another example of the tendency, when alternative courses have long been debated, to do both.[2] Denmark did likewise in October, and Sweden in February 1932. In the months from October 1931 to March 1932, the Netherlands, France, Belgium/Luxemburg, and Switzerland applied across-the-board tariffs, imposed quotas, and in the Swiss case denounced an outstanding German–Swiss trade agreement. The German export surplus, which had reached almost Rm 400 million a month in September and October, fell sharply to 100 million in January and to 97 million in February to remove an expansionary source of spending.

Deflation came not only from abroad but was applied at home. The Acceptance Bank and the Reichsbank provided funds for banks in trouble, the latter furnishing Rm 1.6 billion on the third signature of the former, and brought the rate down from the 10-to-15 percent level of July and August 1931—not, however, a great deal: to 8 percent in October and 7 percent in December. Deflation was still the order of the day.

Luther was a straightforward deflationist. Chapter 7 of his autobiography is entitled "Brüning's Policy: There Was No Alternative,"[3] an expression which Treviranus, in the Brüning cabinet, mocks by quoting the Cockney expression, "Blimey, there's nothing else to do."[4]

2. Keynes himself, however, felt that with sterling off gold, the tariff was unnecessary. See his letter to the *Times* of September 28, 1931, reprinted in J. M. Keynes, *Essays in Persuasion*, 1932, pp. 286–87.

3. Luther, *Vor dem Abgrund, 1930–1933*, pp. 131ff.

4. Gottfried Reinhold Treviranus, *Das Ende von Weimar: Heinrich Brüning und seine Zeit*, 1968, p. 173. Whether alternatives existed or not is debated to this day, as noted in ch. 7, n. 62, in the discussion of whether or not to devalue the Reichsmark. To be sure, that decision seemed to imply a domestic macroeconomic policy of deflation, since the efficiency of foreign exchange control in preventing balance of payments deficits with an overvalued currency (at least in a disciplined country like Germany) was not at that time appreciated.

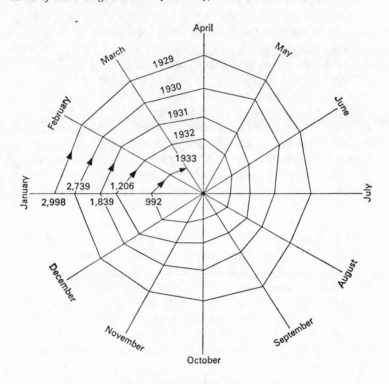

Figure 10. The contracting spiral of world trade, January 1929–
March 1933: Total imports of 75 countries (monthly values in
terms of old U.S. gold dollars [millions]).

(in millions of dollars)

	1929	1930	1931	1932	1933
I	2,997·7	2,738·9	1,838·9	1,206·0	**992·4**
II	2,630·3	2,454·6	1,700·5	1,186·7	**944·0**
III	2,814·8	2,563·9	1,889·1	1,230·4	**1,056·9**
IV	3,039·1	2,449·9	1,796·4	1,212·8	
V	2,967·6	2,447·0	1,764·3	1,150·5	
VI	2,791·0	2,325·7	1,732·3	1,144·7	
VII	2,813·9	2,189·5	1,679·6	993·7	
VIII	2,818·5	2,137·7	1,585·9	1,004·6	
IX	2,773·9	2,164·8	1,572·1	1,029·6	
X	2,966·8	2,300·8	1,556·3	1,090·4	
XI	2,888·8	2,051·3	1,470·0	1,093·3	
XII	2,793·9	2,095·9	1,426·9	1,121·2	
Average:	2,858·0	2,326·7	1,667·7	1,122·0	

SOURCE: League of Nations, *Monthly Bulletin of Statistics*,
February 1934, p. 51.

But there were alternatives. Wilhelm Lautenbach, an official in the Economics Ministry, had a plan for expanding bank credit for public works by several thousands of millions Reichsmarks.[5] These proposals for credit creation were later taken up by Wagemann.[6] Woytinsky for the trade unions, at first alone and later with Baade and Tarnow, became obsessed, as he says, with programs for public works, either international or on a national basis.[7] Luther argued

5. The nearest thing to a text of the Lautenbach plan is his memorandum "Defizitpolitik? Reichsbankzusage als Katalysator. Der Verzweiflungsweg—ohne Auslandskapital!" [Deficit policy? Reichsbank endorsements as catalyst of the way out of despair—without foreign capital!], in Wilhelm Lautenbach, Zins, Kredit und Produktion, 1952, pp. 137–56. This memorandum is printed in the original version of August 9, 1931, and the revised September 9 version in parallel columns to allow comparison of their differences, and it follows an earlier undated essay for the Brauns Commission on Unemployment (on which Röpke also sat) on "Auslandskapital als Katalysator" (Foreign Capital as Catalyst), which dealt with recovery through public works financed from abroad.

Zins, Kredit und Produktion was edited by Wolfgang Stützel after Lautenbach's death and contains a foreword by Röpke with an appreciation of Lautenbach's contribution to economic thought from the Economics Ministry. A full account of Lautenbach's ideas is also found in Grotkopp, Die grosse Krise, which contains thirty-three index citations to the name and a short biography on p. 38, n. 4.

The Lautenbach plan was actively discussed in the Reichsbank in a meeting on September 15, 1931, and opposed by, among others, Salin, Hilferding, and Röpke. After the departure of sterling from gold, however, Salin came to Berlin from Basel on October 3 to argue with Luther for the Lautenbach plan, which he said was supported by some officials at the Bank for International Settlements. See his preface to Luther, Vor dem Abgrund, 1930–1933, p. 23. See also George Garvey, "Keynes and the Economic Activities of Pre-Hitler Germany," 1975.

Borchardt differs with the standard assessment of Lautenbach as a pre-Keynes Keynesian and cites passages in which Lautenbach had called for deflation of costs and prices (before Britain went off gold) and had sharply criticized British abandonment of the gold standard, urging Germany to continue to adhere to it. See his "Zur Aufarbeitung der Vor- und Frühgeschichte der Keynesianismus in Deutschland," 1982.

6. Grotkopp, Die grosse Krise, pp. 179ff. Wagemann's plan was the basis for the German banking reform of 1934.

7. See ibid.; Woytinsky, Stormy Passage, pp. 466ff. Baade states that Woytinsky made the most important contribution to the Woytinsky-Tarnow-Baade plan for domestic public works, which was drafted in December 1931 but not published by the German Federation of Trade Unions (ADBG) until April 13, 1932. See his essay "Fighting Depression in Germany" in Emma S. Woytinsky, ed., So Much Alive: The Life and Work of W. S. Woytinsky, 1962, pp. 64–65. Woytinsky had written Internationale Hebung der Preise als Ausweg der Krise early in 1931, and an article in the International Labor Review, "International Measures to Create Employment: A Remedy for the Depression," at the end of the year. Among his various colleagues

them all down—in this he had plenty of orthodox economic assistance[8]—but the major point was that Brüning had adopted deflation as a means of getting rid of reparations. His detractors suggested that he was a tool of the Reichswehr, having been put in office by Kurt von Schleicher two weeks after the ratification of the Young Plan in March 1930 and removed by von Schleicher on a thin pretext of agricultural policy in May 1932, six weeks before the Lausanne Conference, which ended reparations: 100 meters from the goal, as Brüning claimed.[9]

Whether or not it was part of a conspiracy against the Weimar Republic, as the communists claimed, Brüning's policy from the elections of September 1930 on was first and foremost to concentrate on removing reparations, and to use deflation as a means to that end.[10] As Luther puts it, a foreign policy success was needed to

---

was Gerhard Colm. In *Stormy Passage* (p. 471) Woytinsky quotes Hilferding, whom the trade unions were accustomed to think of as the greatest authority on economic theory since Karl Marx (p. 465) as saying, "If Colm and Woytinsky think they can mitigate a depression by public works, they are merely showing they are not Marxists."

Grotkopp insists that Woytinsky, among others, had a well worked out version of the Keynes-Kahn multiplier and claims originality for them in pushing for public works. But Keynes and Henderson had a version of public spending to counteract depression in a pamphlet, *Can Lloyd George Do It?* in 1929, though without the multiplier; the multiplier was published by Kahn in June 1931 (R. F. Kahn, "The Relation of Home Investment to Unemployment," 1931). Keynes himself, of course, was familiar with this idea as early as 1930 and discussed it publicly in the Norman Wait Harris Foundation lecture in June-July 1931. See his "An Economic Analysis of Unemployment" in Q. Wright, ed., *Unemployment as a World Problem*, 1931. For an account of the development of the multiplier on which Kahn started work in August 1930, see his *The Making of Keynes' General Theory*, ch. 4.

8. Heinrich Dräger, an expansionist and a merchant, wrote bitterly of the solidarity of almost all professors of economics, who regarded the expansion of employment through credit creation as useless, impractical, inappropriate, and at a minimum inexpedient ("unbrauchbar, undurchführbahr, ungeeignet und zum mindestens als unzweckmässig"), quoted by Grotkopp, *Die grosse Krise*, p. 38, n. 3.

9. See Bernhard Menne, *The Case of Dr. Brüning*, 1943, who regards Brüning as a member of a conspiracy against the German republic. That Brüning had army support and was later destroyed by the army is also stated by Vansittart in *The Mist Procession*, pp. 418, 446. Menne quotes Thyssen as having said at a meeting at Haus Hügel of Krupp in the spring of 1929, "I need that crisis now. It offers the only chance of settling wages and reparations questions at one and the same time" (pp. 47–48).

10. Luther, *Vor dem Abgrund, 1930-1933*, pp. 137–38. Brüning, *Memoiren, 1918-1934*, p. 221, speaks of a "seemingly flawless deflationary policy to be followed in order to induce the world at its own initiative to cancel reparations."

take the wind out of the sails of the radicals. The Brüning government had three objectives (in order of priority): (1) foreign policy, to end reparations; (2) economic policy, to eliminate unemployment; and (3) internal policy, to strengthen the center against the extremes. It seemed to Brüning vital to settle reparations before moving on to the next two priority objectives.[11] A default on the Young Plan would lead to new negotiations, which would result in unthinkable internal conditions. It was necessary for Germany to demonstrate to her creditors that it was impossible to pay. Treviranus claims that the plans for government employment lay on Brüning's table and would be used after Germany was free of reparations.[12] Woytinsky thinks Brüning less Machiavellian: "His suicidal policy stemmed from his general philosophy. He feared the phantom of a runaway inflation; he did not like the idea of pampering the unemployed by creating jobs; and he thought that a public works program was a luxury Germany could not afford."[13]

Brüning communicated to Sackett his scenario by which deflation would lead to the cancellation of reparations. Hoover was to call a five-power conference in Washington to address the question of the world economy, and in the course of the conference it would become clear that it was necessary to cancel reparations. According to Brüning's memoirs, Hoover thought enough of the suggestion to send Undersecretary of State Joseph Cotton on an exploratory trip to Europe. Cotton's death on January 27, 1931, brought the effort to a conclusion.[14] But the exact mechanism that would have led from deflation to cancellation is never made clear. Menne is persuaded that bankruptcy was the aim of Brüning's extraordinary campaign of retrenchment, which earned for him the derisive name of "Hunger Chancellor."[15] In his speech on the end of reparations, Brüning is less precise: "The balance of German finance and the German economy stand clear in the world for everyone to see. That is the strongest weapon that the administration can have."[16] Suggestions for devaluation, credit expansion, or public works were rejected out of hand on the grounds that "only through the subsequent carrying out of the deflationary policy could he hope to maintain the goodwill of

11. Luther, *Vor dem Abgrund, 1930–1933*, p. 141.
12. Treviranus, *Das Ende von Weimar*, p. 175.
13. Woytinsky, *Stormy Passage*, p. 466.
14. Brüning, *Memoiren, 1918–1934*, pp. 222–23.
15. Menne, *The Case of Dr. Brüning*, p. 60.
16. Brüning, *Reden und Aufsätze eines deutschen Staatsmannes*, p. 76.

the Allies, and this conviction seemed to him a necessary condition of the final ending of reparations."[17] There is frequent mention of possible Allied objection to the Lautenbach and Wagemann plans, but little explicit detailing of how deflation would end reparations by demonstrating the impossibility of payment.

Whatever Brüning's thought, he proceeded on December 8, 1931, by a fourth emergency decree, to reduce wages, interest rates, and the prices of cartellized industry. Wages were required to be lowered across the board to the level prevailing on January 10, 1927. It failed to help with unemployment. The year-to-year figures, which had shown an increase in unemployment of 1.3 million in August 1931 over 1930 and 1.4 million in September, showed a small decline to 1.1 million over the previous year in January and February 1932 before rising to 1.5 million increases in May and June. The social cement in the country crumbled. The Nazi party continued to gain.

Whether one blames the rise to power of the Nazis on reparations, the occupation of the Ruhr, the 1922–23 inflation, the failure to devalue in 1931, or the Brüning deflation, the verdict is unanimous that Brüning failed. Reparations were canceled de facto at the Lausanne Conference of June and July 1932, but Brüning had been dismissed as chancellor by von Hindenburg in May. His successor, von Papen, adopted the credit creation and spending policies of the reformers, including a device of Lautenbach's to pay for public works with certificates that could be used by business to pay taxes to the Reich in the years 1934–38, when they would presumably be paid off out of budget surpluses. The certificates were negotiable and eligible for discount at the Reichsbank. In addition to the tax certificates, issued to the amount of Rm 1.5 billion, von Papen, after him Gereke, the Reich commissioner for employment, and still later Reinhardt undertook public works on the basis of bills issued to governmental organizations (which were also eligible for discount at the Reichsbank): 300 million under Papen, 600 million under Gereke, and one billion under Reinhardt—prior to Hitler, who took office on January 30, 1933, the numbers reaching 5.5 billion by the end of 1933 and 40 billion by the end of 1939.[18] The reformers were for the most part politically opposed to Hitler and skeptical of his program, which concentrated initially on autobahns (as well as as-

17. Salin in preface to Luther, *Vor dem Abgrund, 1930–1933*, p. 23.
18. C. R. S. Harris, *Germany's Foreign Indebtedness*, 1935, p. 44.

sistance to farmers under Gregor Strasser, who was killed in 1934), and later on rearmament. They furnished him with the ideas Brüning had refused to use.[19]

The end of reparations

In October 1931 Laval paid a visit to Washington to discuss war debts and reparations after the elapse of the year's moratorium. Hoover suggested that European countries might confer to reexamine German capacity to pay reparations and that after a display of Continental initiative it might be possible to reexamine the question of all international debts on the basis of capacity to pay during the depression.

> Insofar as inter-governmental obligations are concerned, we recognize that prior to the expiration of the Hoover year of postponement some agreement regarding them may be necessary covering the period of business depression, as to the terms and conditions of which the two governments make all reservations.[20]

This sentence gave rise to the view a year later that if reparations were further postponed or canceled, similar treatment should be accorded to war debts.

Europe did take the initiative and set up a Special Advisory Committee on the Young Plan to meet in December 1931 under the auspices of the Bank for International Settlements. The committee concluded that the depression had altered the conditions under which the Young Plan had been agreed, and recommended a conference of governments. In an aide-mémoire at the conclusion of the meeting, and periodically throughout the following months, the United States insisted that war debts had no connection with reparations. The conference to settle the question was postponed for the French elections of April 1932 and again for the Prussian elections of May and was finally held in June and July at Lausanne. The meeting was a diffi-

19. Exception has been taken to the suggestion that the German early Keynesians were opposed to National Socialism. Knut Borchardt points out that a number of them were early or later in the Nazi camp ("Zwangslagen und Handlungsspielräume in der grossen Wirtschaftskrise der frühen dreissiger Jahre," pp. 32–33, n. 33). See also Juergens Backhaus, "Economic Theories and Political Interests: Scholarly Economics in Pre-Hitler Germany," 1983, who points out that mainstream German economists were often in support of industrial interests, while the Kiel group, including Neisser and Lederer, favored demand management in behalf of trade union demands (pp. 664, 666).

20. Morison, *Turmoil and Tradition*, p. 425.

cult one, but it resulted in an agreement that all but wiped out reparations. Three billion marks of German debt were issued at 100 to the Bank for International Settlements, which was to sell them commercially on the open market after three years, but not below 90. Any bonds left unsold after fifteen years would be canceled. Ratification of the agreement was delayed to give a chance to settle war debts, mainly those with the United States, but Italian–British and French–British as well. The question of war debts arose in November 1932, when the French and British ambassadors in Washington asked the United States for a review of war debts and for postponement of the December 15 payment. This helped to complicate still further the transfer of power from Hoover, who had been defeated in his bid for reelection to the presidency, to the winner, Roosevelt—a transfer that proved difficult enough.

Britain emerges from the depression

The upturn of the pound began in the first months of 1932. In part it had been oversold as importers had rushed to buy before the prospective import duties were levied. A more significant factor was the recovery of confidence in January 1932, engendered by the knowledge that French holdings of sterling were no longer overhanging the market and that the Bank of England would meet the payments due on the 1931 summer credits without dipping into its gold stock. Another factor may have been the early voluntary payment of income tax due at the end of March, shortly after the issuance of first notices on January 1.[21] The dollar was under evident pressure. In early March the market started to bid the pound up from below $3.50. At the end of the month it reached $3.80.

Einzig regarded the turn in sentiment in favor of the pound as a lost opportunity to stabilize the pound in terms of gold, at such a rate as $3.50 to the dollar, and to reestablish London as a world financial center.[22] This time the rate was important. When it rose

---

21. Einzig, *The Comedy of the Pound*, p. 56.
22. Ibid. This view was not held long. In 1935 Einzig wrote: "The author views with growing suspicion the conversion of some radical economists, such as Sir Arthur Salter, Mr. J. M. Keynes, and Mr. Hubert Henderson, in favour of some form of immediate stabilization . . . this step should not be taken prematurely . . . ingenious traps laid by orthodox adherents of stabilization, who . . . would like to lure Great Britain and other countries into stabilization" (see Paul Einzig, *Bankers, Statesmen, and Economists*, 1935, p. vii).

from $3.50 to $3.80 there was a cry of protest from industrial and exporting circles. But after the difficulties of 1931, Britain was far from ready to reassert a world position. Leadership in free trade was jettisoned in favor of the Import Duties Act of February 1932, levying a 10 percent tariff on most imports but excepting the empire. An Imports Advisory Committee was established to recommend additional duties, and in April this advised doubling the initial level. An Exchange Equalization Account (EEA) was established with £150 million in rights to issue Treasury bills, with the task of holding the pound stable—a euphemism for preventing the rise.[23] It proved a highly useful device for insulating the exchange rate and the London money market from hot money movements, issuing pounds in exchange for gold to those who wanted pounds, and holding gold in readiness to exchange for pounds when the foreign holder reversed the initial process. Equipped with the EEA, the monetary authorities felt no need to stabilize for reasons of national policy. More generally, they had given up any responsibility for the international economic system.

The struggle between parochial and cosmopolitan interests is brought out clearly in an account of the Economic Advisory Council, established under various designations in the 1930s and including such economists as Keynes, Sir Arthur Salter, Lord Stamp, and G. D. H. Cole. There were occasions when the council lifted its eyes from the domestic scene and concerned itself with the rest of the world: in September 1931, in the first report of what was then the Committee for Economic Information, it noted that for Britain to recover, world prices must recover; in March 1932 it observed that the depreciation of sterling might have contributed to the further fall of gold prices; and in July 1932 a Keynes-Henderson plan proposed the issue of an international note by the Bank for International Settlements (closely resembling the Special Drawing Rights of the IMF almost a quarter of a century later in 1966).[24] For the most part, however, discussion of economic policy was conducted as if Britain were a closed economy in partial equilibrium—ceteris paribus—with little if any attention to multipliers, retaliation, feedback, and the like.

23. See Susan K. Howson, "The Management of Sterling, 1932–39," 1980, p. 54.

24. Susan K. Howson and Donald Winch, *The Economic Advisory Council, 1930–1939: A Study in Economic Advice During Depression and Recovery*, 1977, pp. 253, 262, 273–77.

In February 1932 Britain also reversed its deflationary policy, applied with such determination since the abandonment of gold. In six steps from February 18 to the end of June the Bank of England discount rate was reduced from 6 percent, fixed on September 21, to 2 percent on June 30. The main effort, however, was to convert the 5 percent war loan of 1929–47, which held the short-term rate structure up, into a 3.5 percent war loan repayable at the government's option after 1952. It was a major operation, since the issue amounted to £2.085 billion, or 27 percent of the national debt and 38 percent of quoted British securities on the London Stock Exchange.[25] The conversion was a success: 92 percent of the loan was exchanged. The Treasury bill rate dropped from 4.94 percent in January to 0.55 percent in September, and the bankers' allowance on deposits from 4 percent in January to 0.5 percent in June. In the light of modern monetary theory, it is useful to note that the emphasis was on cheap money, not money supply. The latter, as measured by the deposits of the ten London clearing banks, had declined from £1.9 billion in May 1931 to £1.7 billion in September and £1.65 billion in February 1932. It rose sensibly thereafter to £1.75 billion in June and £2 billion in December 1932. But the conscious focus of policy was on cheapening money.

Cheap money made a substantial contribution to British prosperity during the 1930s through its effect on housing. It did not operate in a vacuum, of course. There was a backlog of unsatisfied demand accumulated during the 1920s, when building had been held back by high interest rates. A 1930 housing act gave financial assistance to slum clearance. Improvement in Britain's terms of trade from cheaper imports of necessities gave consumers a surplus to spend. Cheap money assisted. Building plans picked up in the autumn of 1932 after the conversion of the war loan. The increase in private building between 1931 and 1933 amounted to 70 percent. Recent research makes the point that the import tariffs failed to help: when correction of nominal rates is made to derive "effective rates of protection" that take account of tariffs on imported inputs,[26] it becomes clear that two of the bellwether industries of the recovery—steel and construction—were disadvantaged rather than assisted and that the

25. Edward Nevin, *The Mechanism of Cheap Money: A Study in British Monetary Policy, 1931–1939*, 1955, p. 92.

26. Forrest Capie, *Depression and Protectionism: Britain Between the Wars*, 1983.

major lift was given by the fortuitous improvement in the terms of trade.[27]

The improvement in the terms of trade runs contrary to the classical expectation that currency depreciation worsens them. In the classical model, exports are specialized, and more can be sold only at lower prices, whereas the depreciating country has to pay the same price in foreign exchange for its imports. British experience was otherwise. Its import market was so important to so many foreign exporters that it had a monopsony advantage. Attempting to buy less obtained Britain its imports cheaper. Exports fell in price in foreign exchange, but imports fell as much after having fallen much more from 1928 to 1931. Depreciation of sterling put strong downward pressure on world prices expressed in gold, dollars, or other undepreciated currencies, on import prices as much as on export. A direct impact was felt on building costs, which were reduced. In addition, British wage and salary earners had £250 million more in 1932, after buying their food, drink, tobacco, and clothes, than they had in 1924–27, and much of it was spent on housing.[28]

Swedish antidepression policy

Swedish depression and recovery have given rise to widespread debate. It is generally conceded that the depression came from abroad, although the suicide of Ivar Kreuger in March 1932 proved sufficiently upsetting to world markets to constitute a small Swedish contribution to contraction.[29] The more significant issue is the extent to which Sweden recovered through its own efforts, especially through developing a public works policy to accompany cheap

27. Michael Beenstock, Forrest Capie, and Brian Griffiths, "The Economic Recovery in the United Kingdom in the 1930s," 1984, p. 1.

28. See Harold Bellman, "The Building Trades," 1938, p. 432. For a different view that emphasizes changes in policy between the 1920s and 1930s, see H. W. Richardson and D. Aldcroft, *Building in the British Economy Between the Wars*, 1969; and H. W. Richardson, *Economic Recovery in Britain, 1932–39*, 1967, ch. 7, "The Housing Boom."

29. Kreuger organized Kreuger & Toll, a match conglomerate, which lent money to governments on favorable terms in exchange for the grant of match monopolies. When tight credit made it difficult for Kreuger & Toll to borrow the money to relend, Kreuger forged collateral. For a detailed account of his operations and the events leading to his suicide, see Robert Shaplen, *Kreuger, Genius and Swindler*, 1960.

money, and to what extent the recovery represented simple exchange depreciation in excess of that of the pound plus spillover from the British building and later armament boom.

Economic debate had been intense in Sweden since the First World War. The first objective of policy—to restore the gold value of the krona—involved, according to Gustav Cassel, a reduction of prices to the same levels as those of other gold standard countries, or the restoration of purchasing power parity. Knut Wicksell wanted prices reduced to the 1914 level to reestablish the country's old economic structure. But by the end of the 1920s, when prices had fallen 11 percent in the six years from 1924, it had become clear that the gold standard was not suitable for maintaining stable prices, incomes, and employment. When Sweden left the gold standard along with sterling in September 1931, the monetary authorities issued a statement saying that their policy was now to stabilize prices—specifically, to stabilize a newly constructed weekly index. At first, as prices of some internationally traded goods rose with exchange depreciation, tight monetary policy was adopted to hold the overall index steady. Thereafter it was considered sufficient to stabilize internal prices.[30] Gustav Cassel thought that this should be done through monetary policy.[31] Others thought that control of the exchange rate was the key to price stabilization.[32]

The election of a Social Democratic government in September 1932 made possible the adoption of unorthodox budgetary policies. The January 1, 1933, budget of Minister of Finance Ernst Wigfors, based on ideas of Gunnar Myrdal and adopting the Danish device of dividing the governmental budget between current and capital expenditures, called for public works of 160 million kroner to be paid off in four years out of an increase in death duties.[33] The amount of deficit financing in the period to rearmament, however, was small. The public debt rose in five years from the end of 1932 only from 2.202 billion kroner to 2.342 billion. Swedish economists regarded

30. Lundberg, *Business Cycles and Economic Policy*, ch. 5.

31. Lars Jonung, "The Depression in Sweden and the United States: A Comparison of Causes and Policies," 1981, pp. 310–13.

32. Lundberg, *Business Cycles and Economic Policy*, p. 99.

33. Brinley Thomas, *Monetary Policy and Crisis: A Study of Swedish Experience*, 1936, p. 208. Jonung regards the effect of fiscal policy as insignificant ("The Depression in Sweden and the United States," p. 303). Lundberg states that the Swedish advocates of fiscal policy were cautious, conservative, and skeptical (*Business Cycles and Economic Policy*, pp. 117–19).

the favorable "international margin" from an improvement in the terms of trade and the British boom as making recovery through public works possible. The leading economist who has examined the experience is skeptical of the possibility of an independent Swedish economic policy because of the openness of the economy, and insists that the exhaustive theoretical canvas of possible economic policies was put to use to only a limited extent.[34] A younger monetarist economic historian, however, regards the Swedish experience as supporting Friedman and Schwartz against Temin in the monetarism versus Keynesianism debate.[35]

From abroad, and from a Scandinavian rival of Sweden, came the cynical view that Swedish recovery had little to do with policy of any kind. Carl Iversen, the Danish economist, insists that the recovery was due to the "international margin,"[36] what Erik Lundberg calls "international space"[37]—that is, it was due to the balance-of-payments surplus generated by the building boom in Britain. At the time of the Kreuger suicide the Riksbank, with limited reserves, allowed the rate to decline from 18 kroner to the pound to 19.50. Thomas notes explicitly that the advantage of a small country is that it can undertake beggar-thy-neighbor policies of currency depreciation and (moderate) tariffs without eliciting retaliation.[38] Danish exports were restricted in recovery, despite depreciation competitive with that of New Zealand, by British quotas on bacon, ham, and butter, and they increased only from a monthly average of 91 million kroner in 1932 to 107 million in 1935. Besides Japan, Sweden was the only country in the world with a greater increase in exports than in industrial production.[39] The monthly average value of ex-

34. Lundberg, *Business Cycles and Economic Policy*, pp. 122–23.

35. Jonung, "The Depression in Sweden and the United States," p. 311.

36. C. Iversen, "The Importance of the International Margin," 1936.

37. Lundberg, *Business Cycles and Economic Policy*, p. 121. Lundberg's cautious judgment is that Sweden, even if it had no ambitious policies such as the New Deal in the United States, the Blum experiment in France, or the bilateral trading and clearing of Germany, at least *avoided* (his emphasis) mistakes (p. 107).

38. Thomas, *Monetary Policy and Crisis*, p. 154. Marcus claims that the greater depreciation of the krona, while the Canadian dollar appreciated against the pound, enabled Scandinavian countries to offer newsprint, and presumably pulp and paper, in Europe at prices $10 to $12 below Canadian mills (see Marcus, *Canada and the International Business Cycle, 1927–39*, p. 105). The price of Canadian newsprint had fallen from $65 a ton in the spring of 1928 to $32 under NRA in June 1933.

39. H. W. Arndt, *The Economic Lessons of the 1930s*, 1944, p. 215.

ports rose from 70 million kroner in 1932 to 108 million in 1935, or 54 percent compared with 17 percent for Denmark. Finland, without the well worked out theory of public spending, recovered as much as Sweden did with it.[40]

French pressure on U.S. gold

In December 1931 a Reconstruction Finance Corporation was initiated in the United States to provide finance for banks and firms in need of liquidity. The rapid decline in governmental revenue led to a substantial deficit. These factors struck H. Parker Willis, professor of banking at Columbia University, as highly inflationary, and he said so in a famous dispatch to L'Agence Economique in Paris. This disturbed French official and private opinion. Governor Moret of the Bank of France cited it in asking the Federal Reserve Bank of New York to resume the earmarking and shipping of gold. Operations were to be carried out in an orderly way, without undue haste and without adverse publicity, but there were to be two shipments a week.

Harrison was unwilling to ask Moret to stop taking gold. On the contrary, at every stage he offered to assist the Bank of France in converting all or any part of its dollars, which amounted to some $600 million in mid-January. But the Willis view that the United States ran grave risks of inflation produced a reaction. On January 15, 1932, Harrison explained that the country had experienced the most drastic deflation of bank credit in history and that the policy of the Federal Reserve System was not to stimulate inflation but to halt deflation. The next day he added that Kemmerer, Hollander, Taussig, Carver, Seligman, Durand, and Willcox, economists of reputations as conservative and prestigious as Willis's, believed that the general contraction of credit and prices had gone far enough and that what was needed was a liberal policy to encourage the expansion of credit. Moret replied that French opinion still felt some hesitation in forming a judgment about the decisions taken in the United States, but that recent dollar sales had originated in London.[41]

After the gold withdrawals of the autumn of 1931, member bank discounting left indebtedness to the system at $836 million on the

40. Arthur Montgomery, *How Sweden Overcame the Depression, 1930–1933,* 1938, pp. 115–16, 124.

41. Federal Reserve Bank of New York files, January 1932.

average in February, the highest level since November 1929. Free gold of the Federal Reserve System was down to $400 million. While with close to $4 billion the system had more than enough gold to meet the 35 percent gold cover for its liabilities, it lacked the eligible paper needed to make up the difference between 35 and 100 percent and could count only gold in its place. As early as July 1931 the Federal Reserve Bank of St. Louis had stood aside from participation in the system loan to the Bank of England because of a shortage of free gold. By December 1931, free gold was beginning to be a problem.[42] In his presidential campaign in October, Hoover claimed that the United States had come within two weeks of going off the gold standard. This referred to the fact that, before the Glass-Steagall Act of February 27, free gold had fallen to $350 million, with gold losses at a rate of $150 million a week. The Glass-Steagall Act, however, enabled the Federal Reserve System to count government securities together with eligible paper as reserves against the system's liabilities. Its passage was the signal both for a substantial campaign of open market operations, converting net borrowings (gross borrowings minus excess reserves) of $792 million in February to net excess reserves of almost $100 million in July, and for a renewed outflow of French funds. The open market campaign was inspired by congressional pressure, and it was voted for in the Open Market Committee by three to two against strenuous opposition.

On March 1, three days after passage of the Glass-Steagall Act, the U.S. ambassador to France referred to the withdrawals by the Bank of France as inspired politically by the demands of parliamentary deputies nervous over the large loss in sterling, which was then being transferred from the Bank of France to the French Treasury. A week later Moret wrote to Harrison, explaining French devotion to the gold standard; the monetary law of June 1928, which allegedly required the Bank of France to liquidate foreign assets, a difficult task when the French balance of payments was in surplus; and the necessity for the Bank of France to set an example in demon-

42. Wicker, *Federal Reserve Monetary Policy, 1917–1933*, p. 169. Friedman and Schwartz hold that the shortage of free gold did not seriously limit the alternatives open to the system (see Friedman and Schwartz, *A Monetary History of the United States, 1867–1960*, p. 406), but Wicker notes that the references to the free gold issue are too infrequent in January and February 1932 to permit this conclusion (p. 172).

strating the operation of the true gold standard, as opposed to the makeshift arrangements the 1931 crisis had shown to be unsatisfactory. This required liquidation of French holdings of foreign exchange.

By April French conversions of dollars into gold were proceeding at $12.5 million a week. Following the French example, the Netherlands Bank converted $40 million. At the end of May Moret hinted strongly that he would like to increase the rate. Harrison first suggested that he should do what he liked and then, when Moret went to $25 million a week, recommended that he convert the entire $93 million left. This was done, except for $10 million that were left as an exchange reserve. The gold exchange standard was wound up in mid-June 1932 at the bottom of the depression.

It made no difference. Open market operations under the Glass-Steagall Act had belatedly relieved the pressure on the banks—but not equally throughout the system.

The country banks

Simple monetary theory suggesting that business conditions ought to follow the money supply fails to take adequate account of the country banks. Table 15 shows the breakdown of net excess reserves or, with a minus sign, net borrowings from the Federal Reserve System, divided among central reserve city, reserve city, and country banks. The figures are monthly averages for the last month in the quarter from 1929 to 1933 (except for March 1933, when it is necessary because of the bank holiday to use February). In 1929 New York, Chicago, reserve cities, and country banks were all net borrowers from the system to supply the call loan market. With the open market operations following the crash, central reserve cities virtually got out of debt, and by September 1930 reserve cities cut their indebtedness to a low figure. Country banks remained substantially in debt to the system, largely, it is hypothesized, because of the need to carry loans of farmers and small businesses and the lack of government bonds that could be sold off. The increase in borrowings after the pound left gold took place in reserve cities and country banks. Withdrawals of foreign funds occurred largely from New York, but tighter money in that center drew funds from smaller communities. Moreover, open market operations after March 1932 quickly produced excess reserves in central reserve cities and

TABLE 15
FEDERAL RESERVE MEMBER BANK NET EXCESS RESERVES OR NET
BORROWING (−), BY CLASS OF BANK: MONTHLY AVERAGES, END OF
QUARTER, 1929–33 (*in millions of dollars*)

	Total	New York	Chicago	Reserve cities	Country banks
1929					
March	− 915	− 147	− 118	− 414	− 236
June	− 932	− 167	− 62	− 397	− 305
September	− 927	− 159	− 20	− 486	− 260
December	− 753	− 90	− 33	− 339	− 293
1930					
March	− 216	− 7	1	− 60	− 150
June	− 196	− 20	2	− 26	− 153
September	− 129	1	1	− 12	− 119
December	− 264	− 15	3	− 88	− 165
1931					
March	− 110	6	2	− 10	− 108
June	− 58	67	1	− 18	− 105
September	− 160	41	16	− 90	− 137
December	− 703	− 27	− 3	− 344	− 323
1932					
March	− 647	11	3	− 312	− 357
June	− 260	89	57	− 110	− 292
September	− 41	192	82	− 74	− 242
December	245	283	163	− 19	− 182
1933					
February[a]	111	65	169	25	− 174
June	179	69	78	62	− 30
September	572	152	197	160	63
December	671	95	211	246	118

SOURCE: Federal Reserve System, *Banking and Monetary Statistics*, 1943,
pp. 396–99.
[a]March figures incomplete owing to bank holiday.

sharply reduced the net indebtedness of reserve cities. It was much
slower to assist country banks, which remained substantially in-
debted until after the 1933 bank holiday. The figures for December
1932, following the open market program of $1 billion, are of par-
ticular interest: high net excess reserves in New York and Chicago,
small net borrowing in reserve cities, but close on $200 million of
net borrowed reserves of country banks.

These figures cast doubt on the efficacy of open market opera-

TABLE 16
PRICES OF SPECIFIED COMMODITIES, SELECTED MONTHS, 1931–33

	cocoa	coffee	copper	corn	cotton	hides	lead	rubber	silk	sugar	tin	wheat	wool	zinc
	¢ per lb	¢ per lb	¢ per lb	¢ per bushel	¢ per lb	¢ per lb	¢ per lb	¢ per lb	$ per lb	¢ per lb	¢ per lb	¢ per bushel	¢ per lb	¢ per lb
1931														
March	5.41	8.50	9.9	57.5	10.15	9.0	4.28	7.13	2.77	3.28	27.07	76	80	4.01
June	5.17	9.50	8.0	53.8	8.42	10.0	3.76	6.38	2.40	3.32	23.41	76	75	3.40
September	4.47	8.00	7.0	43.2	5.83	9.0	4.22	5.00	2.57	3.41	24.68	71	77	3.74
December	3.97	8.38	6.6	34.5	5.78	7.8	3.59	4.63	2.18	3.14	21.35	74	72	3.15
1932														
March	4.44	9.00	5.8	32.2	6.44	6.4	2.99	3.31	1.71	2.76	21.84	72	69	2.79
June	3.99	10.10	5.1	29.4	4.99	4.3	2.89	2.69	1.27	2.72	19.24	64	54	2.79
September	4.63	15.00	6.0	28.0	7.40	8.1	3.32	3.88	1.89	3.16	24.76	59	63	3.30
December	3.71	10.50	4.8	18.8	5.72	5.5	2.88	3.25	1.60	2.83	22.69	49	55	3.12
1933														
March	3.40	9.25	5.0	20.6	6.19	5.2	3.03	3.03	1.25	2.96	24.34	54	55	3.00
June	4.60	9.00	7.8	40.2	9.28	12.2	4.02	6.09	2.17	3.44	44.21	81	90	4.35

SOURCE: *Commodity Yearbook, 1939*, 1939.

TABLE 17

GERMAN AND U.S. AVERAGE MONTHLY
EXPORT SURPLUS (IMPORT SURPLUS −),
QUARTERLY, 1931 AND 1932

		Germany (in millions of Rm)	United States (in millions of dollars)
1931	I	167	68.5
	II	154	5.0
	III	334	68.3
	IV	302	78.4
1932	I	121	43.7
	II	80	16.1
	III	81	− 0.7
	IV	75	32.4

SOURCE: *Federal Reserve Bulletin.*

tions in relieving the squeeze on the economy outside financial markets. Commodity prices continued to decline, as Table 16 shows. Certain commodities, like sugar and coffee, were unaffected by appreciation of the dollar (depreciation of sterling), but the decline in most was accentuated after September 1931, especially in the last quarter of 1931, when the pound went to $3.30, and again in the last half of 1932, when it dropped from $3.64 in June to $3.27 in December. Wheat and corn were particularly badly hit in the last quarter of 1932.

The price collapse initiated by appreciation was sufficiently fast in both the United States and Germany for export surpluses to be maintained in every quarter but one, as Table 17 shows. The composition of foreign trade helped in both cases, as did the fact that import prices fell sharply while exports of manufactures held up better in price. German foreign exchange control played a role. It remains true that imports fell almost as fast as exports, so that while export surpluses were reduced in 1932, as compared with 1931, they were not eliminated. The German export surplus hardly entered into the discussion as to whether or not the currency should be devalued, since devaluation was thought of, on the external front, as a substitute for foreign exchange controls. In the United States, however, the export surplus was used as an argument that foreign trade

was a force for expansion and that it was beggar-thy-neighbor policy to seek more by depreciation. The error, a normal one in economics, was to confuse partial with general equilibrium. In partial
equilibrium, an export surplus is inflationary compared to balance
or net imports, other things being equal. In general equilibrium, the
appreciation of the exchange rate can be so deflationary that the fall
in income spread through bank failure can wipe out the expected
import surplus. In such a case the surplus cannot be regarded as
expansive.

The export economies

After the initial squeeze from the halt in lending, business decline
in industrial countries spread to the less developed countries of the
world, primarily by means of reduced exports. In these economies,
the level of exports is generally a critical autonomous variable in
the determination of national income—more important than investment, which is often dependent on export sales, and surely more so
than government expenditure, which cannot be independent because
of the lack of a domestic money market at home. As noted earlier,
a country's local population may find a partial cushion in the decline of foreign profits after a fall in exports. In Java foreign plant-
ers suffered more serious losses in income than the native population, which obtained much of its income in kind, and natives
associated with foreign-owned plantations had more serious income
losses than those only loosely tied to the export sector. But the
losses of exports and income were highly impressive in percentage
terms. Triantis prepared a table to show the decline in exports value
by various periods. From 1928–29 to 1932–33 Chile led the list, as
shown in Table 18. How each country fared depended to a great
extent on the character of the products it sold. Triantis divided primary products into four classes: (1) staple foodstuffs, which face
low elasticity of demand; (2) semi-luxury foodstuffs, such as dairy
products, meat, and fruit, which declined less than goods in (1) because of higher price elasticity; (3) raw materials, except fuel, including especially metallic minerals, timber, and hides, which have
very high income elasticity; and (4) materials with low income elasticity, notably oil and paper. In general, the countries specializing
in (3) goods, like Chile, Bolivia, Malaya, and Peru, did worst,
while oil exporters, like Venezuela, were protected by income ine-

TABLE 18

FORTY-NINE PRIMARY-EXPORTING COUNTRIES CLASSIFIED
BY PERCENTAGE OF DECLINE IN EXPORTS, 1928–29 TO
1932–33

Percentage decline in exports	Country
Over 80	Chile
75–80	China
70–75	Bolivia, Cuba, Malaya, Peru, Salvador
65–70	Argentina, Canada, Ceylon, Netherlands Indies, Estonia, Guatemala, India, Irish Free State, Latvia, Mexico, Siam, Spain
60–65	Brazil, Dominican Republic, Egypt, Greece, Haiti, Hungary, Netherlands, Nicaragua, Nigeria, Poland, Yugoslavia
55–60	Denmark, Ecuador, Honduras, New Zealand
50–55	Australia, Bulgaria, Colombia, Costa Rica, Finland, Panama, Paraguay
45–50	Norway, Persia, Portugal, Romania
30–45	Lithuania, Philippines, Turkey, Venezuela

SOURCE: Stephen G. Triantis, *Cyclical Changes in Trade Balances of Countries Exporting Primary Products, 1927–1933*, 1967, p. 19.

lasticity of demand. Exporters of wheat and coffee did less well than those selling butter and meat abroad. Exceptions occurred everywhere. Denmark and New Zealand hurt each other and themselves by engaging in competitive exchange depreciation in 1932 and 1933 in a fight for the British butter market. Britain obtained its butter cheaper from both.[43]

As Table 18 shows, the commodity lottery treated different countries in different ways. Space does not permit a discussion of each country, but the extent of differences can be illustrated by the contrasting experience of Argentina and Brazil. Both countries followed triangular trade patterns: Argentina sold wheat and meat to Britain and bought heavily in North America; Brazil sold coffee mainly to North America and bought from Europe and the United States. Their trading partners behaved differently. Britain exerted its monopsony power to force Argentina to maintain debt service to British investors and to buy more British goods, whereas the United

43. C. P. Kindleberger, "Competitive Currency Depreciation Between Denmark and New Zealand," 1934.

States, through inadvertence or a reluctance to throw its weight around, failed to protest Brazilian default on its foreign bonds, which were held mainly in the United States, or to object to Brazilian bilateral trading with Germany.[44]

In such a country as Canada, depression and subsequent recovery were governed almost entirely by exports. With a branch banking system, Canada suffered no bank failures. Between 1929 and 1933 the supply of money fell only 13 percent, as compared with 33 percent in the United States. But monetary velocity, which fell 29 percent in the United States, declined 41 percent over the same period in Canada, so that the declines in net national product at 53 and 49 percent, respectively, were of the same order of magnitude.[45] Canada gained only limited outlets in Britain from preferences prior to the Ottawa Agreements. The appreciation of the Canadian dollar against sterling and especially against the Scandinavian currencies, which were competitors in newsprint, hurt more than empire preference helped. Despite the depreciation against the United States, exports and industrial production plunged downward after September 1931—exports with a lag—and recovered after April 1932, only to suffer a relapse in the second half of the year and the first months of 1933.[46]

The decline of investment

The emphasis given to stock-market speculation, the halt of international lending, the scramble for liquidity, exchange depreciation, and bank failures suggests a theory of business cycles which is financial to the exclusion of real factors. Some overexpansion was allowed for in a few commodities: sugar, wheat, coffee, and rubber. The decline in housing from 1925 to 1929 has been mentioned. But little notice was taken of the view, which flourished in the later 1930s and for some time after the Second World War, that depres-

44. See Arturo O'Connell, "Argentina into the Depression: The Problems of an Open Economy," 1984, and Marcelo de Paiva Abreu, "Argentina and Brazil during the 1930s: The Impact of British and American International Economic Policies," 1984.

45. Friedman and Schwartz, *A Monetary History of the United States, 1867–1960*, p. 352.

46. Marcus, *Canada and the International Business Cycle, 1927–39*, p. 71.

sion results from an exhaustion of investment opportunities. In one version, this was caused by overshooting normal demand growth, as in commercial building, durable consumer goods such as automobiles and radios, and such materials as newsprint and copper. The overshooting results from the acceleration principle, which relates investment to increases in consumption, so that when consumption levels off, investment must decline and bring income and demand down with it. On this showing, speculative excesses, unwise bank lending, and international complications may account for the depth of the depression and help its spread to the rest of the world; the origin of the cycle, however, lies in an overexpansion of investment in the United States.[47] A further view goes beyond the mechanical connections between multiplier and accelerator into deep-seated factors responsible for the decline in investment: changes in population growth, waves of innovation, and exhaustion of the frontier. These autonomous influences sometimes produce a bunching of investment leading to secular exhilaration, and at other times, as in the late 1920s and early 1930s if they work in concert, a dearth of investment outlets and secular stagnation.[48]

Experience since the 1930s has suggested that investment can be stimulated by fiscal policy—and, in the views of some, by maintaining the money supply stable—and that it is not as intractable as is implied by the stagnation theories. Whether the 1929 depression owes its depth to special circumstances of particularly excessive overexpansion of investment in the 1920s may also be doubted, inasmuch as the boom was not as far-reaching as this would imply. Overexpansion in wheat, copper, rubber, and sugar was a factor in the depression in some countries, but the overexpansion of investment in general hardly was.

If it is difficult to explain the decline in investment except on the accelerator principle combined with financial factors, the fact that gross investment has a limit of zero is useful in explaining that the depression had to end. Gross domestic investment in the United States amounted to $16 billion in 1929; it fell to $1 billion in 1932 and net investment to − $6.6 billion. Inventories declined, durable goods wore out, depreciation reduced fixed capital. At some point

47. Robert A. Gordon, *Business Fluctuations*, 1952, pp. 410ff.
48. Alvin H. Hansen, *Full Recovery or Stagnation*, 1938.

gross investment turns up again and the acceleration principle comes back into its own.[49] With purely financial theories of the business cycle, there is no need for the upturn. Liquidity squeezes, bank failures, and price declines have no natural limits until the monetary system has been entirely wiped out and the system converted to barter. With gross investment close to zero in 1932, the system was ready for the upturn. It was first necessary, however, to have an apocalyptic climax in bank failures.

The 1932 election and interregnum

The depression appeared to be bottoming out in the spring of 1932, after the recovery of sterling from its December 1931 low. Wholesale prices in the United States stopped falling. In July industrial production turned up. Whether one ascribes this to the $1 billion of open market operations, to the end of appreciation, or to the multiplier-accelerator turning point that comes when gross investment hits the bottom, the arrival of the upturn was unmistakable. The suggestion of a world economic conference to plan cooperative recovery, mentioned by Hoover to Laval in October 1931, was revived in May and further discussed at the Lausanne Conference in July. But there was still an election to come in the United States.

In the electoral campaign, Roosevelt charged Hoover with total responsibility for the depression. Its origin, he said, was entirely within the United States. Both as secretary of commerce and president, Hoover had been responsible for the orgy of speculation in the stock market, the overbuilding of industry, and the flood of loans abroad, which caused depression through default. The Smoot-Hawley Tariff Act made it impossible for other countries to pay their

49. W. W. Rostow ascribes the length of the depression in the United States to the importance of automobiles and other durable goods in total spending, and the consequent need to wait for an autonomous rise in consumers' durable goods spending to set leading sectors in motion again. In his view, this altered the business cycle from the nineteenth-century model, in which a fall in interest rates, raw material prices, and money wages could lead to resumed investment; or where population expansion and urbanization at steady rates could make profitable the opening up of new agricultural territories in response to increased demand for grain. See his "The Strategic Role of Theory: A Comment," 1971, p. 84. Of course, the greater the degree of investment plus postponable consumption, the deeper the depression may go, but it is not self-evident that durable goods behave differently from investment in plant, equipment, or inventories in producing the upturn.

debts and gave rise to trade reprisals all over the world. A wildly extravagant government budget produced a huge federal deficit that strangled the country.

Hoover, in reply, insisted that the depression had originated abroad, starting well before the crash of October 1929, and that the heritage of war had led to a financial collapse in Europe, which made it impossible for the United States to collect its debts and had come within two weeks of forcing the United States off the gold standard. Tariffs were necessary to protect American farmers. Agriculture was recovering, employment gaining. The American dollar rang honestly on the counter. Since July 1932 gold had been gained from abroad, and currency and gold were returning from hoarding.

Roosevelt attacked on no other aspect of foreign economic policy than the tariff, nor did he fault Hoover's handling of the banks. On his side, Hoover kept war debts out of the campaign. The two men were united in opposition to deficits and in support of balanced budgets in principle, though Roosevelt characterized Hoover's efforts as inadequate in practice. In a speech at Des Moines on October 4, Hoover described how close the country had come to going off the gold standard. This elicited speculation against the dollar and a reply by Senator Carter Glass that there had never been the slightest danger. There was no hint in the campaign oratory of new experimental policies in either domestic or foreign economic fields, nor of a shift of focus in policy from international to national concerns. Both candidates represented the domestic and middle western wings of their parties; though Roosevelt from New York had connections with internationalists, his foremost advisers, Moley and Tugwell, represented a middle western point of view.[50]

With Roosevelt's sweeping victory in November, two issues requiring urgent attention became caught in the interregnum: one was foreign—war debts; the other domestic—the banks. Neither had played a role in the campaign, but Hoover, the lame duck, wanted to engage Roosevelt's cooperation in their handling for the sake of continuity. Roosevelt was wary of accepting responsibility until he assumed authority.

British and French notes asking for deferment of the payment of December 15 and for a review of the war debt issue were presented

50. Herbert Feis stated that the knowledge of foreign affairs possessed by Roosevelt's assistants seemed to be slighter than their intellectual assurance—see *1933: Characters in Crisis*, 1966, p. 13.

on November 10, two days after the election. Hoover asked Roosevelt to assist in framing the U.S. reply. Conferences on November 17 and 22 and January 20 produced agreement on broad principles of American policy: the debts were a business matter with no connection with reparations or the prospective world economic conference, and each debtor should be treated separately, taking into account ability to pay; and the Allies should pay first and talk later. But this was all. Roosevelt was not as upset as Hoover by the suggestion in the British note that the United States was committed to revision by the terms of the Hoover-Laval communiqué; he would not endorse Hoover's proposal for a review commission made up of executive and congressional representatives; he was not prepared to follow up Hoover's suggestion of exchanging war debts for some specific benefit, such as enlarged markets for U.S. agricultural exports. He issued separate statements and left the task of replying to the British and French to Hoover.[51]

Hoover had strong views on war debts; Roosevelt did not. Tugwell notes that Roosevelt viewed them as a bargaining problem and as a political complication. On the latter score, public opinion, both at home and abroad, was singularly determined: on the one side, not to cancel; on the other, not to pay. This made temporizing necessary. The realities would have their way in the long run, but political considerations had to be taken into account.[52] After January 28, 1933, when Sir Ronald Lindsay, the British ambassador, saw the president-elect in Warm Springs, the British apparently stopped pushing the question. But the Herriot government had fallen over the issue of whether to pay on December 15; the British offered to pay with U.S. agreement that it did not imply resumption of regular payments. The Department of State replied that if payment was made, the debts would undoubtedly be reviewed, but that if agreement to a review was a condition of payment, the United States would have to reject it. The payment was finally made without qualification. There was no agreement and no indication by the United States of what would constitute a solution.

The banking collapse of early 1933 had complex political roots.

51. For a full account of the meetings, which he attended, and the text of Roosevelt's briefing instructions, see Moley, *The First New Deal*, pp. 27ff., 555–56. There are numerous other accounts.

52. Rexford G. Tugwell, *Notes on a New Deal Diary*, pp. 71–73, quoted in Moley, *The First New Deal*, p. 55.

One strand was the attempt of the vice-presidential candidate and Speaker of the House, John N. Garner, to insist that Reconstruction Finance Corporation (RFC) loans to banks be publicized. In July 1932 it had become known that the Central Republic National Bank and Trust Company of Chicago had received a $90 million loan from the RFC. Since this was a Dawes-controlled bank, there was political advantage in charging that the second "Dawes loan" represented political favoritism; but publicity for banks receiving RFC loans would tend to speed up bank runs. Accordingly, when the requirement was enacted in January 1933, banks in trouble stopped seeking RFC aid. On January 17 Hoover asked Roosevelt to advise congressional leaders to stop publication of the names of RFC borrowers. Roosevelt refused.

The January 17 letter contained other requests from Hoover to Roosevelt: that there be no tampering with the currency and no inflation, that the budget be balanced even if it meant more taxation, and that government credit be maintained through limiting government debt. Earlier, in December, the president had called in congressional leaders to propose increased taxes and a cut in expenditures to carry out Roosevelt's campaign promises. In a Lincoln's Day address he asked the president-elect to commit himself to stabilizing currencies and forswearing funny money. These actions were partly a response to the rising tide of demand for inflationary measures by southwestern and western senators, notably Connally of Texas, Thomas of Oklahoma, and Wheeler of Montana, and to the formation of a Committee for the Nation committed to raising prices by monetary means. On January 31 the designated secretary of agriculture in the new cabinet, Henry Wallace, had said, "The smart thing would be to go off the gold standard a little further than England has." Whether markets reacted to the inflationary suggestions or to Hoover's calling them to national attention is not self-evident, but bank failures spread in the Middle West in December, and more widely in January. There was widespread hoarding of currency and, in February 1933, loss of gold. Hoover wrote to Senator Reed on February 10 stating that the panic and gold outflow were the result of a loss of confidence in the new administration.

The Federal Reserve System became gradually demoralized. It undertook contraction in January by selling off government bonds. During the troubles of February, the Open Market Committee did not meet. In response to an express invitation of President Hoover to make suggestions, the board of governors on February 25 had none to offer. On March 2 it was not prepared to recommend a federal guarantee for bank deposits, nor were there any additional measures it felt it would be justified in recommending.[53]

Bank holidays started in Nevada in October 1932, when the state's banks were shut for twelve days. In mid-February, a feud between Henry Ford and Senator James Couzens over two rival groups of Detroit banks required the governor of Michigan to close the banks on February 14 to prevent Ford from withdrawing a large deposit from the rival system. A week later the banks were closed in New Jersey. On the eve of Roosevelt's inauguration, Governor Lehman closed the banks of New York. On March 4, as president, Roosevelt invoked the Trading with the Enemy Act of 1917 to close all banks in the country.

Hoover blames the panic of February–March 1933 squarely on Roosevelt—"the most senseless and easily prevented panic in all history."[54] In his view, Roosevelt wanted to close the banks and blame the debacle on Hoover. But Roosevelt had his hands full, organizing to take power as well as resting after his campaign, and was unwilling to commit himself to any of Hoover's explicit proposals.

The depression had taken its toll on U.S. leadership. Everywhere there was strain and confusion. Antipathy existed between Hoover and Roosevelt, the former regarding the latter as shallow and dangerous, the latter the former as doctrinaire. There was no standard to follow.

53. *The Memoirs of Herbert Hoover*, vol. 3, pp. 211–12.
54. Ibid., p. 215.

9

The World Economic Conference

The inaugural speech

During the campaign and after the election up to the eve of the inauguration, there was considerable question over Roosevelt's attitude toward foreign economic questions. Roosevelt came from an internationalist tradition. As a candidate for vice-president in 1920, he had strongly backed the League of Nations. He was, however, responsive to pressure. When the Hearst press violently attacked the league during 1932, he backed away from it, saying that the league had changed, but went on to hedge by saying that this did not preclude future international cooperation. Tugwell, who with Moley belonged to the nationalist school on Roosevelt's staff, noted that the internationalists in the Democratic party—Baker, Daniels, House, and Hull—were dismayed by his equivocation.[1]

The internationalist leader in the Roosevelt inner group was Norman Davis, a banker who had had wide experience in Europe. Moley was worried that Davis and Henry Stimson, Hoover's secretary of state who negotiated with Roosevelt during the transition on foreign economic matters, might swing Roosevelt into the internationalist camp. The draft agenda for the World Economic Conference, calling for restoration of the gold standard, tariff reduction, and

1. Tugwell, *The Brains Trust*, p. 76.

other measures of international cooperation, in his view threatened to inhibit the program for domestic recovery.[2]

Tugwell and Moley won. The inaugural speech on March 4, 1933, enunciated the commitment of priority to domestic recovery that Moley had sought, and which he took to be "final and irrevocable":[3]

> Our international relations, though vastly important, are in point of time and necessity secondary to the establishment of a sound national economy. I favor as a practical policy the putting of first things first.

While he insisted that his program was not narrowly nationalistic, Roosevelt's attention was inward. The day following the inauguration, Adolf Hitler was given full powers to govern by decree in Germany.

There were campaign promises, but no program. Counsels on the domestic front were divided among at least five groups: (1) the orthodox, who favored putting the economy through the wringer, including Bernard Baruch, an adviser, Lewis Douglas, director of the Bureau of the Budget, Jesse Jones of the Reconstruction Finance Corporation (RFC), and William Woodin, the new secretary of the Treasury; (2) monetary manipulators, including Senators Key Pittman, Elmer Thomas, and Burton Wheeler and Professor James Harvey Rogers of Yale; (3) trustbusters, including Justice Louis Brandeis and Professor Felix Frankfurter of the Harvard Law School; (4) those who believed in government ownership, notably Senator George Norris and Harold Ickes, secretary of the Interior designate; and (5) the planners, including the advisers Adolph A. Berle, Hugh Johnson, Raymond Moley, and Rexford Tugwell, and the new secretary of agriculture, Henry Wallace.[4] Moley was made an assistant secretary of state in charge of economic questions, notably foreign debts, the World Economic Conference, "and such additional duties as the president may direct in the field of foreign and domestic government." He worked from the White House rather than the Department of State and regarded his task in part as preventing foreign considerations from interfering with the domestic program. His nominal superior, Cordell Hull, secretary of state, had

2. Moley, *The First New Deal*, p. 39.
3. See ch. 1, n. 25.
4. Moley, *The First New Deal*, p. 228.

only one formula: stop raising tariffs and start lowering them. But it was hard to see the mechanism by which this could lead to recovery.

First, it was necessary to open the banks. This was done within eight days. The next ninety-two of the "hundred days" of Roosevelt's first administration were devoted to developing programs on a variety of domestic fronts. In agriculture major emphasis was given to production control as a means of raising prices. The Agricultural Adjustment Act (AAA) was passed in May 1933, restricting output and removing surpluses from the market and making direct payments to farmers for reducing production; levying excise taxes on food processors to raise funds for paying benefits; and establishing marketing agreements under government supervision. In June 1933 the National Recovery Act (NRA) provided for industrial agreements or codes on production and prices, but including protection for labor through the specification of maximum hours and minimum wages and a guarantee of the right to join a union. A Tennessee Valley Authority (TVA) was created in May 1933 to establish government authority over the operation of the hydroelectric dam and nitrate plants built at Muscle Shoals on the Tennessee River during the First World War, as well as to coordinate power production, flood control, and river transport. Relief was provided through the Emergency Relief Act of 1933, following similar legislation in 1932 under Hoover but creating a new agency. Later the Civil Works Agency was established for work relief (in November 1933), and this ultimately developed into the Works Progress Administration (WPA) for public works and work relief for the unemployed. Among the more far-reaching items of legislation was bank deposit insurance, resisted by both Hoover and Roosevelt for fear that the weak banks would pull down the strong, and initiated by Congress rather than the Democratic administration.

The two major parts of the program of the hundred days, the NRA and the AAA, were both later declared unconstitutional (in 1935 and 1936, respectively). The AAA was replaced by other legislation, to accomplish the same purpose of holding production down and prices up; NRA, which had been progressively undermined by industrial competition, was quietly forgotten. Neither earned the approval of economists or of ordinary folk: AAA because of the ploughing under of cotton when people were badly clothed and of the killing off of pigs when people were hungry, and NRA because it emerged as industrial cartels policed by government sanction.[5] During the hundred days, however, the measures were looked on by farmers and industry as the way to salvation.

For the orthodox school, Roosevelt cut $400 million in veterans' payments and $100 million in federal employees' salaries to redeem his campaign promise of balancing the budget.

Going off gold

While planners and government owners were occupied with restricting output and the slower process of governmental public works, the monetary manipulators in Congress were at work. Silver interests attached an amendment to the farm bill requiring the president to coin silver at a ratio of 16 to 1 with gold. When the president threatened to veto this Wheeler amendment, the farmer-monetary bloc substituted the Thomas amendment, which allowed the president (1) to issue greenback currency (currency outside the Federal Reserve System not backed by metal) up to a limit of $3 billion, (2) to fix the value of silver in terms of gold, and (3) to fix the weight of gold by proclamation. On the evening of April 18 President Roosevelt announced his decision to accept the Thomas amendment. Lewis Douglas commented later that evening, "This is the end of Western civilization."

In the bank holiday legislation, gold exports had been prohibited except under licence. Until the Thomas amendment, licenses had been issued. Increasingly, as April wore on and the inflationary bloc in Congress grew in strength, the question was raised as to whether this was a good idea.[6] With the acceptance of the Thomas amendment, the decision was taken to stop issuing licenses. The outflow of capital picked up. By April 24 the pound had risen from $3.24 in the first half of April to $3.86.

In January twenty economists had recommended that the United States should settle war debts, reduce tariffs, and cling unflinch-

5. The National Industrial Recovery Act has come to be regarded by 1980s monetarists as a major part of the explanation why the expansion of the money supply after 1933 produced increases in prices and wages rather than a far-reaching reduction in unemployment. See Michael M. Weinstein, "Some Macroeconomic Impacts of the National Industrial Recovery Act, 1933–1935," 1981, and especially the commentary by Phillip Cagan, 1981, and Karl Brunner, "Epilogue," 1981, p. 350.

6. See the excerpt from James Warburg's oral history statement in Jordan Schwartz, *1933: Roosevelt's Decision: The United States Leaves the Gold Standard*, 1969, p. 141; and Herbert Feis, *1933*, p. 121.

ingly to the gold standard.[7] At the time of the bank holiday, Paris saw it as utter madness for the United States to attempt to go off gold. It would solve nothing and would only bring U.S. internal problems to a world level.[8] On March 7 the *Times* in London declared the abandonment of the gold standard by the United States so unlikely as almost to be left out of account. None of the causes that drove the United Kingdom off gold were to be found in the United States. There was no run on U.S. funds or securities by foreign creditors. There was no remedy for any problem in devaluation.[9] At the same time, a cynical Frenchman, Edouard Daladier, who replaced Paul-Boncour as prime minister of France at the end of January, thought that going off gold was the inevitable response of the dollar to the fluctuating pound.[10]

The pound was comfortable. In his annual speech, Chairman of the Midland Bank Reginald McKenna opposed Britain returning to gold, claiming that it had been off the gold standard for sixteen months and that nothing catastrophic had happened.[11] On January 28 Neville Chamberlain, chancellor of the Exchequer, said that the United Kingdom would return to gold only when it felt assured that the system would work well.[12] However, while Ramsay MacDonald was en route to Washington to discuss preparations for the World Economic Conference with Roosevelt, the United States halted gold exports. This changed the bargaining position dramatically.

Preparing for the World Economic Conference

The idea of a world economic conference to formulate recovery plans goes back perhaps to a discussion of December 1930 between

7. *New York Times*, January 3, 1933, p. 1.

8. *New York Times*, March 3, 1933, p. 21. This conclusion was insufficient to free French officials of thought of what would be required in the event of devaluation of the dollar. At French-British discussions headed by Neville Chamberlain, chancellor of the Exchequer, and Georges Bonnet, French minister of finance, in London on March 17 to discuss the World Economic Conference, it was agreed that further discussions would be useful if the dollar were to be devalued (see *Documents diplomatiques français, 1932–1939*, 1966, vol. 3, no. 1, p. 12).

9. *New York Times*, March 7, 1933, p. 6.

10. Department of State, *Foreign Relations of the United States, 1933*, vol. 1, p. 576.

11. *New York Times*, January 28, 1933.

12. *New York Times*, January 30, 1933.

the U.S. Ambassador, Sackett, and Chancellor Brüning in Germany, in which the latter suggested the possibility of a conference in which the great related questions of disarmament, reparations, debt retirement, and international loan requirements could be dealt with as one package and settled on a political basis rather than treating each question separately by economic experts.[13]

The more proximate origin of the conference, as noted earlier, was the Laval-Hoover discussions of October 1931 and the Hoover-MacDonald exchange of May 1932. On the latter occasion the British government had expressed some concern that gold prices had suffered a further fall. Stimson's reply to MacDonald on behalf of President Hoover had indicated that the conference should have two purposes: (1) to raise commodity prices by easier credit, and possibly by some program of synchronized public expenditure, and (2) to encourage private business groups throughout the world.[14]

The conference was formally called by the Lausanne Conference resolution of July 9, 1932, following up an International Labor Office (ILO) proposal adopted by the League of Nations on May 21. Its official title was International Conference on Monetary and Economic Questions, after the United States had objected to calling the questions "financial and economic" on the grounds that "financial" would allow the discussion of war debts, which it sought to keep off the agenda. The Lausanne resolution provided for an organizing committee and a preparatory commission of experts to draw up an agenda. The topics to be covered were designated under (1) monetary (and financial) questions: monetary and credit policy, exchange stabilization and the level of prices, and the movement of capital; and (2) economic questions: improved conditions of production and trade, with particular attention to tariff policy, quantitative restrictions, and agreements among producers.

The organizing committee stayed away from substance, and the

13. Bennett, *Germany and the Diplomacy of the Financial Crisis, 1931*, p. 32. James M. Cox, the former governor of Ohio and presidential candidate on the Democratic ticket in 1920, traces the origin to a resolution of the Democratic Congress elected in 1930, calling for international action to reduce excessive duties and eliminate destructive and unfair trade practices by means of an international economic conference on the one hand and reciprocal trade agreements negotiated by the president on the other. The resolution was, of course, directed against the president's signature of the Smoot-Hawley Tariff Act. President Hoover vetoed it. See Cox, *Journey Through My Years*, p. 353.

14. Feis, *1933*, pp. 21, 23.

preparatory commission of experts did not do much better. Professor John H. Williams, who with E. E. Day served as one of the U.S. experts, reported to W. Randolph Burgess of the Federal Reserve Bank of New York after the first meeting of the experts in Geneva in November that the discussion started with the British asking: "How can prices be raised?" and the others replying, "When will sterling be stabilized?" The British were reluctant to discuss the second question at any length but indicated that there would be no stabilization until prices were higher, or at least until war debts were settled.[15]

Roosevelt's primary response was to delay the conference, at least until he took over and his domestic programs had had an opportunity to take hold. Like Hoover, he was against allowing war debts into the discussion.

The second meeting of the preparatory commission took place in January and February, before the bank holiday and before the dollar went off gold. Leith-Ross stated for the British that the world economy had deteriorated since the previous meeting, that a premature restoration of the gold standard would be extremely dangerous, and that there was need to close the gap between costs and prices before restoring gold, not to mention clearing up war debts and reparations, undertaking monetary reform to economize gold, providing for financial reconstruction, and lowering tariffs and quotas.[16] Emile Francqui of the National Bank of Belgium proposed a plan for an international credit institute that would make short-term funds available to countries running temporary balance-of-payments deficits in the course of stabilizing their currencies and undertaking domestic recovery measures. An ILO plan for international public works fi-

15. Federal Reserve Bank of New York files, memorandum from Burgess to Harrison, November 23, 1932.

16. Federal Reserve Bank of New York files, memorandum of January 7, 1933. An account of the opening session is also contained in *Documents diplomatiques français*, vol. 2, no. 180, Geneva to Paris, p. 386, and notes that Professor J. H. Williams, the U.S. expert, called Great Britain and Germany "key countries," anticipating his "key currency" view of ten years later. The key countries notion goes back at least to 1922 and Governor Benjamin Strong of the Federal Reserve Bank of New York. Strong favored a country-by-country approach to the stabilization of European currencies and opposed "any plan that would seek to stabilize all currencies simultaneously and also to great international conferences for this purpose" (Chandler, *Benjamin Strong*, p. 278, and Clarke, "The Reconstruction of the International Monetary System," p. 15).

nanced by a common credit pool followed the lines of Woytinsky's proposal noted in the previous chapter. Echoes of the 1930 Kindersley or Norman plan were heard at the conference. But the experts ultimately put aside these ideas in favor of, first, raising prices directly insofar as it could be done with balanced budgets and sound monetary measures and, second, dismantling the system of national defensive measures based on concerted action over a broad front— the United Kingdom would stabilize the pound, although it was agreed that the timing and the rate posed tricky questions; Germany would relax foreign exchange control; France would reduce its quota restrictions; and the United States would settle war debts and lower the tariff.[17] Herbert Feis, in a memorandum of January 29, stated that this program was impracticable because workers and politicians in the United States wanted bolder monetary and banking measures and that stabilization at present rates of the franc and pound would be premature. This statement led to an angry intellectual brawl.[18]

It was agreed that the meeting would be held in London. Ramsay MacDonald hoped to go out in a blaze of glory at the conference.[19] In his memoirs Warburg says that this was a mistake and the conference should have been held in Washington.[20] As a preliminary, the heads of various delegations came to Washington to confer with President Roosevelt. "For a time it seemed that America was assuming the leadership in an enterprise that held out every hope of success."[21]

17. Department of State, *Foreign Relations of the United States, 1933*, vol. 1, p. 462.

18. Feis, *1933*, p. 116.

19. Department of State, *Foreign Relations of the United States, 1933*, vol. 1, p. 477.

20. Warburg, *The Long Road Home*, p. 122. A desire to hold the conference in Washington was expressed by Roosevelt to the French ambassador, Claudel, on February 21 and the possibility was again taken up by Ramsay MacDonald and the French premier, Edouard Daladier, in Paris on March 10. It was stated that President Roosevelt was willing to send a delegation to London but preferred Washington as a site. The French had no preference, and MacDonald asserted that he would go to Washington if it would help, but the prime minister of Britain could hardly spend several months across the ocean. Sir John Simon, the foreign minister, added that Washington was hot in summer. At the March 17 meeting between Chamberlain and Bonnet, it was noted that London was a preferable location for the time of year but that Washington would have helped to educate United States public opinion. See *Documents diplomatiques français*, vol. 2, nos. 318 and 392, February 21 and March 10, on pp. 671 and 778, respectively, and vol. 3, no. 1, March 17, p. 3.

21. Cox, *Journey Through My Years*, p. 355.

Roosevelt, Hull, and Moley took only a minor part in the consultations, however. Warburg handled financial questions, Feis tariff and trade, and Bullitt handled politics.

The departure of the dollar from gold while MacDonald and Herriot were at sea shifted the focus from war debts to stabilization. Warburg seized the initiative and with agreement from President Roosevelt proposed a stabilization plan in which the United States would depreciate the dollar by 15 to 25 percent, and thereafter the three currencies would be stabilized and managed by a three-country stabilization fund. Leith-Ross for the British was shocked by a depreciation of the dollar as high as 15 percent. He felt the United States could easily maintain its old gold parity and stated as a final position that, if the stabilization of the dollar took place at a lower rate, the pound would be lowered to a parallel extent.[22] Charles Rist for the French thought it would be impossible to get the Chamber of Deputies to agree, since francs might be used to buy dollars and these might subsequently depreciate to saddle the French Treasury with a loss. These discussions took place over the period April 26–30 with the dollar steady and the pound moving down from $3.85 on April 25 to $3.73 two days later and back again to $3.85 on April 29. President Roosevelt expressed relief when the stabilization proposal fell through.[23] The communiqué issued by the president

22. This was apropos of a suggestion that the U.S. dollar might be depreciated by 15 percent in respect of gold, and the pound held at $3.75. See *Documents diplomatiques français*, vol. 3, no. 190, Washington to Paris, p. 328.

23. Feis, *1933*, pp. 144–47. Jeannette P. Nichols claims that Bonnet as minister of finance in Paris rejected the agreement as likely to be interpreted as inflationary (see "Roosevelt's Monetary Diplomacy, 1933," 1951, p. 302). This seems less compelling than the fear of loss cited by Governor Moret of the Bank of France in 1932. No explicit message on Paris's reasoning is contained in *Documents diplomatiques français*, in which a statement of a position against the common stabilization fund is given in vol. 3, no. 258, note of the Section on Commercial Policy (Paris), p. 457. Bullitt later expressed the discouragement of the U.S. government over the restrained attitude of the British government and the lack of response of the French to the common stabilization fund (vol. 3, no. 262 of May 10, p. 465). In reply, the French Foreign Office expressed the willingness of its government and the Bank of France to enter into immediate conversations on tripartite monetary cooperation as soon as they were approached (vol. 3, no. 274 of May 14, p. 482). The French ambassador in London asked for immediate stabilization discussion on May 17 (vol. 3, no. 288, p. 500). He was told that the British thought that too little time had elapsed since the dollar had gone off gold. It took six months for sterling to find a certain equilibrium. As much would be required of the dollar, especially in light of the conflicts between Wall Street and Washington and between the president and Congress.

and Guido Jung of the Bank of Italy, however, came out in favor of currency stabilization.

As the dollar fell on international exchanges in May—going from $3.85 to the pound on April 29 to $4.00 on May 31—Roosevelt became less and less interested in stabilization. Moley records that he experienced a "dangerous euphoria." He was prepared to agree on the date of the conference—in mid-June. Nothing else was decided.

Hull and Feis worked on the tariff truce. It was difficult to the point of impossibility to give it content. Every country wanted exceptions. The United States wanted to put up tariffs on agricultural commodities subject to a processing tax under the AAA. Britain had some unfinished tariff increases on eggs and bacon under the Ottawa Conference of 1932. France reserved its position until it saw whether prices in the United States rose the full amount of the depreciation of the dollar; otherwise they would be obliged to apply import surtaxes. But when Brazil demurred to the tariff truce, stating that it had some increases in process, Feis told them sharply that all countries had to make sacrifices in the general interest.[24]

The Washington consultations brought up a number of points of national economic interest. Schacht asked for access to colonies and hinted that Germany might cut off external debt service unilaterally. On May 20 service in fact was suspended on debts amounting to perhaps $5 billion.[25] An Australian submission pointed out that gold prices for the country's exports had fallen to 30 percent of the 1928 level and sterling prices to 42 percent, imposing a heavy burden of debt service in sterling and gold currencies. Interest alone absorbed one-third of a greatly increased volume of exports.[26] T. V. Soong, the Chinese minister of finance, was disturbed at the rising price of silver since China was stabilized on a silver standard and the rising price drained the country of money;[27] this was the case with Mexico as well. The Japanese representative made it clear that under no circumstances in a world stabilization agreement would his country al-

24. Department of State, *Foreign Relations of the United States, 1933*, vol. 1, pp. 515, 587, 608. The text of the truce, with some of the reservations verbal, was announced in London by the Organizing Committee of the Conference, but was good only for the duration of the conference.

25. Ibid., pp. 532, 534.

26. Ibid., p. 511.

27. Ibid., pp. 532, 763ff.

low the yen to go back to 49 cents: 20 cents would be all right, and it might compromise at 25 cents if it could not go lower.[28]

The Swedish minister could not understand how the dollar needed to be protected by a gold embargo when the balance of payments was in surplus. Ambassador Lawrence Steinhardt, working with Warburg, explained that the United States had been experiencing a capital flight based on the possibility that the dollar might be devalued and on that account had to devalue.[29]

Of more far-reaching importance were the answers given to the Japanese and the Poles on international public works. Mr. Tsushima of the Japanese delegation stated that he understood that the International Labor Office at Geneva was going to propose some international program of international public works. Mr. Warburg said that the United States felt that each nation must raise its own funds. "We would oppose without any ambiguity a proposal that we finance someone else's program."[30] The Polish ambassador found the

28. Ibid., pp. 536, 538. *Documents diplomatiques français*, vol. 3, no. 242, Tokyo to Paris, May 4, 1933, p. 423, sets out the Japanese attitude before the arrival of Viscount Ishii in Washington: without rejecting a return to the gold standard, Japan considers this measure should be subordinated to a redistribution of world gold and increases in reserves in all countries. It should also be connected with free circulation of capital. "In other words, Japan is not proceeding otherwise than other governments, and under its adherence to principles, it is easy to discern the concern to safeguard above all its national economic interests. It refuses to lower its tariffs significantly, objecting that it has not, unlike other countries, significantly raised them since the war. At the same time, and in apparent contradiction, it refuses to revalue its exchange rate for fear of upsetting the conditions of exporting."

29. Department of State, *Foreign Relations of the United States, 1933*, vol. 1, p. 566.

30. Ibid., p. 538. In this the United States was following the French, who, as reported by Cochran (Department of State, *Foreign Relations of the United States, 1932*, vol. 1, p. 831), with regard to the work of the Preparatory Commission had stated their objection to the Francqui and Kindersley plans: "If she is called upon to make a big investment, she desires to be free to make her own terms as she has done before. She looks on loans as political as well as trade means and desires her independence of action. She is not willing to help the British or Americans retrieve bad loans unless her funds are involved." (The Francqui plan was referred to earlier. The Kindersley plan is probably the same as the Norman plan, noted in the previous chapter.) In addition to the International Credit Institute proposed by Francqui, the Preparatory Commission also discussed, and was cool toward, a Monetary Normalization Fund, first brought forward at the Stresa Conference for the Economic Restoration of Central and Eastern Europe, held September 5–20, 1932, and an ILO proposal for financing international public works, probably along the lines of Woytinsky's article in the *International Labor Review* discussed above. See James

proposals of the American government too indefinite to provide any basis for understanding between the two governments. Dr. Feis replied that the United States did not want to enter the conference with a program binding itself to a series of propositions. It was not an American conference, and the United States had less to gain and less to lose than other countries. The ambassador referred to the question of the synchronization of public works undertaken for the purpose of increasing employment and trade and asked how funds would be provided.

> He was informed that proposals had been made for the creation of an international fund. . . . The United States could not participate in such a fund. In the first place, it would be impossible to come to any international agreement. . . . An international fund of the nature proposed would only cause greater dissension among the countries. In the second place, the United States could not possibly participate in such a fund since the Congress would not provide money for that purpose. American experience with respect to international loans has not been sufficiently happy to encourage it to enter into additional ventures.[31]

In talking to the Polish ambassador, Feis mentioned a proposal put forward by the Special British Mission. This is referred to in a brief memorandum of conversation by Feis. The British financial attaché in Washington, Kenneth S. Bewley, waited on Feis with a memorandum on April 15 but did not leave it with him. The British government proposed the creation of an international fund of between $1 billion and $2 billion by the contribution of various governments for the purpose of making loans to central banks, which in turn would end exchange controls and reduce trade barriers. Bewley and Feis agreed that there were three questions that would have to be answered with respect to the suggestion: (1) was it practical? (2) would it achieve the desired end of reducing trade barriers and raising prices? and (3) would it be politically possible to win support for it in the United States? Feis suggested that there was doubt on all three issues, especially the third in light of the opposi-

---

W. Angell, *The Program for the World Economic Conference: The Experts' Agenda and the Document,* 1933, p. 52, and Department of State, *Foreign Relations of the United States, 1933,* vol. 1, p. 457.

For a reference to a Turkish proposal for an International Credit Bank, see Department of State, *Foreign Relations of the United States, 1933,* vol. 1, p. 570.

31. Department of State, *Foreign Relations of the United States, 1933,* vol. 1, pp. 560–61.

tion in the United States to proposals under which the government would obligate itself to furnish any more money to foreign governments—particularly in light of threatened default on all past loans. Bewley was so impressed that he left, taking with him the copy of the British government's memorandum.[32]

The Bewley proposal represents a watered-down Treasury version of a memorandum by Hubert Henderson, which was adopted by the Economic Advisory Council in its fourth report and revived when the prime minister asked an EAC Committee on International Economic Policy, consisting of Sir Charles Addis, Lord Astor, Sir Basil Blackett, Lord Essendon, Keynes, Layton, Salter, Stamp, and Henderson, for advice on the World Economic Conference. It strongly resembles the Henderson "Monetary Proposal for Lausanne," dated May 12, 1932, which called for special currency international certificates to be issued by the Bank for International Settlements, to the value of 50 percent of a country's gold value exports in 1928 (as an illustration),[33] and the Keynes proposal published in letters to the *Times* in March and April 1933 and reproduced as Chapter 5 of *The Means to Prosperity*.[34] The Keynes proposal provided for $5 billion in paper gold to be issued to countries of the world based on their gold holdings at the end of 1928, but with an upper limit of $450 million to be granted to Great Britain, the United States, France, Germany, Spain, Argentina, and Japan.

The Henderson memorandum for the EAC is dated July 1, 1932, and calls for the issue by the Bank for International Settlements of new notes, equivalent to gold, in the amount of £1 billion.[35] The basis for distribution is not stated. Of particular interest, however, is the analysis leading up to the proposal. Henderson recalled the central theme of Bagehot's *Lombard Street* of the danger of a run on London and the necessity to curb it by suspending the Bank Act of 1844 (which limited the note issue). He stated that Britain used

32. Ibid., pp. 574–75.

33. See Hubert Henderson, *The Interwar Years and Other Papers*, 1955, pp. 103–6.

34. My personal copy has the date of May 1, 1933, written in it.

35. See Howson and Winch, *The Economic Advisory Council, 1930–1939*, pp. 273–77. Ralph G. Hawtrey also stated contemporaneously the need for an *international lender of last resort* (his emphasis), adding, "Perhaps some day, the B.I.S. ... But as things are, the function can only be undertaken by a foreign central bank or by a group of foreign central banks in cooperation" (*The Art of Central Banking*, 1932, p. 228).

to assist in maintaining solvency everywhere in difficult times by shipping gold to centers of financial crisis and by drawing gold from centers that were not affected:

> It is of the essence of the present world difficulties that London has failed in the discharge of that vital function, and that no other centre has been willing and able to discharge it.[36]

Henderson suggested that the departure of Great Britain from gold had had national advantages, but from the general world standpoint had seriously intensified the instability of international financial relations.

> General lack of confidence serves to render precarious even currencies like the dollar which are impregnable against a purely external drain. This makes it impossible for the United States and perhaps for any country to step into the breach and discharge the functions of a world banker by advancing money to embarrassed countries.[37]

Henderson recognized that to issue new money on a uniform basis to all governments, debtor and creditor alike, would be a departure from Bagehot's principle of making notes available in internal panics to applicants, but he thought it would be effective. The resemblance to the Special Drawing Rights of the International Monetary Fund, agreed on in 1968, is striking. But whether or not the United States could participate in such a scheme, it would not. Bewley's conversation with Feis, based on the cut-down version of the Henderson report, was enough to kill the idea.

Earlier Chamberlain had sounded out Bonnet on the Keynes version of the plan, including the provision for public works, in a London meeting of the two financial heads on March 17. He introduced the subject by stating that Keynes was not infallible, briefly described the Keynes proposal for public works by the United States, France, and Great Britain, together with the creation of purchasing power, noted that since the war Great Britain had undertaken public works without the results forecast by Keynes, and asked for Bonnet's views. Bonnet replied that there had been little British help for Daladier when he had supported a program of international public works at Geneva in October 1932. Bonnet worried about the financing but was not reassured by the discussion of new credits put at the

---

36. Henderson memorandum, p. 4. D. E. Moggridge has kindly furnished me with a copy of the memorandum, and he has also traced the history of the Bewley memorandum for me in the Public Record Office.

37. Ibid., p. 5

disposition of central banks. He asserted that France had practiced public works programs for several years without any noticeable increase of prices. The budgetary deficits disquieted the minister of finance. The real need was to restore confidence.[38] There was no support for the feeble British initiative from this quarter.

Apart from Hull, who was to head the delegation and who thought exclusively about tariff truce and long-run tariff reduction, there was little enthusiasm for the conference as the date grew near. Norman Davis kept cabling from London that while MacDonald was away in Washington there were grave doubts at home whether Britain might not do better to move to an empire rather than a world solution. The country wanted to cooperate, but its only interest was war debts, now widened by the unhinging of the dollar.[39] In a speech made over the radio on May 20 and approved by Roosevelt, Moley suggested that not much would result from the World Economic Conference apart from comparing domestic experience:

> Too many people are likely to think that because the depression is worldwide, its causes rest solely on international conditions or that the solution for this worldwide depression is solely through international remedies. . . . The fact is that a good many of the economic ills of each country are domestic. . . . They are predominantly internal, not external. Much of the remedy, then, must be what the nations do themselves.[40]

38. *Documents diplomatiques français*, vol. 3, no. 1, London to Paris, March 17, 1933, p. 607.

39. Ibid., pp. 586, 598–99.

40. Moley, *The First New Deal*, pp. 404–5. The sardonic Lord Vansittart, who accompanied MacDonald to Washington, put it thus: "We find that discussion of war debts, reparations and tariffs might be difficult at the World Conference. We could present *Hamlet* without the Prince of Denmark, Ophelia and Polonius; it would be shortened. So would the Conference. Failure was assured" (*The Mist Procession*, p. 465).

At the time he sought to arrange Washington talks, Roosevelt expressed to Claudel, the French ambassador, his concern that the program was insufficiently prepared and the assemblage too large, exposed to publicity, and divided by irreconcilable views (*Documents diplomatiques français*, vol. 3, no. 54, Washington to Paris, March 27, 1933, p. 94). The Washington talks helped to remedy these defects but little. See also *The Economist*, June 10, 1933, p. 1229: "France is sceptical; the American delegation, perplexed by an extremely complex situation at home, is new to the international game; while Germany is deeply absorbed in her ideas of national revival at home. England, in her turn, shows signs of a dangerous complacency, due perhaps to the happy chance that she has escaped the worst crises of the past year" (quoted by Abdul Hasib, *Monetary Negotiations in the World Economic Conference*, 1958, p. 82).

War debts were separated from the agenda of the conference, and so was currency stabilization, although Governor Harrison of the Federal Reserve Bank of New York, O. M. W. Sprague, a former adviser to the Bank of England, and Warburg were to negotiate an agreement on stabilization among the central banks parallel to the general conference. U.S. instructions to the delegation called for action along six (overlapping) fronts and furnished draft resolutions:

(1) A tariff truce.
(2) Coordinated monetary and fiscal policy, with the monetary policy consisting of open market operations (to which the French objected) and no content given to coordinated fiscal policy, which was to be the object of study.
(3) The removal of foreign exchange restrictions.
(4) Laying the groundwork for an adequate and enduring monetary standard.
(5) Basic agreement on the gradual abolition of barriers to trade.
(6) Basic agreement on the control of production and distribution of world commodities.[41]

As the Polish ambassador commented, the degree of specificity was low.

The World Economic Conference

Meeting in London on June 12, the conference was thronged with prime ministers: Daladier of France, Beneš of Czechoslovakia, Bennett of Canada, Dollfuss of Austria, Smuts of the Union of South Africa, Bruce of Australia; foreign ministers, such as Hull of the United States, Colijn of the Netherlands, Litvinov of the Soviet Union; ministers of finance, including Neville Chamberlain, British

---

41. *Foreign Relations of the United States, 1933*, vol. 1, p. 623. At an earlier stage, when the United States was still committed to the gold standard, proposals for monetary reform—put forward by the United States as a basis of discussion—included a reduction of gold reserve requirements to a uniform 30 or 25 percent, the abandonment of internal convertibility of currencies into gold, and the adoption of fixed gold points, perhaps 5 percentage points apart, rather than gold points that varied with such circumstances as geographical distance. See *Documents diplomatiques français*, vol. 3, no. 106, Washington to Paris, April 8, 1933. With the abandonment of the gold standard, this proposal dropped by the wayside. The suggestion regarding open market operations goes back to the second Preparatory Commission, but it was difficult to have much faith in open market operations in the United States with excess reserves of over $1 billion.

chancellor of the Exchequer, Bonnet of France, T. V. Soong of China; presidents of central banks, among them Hjalmar Schacht of Germany, Trip of the Netherlands, Kienbock of Austria, Jung of Italy. The U.S. delegation, headed by Hull, included an odd assortment of personalities and experts, among them three isolationists who were ultimately pleased with the conference failure—Key Pittman and James Couzens, senators respectively of Nevada and Michigan, and an industrialist named Morrison. There was a round of opening speeches. That of Hull had to be delayed while it was rewritten in Washington to play down international solutions to the depression, provided in the Hull draft, and to emphasize domestic ones. MacDonald scandalized the American delegation by mentioning war debts.

In the course of organization, a contest emerged between James Cox of the United States and Georges Bonnet of France for the post of presiding officer of the financial committee. The French suggested that it was inappropriate to have the representative of a country that had left the gold standard presiding; in reply, it was pointed out that it was unsuitable to elect the representative of a country that had repudiated its debts. The British had paid the June 15 installment on war debts by transferring silver they were able to buy in the market at half the price for which they were credited. The French defaulted. Feis notes that Roosevelt showed no animus against the French on this score and shelved the issue for the duration of the conference. He added, "It is probable that the default washed away the remnants of Roosevelt's tolerance for the French effort to cause us to return to the international gold standard."[42]

The first business was to take place outside the conference: the conclusion of an agreement to stabilize the pound and the dollar in terms of gold for the duration of the conference. This had been agreed on May 31, when the pound was $4.00. On June 12 as the conference opened, the rate was $4.15. More important, while the dollar was falling from $3.42 to the pound to $4.00, Moody's index

42. Feis, *1933*, p. 182. Roosevelt had been urging the French to make a gesture of a token payment in arrears for the December 15, 1932, installment, but without promising them anything concrete in exchange. See *Documents diplomatiques français*, vol. 3, no. 86, Washington to Paris, April 5, pp. 148–49, apropos of Herriot's visit: "For the due date of 15 June, I hope in one way or another to have the necessary powers, but France must understand that it is impossible for me to undertake any explicit engagements now."

of staple commodity prices had risen from 86 to 120, and the Dow-Jones industrial stock index from 56 to 90. By June 12 the two indexes were 124 and 97, respectively.

The deal worked out among the financial representatives called for the dollar to be stabilized at $4.00 to the pound and 0.04662 to the franc, with a 3 percent spread on either side, from $3.88 to $4.12 for the pound and 0.04893 to 0.047331 for the franc. Each of the three central banks would support its currency by selling gold, up to a limit of four or five million ounces, equivalent to $80–$100 million. When this was used up, the agreement would be reexamined.

The news of stabilization leaked to the press, and the exchange market firmed from $4.12 to $4.02; the commodity and stock markets declined. The Committee for the Nation sent President Roosevelt a telegram calling for the dollar to be cut 43 percent, based on calculations for restoring U.S. prices, which implied a pound rate of $5.70. Roosevelt sent the delegation telegrams on June 17 from Washington and on June 19 and 20 from the destroyer U.S.S. *Ellis* (which was accompanying him sailing) saying that $4.00 was unacceptable. While stabilization was an ultimate objective, one needed worldwide action to achieve it, not just the action of three or four countries. It was as well to avoid even a tentative commitment to a definite program to control fluctuations in the dollar. When the pound reached $4.25, the United States would contemplate unilateral action to hold the level. As an afterthought, he added that he would consider a median rate of $4.15. Too much importance was attached to stabilization by banker-influenced cabinets. In the case of the United States, "it means only a very small (perhaps 3) percent of our total trade."[43] He then took off for a sailing vacation which made communications with both Washington and London difficult.

The rejection of the stabilization agreement on June 17 restored the downward progress of the dollar and the upward march of commodity and stock prices. Harrison returned from London. In London Warburg began to draft a new stabilization agreement. Moley flew from Washington to Martha's Vineyard to confer with Roosevelt aboard his boat and then returned to New York to sail for Lon-

43. Department of State, *Foreign Relations of the United States, 1933*, vol. 1, pp. 646, 649, 650.

don on June 21. In the Federal Reserve Bank of New York, J. H. Williams suggested that if the French, and to some extent the British, insisted on stabilization and the United States that currency stabilization must not be allowed to interfere with the domestic program of raising prices, "we say to the British what they said to us at Geneva last fall: we cannot undertake currency stabilization except as part of a general program, to be entered into by at least three leading countries, to raise prices by means of credit expansion, public works and other suitable measures, and that any stabilization agreement must be flexible and subject to change in accordance with domestic and international forces, especially relative changes in price levels."[44] The gold bloc told the British that unless something were done to stabilize the dollar, it would have to go off gold.

Moley arrived in London on June 28 and went to work with Warburg to effect a compromise. He referred to a declaration drawn up by Cox, Warburg, and Sprague and agreed to by the French, Dutch, and Italians—largely a paraphrase of Warburg's instructions from Washington, with no mention of rates and stabilization mentioned only as an ultimate objective—and called it unconditional surrender on the part of the gold bloc countries.[45] Bonnet's report to his government suggested that he drew up the statement in response to a request by MacDonald and transmitted a copy before the British and American delegations signed it, which they ultimately did on June 30.[46] The agreement provided for appropriate measures to limit speculation and for central bank cooperation in stabilization on an interim basis. It is hard to understand Moley's characterization of the agreement as unconditional surrender.

The draft was cabled to Washington and to Roosevelt in his Campobello summer home in New Brunswick, Canada. Baruch, Woodin, and Acheson supported the plan from Washington. Roosevelt, who had no advisers with him, only Henry Morgenthau of the Farm Credit Board as a friend and Louis Howe, his secretary, twice rejected the compromise. By this time the dollar had reached $4.33 against the pound, commodity prices had risen to 130, and the Dow-Jones industrial average reached 100. On July 1 Roosevelt

44. Federal Reserve Bank of New York files, J. H. Williams memorandum to Secretary of the Treasury Woodin, June 19, 1933.

45. Moley, *The First New Deal*, p. 435.

46. *Documents diplomatiques français*, vol. 3, nos. 426, 436, 438, Bonnet to Paris, pp. 776, 795, 799, respectively.

stated that stabilization was a matter for private (i.e., central) banks, not governments, that it would permit unbalanced budgets, and that he could not obligate the United States now or later to approve the export of gold. A second message on July 3 was worded more pungently for public release.

> I would regard it as a catastrophe, amounting to a world tragedy, if the great Conference of Nations . . . should . . . allow itself to be diverted by the proposal of a purely artificial and temporary experiment affecting the monetary exchange of a few nations only. . . . I do not relish the thought that insistence on such action should be an excuse for the continuance of basic economic errors that underlie so much of the present worldwide depression.
>
> The world will not long be lulled by the specious fallacy of achieving a temporary and probably an artificial stability in foreign exchange on the part of a few large countries only.
>
> The sound internal economic situation of a nation is a greater factor in its well-being than the price of its currency. . . .
>
> The old fetishes of so-called international bankers are being replaced by efforts to plan national currencies with the objective of giving those currencies a continuing purchasing power. . . . The U.S. seeks the kind of dollar which a generation hence will have the same purchasing power and debt-paying power as the dollar value we hope to attain in the near future. . . .
>
> Our broad purpose is the permanent stabilization of every nation's currency. . . . When the world works out concerted policies in the majority of nations to produce balanced budgets and living within their means, then we can properly discuss a better distribution of the world's gold and silver.[47]

The message had an explosive effect. Criticized for its rhetoric, which Roosevelt later admitted was excessive, its substance has been debated to this day. It broke up the World Economic Conference, which limped along at U.S. insistence for a week or two before closing up shop with one agreement on silver, pushed through by Senator Pittman. British Empire countries met in a formal conference and formed the sterling area. The gold bloc organized itself defensively more fully. A number of economists—notably Harrod, Meade, and Keynes, who called Roosevelt "magnificently right"— approved. They could hardly have approved the analysis, which

47. Department of State, *Foreign Relations of the United States, 1933*, vol. 1, pp. 673–74.

Figure 11. Daily exchange rates, commodity prices, and stock prices, New York, April–July 1933.

Figure 11, continued

		Moody's Daily Index of Staple Commodity Prices	Exchange rate on the £	Dow-Jones Industrial Average closing
		(Base: 100 = 31 Dec. 1931		
1933:				
April	1	86·4	3·42	55·7
Sun.	2	X	X	X
	3	86·7	3·42	55·7
	4	86·8	3·42	56·1
	5	87·5	3·42	57·5
	6	88·8	3·42	58·8
	7	88·5	3·42	58·8
	8	87·9	3·42	59·3
	9	X	X	X
	10	88·6	3·41	62·1
	11	90·2	3·41	61·2
	12	89·7	3·41	60·3
	13	90·9	3·41	62·7
	14	Holiday	3·44	X
	15	Holiday	3·45	62·9
	16	X	X	X
	17	91·3	3·49	61·6
	18	92·5	3·45	62·7
	19	95·1	3·49	68·3
	20	99·9	3·61	72·3
	21	99·7	3·84	69·8
	22	100·5	3·81	72·2
	23	X	X	X
	24	102·9	3·86	73·7
	25	102·2	3·85	72·4
	26	102·4	3·79	72·6
	27	102·4	3·73	71·7
	28	101·5	3·77	73·1
	29	103·8	3·85	77·7
	30	X	X	X
May	1	105·9	3·88	77·8
	2	106·6	3·88	77·3
	3	108·1	3·91	77·4
	4	109·0	3·91	79·2
	5	110·0	3·98	79·8
	6	109·8	3·99	77·6
	7	X	X	X
	8	111·0	3·97	76·6
	9	110·9	3·94	77·2
	10	111·6	3·93	80·8
	11	114·1	3·96	82·5
	12	115·6	3·98	82·1
	13	115·8	3·97	80·9
	14	X	X	X
	15	115·0	3·96	79·7
	16	115·3	3·94	81·3
	17	116·4	3·91	82·6
	18	116·0	3·90	82·6
	19	114·9	3·88	81·8
	20	113·7	3·87	80·2
	21	X	X	X
	22	113·6	3·89	79·9
	23	114·7	3·91	83·1
	24	115·7	3·92	84·3
	25	115·4	3·92	83·7
	26	116·9	3·91	86·6
	27	118·5	3·97	89·6
	28	X	X	X

		Moody's Daily Index of Staple Commodity Prices	Exchange rate on the £	Dow-Jones Industrial Average closing
		(Base: 100 = 31 Dec. 1931		
	29	119·5	3·97	90·0
	30	Holiday	X	X
	31	120·7	4·00	88·1
June	1	120·3	4·00	89·1
	2	120·9	3·99	92·2
	3	120·5	4·01	90·0
	4	X	X	X
	5	120·2	4·01	91·9
	6	120·9	4·02	91·9
	7	121·4	4·06	93·0
	8	120·6	4·12	93·5
	9	121·6	4·10	94·3
	10	122·7	4·14	94·4
	11	X	X	X
	12	123·7	4·15	96·8
	13	123·8	4·14	94·8
	14	121·8	4·09	94·1
	15	120·1	4·06	88·9
	16	120·1	4·07	89·2
	17	119·5	4·07	90·2
	18	X	X	X
	19	121·7	4·14	96·0
	20	121·7	4·18	95·2
	21	121·9	4·16	95·9
	22	122·4	4·23	92·9
	23	122·7	4·22	95·5
	24	123·4	4·22	95·7
	25	X	X	X
	26	127·4	4·21	98·5
	27	130·3	4·24	98·7
	28	128·9	4·34	97·7
	29	128·8	4·30	97·0
	30	128·6	4·26	98·1
July	1	129·9	4·33	100·9
	2	X	X	X
	3	132·4	4·41	103·8
	4	Holiday	X	X
	5	132·9	4·52	102·7
	6	134·6	4·47	105·0
	7	135·4	4·73	105·4
	8	135·5	4·70	105·2
	9	X	X	X
	10	136·9	4·80	104·1
	11	139·0	4·74	103·1
	12	142·6	4·68	104·6
	13	143·0	4·77	105·5
	14	143·7	4·78	105·0
	15	145·3	4·78	106·1
	16	X	X	X
	17	148·5	4·78	108·3
	18	148·9	4·84	108·7
	19	145·2	4·83	103·6
	20	137·8	4·75	96·3
	21	134·1	4·65	88·7
	22	133·5	4·64	88·4
	23	X	X	X
	24	135·4	4·64	94·3
	25	135·2	4·68	92·8
	26	137·4	4·61	95·1

Figure 11, continued

		Moody's Daily Index of Staple Commodity Prices	Exchange rate on the £	Dow-Jones Industrial Average closing
		(Base: 100 = 12/31/31)		
	27	140·0	4·56	96·0
	28	137·4	4·48	94·5
	29	135·3	4·53	X
	30	X	X	X
	31	132·1	4·53	90·8
August	1		4·41	
	2		4·45	
	3		4·53	
	4		4·50	

SOURCE: *Commercial and Financial Chronicle*, 1933, various issues.

contained some unusual economic ideas and even non sequiturs: fear of gold losses, when the United States had one-third of the world stock; concern that two or three currencies only would stabilize, when the rest of the world could stabilize only in terms of key currencies; distinctions between governments and central banks, which make it appropriate for the latter to undertake agreements the former should avoid; the unimportance of trade to the United States, but the crucial importance of a declining dollar; and the suggestion that stabilization leads to unbalanced budgets, which are in themselves abhorrent. Nor could they have endorsed reasoning that spoke of stabilizing currencies in terms of purchasing power from generation to generation when it was evident that Roosevelt's agreement to stabilize gave way under the impact of a decline in the stock market from 96.8 to 89.2 in four days in mid-June. Moley talked to Lippmann and Keynes in London about a proposal for a new international currency unit—the *dinard*—the value of which would be stabilized in terms of many commodities and not merely gold. "None of them knew how this could be done."[48]

Presumably Roosevelt was saying that the United States was not ready to enter into international agreement until it had pushed further with attempting to raise prices by exchange depreciation. The experiment did not last long. On July 17 the pound approached $4.86, and Roosevelt ordered the Federal Reserve Bank of New

48. Feis, *1933*, p. 211.

York to support the dollar, up to perhaps $30 million, in an effort to fend off possible retaliation.[49] The bank bought only $1.3 million when the exchange, commodity, and stock markets all turned around. The dollar rose substantially, and the commodity and stock markets fell. As Figure 11 shows, however, the rise in the stock market did not keep up with the depreciation of the dollar, and the decline went further than the depreciation. The pound went to $5.15 in the autumn; the stock market did not reach its July 1933 peak again until well into 1934.

The official reaction was well expressed by MacDonald, who cabled Roosevelt that Europe had no desire to interfere with domestic American policies but had counted on the United States to find an arrangement that would not bring chaos to Europe as the price of American success. Jung of Italy added that Europe could not throw overboard the accumulated experience of centuries for an untested theory and would have to leave such experimentation to those with sufficient resources to be able to afford it.[50]

Experimenting with the gold price

The collapse of the conference and the rise of the dollar set prices down again, and Roosevelt looked around for a new expedient. It was not far to seek. Henry Morgenthau, who was with him at Campobello and on the return trip to Washington on the *Indianapolis*, brought Roosevelt charts showing weekly prices of agricultural commodities and of gold prepared by Professor George Warren, an agricultural economist of Cornell. Warren's views had been formed while working on a book with Frank Pearson that studied the behavior of prices in the greenback period in the United States from the

---

49. Federal Reserve Bank of New York files, Crane memorandum, July 20, 1933.

50. *Foreign Relations of the United States, 1933*, vol. 1, pp. 682–83. Roosevelt's reply to MacDonald was unenlightening: there is no inconsistency between the U.S. program for economic recovery and international cooperation for the purpose of restoring prices, maintaining purchasing power stable over a generation, stimulating business activity, public works, managed farm production, increased purchasing power through high wages, and balanced expenditure and government taxes. The program might be jeopardized by exposure to concerted competition. The United States wanted to stop the drift to nationalist exclusionism. There could be no other response than the present program until a general international program was worked out (p. 686).

Civil War to 1879.[51] The connection between the price of gold and the general price level, however, was not as direct as Warren seemed to think, but went through the exchange rate. It assumed a fixed price of gold and steady commodity prices abroad in the world's leading financial center of the time, London.

A week after the July 3 message, Roosevelt had Warren to tea. Roosevelt was impressed. On August 16 he told Morgenthau that he would like to buy gold in the open market at more than the prevailing price in an effort to raise commodity prices. The day before, he had authorized Warburg to form a monetary study group consisting of Acheson, Eugene Black, Douglas, Harrison, James Harvey Rogers, Sprague, and Walter Stewart. This group urged strongly against the Warren Plan but had no alternative to offer. Accordingly, on September 8 Roosevelt raised the domestic price of gold from $20.67 an ounce, where it had been for more than a century, with the exception of twenty years during and after the Civil War, to $29.82.

The initial results were satisfactory. Sterling rose above $5.00 and, with the depreciation of the dollar, stocks and commodities went up. Warburg's diary for September 21 records a conversation with the president in which he accused the president of always wanting a lower dollar than existed. In April, when the dollar was $3.75 against the pound, he wanted $3.85. In May, when it was $3.85, he said he would be satisfied with $4.00. On June 17, when he was offered $4.00, he wanted $4.25. In August, when the pound was $4.50, he wanted $5.00. The process could go on indefinitely. Roosevelt's reply was, "Well, what would you do?" Warburg had to confess that he and his study committee had no panacea.[52]

But prices fell again, and in October, after some weeks looking for the requisite authority, Roosevelt undertook to buy newly mined gold on the open market through a subsidiary of the RFC. The policy was announced in a fireside chat on October 22. The permanent value of the dollar would not be fixed until the price level had been restored. The United States must take firmly into its own hands the control of the gold value of the dollar, too greatly influenced by the accidents of international trade. The new gold purchases were a policy and not an expedient. Morgenthau reported that the president

51. George F. Warren and Frank A. Pearson, *Prices*, 1933.
52. Warburg, *The Long Road Home*, p. 147.

was not surprised or upset by the skepticism of the press or the angry uproar of the gold bloc, and laughed at the news from Harrison that Governor Norman—"old pink whiskers," as he referred to him—had complained that the whole world would be put into bankruptcy.[53]

Beginning on October 25, Morgenthau, working with Roosevelt, set the price higher each day by amounts that varied arbitrarily and about which they joked.[54] They began by buying only newly mined domestic gold, but it proved impossible to get the London price up the full amount of the rise inside the United States. On October 29, therefore, the RFC started to buy gold abroad. Harrison and Black were worried that the move would push France off the gold standard.[55] The president, however, was insistent that the time had not come to stabilize the dollar.

It came quickly. Farm prices sagged again in November and December, and the gap between the New York and the London gold prices widened. Morgenthau, appointed acting secretary of the Treasury in November to replace Woodin, who was gravely ill, telephoned Harrison asking him to approach Governor Norman to ask whether the British government would join the United States in de jure stabilization of the pound and the dollar. Two days later Norman reported that he had consulted Leith-Ross and that the British government would not be willing to stabilize de jure, nor would it be willing to give any commitment as to a minimum rate in future. They would be glad to consider, however, de facto stabilization for

53. Blum, *From the Morgenthau Diaries*, vol. 1, p. 73. Feis comments that Morgenthau had a juvenile sense of humor (*1933*, p. 287).

54. Morgenthau reported that Roosevelt once proposed raising the price 21 cents because it was three times 7 cents and seven was a lucky number. Morgenthau claims Roosevelt was making a joke to relieve a tense and gloomy moment (Blum, *From the Morgenthau Diaries*, vol. 1, p. 70). Moley, on the other hand, comments that Roosevelt gravely marred his image as a responsible statesman by his early morning bedside guesses as to what the price of gold would be that day (*The First New Deal*, p. 303).

55. The Board of Directors of the Federal Reserve Bank of New York contemplated refusing to assist the RFC in its foreign purchases. Owen D. Young, the chairman, expressed the sense of the directors that they were determined not to cooperate in any monetary program that threatened the government credit to such an extent as to make the issuance of fiat money inevitable. Harrison, the president, however, argued against any action to terminate the bank's participation while even a slight hope remained of a program of dollar stability. See Federal Reserve Bank of New York files, Board Minutes, November 10, 1933.

a temporary period, through the use of an agreed amount of gold. By December, when the dollar strengthened, Harrison reported to Norman that it was impossible to press the scheme. It no longer mattered. Roosevelt and Morgenthau were bored with changing the gold price and wanted to fix it permanently. On January 15, 1934, the President sent a special monetary message to Congress. The Gold Reserve Act was passed on January 30. On February 1 the President fixed the price of gold at $35 an ounce.

It is not entirely clear why. Morgenthau's account has an assortment of not very compelling reasons, judged in the light of the past. Exchange fluctuations could not be permitted to disrupt trade. A fixed price for gold was necessary if the government was to realize a profit for gold and use it to create a stabilization fund. The dollar was again appreciating, and Jacob Viner reported that the American gold purchases abroad were inadequately large to hold down the value of the dollar or inflate the domestic price level.[56] Flexibility was less important than the continuous harassment by the Committee for the Nation, the populist radio priest Father Coughlin, and other inflationary groups. The policy had not worked. It was necessary to move on.

Raising prices

A large number of economists have denounced the United States for abandoning the gold standard and devaluing the dollar when it had an export surplus. To Röpke, for example:

The abandonment of the gold dollar by the Roosevelt administration must, indeed, be viewed as one of the most disastrous acts of any government and any country in recent times, disastrous both for the country itself and the rest of the world.[57]

In the previous chapter, however, it was indicated that the appreciation of the dollar was exercising a deflationary force in the United States that was keeping ahead of any decline in exports and leaving a small export surplus. It may be granted that Roosevelt and

56. Blum, *From the Morgenthau Diaries*, vol. 1, p. 120.
57. Röpke, *Crises and Cycles*, p. 167. See also Ragnar Nurkse, "International Monetary Equilibrium," 1945: "A country with a surplus in its balance of payments should never resort to devaluation; on the contrary, it might be asked to appreciate its currency" (p. 13).

his closest advisers—especially Morgenthau and Howe—often had no clear idea of what they were doing. In the end, the policy may have been a good one.

Once it is agreed that it is important and necessary to raise world prices,[58] two means are available. The first is for the countries of the world to embark simultaneously on programs of government spending, either so carefully articulated in amount and timing that each country's exports grow at the same rate as its imports or, more probably, with a fund contributed jointly to ensure that any country whose imports got ahead of its exports—in the pursuit of the common program, and not in an effort to acquire resources—would be financed temporarily. Such a program was impossible in 1933, though not because it had not been thought of—the elements were all available in the Kindersley, Francqui, ILO, and Keynes plans. It was simply that all governments (and most politicians and economists) were opposed to government deficits, and the United States was not prepared to take the leadership in making fresh money available for a Monetary Normalization Fund or International Credit Institute or to take the daring step of creating new international money by fiat.

The other possibility is for all countries to devalue in terms of gold simultaneously and in the same proportion, maintaining exchange rates and creating gold profits that would be available for spending.[59] When the spending occurred, prices would rise. They might even reverse direction and start upward in expectation of increased spending. This idea had been expressed. Feis had written a

58. Feis records a view of Keynes's that the gold bloc sees no virtue in a rising price level, putting their faith in a revival of confidence that is to come somehow by itself through businessmen gradually deciding that the world is safe for them (1933, p. 236).

59. This is presumably what Jacobsson meant when he approved of Roosevelt's devaluation but suggested that it would have been advantageous if it had occurred in 1931, two years earlier (Per Jacobsson, *Some Monetary Problems, International and National*, 1958, pp. 117, 124). But the text is not altogether clear. On p. 118 he states that other means to raise prices than depreciation were not available. But Britain and the United States could not depreciate simultaneously against one another's currencies—only against gold. If all countries had depreciated against gold, with exchange rates unchanged, there would have been no lift to prices from the exchanges, and prices would have been raised, if at all, only from the spending of profits on gold reserves and enlarged gold production.

memorandum to this effect on March 3.[60] The Lippmann-Keynes discussion of a new currency encompassed the outlines of a program for general devaluation. But there was almost no possibility of getting opinion to understand and agree on such a program, especially since there would be much objection that it was highly inflationary.

In no event is it likely that world economic recovery could have been accomplished by truces in the fields of tariffs and exchange depreciation.

If a simultaneous depreciation of the world's major currencies in terms of gold with the profit spent might raise prices, what of a seriatim depreciation of one currency followed by another, with the pattern of exchange rates restored at the end of the process?[61] This is by no means the same thing. It was noted earlier that depreciation in a single country can leave world prices unchanged and raise domestic prices, leave domestic prices unchanged and depress world (gold) prices, or partly raise domestic and lower world prices. Successive depreciations that ultimately restore the original set of exchange rates thus have the possibility of being either inflationary or deflationary on balance. In the 1930s the successive depreciations by Britain and the sterling area, Japan, Canada, and so on, operated like a ratchet to lower world prices on balance, just as the system of floating rates in the 1970s, with overshooting first in one direction, then in the other, produced an inflationary ratchet. Some part of the difference may turn on domestic macroeconomic policies in the depreciating countries. In the 1930s Britain, Sweden, and other countries applied the brakes as they abandoned the gold standard; in the 1970s most of the depreciations occurred in countries suffering from overheating. But world conditions count too. In a world poised

60. Feis, *1933*, p. 119. Feis also records that he wrote a memorandum in May 1932, when the first discussions took place between Hoover and MacDonald about a world economic conference, suggesting that all the main currencies be devalued as a preliminary to stabilization (p. 113). The proposal was disliked by Ogden Mills and so was not put forward as a suggestion to the British. It is not clear from his account, however, whether Feis implied, in 1932 as in 1933, devaluation in gold but no stimulus for any country from lower exchange rates. Or perhaps he wanted the pound sterling rate to be returned from $3.675 in May 1932 back to $4.86.

61. Sidney E. Rolfe and James L. Burtle insist that the successive devaluations from 1931 to 1936 did not restore the old pattern of exchange rates (*The Great Wheel: The World Monetary System*, 1973).

on the edge of deflation, depreciation is deflationary for the countries whose currencies rise in value. In a seller's world market, on the contrary, exchange depreciation is inflationary for the country that undertakes it. The confidence of many economists that exchange rate floating is the cure for balance-of-payments difficulties, with little or no macroeconomic impact at home or abroad, seems badly misplaced.

What is still baffling today is why the depreciation of sterling and the yen were strongly deflationary for gold prices in 1931, especially for the gold bloc, the United States, and Germany, while the depreciation of the dollar in 1933 raised prices in the United States but did not depress them abroad. It is sometimes said that the U.S. going off gold was deflationary for the gold bloc.[62] The judgment is not supported by the evidence. Table 19 shows French prices declining in 1931 and 1932 under the impact of sterling depreciation, but holding steady when the dollar was devalued in 1933.

That devaluation did not push world prices lower is possibly the result of a sea change in expectations in the United States, not to mention the fact that gross investment was already approaching zero and could not go lower. When the gold bloc finally devalued in 1935 and 1936, general all-around devaluation had taken place—a slow and painful process. The U.S. devaluation, inept and graceless as it was, can be regarded as useful, in the absence of intellectual and political readiness to move by more efficient methods to general expansion.

But this is serendipity. Surely the Roosevelt policy was clumsy in letting the World Economic Conference go forward and then killing it in what appeared to be a vindictive way, citing the purchasing power of generations while reacting to the fall in market prices of a few days. Morgenthau's defense is puerile:

> Compared to what Roosevelt might have done in setting a $40 price for gold, printing $3 billion in paperbacks, remonetizing silver, the gold-buying program was modest. European countries resented the policy, but no nation had for several years

---

62. See for example, Gottfried Haberler, "Die Weltwirtschaft und das internationale Währungssystem in der Zeit zwischen den beiden Weltkriegen," 1976, p. 220. This essay has been published in English by the American Enterprise Institute and is in course of republication, along with another Haberler work on the Great Depression, in *Selected Essays of Gottfried Haberler*, 1985.

TABLE 19
SELECTED FRENCH EXCHANGE RATES AND COMMODITY
PRICES (*July 1931–December 1933*)

	Exchange Rates (monthly averages)	Wholesale Prices (126 commodities) (1913 = 100)
1931	Sterling Rate (in francs per pound)	
July	123.89	500
August	123.93	488
September	115.42	473
October	99.67	457
November	94.73	447
December	85.83	442
1932	Sterling Rate (in francs per pound)	
January	87.36	439
February	87.30	446
March	92.12	444
April	95.18	439
May	93.16	438
June	92.68	425
July	90.62	430
August	88.78	415
September	88.59	412
October	88.63	412
November	83.60	413
December	84.00	413
1933	Dollar Rate (in francs per dollar)	
January	25.62	411
February	25.49	403
March	25.40	390
April	24.36	387
May	21.70	383
June	20.77	403
July	18.25	401
August	18.62	397
September	17.23	396
October	17.13	397
November	15.97	402
December	16.31	406

SOURCE: Alfred Sauvy, *Histoire économique de la France entre les deux guerres*, vol. 2: *1931–1939*, 1967, tables IV, ii, p. 489; V 4, p. 496.

shown much regard for the economic convenience of others, and in 1933 the pressure on the President was such that he had to do something.[63]

The Democratic administration was prepared to experiment until it achieved recovery on the home front. It had little interest in or knowledge of the world economy, and it lacked confidence in facing it. The memoirs are full of hesitations in dealing with the British: "Every time we take the British into our confidence, they give us a trimming."[64] Moley characterized the U.S. delegations to the World Economic Conference as "Untrained and unbriefed ... pitted against foreigners who knew what they wanted."[65] Pierrepont Moffat reported that the President wondered whether his July 3 message had been too strong; but he did not regret it. "It counteracts an impression widespread throughout the country that at every conference we come out a loser."[66]

It would be three years before the administration felt a responsibility for the operation of the international economic system.

63. Blum, *From the Morgenthau Diaries*, vol. 1, p. 75.

64. Ibid., p. 71; see also p. 141: President Roosevelt said, "The trouble is that when you sit around the table with a Britisher he usually gets 80 percent of the deal and you get what's left."

65. Moley, *The First New Deal*, p. 432.

66. Feis, *1933*, pp. 246–47.

10

The Beginnings
of Recovery

World economy in disarray

The upturn from the depth of the depression began in 1933, but it
was neither widespread nor rapid. In particular, the world economy
lost its cohesion.[1] The gold bloc sank still further into depression.
Germany and Italy of the Axis pursued independent economic
paths, cut off from the world economy by a system of controls. On
the other side of the world, Japan was recovering on its own with
speed and verve. The British Commonwealth, together with a number of other countries linked to sterling, proceeded, turning inward
along its own recovery path. In the United States and Canada recovery was under way, but unevenly and, on balance, slowly. The world
capital market was moribund. Debt service for less developed countries was heavy. Default spread.

But the turn had been made. Outside the gold bloc, 1934 and
1935 saw increases in prices, exports, industrial production, and
national income. The largest part of this improvement came in
1934, after some recovery but also much uncertainty the previous
year. In 1935 the movement slowed to barely perceptible gains.

There were, of course, more exceptions than the gold bloc. The

1. A German economist, expatriated in Switzerland, wrote of "international economic disintegration." See Wilhelm Röpke's book of that title, 1942.

most notable was the foreign trade of the Soviet Union, which found more and more difficulty in exporting to European countries with foreign exchange control and was obliged in consequence to squeeze down imports in 1934 and 1935 one-third below the 1932 low level.

Recovery in the United States

The position of the United States was significant for the world economy and illustrated the unevenness of the pattern. The rapid rise in industrial production from 59 in March 1933 (on the basis of 1923–25 as 100) to 100 in July was not sustained. Based on inventory accumulation rather than long-term investment, with excess capacity in many lines of activity, it fell to 71 in July 1934, well below the peak of the previous year but at the same time off the depression bottom. From this level it worked its way to 90 in July 1935 and to 100 by the end of the year. The movement in prices was broadly similar but dampened: from 63 in March 1933 (1929 = 100) to 74 in July, off again to 71, and then back to 75 in 1934 and 76.5 in 1935. Unemployment declined on one measure from more than 25 percent of trade union membership to less than 17 percent, but the American Federation of Labor estimate of the number of unemployed went down only from an average 13.7 million in 1933 to 12.4 million in 1934 and 12 million in 1935. The Agricultural Adjustment Act and the National Recovery Act (NRA) were declared unconstitutional by the Supreme Court, and spending for relief under the Works Progress Administration increased. Fiscal measures to expand employment were limited, however, since the Democratic administration under President Roosevelt remained committed to balanced budgets.

NRA left a strong imprint on the country, however, in its effect on union membership. Since NRA suspended antitrust action against industrialists, it was felt necessary also to allow workers to combine as a means of promoting industrial peace. Union membership rose from under 3 million in 1933 to 3.6 million in 1934 and 3.9 million in 1935. The Committee for Industrial Organization (CIO) split off from the American Federation of Labor (AFL) to organize along industrial and across traditional craft lines. Among its leaders were John L. Lewis of the United Mine Workers, Walter Reuther of the United Automobile Workers, and Sidney Hillman

and David Dubinsky of the needle trades. Labor and antilabor violence followed in a variety of strikes in 1934 and 1935, which the
National Labor Board and its 1934 successor, the National Labor
Relations Board, sought ineffectively to contain. Sit-in strikes in
automobile plants in Detroit added a new technique to the show of
force in industrial and subsequently other types of disagreement. In
1935, after NRA had been declared unconstitutional, the National
Labor Relations Act reenacted the labor provisions of NRA to apply
in interstate commerce. Parallel state laws in a number of jurisdic-
tions extended the coverage to intrastate activity.

The National Labor Relations Act, considered by the Supreme
Court to be constitutional in early 1937 following President Roosevelt's attack on the court at the end of 1936, was a signal to labor to
extend its membership and its aggressive bargaining tactics. It
marked the arrival of what was later called a "laboristic" economy
in the United States and stimulated fears of inflation from higher
wages, which led, in 1936 and early 1937, to industrial orders to
build up inventories before prices rose too far. We return to this
experience in Chapter 12.

In the relations of the United States to the world economy, the
stabilization of the dollar in February 1934 has already been noted.
This seems to have been less part of a positive design for foreign
economic policy than an attempt to bury an experiment (judged to
have failed) to raise prices by changing the price of gold. President
Roosevelt seems to have been reluctant to admit the failure, although he was clearly relieved to turn from it to domestic policy
concerns.[2]

The monetary experiment with silver was continued longer. Domestic purchases had begun under the Thomas amendment, and the
only agreement to emerge from the World Economic Conference in
December 1933 extended them to the world. The price was set at
64.64 cents, or half the $1.29 price, which was one-sixteenth of
$20.67, the March 1933 price of gold. It was 19 cents above the

---

2. See Blum, *From the Morgenthau Diaries*, vol. 1, p. 132. Roosevelt was not
opposed to de facto stabilization, but he was not excited by it either. Morgenthau
also records (p. 126) that Roosevelt contemplated changing the price of gold in January 1935, when the Supreme Court considered the gold clause case. Such a change
would, according to Morgenthau, have been for political, not economic, reasons.
The same source records that Roosevelt in August 1935 suggested changing the gold
price, "partly in fun, partly to test him [Morgenthau]."

market. In the eyes of the silver bloc, it was not high enough. The price of gold had been raised substantially, and in February 1934 it was set at $35 an ounce. The bloc turned up the pressure. In June 1934 President Roosevelt submitted to Congress a bill, quickly passed, to buy silver at home and abroad until the price reached $1.29 or until silver, valued at $1.29, amounted to a quarter of the government's monetary reserve.

Silver purchases abroad provide a brilliant example of world economic irresponsibility on the part of the United States. Chapter 5 of the Morgenthau diaries records how Roosevelt and Morgenthau embarked on the policy of appeasing the silver bloc at the cost of monetary disorders to Mexico and China, both being countries that based their currencies on silver and found their money supply drained as the price of silver rose. Morgenthau's initial reaction was to blame the Mexicans and Chinese for creating difficulties, for failure to guard their currency system, or for their standards of personal and public morality.[3] In due course he became indignant at the action of "speculators" who sold them silver at the high prices the Treasury set, and he set out at the end of 1935 with high moral resolve to drive the price of silver down again. "All in all, the silver program was a fiasco."[4] But it was more: it represented a beggar-thy-neighbor policy, where the hurt to the neighbor was wanton and provided no domestic economic and little political benefit.[5]

The Reciprocal Trade Agreement Act of 1934 was the very opposite: an act of piety in which the Roosevelt administration had little faith but which it undertook out of tradition and to appease the secretary of state, Cordell Hull. During the political campaign Roosevelt had paid little heed to the issue, though he had condemned the Smoot-Hawley tariff. When Hoover accused him of plans to reduce tariffs on agricultural products and plunge the

3. Ibid., pp. 204, 209. Morgenthau said (p. 202) that he wanted to help Mexico but that he was concerned for his own country. At another stage he told the protesting Chinese that they should complain to the Congressmen who wrote the law (p. 207).

4. Broadus Mitchell, *Depression Decade: From New Era Through New Deal, 1929–1941*, 1947, p. 150.

5. Some unintended benefit may have accrued to India, which, after importing silver for hoarding for almost a hundred years, turned to exporting it at the higher price. Estimated imports from 1874 to 1932 amounted to 2.9 billion ounces. No estimates are available for the subsequent exports, since most of it was smuggled abroad at a rate believed to run roughly between 20 and 25 million ounces a year. See *Green's Commodity Market Comments*, October 21, 1970.

farmer still deeper into depression, he provided assurance that he would not. Hull, however, was "almost fanatical" in his dedication to lower tariffs. Ernest Lindley said he had only one formula.[6] After returning from the World Economic Conference, he four times took to cabinet meetings proposals for tariff reductions, but once there he mumbled his views and did nothing more when they were ignored.[7] In due course, though, a proposal for reducing tariffs by executive agreement on a reciprocal basis was sent to Congress, and it was enacted into law. Hull's "rambling, lisping speeches on the evils of protection," as Tugwell characterized them, ultimately produced the legislation that started the reversal of fifty years of rising protection, the last three of them at an unprecedented rate. It is characteristic of the chaos of Roosevelt's administration that the president decided in favor of a trade agreements program in November 1933 but appointed George Peek, an agricultural restrictionist, to be chairman of the Executive Committee on Commercial Policy, which was charged with drafting the bill. A draft was completed under the leadership of the State Department in February 1934 and approved by the president at the end of the month. It passed the House on March 20 and the Senate on June 4, despite its provision for negotiation by executive agreement, which did not have to be ratified by the Senate, instead of trade treaties, which did. It was signed into law on June 12.[8]

The comparison and contrast are with the repeal of the Corn Laws in Britain in 1846. The fundamental cause for the change in commercial policy was in each case a change in the structure of the economy and the rise to political dominance of the group that benefited from lower tariffs: manufacturers in Britain and mass production in the United States—that is, Manchester and Detroit, respectively. In the United States, however, there was no Cobden or Bright to articulate the interest of the dominant group. On the contrary, the Republican party of the northern manufacturers went ahead with two tariff increases in 1921 and 1930, after much of its clientele had changed from import-competing to exporting in the First World War; and the spokesmen for lower tariffs were the Democrats from the agrarian South, which was on the verge of becoming industrialized and a potential beneficiary from protection. Nor was there a

6. Moley, *The First New Deal*, pp. 90, 92.
7. Feis, *1933*, p. 262.
8. *The Memoirs of Cordell Hull*, vol. 1, 1948, pp. 353–57.

causa proxima like the potato famine of 1845. The Reciprocal Trade Agreements Act of 1934 was sold on the basis of employment, although there is a theoretical basis for believing that a balanced increase in exports and imports—the one capital-intensive, and the other labor-intensive—would increase unemployment. The action was tentative and required execution under safeguards in separate negotiations with foreign countries. It remains a tribute to a statesman with a one-track mind with whom history has not in other respects dealt generously.

Support for the Reciprocal Trade Agreements Act came especially from U.S. traditional opposition to preferences and concern that the Ottawa Agreements might isolate the country and lose British markets to Commonwealth farmers and jobs to American firms that had established plants in Canada to come within the preference system. By the end of 1937, sixteen agreements covering a third of American foreign trade had been negotiated. The act was renewed in 1937, in 1940, and again on frequent occasions after the Second World War. The 1934 act, at the faint beginnings of recovery, remains a remarkable and unpredictable step reversing the direction of movement in the world economy.

Much of the tariff reduction under the program consisted in the lowering of redundant or ineffective duties. Half the early agreements under its authority were with Latin American countries, most of whose exports to the United States consisted of duty-free tropical products and raw materials. Other early agreements were with countries of highly specialized manufactured exports that were not directly competitive with U.S. manufactures—Finland, Sweden, and to a lesser extent, Switzerland. There were, however, major accomplishments: two agreements with Canada, in 1935 and again in 1938, and in the latter connection, a far-reaching agreement with the United Kingdom in 1938, which went some way toward reversing the inward-turning policies of the Commonwealth.[9]

Attempts were made at negotiation with Spain and Italy, though

9. By the outbreak of war, twenty agreements in all had been concluded, reducing the nominal unweighted (equal weights) average of U.S. ad valorem duties on dutiable products from 52 percent in the Smoot-Hawley schedule to 35 percent. This was below the Payne-Aldrich (1909) average of 40.8 percent and the Fordney-McCumber (1921) level of 38.5 percent, but still above the 1913 Underwood average of 27 percent. See Carl Kreider, *The Anglo-American Trade Agreement: A Study of British and American Commercial Policies, 1934–39,* 1943, pp. 170ff.

without success. Not even attempts were undertaken with Japan and Germany. A trade agreement with the Soviet Union in 1935, exchanging most-favored treatment for promises to purchase U.S. products up to a given amount, carried forward the Roosevelt policy of economic intercourse that had begun with diplomatic recognition in 1933. It was an empty gesture.

In addition to these actions, negative and positive, there was a movement away from involvement in world affairs, a ritualistic locking of the barn door after the horse was stolen. The Johnson Act of 1934, named after Senator Hiram Johnson, an isolationist from California, denied the right of countries that had defaulted on their war debts to borrow in U.S. markets. In August 1935, as Mussolini prepared to invade Ethiopia, Congress passed the Neutrality Act forbidding the shipment of arms to either aggressor or victim. The legislation was strengthened after the outbreak of the Spanish Civil War a year later. "The Unbrave New World"[10] was afraid of contamination by the Old.

The Axis countries

Hitler's accession to full power in March 1933 was a forecast of far-reaching changes in the German economic system. In Munich in 1920, the National Socialist party had laid down a list of twenty-five points, largely economic and social, directed against capitalism, "interest slavery," and the like and in favor of colonies, land reform, pensions for old people, and the development of the middle class through assistance to shopkeepers. A four-year plan announced in the spring of 1933 promised the rescue of the peasant and the worker, the latter by an attack on unemployment. Agriculture was to be reformed through the establishment of the *Reichsnährstand* (Food Estate), which controlled prices and then production. Unemployment was attacked through conscription (in March 1935), the development of parastatal bodies, such as the storm troopers and the SA, and especially in spending on public works and armaments. But the anticapitalism of the initial stages did not survive for long. The purge of June 30, 1934, was not economic in origin, but it nonetheless had the effect of moving party doctrine in a more conservative direction in respect of income distribution, if

10. An expression of Vansittart's; see *The Mist Procession*, p. 467.

not of control of industry. Control was provided by the law of February 27, 1934—"Gesetz zur Vorbereitung des organischen Aufbaus der deutschen Wirtschaft" (Law for the Preparation of the Organic Constitution of the German Economy)—which laid out a crisscross pattern of industrial and regional *Überwachungsstellen* (Control Offices). Initially, these Control Offices regulated imports on the basis of goods quantities, but this task was eventually turned over to the Reichsbank and operated through foreign exchange controls.

On May 2, 1933, the SS seized all offices of trade unions in Germany; officials were arrested, and union property was confiscated. The property was incorporated into the Nazi-controlled *Deutsche Arbeitsfront* (German Labor Front), which included entrepreneurs and professionals as well as workers. Wages and working conditions were regulated by *Treuhänder der Arbeit* (Labor Trustees) appointed for each district. The German Labor Front included Social Honor Courts to deal with abuses by employers or agitation by workers; and *Kraft durch Freude* ("Strength through Joy"), which organized workers and youth in holidays through taxes on workers' salaries. In particular, workers were required to carry a work book by which both their jobs and movements were controlled.[11]

Since an early task was to eliminate unemployment, the National Labor Service was established for a variety of projects ranging from agriculture, reclamation, road construction, and ultimately, military installations. It was made compulsory in June 1935. Industrial workers who had agricultural training were dismissed and sent back to farms. All labor was frozen in National Labor Service jobs in 1934. A campaign was undertaken to drive women from gainful employment and back to the hearth. These efforts, it was later thought, prevented Germany from undertaking full mobilization after 1938 and during the Second World War.[12]

Hjalmar Schacht fought hard to prevent deficit financing from rising above a dangerous level until 1938, when he resigned. But spending for public works, including autobahns, was undertaken through special paper discounted by banks. The effect was rapidly to reduce unemployment from 6 million in October 1933 to 4.1 million a year later, 2.8 million in February 1935, 2.5 million in Feb-

11. Stolper, *German Economy, 1870–1940*, part 5.
12. Edward L. Homze, *Foreign Labor in Nazi Germany*, 1967, pp. 7ff. See also Burton H. Klein, *Germany's Economic Preparations for War*, 1959, pp. 60, 73.

ruary 1936, and 1.2 million in February 1937. At the time the Second Four-Year Plan was introduced by Hitler in a speech at Nuremberg in September 1936, and formally in October by Hermann Göring, anti-depression policy was a thing of the past. Women who had received marriage loans were allowed to take jobs. The forty-hour week was ignored, although the forty-eight-hour week did not come in until August 1938. In June 1938 the Compulsory Labor Decree (*Dienstpflichtverordnung*) provided that any inhabitant of the Reich had to accept any work or vocational training assigned to him or her by the Labor Front.

The Second Four-Year Plan also turned policy definitely away from unemployment toward preparation for war. It still contained schemes for public buildings and autobahns, but the emphasis was on providing synthetic industries in rubber, oil, fats, and so on to protect Germany against blockade in time of war.

German foreign trade moved slowly during the period. Clearing and payments arrangements, begun to conserve scarce foreign exchange, were slowly developed into devices for obtaining real resources. The suggestion that Germany bought petroleum, grain, and fattened hogs from southeast Europe in exchange for harmonicas and aspirin is exaggerated, as is the view that Germany used such clearing to manipulate the terms of trade strongly in her favor.[13] It is nevertheless true that Germany's monopsony position as an important market for the goods of southeastern Europe, together with the closing of the markets of France and Britain to these products, meant that these countries were helped by selling their foodstuffs and raw materials to Germany on clearing account and that they were willing to wait some time to get manufactured goods in exchange, often at high prices. German clearing arrangements with Latin America succeeded in bringing back trade almost to the levels of the 1920s. With Western Europe, the Commonwealth, and North America, it remained at a low level, handicapped by the complex clearing arrangements.

The corporate state, undertaken in the February 1934 law, was already far advanced in Italy. Its proximate origin was the Rocco Law on Corporations of April 1926, named after the minister of justice. This established machinery for relations between confeder-

13. See Larry Neal, "The Economics and Finance of Bilateral Clearing Agreements: Germany, 1934–38," 1979.

ations of employers on the one hand and of workers on the other, with the state occupying a position in the middle. Strikes and lock-outs were forbidden, and contracts reached in bargaining were deposited with the Ministry of National Economy.

During the depression, Italy held the lira at a high level but employed tariffs, quotas, prohibitions, and subsidies to stave off the deflationary pressures from abroad through reduced exports and direct price effects via appreciation. The breakdown of mixed banking and the limited profits of Italian industry available for self-financing led the government to create an Istituto Mobiliare Italiano (IMI) in December 1931, which took effect from the beginning of 1932. The task of clearing up the frozen industrial bank loans had been pursued on an ad hoc basis through the crises of 1914, 1921, 1926, and 1929–30. Finally in January 1933, the various securities taken over from the banks by these expedients were assembled in an Istituto per la Ricostruzione Italiana (IRI). Started on a temporary basis, IRI gradually evolved into a new sort of institution in the fields of industrial organization and finance. In its first year it found itself with capital funds of 10.3 billion lire, or 21.5 percent of the nominal capital of Italian firms, and with interests in firms that controlled almost half the capital of the country.[14] By March 1934 IRI was organizing industries into giant concerns that were easy to finance and plan. This was undertaken in shipping, steel, shipbuilding, machinery, and munitions.[15] Since much of Italian industry was conducted in very small firms, especially in the south, the effort at concentration consolidated Italy into a dual economy. In 1936, in a move that had an effect similar to that of the Glass-Steagall Act of 1936, which separated commercial and investment banking in the United States, the Italian authorities outlawed mixed banking, forbidding the so-called ordinary banks from dealing in industrial equity securities.[16]

In October 1935 Mussolini launched his attack on Ethiopia. It proved fateful for the League of Nations, which sought to impose sanctions on the extension of credit to Italy and the provision of raw

14. Toniolo, *L'economia dell' Italia fascista*, pp. 248–49; and by the same author, "Crisi economica e smobilizzo pubblico delle banche miste (1930–34)," esp. pp. 330–48.

15. Clough, *The Economic History of Modern Italy*, p. 249.

16. Sabino Cassese, "Introduzione al dibattio," 1981, pp. 99–103, and Franco Belli, "Le legge bancarie del 1926 e del 1936–38," 1981.

materials or munitions. It has been claimed that the sanctions failed because they were disregarded by the major petroleum companies.[17] Feis's account exonerates the large international oil companies but makes it clear that the high prices for oil generated by the refusal of the business induced hundreds of small business operators to charter tankers and deliver fuel not only to Italy but also to Red Sea ports.[18] The United States was not a member of the league, and it merely asked for the cooperation of American business over sanctions rather than requiring that they be observed. Lacking any strong lead from the United States or Britain, sanctions failed. By May 1936 the Ethiopian forces had been overcome and the league withdrew the sanctions. Their failure contributed to Japanese readiness to invade Manchuria in 1937.

Like Germany, Japan enjoyed uninterrupted expansion in the years 1934–36, with wages steady and prices rising at the rate of world prices. Unlike Germany, however, much of the impetus for the expansion came from the international margin as a result of the undervaluation of the yen. The terms of trade were strongly unfavorable, rather than favorable as was the case with Germany. Japanese internal spending was dominated by military disbursements. When the attempt was made at the end of 1936 to curb them after full employment had been reached so as to prevent inflation, the minister of finance was assassinated by a military fanatic.

United Kingdom

The first major country to surpass its 1929 performance in industrial production was the United Kingdom, which reached 116 in the last quarter of 1934, compared with 114 in the last quarter of 1929 (1924 = 100). The fact reflects partly the efficacy of British recovery under the impact of depreciation and cheap money and partly the weakness of the expansion of the 1920s. Unemployment declined only slowly from 17.6 percent in 1932 to between 12 and 13 percent in 1935. This was highly concentrated in depressed areas specializing in coal, shipbuilding, and cotton textiles. In some of them unemployment rose as high as 50 percent. Recovery was especially strong in motorcars, electrical industry, chemicals, and housing,

17. Clough, *The Economic History of Modern Italy*, p. 254.
18. Herbert Feis, *Seen from E.A.: Three International Episodes*, 1947, pp. 305–8.

and in southern and southwestern England as opposed to Wales, southwest Scotland, Northern Ireland, and the Clyde, Tyne, and Mersey river areas.

A slow movement of population southward and eastward helped to relieve the depressed areas. The Special Areas (Development and Improvement) Act of 1934, amended in 1937, undertook to provide facilities for light industries in the areas and to assist firms settling there. In 1935 the government brought pressure on Richard Thomas to build its new steel strip mill not in Lincolnshire, as economic considerations dictated, but in the depressed area of Ebbw Vale in South Wales.

In addition to the depressed industries and areas and the verve of rising production in mechanical, electrical, and chemical lines, the 1930s in Britain were characterized by a movement away from competition. "Trade associations and price fixing were the rule in British industry between the wars. . . . The limited, exiguous, emasculated, etiolated competition of the 1930s was too little for good economic health ... and ... produced unenterprising habits."[19] This was particularly the case with chemicals, soap, oil, wallpaper, tobacco, and steel. The steel industry had obtained generalized protection in early 1932 and a special rate of 33.33 percent in the spring of that year. The organization of the European steel cartel in 1933, however, led to dumping in the British market, especially of basic Thomas steel. The industry turned to the Import Duties Advisory Committee for an increase in tariff to 50 percent and was able to reach agreement with the European cartel for a limited import quota. By 1937, when the rearmament boom flourished, this quota was exceeded.

But the major economic success of the period was housing under the influence of government assistance, a substantial backlog, migration, lower building costs, cheap money, cheap food, and development of the automobile, which stimulated movement to the suburbs and perhaps a change in spending habits.[20] The boom increased the demand for building materials and household furnishings. As was noted in Chapter 8, the spillover into import demand was the basis for the spectacular recovery in Sweden.

British exports shifted, together with domestic production, from

19. Youngson, *The British Economy, 1920–57*, pp. 133, 134.
20. See Richardson and Aldcroft, *Building in the British Economy Between the Wars*.

the staple trades—coal, ships, iron and steel, and cotton textiles—to the new industries—electrical equipment, automobiles, chemicals, and so on—which rose from 13.6 percent of total exports in 1929 to 17.6 percent in 1937.[21] The change received little help from long-term lending. Long-term loans for new money from 1931 to 1938 amounted to an annual average of £33 million, as compared with £117 million from 1924 to 1930, during much of which capital lending was restricted. A complete embargo on foreign loans was applied in June 1932. Shortly after the success of the war loan conversion, the embargo was relaxed to permit domestic and empire conversions, and in October 1932 it was still further dismantled to apply only to new issues for borrowers outside the empire. In July 1934, sterling countries were encouraged to borrow for adding to reserves or for imports from Britain. The stimulus thus afforded to exports was limited. The Export Credit Guarantees Department, begun immediately after the war but reorganized thoroughly in 1928, was twice expanded from its original limit of £25 million, reaching £75 million in 1938. The terms under which export credits were guaranteed or loans provided were improved through lowering rates and extending the period. But amounts were small—no more than £10 million a year.

Less developed countries

Within the British Commonwealth, economic recovery was assisted by the rise of prices in 1933 and 1934, especially in those countries that had depreciated against sterling. On a 1929 base, Australia and New Zealand, respectively, had reached the 80s and 95 by 1935. With the help of the sizable increase in the price of gold and expansion in output—restrained, however, by a new tax system that encouraged the working of low-grade ore—prices in the Union of South Africa also reached the 80s. The recovery in British India prices was much less extensive—from 58 in March 1933 to 65 in 1935 and 1936. The performance in the Netherlands East Indies, which remained tied to the gold bloc through the Dutch guilder, was still worse. From a price level of 49.6 in March 1933 (on the basis of 1929 = 100), the index declined slowly to 46 in 1935 and 44 in 1936, despite the recovery in world prices.

21. A. E. Kahn, *Great Britain in the World Economy*, 1946, table 8, p. 109.

The Latin American experience was varied, dependent on a number of factors: the "commodity lottery," the extent of exchange depreciation, whether or not the balance of payments had been relieved by default on foreign debt, the extent to which import substitution policies had gotten a start in the First World War and were furthered by active policies, the extent of new foreign direct investment, and the like. In Central America, for example, in a trend that began as early as 1926 and lasted into the 1930s, bananas did comparatively well in price, helped by a fall in volume due to plant disease, but coffee did badly.[22] In Argentina, despite the fact that both beef and wheat were marketed by concentrated export houses in Buenos Aires, which were almost exclusively foreign-owned, wheat did badly because of lack of storage space, and beef did well. The Roca-Runciman agreement negotiated with Britain forced Argentina to spend its sterling for debt service instead of imports. Later in the decade, however, it was helped by the 1936 and 1938 droughts in the United States, which opened up the U.S. market to Argentine corn. Wheat difficulties led through market processes to new agricultural products for the domestic market—sunflower seed, cotton, peanuts—a sort of export-substitution that grew in output at 30 percent per year, compared with 5 percent for exported agricultural staples.[23]

Cuba, in sugar, and Chile, in copper, were not too badly off, since a portion of their gross loss in income was offset by a decline in payments to foreign investors in those products. Having made a start in import substitution during the First World War, Brazil was further along than Argentina in reducing dependence on foreign markets, and it was in a strong position to continue the process during the Second World War.[24] Mexico suffered from the early decline in silver prices, but in the end it benefited from the substantial seignorage it earned by coining its own silver and, after reorganization of the Banco de México in 1936, by keeping its paper notes in circulation.[25]

22. Victor Bulmer-Thomas, "The Central American Economies in the Interwar Period," 1984.

23. O'Connell, "Argentina into the Depression." See also Albert Fishlow, "Origins and Consequences of Import Substitution in Brazil," 1972.

24. Flavio Rabelo Versiani, "Brazilian Industrial Growth: The 1920s and the Depression," 1984.

25. E. V. K. Fitzgerald, "Restructuring in a Crisis: The Mexican Economy and the Great Depression," 1984.

The depression years were a period of stress and change in Latin America: revolutions were pandemic; new crops and new industries sprang up continuously. In due course governments abandoned what had been essentially a passive response to economic events abroad and explored the possibilities of directing their own economies. But the experiences of separate countries were far from uniform, and generalization about Latin America as a whole is fraught with danger. While discussion of Latin American economic dependence became popular after the Second World War, a case can be made that following its beginnings in the First World War, independence made great strides during the depression.[26]

As Figure 2 shows, beginnings were made in this period in getting burdensome commodity stocks reduced in general, especially in tin, wheat, cotton, silk, and sugar. This was only to a slight extent accomplished through actual reductions in production. In raw materials, increased business activity led to increases in demand. In foodstuffs, population growth and increased incomes helped. In both groups attempts were made at international commodity agreements, which functioned for a time in wheat, sugar, rubber, tin, and cotton but were not sustained.

On the whole, however, with one or two exceptions, such as the Union of South Africa, the less developed countries had a difficult time in the 1930s. Unable to borrow to sustain their investment programs and with heavy burdens in debt service from low prices in gold currencies and sterling, their balances of payments remained under pressure. Foreign exchange controls and depreciation persisted, and tariffs remained high, despite the attempt by the United States to bargain them down under the Reciprocal Trade Agreements Act. In many parts of Africa and Asia the depreciation of the yen and the pushing of Japanese textile and other exports led to specific import controls to protect simple industry and to safeguard the traditional markets of metropolitan Britain and France. Recovery was hesitant, limited, and unsatisfactory.

Like the Axis, the Soviet Union went its own way, largely cut off from the world economy, pursuing the collectivization of agriculture and the construction of heavy industry and importing to build autar-

26. See Rosemary Thorp, "Introduction," 1984; Díaz Alejandro, "Latin America in the Depression, 1929–1939," and ibid., "Latin America in the 1930s." Díaz Alejandro divides the Latin American countries into the passive and the reactive and asserts that the latter did better economically than the former.

chy and freedom of dependence on raw material imports. The motive was partly military defense and partly the protection of socialism against contagion from world depression. Soviet trade statistics are kept on an arbitrary basis, but they show declining exports going from a monthly average of 180 million new (1935) rubles in 1932 (compared with 296 million at the peak in 1930) downward each year to 75 million in the early months of 1936. The change from old to new rubles in the latter year had no effect on trade, which is conducted on a negotiated basis in foreign prices. Expanded diplomatic and commercial relations with the West led to a rapid increase in recorded export trade after the middle of 1936.

In short, world recovery in 1934 and 1935 was limited and fragmented. It excluded the gold bloc.

11

The Gold Bloc
Yields

The gold bloc

The gold bloc began to take shape at the time of the depreciation of
sterling, when the central banks of Belgium, France, and the Netherlands all suffered exchange losses. It was formally constituted in
a meeting of July 3, 1933, when President Roosevelt's letter denouncing stabilization of the dollar effectively broke up the World
Economic Conference. It had little cohesion and no organization.
Some basis of tradition went back to the Latin Monetary Union of
1865, when the French, Belgian, and Swiss francs were equiva-
lents. This had been broken up by the First World War and the varying degrees of inflation and depreciation that followed. The Dutch
and Swiss clung to gold at the old parity as an act of faith.[1] Having
devalued by large amounts during the 1920s at substantial cost to
the rentier classes, France and Belgium were determined to resist
inflation. It was not clear whether Italy was a member or not.

For five years prior to 1931 France, the leader of the gold bloc,

1. But see G. M. Verrijn Stuart, "The Netherlands During the Recent Depression," 1937, p. 249: "Until then [June 1933] I still hoped that some form of international understanding might lead to putting into effect a policy of 'reflation within
gold.' The deplorable results shown by the London Economic and Financial Conference in the first month convinced me that the only way for the Netherlands to escape
from the difficulties was to give up the gold base of the guilder and devalue."

had been an independent monetary force. Its large gold reserves, buoyant trade, and budgetary surpluses had made it impervious to the troubles that affected Germany, Britain, and even the United States. But 1931 and especially 1933 changed all that. As the world broke up into sterling, dollar, blocked-currency, and gold blocs, it was the last which went on the defensive, embracing the difficult and, as it proved, impossible task of deflating to maintain its trade balance and its gold reserves.

Deflation as a cure for disequilibrium

If recent history would not permit depreciation and pride forbade exchange control (except in the case of Italy), the remaining remedy was deflation. Sauvy chooses to illustrate the overvaluation of the franc by retail prices in France and Britain, adjusted to an overvaluation of 22 percent in February 1935, as shown in Figure 12.[2] The peak of overvaluation was reached in February 1934 at 26 percent. The pressure on French exports was severe. Monthly average exports declined from 3.6 billion Poincaré francs in 1930 to 1.5 billion in 1932 and 1.3 billion in 1935. Average monthly imports for the same period went from 4.4 billion francs to 2.5 billion and 1.7 billion. The declines from 1932 to 1935 occurred despite the expansion of world trade. French exports of textiles, clothing, and leather goods were hit more sharply than iron and steel or motor vehicles. Consumer categories suffered more from tariff and quota restrictions. But the price disadvantage was severe, since it proved impossible to reduce costs and prices to make up for the appreciation of the currency.

The patterns of attempts to deflate were similar. As prices declined, wholesale prices falling from 462 in 1931 to 407 in 1932, 388 in 1933, 366 in 1934, and 347 in 1935 (July 1914 = 100), successive governments would try to balance the budget by cutting expenditure, especially by reducing payments to pensioners and veterans and the wages of government employees. These efforts were strongly opposed. Pensioners, veterans, and functionaries experi-

2. See Alfred Sauvy, *Histoire économique de la France entre les deux guerres*, vol. 2: *1931–1939*, 1967, pp. 400–401, 508–9. Sauvy is aware of the theoretical and practical difficulties of accurate measures of overvaluation and undervaluation of the exchange rate. The account given in this chapter relies heavily on Sauvy's detailed history of France in the 1930s.

Figure 12. Relationship between French and English prices, 1930–39.

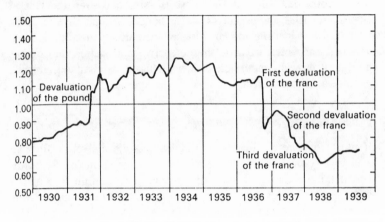

	1931	1932	1933	1934	1935	1936	1937	1938	1939
January	0·86	1·13	1·15	1·22	1·21	1·12	0·95	0·77	0·71
February	0·87	1·13	1·16	1·26	1·22	1·12	0·96	0·75	0·72
March	0·88	1·05	1·15	1·25	1·23	1·14	0·97	0·73	0·72
April	0·88	1·10	1·17	1·25	1·21	1·14	0·94	0·72	0·72
May	0·89	1·09	1·16	1·24	1·16	1·13	0·93	0·67	0·72
June	0·87	1·10	1·13	1·22	1·13	1·12	0·93	0·66	0·71
July	0·87	1·14	1·15	1·22	1·12	1·13	0·79	0·66	0·72
August	0·86	1·17	1·19	1·23	1·12	1·16	0·80	0·66	0·73
September	1·07	1·14	1·23	1·22	1·11	1·15	0·76	0·68	
October	1·04	1·20	1·20	1·19	1·10	0·86	0·73	0·68	
November	1·14	1·21	1·15	1·19	1·10	0·90	0·74	0·69	
December	1·18	1·18	1·17	1·20	1·12	0·92	0·75	0·71	
Average	0·93	1·13	1·16	1·22	1·15	1·07	0·85	0.70	0·73

SOURCE: Alfred Sauvy, *Histoire économique de la France entre les deux guerres*, vol. 2, 1967, p. 401.

enced money illusion and regarded their incomes as determined by the money amounts received, taking no account of the decline in prices. Or those who understood that they had gained in real income through falling prices despite fixed incomes in francs were unwilling to share with their less fortunate compatriots. The social cement in the system was crumbling. From 1930 to 1935, disposable income declined from 331 billion francs to 221 billion in money terms, but only to 291 billion in real terms—13 percent real instead of 33 percent nominal.[3] Pensioners' real income increased 46 percent, that of government employees 18.9 percent and of weekly occupied workers 18.5 percent (more in certain industries, such as coal). Landlords' real income went up 11.5 percent. The main burden fell on the unemployed and on agriculture. The unemployed never reached very large numbers, amounting only to 500,000 receiving assistance in February 1935 on a rather restricted definition. This was perhaps because a million Polish, Italian, and Algerian workers had left France or been rounded up and deported. In addition, many workers left the city for the farm, where, despite the decline in income—amounting to almost 32 percent—it was possible to sleep and eat.[4] The reversal of the normal movement from countryside to city occurred widely in the world during the depression, especially in the United States. An analogous return to familiar surroundings took place in net return migration from the Commonwealth to Britain.

The minister of finance would propose expenditure cuts and occasionally new taxes. Sometimes these would pass. More often the government would fall. In 1932 and 1934 there were four governments; in 1933 three. In June 1935 Laval undertook to produce deflation by decree, as Brüning had in Germany four years before. He issued decrees in three groups in July, August, and October.

Malthusianism

Apart from the attempts to reduce wages and pensions by decree, French governments up to 1935 were obliged to worry about agriculture. For the most part, they followed policies which French economists described as "Malthusian." This term is unfair to the memory of Thomas Malthus, known elsewhere for his law of population and his pioneering insight into macroeconomic analysis. In the French context, Malthusian policies are those of raising prices by restriction, prohibition, subsidy, minimum prices, or other interference in the market process. The French revival of the ancient practice of prohibitions and quotas instead of tariffs, to make sure of cutting off imports, was Malthusian, as was the establishment of

3. Ibid., p. 575.
4. Ibid., pp. 133, 135, 137.

minimum prices for wheat and wine above the market clearing
level, leading to black markets in these two commodities. Steps to
retire married women from the labor market and to lower the retirement age for men belong in the same category, together with the
prohibition by a new law of a shoe plant projected by the Czech
manufacturer, Bat'a, in March 1936, in an effort to protect the small
shoe manufacturer and retail distribution.[5]

Malthusianism was an ancient tradition in France, which believed
in the decent wage and the just price and after the depreciations of
sterling and the dollar sought to shut itself up by closing down on
imports. Keynesianism, which was detected by Germans in 1931
and broadcast to the world in *The Means to Prosperity* of 1934,
before the *General Theory of Employment, Interest, and Money* of
1936, was not available in France as an alternative to Malthusianism. Since Keynes had shown himself unfriendly to France by writing *The Economic Consequences of the Peace* and had wrecked
French chances of obtaining reparations from Germany, no French
economist would study him until time was to hang heavy on their
hands during the German occupation.[6]

Belgium devalues

While French economists were advocating deflation, opposing both
foreign exchange control and devaluation, Italy defended itself with
controls and Belgium devalued. Italy found itself unable to devalue
because of Mussolini's pride in the currency, and it was unwilling,
with high unemployment, to deflate. With increasing ties to Germany, with which it had clearing arrangements, it gradually defended the international payments position with exchange control.
The Belgian devaluation, which represented a real defection from
the gold bloc, was taken in cold blood.

The contrast is with the British and U.S. depreciations: the one
under pressure, the other offhand or even quixotic, and both highly
casual about the rate. In Belgium the University of Louvain had or-

5. Ibid., p. 372.
6. Pierre Lalumière, *L'inspection des finances*, 1959, pp. 179ff. This is an exaggeration, as there had been French translations published of *A Revision of the Treaty*,
Monetary Reform, and *Essays in Persuasion*. A translation of *The General Theory of
Employment, Interest, and Money* had been arranged in 1938. It was not finally produced, on account of the war, until 1942.

ganized an economics institute, led by Professors Dupriez, Baudhuin, and Paul Van Zeeland and, among research assistants, Robert Triffin. A study of 1933 suggested that the Belgian franc was overvalued by some 25 to 30 percent and that deflation was impossible.[7] In September 1934, Professor Baudhuin took a post with the Treasury and privately advised it to devalue. In March 1935 in a public speech he stated that devaluation was inescapable and the only way to rescue the Belgian economy. This led to an outflow of capital, a government crisis, and a new cabinet, headed by Van Zeeland. On March 29 Van Zeeland sought and obtained emergency powers from the Belgian Parliament, and on April 2 he devalued by 28 percent.[8] Prices bounded up from 54.5 in March to 68 at the end of the year and 75 a year later. Production, exports, and gold stocks of the National Bank of Belgium all recovered. France was not moved.

The Popular Front

French workers demonstrated against the deflationary policies recommended by the experts and put into effect by Laval. Socialists joined with Communists in a Popular Front, and the general trade union merged with the communist labor organization. There were sit-in strikes in shipyards, ports, and truck plants and a general strike in the metals industry in the Paris region. This brought down the Sarrault government, which had taken over from Laval in January. During the course of the unrest, Hitler's army marched into the Rhineland and started its fortification.

The Popular Front had no real economic program. It advocated control of trusts, repression of agricultural speculation, suppression of fraud, elimination of tax evasion, extension of the school-leaving age, respect for pensions and the rights of veterans, maintenance of social security, and especially the repudiation of deflation and the introduction of the forty-hour week. There was no mention of devaluation. The Socialists were prepared to contemplate it, but the Communists were vehemently opposed, stating it as contrary to the workers' interests. The implicit model was not spelled out. If there

7. See Robert Triffin, "La théorie de la surévaluation monétaire et la dévaluation belge," 1937.

8. Sauvy, *Histoire économique de la France entre les deux guerres*, vol. 2, pp. 105–6.

was any program for recovery, it came from a view that the forty-hour week, with no change in pay, would contribute purchasing power sufficient to enable the economy to move upward. There was no provision for coping with the balance of payments or the capital outflow stimulated by the sit-in strikes. It was as if the Popular Front had been dealing with a closed economy. As he took office Blum promised that the country would not wake up one morning and find the hoardings covered with an announcement of devaluation. In his memoirs Auriol, the minister of finance, suggested that foreign exchange control would have suited the temperament of the Popular Front, but that nothing was ready, 30 billion francs in gold had already left, it was necessary to have control of the credit mechanism, and foreign exchange control would have separated France from its western allies. In addition, he wrongly thought that foreign exchange control implied devaluation, which the Communist allies opposed.[9] The opposition to devaluation at the start of the Popular Front has its modern parallel in the decision by the British prime minister, Harold Wilson, not to devalue in the autumn of 1964.

The first step taken by the Popular Front was to force employers to sign the Accord de Matignon guaranteeing wage rises, a three-week annual holiday with pay, and the forty-hour week. Like the decision on devaluation, it has a modern parallel: the Accord de Grenelle of 1968, which raised wages after the disturbances of May and June in the universities and the accompanying general strike. Again like the decision on devaluation, it constituted a poor precedent.

The Accord de Matignon was a humiliation for the employers and a disaster for everyone. Wages were raised by 15 percent for the lowest-paid workers and by 7 percent for the highest, with a 12 percent average being representative of many plants. Holidays with pay and the forty-hour week also raised costs. Wholesale prices rose from 375 (on the 1913 base) in May to 420 in September, and retail prices from 76.4 (base 1930) to 80.5. Exports failed to recover after the strikes. The stock market declined, the capital outflow picked up. Devaluation was forced on France. It was undertaken by agreement with the United States and Britain to prevent retaliation. The significance of the Tripartite Monetary Agreement for the interna-

9. Vincent Auriol, *Hier et aujourd'hui*, 1945, pp. 38–39, quoted by Sauvy, *Histoire économique de la France entre les deux guerres*, vol. 2, p. 200. For doctrinaire Marxist opposition to devaluation in Germany, see above, pp. 161–62.

tional economic system will be discussed presently. For France and the rest of the gold bloc, it provided an international cover for a retreat from an impossible position that had been held for far too long.

After devaluation

In the Netherlands and Switzerland, like Belgium before them, limited devaluations corrected the overvaluation and allowed the economy to snap back into line with the rest of the world economy. Trade in the Netherlands rebounded vigorously, with exports rising from 45 million guilders a month in the first nine months of 1936 to 90 million by June 1937. Swiss recovery was almost as extensive, from 68 million Swiss francs to 123 million in September 1937. The Italians used the occasion to devalue the lira rate, adjust exports and imports upward, and reduce the force of foreign exchange control.

In France, however, the forty-hour week became a symbol of the workers' pride and independence. Serious consideration was given to moving upward to a forty-five-hour week, especially as hours were lengthened in the German armament industry, ultimately going to fifty-four hours a week in aviation. This was rejected. The forty-hour week was extended to coal mines and metallurgical plants, which had originally been exempt.

It proved impossible to restore the trading position or the confidence of the rentier with the forty-hour week, or to quiet the worker without it. In March 1937, 10 billion francs were sought as a loan, with a dollar guarantee. It failed to build confidence on the right. Another crisis of confidence and capital outflow led to gold losses in June. Blum again sought to govern by decree, was refused, and left power; Chautemps took over as premier and Bonnet as minister of finance. They turned the franc loose from the Monetary Law of October 1, 1936, with the result that it again declined below 4 cents. In March 1938 the Chautemps government proposed a modern statute of conditions of work, providing for collective bargaining, conciliation, and arbitration, plus, at the demand of labor, escalation clauses in work contracts. It passed. Chautemps then asked for powers to restore the budget by decree. These were denied. The Chautemps cabinet was followed briefly by a second Blum cabinet. During this period, Hitler proclaimed the *Anschluss* and marched

German troops into Austria. The Blum cabinet fell. Daladier took over, devalued the franc once again in May, and governed by decree. The last of four sets of decrees beginning in November 1938, after Munich, was prepared under the aegis of a new minister of finance, Paul Reynaud, a confirmed liberal. He reversed the trend.

Reynaud killed the five-day week, levied new taxes, adopted budgetary economies, instituted a more liberal regime for prices, credit, and conditions of work. He especially attacked fiscal fraud. With the rate of the franc at 178 to the pound, a new convention between the Finance Ministry and the Bank of France revalued the latter's gold at 170 to the pound, transferring the profit to the ministry. A threatened general strike fizzled out. Six billion francs of capital returned from abroad. Production picked up by leaps and bounds, with a 15 percent rise between November 1938 and the following June. Too late, Reynaud served up a repetition of the economic miracle of Poincaré—one which a number of countries of Europe were to experience after the Second World War.

Sauvy claims that the malaise from 1936 to 1938 was entirely owing to the forty-hour week.[10] The idea was economically Malthusian, despite its positive social roots in the twelve-to-thirteen-hour day of the nineteenth century. It was not perhaps worse than the doctrinaire view of the right on budgets. Sauvy's text is replete with balanced homilies of this kind: "The right reduced expenses, but the deficit formed again; the left reduced the working day, but unemployment came back into existence."[11]

To a certain extent, Sauvy is justifying his opinion at a time when, from a position in the bureaucracy, he vigorously opposed the forty-hour week in the face of opposition from his superiors. A somewhat later observer is disposed to believe that the forty-hour week can be useful as a short-run measure of spreading the work but that it was wrongly applied in a country such as France, where unemployment was not substantial.[12] Within six months of the serious application of the law in September 1936, the economy had brought unemployment down to the amount appropriate for transitional needs. The forty-hour week then proved disastrous, but it was so in conjunction with other French policies of all political colors,

10. Sauvy, *Histoire économique de la France entre les deux guerres*, vol. 2, esp. pp. 209, 297, 305, 334.

11. Ibid., p. 468; see also pp. 253, 269.

12. Arndt, *The Economic Lessons of the 1930s*, p. 147.

especially the refusal to devalue and the insistence on budget balance. Léon Jouhaux noted that the forty-hour week would have had to be internationalized if it was to succeed. Twenty years later, Michel Debré said the same thing about French planning. Idiosyncratic remedies encounter difficulties in a connected world. The essence of the French difficulty, however, lay in the loss of social cohesion. Neither right nor left worked in terms of a national solution, but only in those of its own interest. The right was prepared to strike through tax fraud and capital export if it did not get its way; the left behaved identically with different weapons. Reynaud succeeded, under the rising threat of Germany after Munich, partly because his policies were more liberal but also because he attacked the forty-hour week indirectly by granting exceptions of fifty hours, and later sixty hours, to armament industries and then to the industries supplying them. The principle of the forty-hour week was retained, its use abandoned. It did not survive the war.

The Tripartite Monetary Agreement

Sauvy dismisses the Tripartite Monetary Agreement curtly: the three central banks agreed to nothing.[13] Morgenthau said: "If this goes through it is the greatest move taken toward peace in the world since the World War. . . . It may be the turning point for again resuming [*sic*] rational thinking in Europe."[14] Each view contains a grain of truth. The Tripartite Monetary Agreement committed the major powers to almost nothing, but it constituted a significant step in rebuilding the international economic system.

Neither President Roosevelt nor his secretary of the Treasury, Morgenthau, understood well what they were doing in the international monetary field. Roosevelt kept coming back to his message to the London World Economic Conference, which he thought should be the text and bible of U.S. monetary policy. When asked

13. Sauvy, *Histoire économique de la France entre les deux guerres*, vol. 2, p. 224. Whitehall (the British civil service) in 1936 thought the Tripartite Declarations "an elaborate piece of political obfuscation that allowed Henry Morgenthau, Jr., to parade as a great thinker and world pacifier, and Blum and Auriol to escape from the trap they had constructed for themselves when they promised never to devalue the franc" (Ian M. Drummond, "London, Washington, and the Management of the Franc, 1936–39," 1979, p. 53).

14. Blum, *From the Morgenthau Diaries*, vol. 1, p. 171.

whether he was willing to sell gold to the British against dollars, he started a "long harangue that he thought the United States should have a secret commodity index with which it could manage the dollar."[15] Later he was fearful that the Tripartite Monetary Agreement might be interpreted as a departure from the monetary policy set out at the time of the London conference.[16] Morgenthau's opinions on the dollar veered about in chaotic fashion, if one is to believe his diary and his biographer. At one time he defends devaluation; at another, he states that it did not fail but offered no future benefits. He was not prepared to sacrifice any freedom in monetary policy that domestic developments might require, but he recognized his responsibility for preventing competitive international devaluation and the disorder it would involve. He told the press that American monetary policy was on a twenty-four-hour basis, but he urged stabilization, and when the British responded to his stabilization feeler by saying that it reserved the right to devalue for domestic reasons, he felt encouraged.[17] Lacking any real understanding of the international monetary mechanism, but excited by dabbling in esoteric affairs of state, he overreacted to the unfolding course of events: becoming infuriated at a speculative attack on francs; his blood boiling because the State Department (probably Feis) favored an exchange rate of $4.86; taking the credit for saving France with a $33 million credit in May 1935; becoming shaky at the knees over the draft of the Tripartite Monetary Agreement—a great victory over Feis—because it was so important; and breaking out into a cold sweat over a French suggestion that the American Treasury should run its unconverted French balances up to $5 million or $10 million, saying that it was like kiting a check.[18] The prize example of misunderstanding and overreaction was his denunciation of the Soviet Union for selling £1.2 million in the New York market and driving the rate down from $5.02 until the Treasury stabilized the market at $4.91. This took place on September 26, 1936, a Saturday and a half-day, when London was closed and the New York market thin. The Russians, Morgenthau claimed, were trying to undermine the capitalist system, and he prevented it. The Russians, in turn, indi-

15. Ibid., p. 144.
16. Ibid., p. 168.
17. Ibid., pp. 125, 133, 138, 142.
18. Ibid., pp. 129, 132, 138, 167, 455.

cated that they owed $6 million to Sweden and were only trying to convert pounds to dollars before the market fell, as was likely to happen if the return flow of funds from London to Paris reversed the upward pressure on the pound. Morgenthau claimed that the American Treasury would make a profit on the transaction. When the market opened on Monday at $4.86—the rate the Department of State had advocated—Morgenthau was unable to close out the £900,000 he had bought at $4.91 with a profit. For years thereafter the 0.25 percent handling charge on gold bought and sold was credited to the account to eat up the loss. John Morton Blum contends that the Russians did not need dollars to pay dollars in Stockholm; they could have paid in pounds.[19] The political historian is on dangerous ground in rewriting old exchange contracts. Blum continues: "Or, as Morgenthau contended, they could have waited to convert the pounds until all the money markets were open." But this would have meant a loss of 11 cents, or perhaps up to 16 cents, on each of £1.2 million. Morgenthau's understanding of the intricacies of international finance, and his enthusiasm for them, make trying reading, but the Tripartite Monetary Agreement was nonetheless a milestone.[20]

The agreement provided very little in the way of cooperation. Each treasury, and much was made of the fact that the agreement ran between stabilization funds rather than central banks (though the detail was trivial except in institutional terms), would be prepared to execute support orders for the other and hold the exchange for twenty-four hours, when it could ask for conversion into gold. The United States was ready to make gold available against dollars, and the obverse for Britain and France when they were not on the gold standard. This was a technical facility of some value, relieving Britain, for example, of the need to deal in dollars via the London gold market and of reliance on private arbitrage.

The French gained assurance that the United States and Britain

19. Ibid., p. 176.

20. For an illuminating and detailed account of the negotiations leading to the Tripartite Agreement, see Stephen V. O. Clarke, "Exchange-Rate Stabilization in the Mid-1930s: Negotiating the Tripartite Agreement," 1977, esp. pp. 11–14. Clarke brings out the fact that Roosevelt and Morgenthau had "no very clear idea about the nature of the international monetary system that should replace the gold standard," and he brilliantly illustrates Morgenthau's "abysmal ignorance of the workings of exchange markets" by including a transcript of a telephone conversation between Morgenthau and Merle Cochran, financial secretary of the U.S. embassy in Paris.

would not indulge in competitive exchange depreciation, although the reversal of the capital flow out of Paris inevitably caused some adjustment in the pound rate, which had been allowed to rise when capital was coming out of Paris so as to divert much of the flow to New York and away from the high-priced pound. The French also had an international context in which to undertake a necessary domestic adjustment.[21]

The British did not agree to stabilize the pound. On the contrary, they said they had no intention of so doing.[22] But for the first time since June 1933, exchange rates were discussed, technical arrangements made, and international cooperation built in the monetary area. The agreement was the origin of the ultimate swaps, when the holdings of one another's currency, which in 1937 made Morgenthau break out into a cold sweat because it was like kiting a check, would be undertaken up to billions of dollars at a time.

The idea of central bank cooperation to maintain exchange rates in the face of hot money was not new. In 1933 Jørgen Pedersen, professor of economics at the University of Aarhus in Denmark, put forward the idea in an offhand set of remarks at a study conference of the League of Nations, held in London two weeks before the World Economic Conference:

> It ought to be possible to neutralize the effects of such a movement of [short-term] capital from one country to another—this flight of capital—by a pooling of the resources of the different Banks of Issue. . . .
> If for instance, there had been perfect cooperation between the American Central Banking system, the Bank of France and the Bank of England in 1931, I do not see why Great Britain should have been forced off the Gold Standard at all. Perhaps she intended to be forced off the Gold Standard, in which case

21. This point is made in one of the few documents on the subject in the French diplomatic papers. See *Documents diplomatiques français*, 1968, vol. 3, no. 240, Paris to Washington and London, September 8, 1936, p. 348. The reason, of course, is that the telephone had taken over from the telegraph.

22. Stephen V. O. Clarke analyzes the views of Jacob Viner, Harry Dexter White, and John H. Williams, economists who gave advice to the Treasury, and those of Henry (later Sir Henry) Clay, Hubert Henderson, J. M. (later Lord) Keynes, and Sir Arthur Salter. He asserts that the major influence in the British decision to forbear from stabilizing the pound was that of Keynes. See Clarke, "The Influence of Economists on the Tripartite Agreement of 1936," 1977, p. 388.

of course it was fortunate that it appeared, at least, to be so necessary. . . .

If we can ensure that cooperation between central banks will be possible in the future, then the movement of short-term capital does not seem to present any danger at all.[23]

In the discussion that followed, William Rappard, of the Institute of Advanced International Studies in Geneva, noted that the Federal Reserve Bank of New York and the Bank of France had opened credits in favor of the Bank of England. Pedersen replied that these were insufficient, that the banks that lent money to Britain did so in a half-hearted fashion. The Tripartite Monetary Agreement was also half-hearted, or perhaps only an eighth-hearted. But the statement in the Tripartite Declaration that the "constant object of policy is to maintain equilibrium in international exchange and to avoid utmost disturbance there by monetary action" represented a fundamental change.

Morgenthau and Roosevelt were not the only personalities whose thoughts had evolved between 1933 and 1936. On hearing the president's message of July 3, 1933, to the World Economic Conference, Keynes had said: "Roosevelt was magnificently right." (It was suggested that he should have said: "Roosevelt was magnificently left.") In the *Yale Review* for 1933 comes the famous quotation:

Ideas, knowledge, science, hospitality, travel—these are the things which should of their nature be international. But let goods be homespun whenever it is reasonable and conveniently possible and, above all, let finance be primarily national.[24]

By the spring of 1936, according to a report of Harry White,

23. League of Nations, Sixth International Studies Conference on "The State and Economic Life," 1934, pp. 132–33. A colloquy between a director of the Bank of France and the economist Michel Chevalier in 1865 furnishes a still earlier example of the essential idea behind the "swap network" that finally came into effect in March 1961, also foreshadowed in Pedersen's remark. See Ministère des Finances et al., *Enquête sur les principes et les faits généraux qui régissent la circulation monétaire et fiduciaire*, vol. 3, 1867, pp. 102–5.

24. J. M. Keynes, "National Self-Sufficiency," 1933, p. 758. Lord Robbins, *Autobiography of an Economist*, p. 156, referring to this article, wrote: "Even Keynes succumbed to the current insanity . . . a sad aberration of a noble mind" (quoted in Haberler, "Die Weltwirtschaft und das internationale Währungssystem in der Zeit zwischen den beiden Weltkriegen," p. 217).

Keynes believed strongly that de facto stabilization was desirable and possible through cooperation among treasuries.[25] This was a long way from the restoration of freer trade and international capital movements of the 1946 posthumously published article in the *Economic Journal*. It was also a long way from 1933.

25. Blum, *From the Morgenthau Diaries*, vol. 1, pp. 139–40.

12

The 1937
Recession

The 1936–1937 boom

Production and prices, which had been rising evenly in 1934 and 1935, turned sharply upward in the second half of 1936. In the gold bloc, the movement was stimulated by depreciation, but this had no deflationary impact elsewhere as the world as a whole felt the stimulus of rising economic activity. The price movement was perhaps most pronounced in Japan, which had reached full employment through steady and rapid expansion from early 1932. It was nevertheless general.

In the United States, commercial loans had finally in March 1936 reversed their long decline from 1929. The upswing was further stimulated by the payment of $1.7 billion in bonds as a bonus to the veterans of the First World War. President Roosevelt had twice vetoed congressional votes for the bonus, once in May 1935 and again in January 1936. On the second occasion, Congress had passed the bonus over the veto, with a two-thirds majority. Payment was effected on June 15. The administration urged veterans to retain the bonds. Of them, $1.4 billion had been cashed and spent by the end of the year. This led to an upsurge in automobile production and residential housing.

A further stimulus to expansion was provided by the organizing campaigns of labor under the Wagner Act of 1935. Wage rates rose in bituminous coal in April 1936 and generally in manufacturing after October of that year. The rise in wages and prices, moreover, led industrialists to step up production before costs rose further. By mid-1937, gross national production had risen above the 1929 level. The rise was uneven: in consumers' nondurable goods the 1929 peaks had been exceeded by 10 percent; in residential construction, despite the fillip provided by the bonus, output remained 40 percent below 1929, itself well under the peak of 1925. Other construction projects were 50 percent below 1929. The surpassing of the overall output of 1929 was not a striking accomplishment in view of the increase in working population of some 10 percent and increased productivity of perhaps 15 percent. Nor was it to last.

In the spring of 1937, President Roosevelt expressed concern that speculation was becoming excessive and that commodity prices were being bid up to heights that could not be sustained. According to the report of the Bank for International Settlements for May 1938:

> Rubber producers are generally thought to be satisfied with a price of 9d. and in April 1937 the price reached 13d. For tin, £200 per ton is usually regarded as a fair price, but in the spring of 1937 it went above £300. It is believed that in Rhodesia, where conditions of copper production are most favourable, a profit can be made on copper at a price of £30 to £35 a ton, and the market price went to £80. As compared with the 9-cents-a-pound loan on cotton which had been granted in the United States, the market price touched 15 cents in March 1937. These examples could be multiplied many times.[1]

The results were brought about by increases in demand, as supplies grew rapidly. In 1937 the cotton crop in the United States hit a record peak of 19 million bales. Export quotas for rubber and tin were enlarged from 60 percent and 85 percent at the beginning of 1936 to 90 percent and 110 percent of stated quotas, respectively.

1. Bank for International Settlements, Eighth Annual Report, covering the year ending March 31, 1938, p. 26. President Roosevelt's message of April 14, 1938, also reasoned in terms of "fair prices," remarking that the price of copper had been pushed from 10–12 cents where production was profitable to 17 cents a pound (see *The Public Papers and Addresses of Franklin Delano Roosevelt*, vol. 7: *The Continuing Struggle for Liberalism*, 1941, p. 223).

Tin, copper, zinc, rubber, cotton, wheat, and sugar exceeded 1929 world output levels in 1937, and lead, wool, and tea came close.[2]

The outcome was a rapid rise in exports and income in the bulk of the developing countries, especially for the twelve months after the summer of 1936. But much of the production and exports was for stocks. An investigation of the Cleveland Trust Company suggested that inventories of raw materials in September 1937 were 50 percent above the level of 1929. They were out of line.

Gold dishoarding

The Tripartite Monetary Agreement was not only a signal for a rapid expansion of prices, wages, and output. It led also to dishoarding of gold. European investors who had clung to gold because of distrust of currencies undertook to cash in and buy securities. Many of these were small savers. The Swiss National Bank reported that of 8,840 persons who turned in gold to its Zürich office between September 30 and November 30, 1936, 87 percent had amounts under 500 Swiss francs, and 46 percent were for amounts of less than SFr 100. But the total amount of dishoarding was substantial. Much was invested in the United States. In addition, Europeans bought United States securities by drawing down dollar balances. Industrial com-

2. Bank for International Settlements, Eighth Annual Report, p. 27, which presents the following table:

WORLD PRODUCTION OF PRIMARY COMMODITIES

Year	Tin	Copper	Lead	Zinc	Rubber
			(in thousand tons)		
1929	192	1,915	1,725	1,450	868
1932	99	886	1,162	778	709
1936	179	1,684	1,469	1,473	862
1937	199	2,141	1,642	1,620	1,140

Year	Cotton	Wool	Wheat (millions of bushels)	Tea (millions of pounds)	Sugar (millions of tons)
	(in billion lb.)				
1929	12.7	3.915	3.566	968	27.34
1932	11.4	3.857	3.812	932	24.13
1936	15.0	3.713	3.491	844	28.67
1937	18.5	3.880	3.751	850	30.96

mon stocks rose from 121 in June 1936 (Standard Statistics index, 1926 = 100) to 130 in September 1936 and 152 in February 1937.

Gold continued to move to the United States. Instead of a reversal, such as one might have expected after the stabilization of European currencies, the movement dropped off after the heavy inflow of October 1936, the counterpart of capital flight preceding the agreements. But it did not halt. The amounts were becoming embarrassing. From the $6.8 billion revalued figure of January 1934, the gold stock of the United States passed the $11 billion mark in October 1936. Reserves in excess of Federal Reserve requirements reached $3 billion, or half of total reserves, in November 1935 and again twice in 1936, before the summer increase in reserve requirements. This last action reduced excess reserves; they started back up.

In December 1936 the Treasury undertook a program of gold sterilization to prevent further inflows of gold from adding to excess reserves, which had reached 50 percent of the total. Sterilization was called for partly because the Stabilization Fund was incapable of offsetting the gold inflow and partly because the open market portfolio of the Federal Reserve System, at $2.43 billion, was required to provide income to cover the expenses of the system and could not therefore be reduced. The Exchange Equalization Account in Britain could finance a gold inflow because it was equipped with power to borrow sterling; when it bought gold it issued Treasury bills. The U.S. Stabilization Fund, however, possessed only gold. To get dollars to buy gold from abroad, it had to sell currently owned gold to the Federal Reserve System. The foreign gold might just as well be sold directly to the Federal Reserve. On this account, if it was useful to borrow the money from the market to hold gold out of the credit bases, the Treasury was obliged to undertake it since the Stabilization Fund had no authority to do so.

A few days before the program of Treasury sterilization of gold, the Bank of England reduced the fiduciary issue of the Issue Department by £60 million and replaced it with gold bought from the Exchange Equalization Account (EEA). This indicated to the world that the EEA was filled with gold and had no margin of borrowing capacity.

In January 1937 the Federal Reserve Board again raised reserve requirements. On top of the 50 percent increase of August 1936 was placed a 33.33 percent increase to take effect in two steps, half on March 1 and the other half on May 1, 1937. The effect of the two decisions and the three distinct increases was to double reserve requirements between July 1936 and May 1937. Central reserve city reserves on demand deposits went from 13 to 26 percent, those on reserve cities from 10 to 20 percent, and on country banks 7 to 14 percent. The requirement on time deposits was raised from 3 to 6 percent. The statement accompanying the decision referred explicitly to the $4 billion in gold imports from the bank holiday in 1933 to the Treasury sterilization program of December 1936.

The evident burden of gold imports into Britain and the United States gave rise to concern that the price of gold might be reduced. This led to more dishoarding. At the time of the Tripartite Declaration, gold hoarded in Europe amounted to $1.5 to $2 billion, as estimated by the *Federal Reserve Bulletin*. Two-thirds of this was held in London, largely for the accounts of nationals of countries other than Britain.[3] From September 1936 to July 1937, more than $1 billion came out of these private hoards, and insofar as it was possible to estimate, largely from stocks held in London. During the winter and spring of 1937, dishoarding built up until in March and April small central banks, fearful that the price of gold would be reduced and they be caught with losses as in September 1931, joined in. The amounts were limited in the main to part of the gold held in stabilization funds, so that the published gold reserves of the national banks show a decline in these months only for the Swiss National Bank, which disclosed a reduction of only $22 million. By acting like private holders, however, the national banks of a number of the smaller countries underlined the distinction between the private national interest of the small country and the larger public interest of larger countries that, whether they wanted it or not, had responsibility for stabilizing the system.

At the height of the gold scare in April 1937, gold arbitrageurs were so certain of a cut in price that they were unwilling to risk their money for the five days it took, on average, to complete the transaction of buying in London and selling in New York. The gold export point in London, involving a combination of sterling-dollar rate and sterling-gold price at which it was profitable to buy gold

3. *Federal Reserve Bulletin*, vol. 23, no. 8 (August 1937), p. 704.

for shipment to New York and sale to the Treasury, dropped to a sizable discount. This accentuated the dishoarding. Since the gold price held steady, the discount took the form of a rise in the sterling exchange rate, itself aided by economic and political disturbances in France that resulted in a renewed capital outflow.

In the autumn of 1936 the gold flow to the United States represented a movement of European money into American securities. It caused President Roosevelt to set up a committee of the secretary of the Treasury, the chairman of the Board of Governors of the Federal Reserve System, and the chairman of the Securities and Exchange Commission to explore methods of restricting the inflow of capital. Nothing came of it. In the spring of 1937 there was no European interest in securities. If anything, the prospect of a lower price for gold, as seen by the speculators, induced weakness in commodity and security markets, and Europeans tended to sell American securities. The movement was a simple one of selling gold for dollars.

The "Golden Avalanche," as it was later called, produced a substantial literature for and against policy steps. There was widespread recommendation for a reduction in the gold price, whether on a negotiated basis internationally, as R. H. Brand recommended,[4] or by the United States alone, leaving to other countries the decision whether to change the gold price or allow their currencies to depreciate.[5] Short of such steps were proposals for regulating gold output and exports, reintroducing gold coins into circulation, and introducing a two-price system for gold—one at $35 an ounce for central bank metal and the other, presumably lower, at whatever the market determined. As secretary of the Treasury, Morgenthau went so far as to explore the possibility of negotiations with the Soviet Union on restricting the sale of gold to the West. His object was primarily political, and only secondarily was it to "ease the temporary decline in the international value of gold that occurred in the spring of 1937."[6]

4. R. H. Brand, "Gold: A World Problem," 1937.

5. Frank D. Graham and Charles R. Whittlesey, *Golden Avalanche*, 1939, ch. 9.

6. Blum, *From the Morgenthau Diaries*, vol. 1, p. 467. Curiously enough, Morgenthau had nothing more to say about the gold scare, which surely was a central issue to the Treasury in the spring of 1937. His diaries are full of accounts of his differences with Governor Eccles of the Federal Reserve System about interest rates, which he appears to think had importance for the subsequent recession.

One objection to reducing the gold price was that, instead of the profits made from raising the gold price, there would be a loss. The technical aspects of this objection are disposed of by Nurkse, who suggests that such loss can easily be offset by some accounting device, such as the creation of a government debt to the central bank in place of the amount by which the gold reserves were marked down.[7] Feasible technically, such devices recommend themselves slowly to politically sensitive bodies, which give the public little credit for sophistication and doubt whether it can disregard a mere bookkeeping entry that raises the government debt.

President Roosevelt stated on April 9, 1937, that the United States had no plans to reduce the price of gold. This failed to calm the market. Among other reasons, the Bank for International Settlements uttered a Delphic statement about lowering the price of gold in its annual report, which appeared on May 3.[8] The monthly inflow of gold, which had reached $216 million in April 1937, the highest since the inflow of $219 million in October 1936 caused by the pressure on the gold bloc prior to the Tripartite Monetary Agreement, went to $262 million in June. This was the worst month, however, until Munich. The movement subsided in June, partly owing to weakness in raw material prices, which was thought to discourage any official plan to reduce the gold price—if there was one, as seems entirely unlikely. In addition, the market was quieted by the action of the British in adding £200 million to the borrowing

7. League of Nations (Ragnar Nurkse), *International Currency Experience*, p. 133.

8. Bank for International Settlements, Seventh Annual Report, covering the year ending March 31, 1937, p. 56:

It can hardly be doubted that at present a lowering of the price of gold would help to cope with the serious problems resulting from overabundant production. It would, however, cause certain difficulties with regard to valuation of existing gold reserves and the relative position of currencies (the latter, insofar as equilibrium has already been attained, should be disturbed as little as possible). It would, moreover, involve the danger of manipulation of currencies in the future, which would add an element of instability and distrust to the monetary structure.

In the discussion of a reconstruction of the world's monetary system these various questions, difficult though they might be, cannot be avoided. Also from the point of view of the gold producers, it is important to establish conditions which will render gold continuously useful as a basis for currencies, instead of concentrating attention on immediate profits.

authority of the Exchange Equalization Account in June 1937: an
indication, after imports of $1.2 billion in 1936 and close to $210
million in the first half of 1937, that it expected to continue absorbing gold.

The American record does not indicate how seriously the question of a reduced gold price was taken. British Treasury files, however, show that its Washington representative had undertaken a series of discussions with Morgenthau in the spring of 1937 at
Morgenthau's cottage in Georgia, without any of the U.S. advisers
present. In these discussions Morgenthau raised the question of a
tax on gold imports and of a reduction in the price of gold as a
means of reducing imports. Bewley treated these proposals, together with others relating to limiting foreign purchases of U.S. securities, as "only canvassing possible courses of action in the future." He suggested in his report to London that Morgenthau was
basically ignorant of financial matters and more cautious in what he
did than what he said, and that the proposals, which he had not
thought out, would probably be dropped under the influence of his
advisers.

The British Treasury was sufficiently stirred by the prospects,
however, to elect to pursue the question further, and when Sir John
Simon replaced Chamberlain at the Treasury, he cabled Morgenthau
suggesting a visit by the top Treasury civil servant, Sir Frederick
Phillips, in September. In the message, he stated that his mind was
not made up on the subject of a reduction in the gold price but that
his first reactions were unsympathetic, given the public's tendency
to associate the reduced price of gold with deflation. He therefore
proposed to do nothing for the immediate future.

When Phillips's instructions were drawn up in mid-July, they did
not rule out a reduction in the price of gold by concerted international action as a "long-term possibility" in case of inflation; but
given the need for higher commodity prices, it was not called for
currently.

Morgenthau told Phillips in September 1937 that he got several
callers a day with ideas on gold but "paid no attention to them."
The subject was not discussed in open meetings with Morgenthau,
Riefler, and Viner, but as Phillips left Morgenthau privately informed him that he had just discussed gold with the president and
that "whatever course of action might be required in connection
with gold imports, a lowering of the price of gold was definitely not

part of it." Phillips accepted this, according to British records, and concluded that Morgenthau's "whole inclinations are against a change in the price and in favor of limiting output."[9]

It is not clear from the record whether the lack of real consideration given to lowering the price of gold as a means of reducing the burden of absorbing the gold supply was the result of inattention, lack of imagination, or the concern for the stability of the U.S. economy or for that of the world monetary structure indicated in the quotation from the BIS report above. At the working level, economists in the Treasury Department, Federal Reserve Board, and the Federal Reserve Bank of New York were producing proposals for an ultimate demonetization of gold and suggestions of taxes and other devices to contain hot money. The former were hedged after September 1937, with the proviso that any reduction in the price of gold be postponed until the economy had recovered from recession. The latter were qualified with doubts as to their practicality. The Roosevelt committee on hot money met as late as April 1937 without producing useful proposals. By that time the problem had altered from one of slowing down the movement of European funds into the New York stock market to countering speculation against gold. But the interest and excitement in the gold scare at the bureaucratic level and in the financial press did not communicate itself to, say, the public papers and addresses of Franklin D. Roosevelt or the Morgenthau diaries. At the very least, Roosevelt and Morgenthau had learned enough about the international monetary system not to go off half-cocked with half-baked proposals, as they had in 1933. On a more generous interpretation, they and the British were prepared to ride out the destabilizing forces, no matter how uncomfortable, in the interest of maintaining relative exchange rates, which were broadly back to the 1929 pattern, and of stability of the international monetary structure. There are times, perhaps as in 1933, when it is appropriate to respond to the slogan later attributed to John Foster Dulles, "Don't just stand there: do something." On the other hand, there are also occasions when the system is best served by reversing it to, "Don't just do something: stand there."[10]

9. British Treasury records, files of Sir Frederick Phillips, kindly summarized for me by D. E. Moggridge.

10. This was the later conclusion of G. Griffith Johnson, Jr. (but not of Graham and Whittlesey), in *The Treasury and Monetary Policy, 1933–1938*, 1939, p. 159:

Apparently the most promising course is a waiting one . . . in the hope of a

The recession

Business had gone sideways from March to August 1937. A few prices, especially grains and cotton, had fallen. With a record crop, the price of cotton had dropped from 15 cents in March to 9 cents in August. Foreign trade was steady, with imports up more than exports. Markets were uneasy but calm. Then in mid-August the stock market started off. In September trading increased and prices fell precipitously. From 141 on August 25, the Standard Statistics industrial index (based on 1926 as 100) went to 125 in two weeks. By the end of the month it was 30 percent below the March highs. On September 13 the Open Market Committee took cognizance of the turn of events and of the possibility that the reduction of excess reserves of member banks from more than $3 billion in July 1936 to less than $700 million in early August had had something to do with it. It requested the secretary of the Treasury to release $300 million from the Inactive Gold Account set up under sterilization, and this was done. It helped but little. In October the stock market declined still further, with a Black Tuesday on October 19, bringing the industrial share average to 102. Commodity prices fell sharply, as did industrial production. The Federal Reserve index of industrial production slipped from 116 of the 1923–25 average in the first eight months to August to 106 in September, 99 in October, 86 in November, and 83 in December. Steel dropped from 85 percent of capacity in August to 38 percent of capacity in November and 26 percent in December. This was the largest decline. The next largest occurred in cotton textiles, which fell from 143 percent of the 1923–25 average in March, when three-shift working was normal, to 116 by August and 81 by December. Prices of farm products fell by 24 percent between April 3, 1937, and the end of the year. Prices of durable goods did not decline substantially, but those of nondurables were off 10 percent or so. All commodities fell in price by 8 percent.

For a considerable time there was no understanding of what had happened. Then it became clear. The spurt in activity from October

---

rising price level, . . . a return of capital to France, a renewal of absorption in the Orient, . . . and a restoration of international trade and lending. It may be argued that these happy conditions are unlikely to occur, but if that is so there is little that can be done now to solve the gold problem without bringing greater difficulties.

1936 had been dominated by inventory accumulation. This was especially the case in automobiles, where, because of fears of strikes, supplies of new cars had been built up. It was the same in steel and textiles—two other industries with strong CIO unions. When it became evident after the spring of 1937 that commodity prices were not going to continue upward, the basis for the inventory accumulation was undermined, and first in textiles, then in steel, the reverse process took place. Long-term investment had not been built to great heights and did not fall far. The steepest economic descent in the history of the United States, which lost half the ground gained for many indexes since 1932, proved that the economic recovery in the United States had been built on illusion.[11]

One particular deception had occurred in foreign trade. The excess of exports over imports in the U.S. accounts had been worked down from $478 million in 1934 to $235 million in 1935 and $33 million in 1936. In the first six months of 1937 there was an import surplus of $148 million. A considerable part of the increase in imports, however, was intended for stocks and was borrowed from future imports. In the second half of 1937 imports fell from a peak of $307 million in March 1937 to $209 million in December and $141 million at the bottom in July 1938. The export surplus for 1937 rose to $265 million and that for 1938 to $1.1 billion. Foreign withdrawals of dollars after October 1936 were partly based on disillusionment with the New York stock market; in great measure, they went to pay for the U.S. export surplus. The widespread view that U.S. balance of payments was coming into adjustment proved false.

Some part of the recession—how much is debated—was the result of the sharp change in fiscal policy.[12] The 1936 deficit had been large. Swollen by the $1.7 billion bonus payment, the excess of ex-

11. Monetarists may be interested in contemplating a quotation from the *Federal Reserve Bulletin* of June 1938, p. 437: "The events of 1929 taught us that the absence of any rise in prices did not prove that no crisis was pending. 1937 taught us that an abundant supply of gold and a cheap monetary policy do not prevent prices from falling."

12. The most detailed account, by Kenneth D. Roose, *The Economics of Recession and Revival: An Interpretation of 1937–38*, 1954, attributes more importance to the change in fiscal policy and less to inventory accumulation, some considerable portion of which, he claims, was involuntary (p. 191). He also ascribes importance to the uncertainty of business expectations, based on the "serious political conflict between the New Deal and business" (p. 238). This interpretation, however, was written at the height of faith in Keynesian doctrine.

penditure over receipts in the general and special accounts of the U.S. Treasury had been $4.6 billion in fiscal 1936. In fiscal 1937 it was off to $3.1 billion, and in fiscal 1938 down to $1.4 billion. The decline in the deficit for calendar years was $2.2 billion between 1936 and 1937.[13]

Whether the recession owed more to inventory accumulation and its reversal, tighter money (not actually tight) as a consequence of increases in reserve requirements, or to a sharp reversal in fiscal policy, it produced a change in the intellectual climate. Hitherto resisting the Keynesian revolution in analysis, the leading figures below the cabinet level became much more interested in the message of *The General Theory of Employment, Interest, and Money*. Whereas on October 12 Roosevelt was still urging congressional leaders to wipe out the predicted deficit in the budget for the fiscal year 1939, market collapse a week later produced a change of view.[14] In the Treasury, White, Oliphant, Magill, and Selzer, but not Morgenthau, began to think in Keynesian terms. Elsewhere Eccles, Henderson, Hopkins, and Currie were among the leaders.[15] The president was gradually won over. By April 14 a program was worked out that embraced positive fiscal policy as a measure to stabilize the economy. It was announced in a message to Congress and in a fireside chat on the same evening.

The dollar scare

While the recession ended the gold scare that the price of gold would be reduced, it gave rise to the opposite fear that the dollar would again be devalued. The prospect was not very real. In November, Morgenthau told Roosevelt that he was planning to assemble a group of people over the weekend to discuss gold—meaning a further undoing of the sterilization program of December 1936.

13. Marriner S. Eccles, the chairman of the Board of Governors of the Federal Reserve System, refers in his memoirs to a $4 billion impact of the change in government budget on disposable income between the first four months of 1936 and those of 1937. See his *Beckoning Frontiers: Public and Personal Recollections*, 1951, p. 295.

14. Blum, *From the Morgenthau Diaries*, vol. 1, pp. 385–86.

15. Eccles refers to the "famous memorandum" of Lubin, Henderson, and Currie on how the change in government spending produced the depression, which was written for a decisive White House meeting of November 8, 1937 (*Beckoning Frontiers*, p. 304).

Misunderstanding him, Roosevelt said that he would not raise the price of gold.[16] That line of action was not contemplated. In a press conference on February 18, discussing raising prices but especially restoring balance in relative prices and raising those that had fallen but not those that had been steady through the recession, he declared:

> Somebody else with a mind full of generalities will ask ...
> "Does this mean inflation?" No, the policy is to help restore balance in the price structure.
>   Somebody will say, "Are we going to have further deflation [*sic*] of the dollar?" The answer is, "No."[17]

The dollar scare was neither serious nor prolonged. To a considerable extent it represented mainly the undoing of bear speculation against gold from Europe, especially the United Kingdom, Switzerland, and the Netherlands. Between the end of September and the end of the year $575 million were withdrawn from United States banks. But these large-scale movements of hot money did not upset the system. The increase in gold hoarding was easily met by ending the program of sterilization that gold dishoarding had occasioned.

The recovery program

The recovery program of April 14, 1938, had a money-and-banking component: a reduction of reserve requirements by approximately $750 million effective from April 16 and the discontinuance of the Treasury's inactive gold account with its remaining amount of $1.183 billion. The major proposal was to increase spending. Works Progress Administration funds were raised by $1.25 billion for the largest amount. Next came $550 million to be loaned by the Treasury to states for public works, $450 million to be spent on public works by the Federal Government, and $300 million available for loan by the U.S. Housing Authority. All in all, spending of over $2 billion and loans to other spending bodies of almost $1 billion were proposed. The budget implications explicitly involved acceptance of deficits. The Keynesian doctrine of spending for stability was finally accepted after having been resisted for seven years of depression by both Hoover and Roosevelt.

16. Blum, *From the Morgenthau Diaries*, vol. 1, pp. 390–91.
17. *The Public Papers and Addresses of Franklin D. Roosevelt*, vol. 7, pp. 105–6.

TABLE 20

INDEXES OF INCOME, EMPLOYMENT, PRODUCTION, AND OTHER BUSINESS ACTIVITY OF THE UNITED STATES, 1937–39 (adjusted for seasonal variation, except as noted)

	Base period	1937	1938		1939	Jul. '37 Jun. '38	Jun. '38 Aug. '39
		July	Mar.	Jun.	Aug.	(percent change)	
Income payments	1929	89	81	79	85	− 12	+ 8
Factory							
employment[a]	1923–5	111	91	84	96	− 24	+ 14
Factory payrolls[a]	1923–5	105	78	71	90	− 32	+ 26
Industrial production							
Total	1935–9	120	84	81	104	− 33	+ 28
steel		142	53	49	111	− 65	+ 127
automobiles		144	57	49	84	− 66	+ 71
cotton textiles		118	81	81	114	− 31	+ 41
woollen textiles		97	53	68	106	− 30	+ 56
shoes		108	93	88	107	− 19	+ 22
Freight car loadings	1923–5	80	60	58	70	− 28	+ 21
Construction							
contracts	1923–5	67	46	54	73	− 19	+ 35
residential		44	33	42	67	− 5	+ 60
other		86	56	64	78	− 26	+ 22
Department store sales	1923–5	92	86	82	89	− 11	+ 9
Wholesale prices[a]	1926	87.9	79.7	78.3	75.0	− 11	− 4

SOURCE: Franklin Delano Roosevelt, *The Public Papers and Addresses of Franklin Delano Roosevelt*, vol. VII, 1941, p. 235.

[a]Not adjusted for seasonal variation.

The commitment was both belated and faint-hearted, as Cary Brown has shown, in that casual impressions of the New Deal greatly exaggerate its devotion to deficit spending.[18] Early deficits were reluctantly accepted as the result of shortfalls in taxes or expenditures that the administration had been unable to reduce. The recession was needed to demonstrate the efficacy of Keynesian ideas, which would make a deep national depression never again possible, and the commitment of the United States to steady support for the international system, such as it was, in one sort of disturbance and another.

The recovery from the recession lows took place quickly, though not as speedily as the recession which preceded it. In a note attached to the April 14 message to Congress in his papers and addresses, Roosevelt included a table showing the decline from July 1937 to March and June 1938 and the recovery to August 1939 (Table 20). It sums up rather neatly how the recovery commenced unevenly in the spring of 1938, with certain items, like construction, rising immediately and others not reaching their lows until June; the uneven path of recovery; and the continued if gentle slide in prices. It does not indicate the part played in recovery in foreign orders for arms as against domestic spending programs. But it emphasizes the recession, which was needed in addition to the depression to provide the intellectual basis for stabilizing the economy.

"The basic reason the depression lasted so long was, of course, the economic ignorance of the times."[19] This answer, as we hope to have demonstrated, is inadequate on a world basis. It fits very well for the United States.

18. E. C. Brown, "Fiscal Policy in the Thirties: A Reappraisal," 1956.
19. Gilbert Burck and Charles Silberman, "Why the Depression Lasted So Long," 1955, reprinted in Stanley Coben and F. G. Hill, eds., *American Economic History: Essays in Interpretation*, 1966, p. 496.

13

Rearmament in a
Disintegrating
World Economy

In 1937, unlike 1929, there was no doubt where the trouble started. The recession originated in the United States. Moreover, in a world not closely knit by trade and payments its impact was felt unevenly. After the upcoming war, Sir Dennis Robertson was to state that when the United States sneezed, Europe caught pneumonia. In 1937–38, the impact of the recession was felt mainly in the less-developed countries. Busy preparing for war, Europe and Japan suffered no more than a few sniffles.

The industrial countries felt, first, a decline in security prices. This was largely psychological. The nosedive in New York made the world's capitalists uneasy, and some liquidation elsewhere was required to make good the liquidity lost on the New York Stock Exchange. With easy monetary policy, however, and substantial spending for public works, the dip did not develop into anything serious. In some markets, such as the Swiss, it did not occur at all.

Second, there were two effects in foreign trade: (1) a loss in exports to the United States as well as to customers of the United States that were forced to cut back on imports because their exports to the United States had fallen and (2) a reduction in the prices of imported raw materials. Prices of European and overseas commodities moved disparately. From 1928 to 1938, European import values as a whole fell from 100 to 73, constituting the trend. Extra-

European commodities, such as cocoa beans, sugar, coffee, wool, cotton, fats and oils, and silk, fell by more than the trend by percentages clustering around 40 percent, whereas raw materials of European origin—wood pulp, coal, iron ore, iron and steel, cement—rose relative to trend by 45 to 75 percent.[1] The divergence originated in the decline in U.S. demand for the first group of commodities and in rapidly rising European expenditure for armaments and for plants to build armaments, which affected the second commodity group.

Part of the improvement in Europe's terms of trade in 1938 over 1937 resulted from a decline in freight rates. This took place not at the expense of Europe's suppliers but of shipowners, themselves largely European. The scramble for raw materials to be added to inventories in the United States, against the background of years of failure to replace ships, almost doubled the freight index between the first half of 1936 and the third quarter of 1937. Nine months later it had fallen 50 percent. The decline of 35 percent in the U.S. demand for goods from 1937 to 1938 relieved the inflationary squeeze in shipping and helped to make overseas imports cheap again.

If it did not greatly disturb the industrialized countries, or even aided them in a few respects, the U.S. recession was harsh on suppliers of raw materials. The price decline did not cumulate, as it had after 1929, and rearmament demand from Europe provided something of a cushion. To support prices, attempts were made to set in motion the machinery of export quotas, so laboriously constructed during the middle 1930s. It did not help greatly. The Pan-American conference on coffee broke down in August 1937, before the recession struck in September, and Brazil gave up its attempt to stabilize the price of coffee the following November. Despite a rapid closing down of export quotas in rubber, tin, copper, and wheat, prices fell sharply in these materials. The decline in U.S. consumption between January 1937 and January 1938—illustrated by such figures as 30 percent in silk, 35 percent in cotton, 40 percent in rubber, 60 percent in tin and wool—proved too severe.

Nor did less developed countries receive help from a countercyclical revival of long-term lending. Instead of sending capital

1. C. P. Kindleberger, *The Terms of Trade: A European Case Study*, 1956, pp. 182–83.

abroad, the United States was receiving it. The world economy functioned poorly in trade, the capital market, and in payments. Separate countries were on their own.

The disarticulated world economy

The lack of coherence of the world economy in the 1930s is illustrated by changes in industrial production in the upswings of 1925 to 1929 and 1932 to 1937, on the one hand, and in the one-year declines from 1929 to 1930 and from 1937 to 1938 on the other. These are shown in Figure 13. On the upswing, the range of the selected countries runs from +12 percent to +55 percent in the 1920s, and from +14 percent to +120 percent in the 1930s. On the downside, the spreads are +3 to −19 percent and +8 to −22 percent, respectively.

The relationship of foreign trade to domestic production, measured by the ratio between the volume of imports and that of industrial production in 1938 as compared with 1929, held up for a few countries, notably France and the United States, but declined 10 percent in Britain, nearly 20 percent in Canada, and 25 to 40 percent in Japan, Germany, and Italy.[2] Within the foreign trade totals, moreover, trade was balanced less multilaterally. In 1928, according to Hilgerdt's calculations, bilateral balancing between exports and imports between pairs of countries on the average covered 70 percent of merchandise trade, with about 5 percent more covered by exports or imports of services or capital movements and 25 percent balanced multilaterally.[3] The drying up of the international capital market, tariff discrimination, foreign exchange controls, and clearing and payments arrangements sharply reduced the proportion of multilateral payments.[4] Trade increasingly took place bilaterally and, to the extent it continued to be multilateral, was contained

2. League of Nations (James E. Meade), *World Economic Survey, 1938–39*, 1939, p. 108.

3. See League of Nations (F. Hilgerdt), *The Network of World Trade*, 1942, pp. 87ff. Hilgerdt does not give a figure for the percentage bilaterally balanced in 1938 (nor the method of calculating the 1928 figure). Tables 44 and 48 and diagrams 6 and 10 on pp. 77, 78, and 90, however, demonstrate the extent of shrinkage in regional multilateral clearing, and the fact is referred to throughout the text.

4. By the end of 1937, the number of clearing agreements had reached 170 (see League of Nations [James E. Meade], *World Economic Survey, 1937–38*, 1938, p. 161).

Figure 13. Changes in industrial production in selected countries, 1924–29, 1932–37, 1929–30 and 1937–38 (index numbers with specified bases).

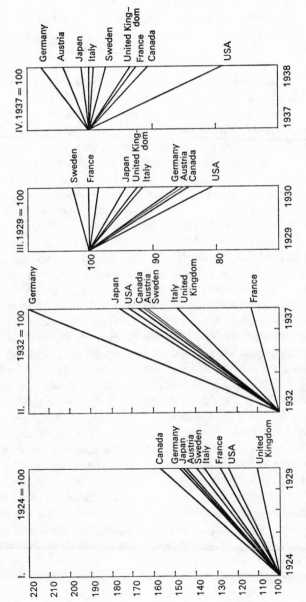

SOURCE: League of Nations, World Economic Survey, 1938–39, 1939, p. 107.

within bloc lines. The United Kingdom, for example, sold 62 percent of its exports to the Commonwealth and sterling bloc in 1938, compared with 51 percent in 1929, and bought 55 percent of its imports within the bloc in the later year, as compared with 42 percent in the earlier year. German trade with southeastern Europe over the same period grew from 5 to 13 percent in exports and from 4.5 to 12 percent in imports. The most remarkable shift took place in Japan's trade with the "yen bloc" of Korea, Formosa, Kwantung, and Manchuria, where exports rose from 24 to 55 percent between 1929 and 1938 and imports from 20 to 41 percent.[5]

Not only had the structure of trade altered. The adjustment mechanism no longer worked. Income changes produced disequilibrium in trade and payments rather than being induced in response to them. To the extent that adjustment was inescapable because of the lack of foreign exchange reserves, it was brought about by tariffs, quotas, and foreign exchange controls. Tariffs were raised widely in 1938, reversing the liberalizing movement that had begun in 1937. The Hague convention of 1937 to lower tariffs among Scandinavian countries and Belgium and the Netherlands was allowed to lapse the following year. One country after another tightened up exchange regulations, and where they were already tight a few countries added the death penalty, as did Germany in 1936 and Italy in 1939.

As already observed, the private capital market remained moribund. U.S. investors had had their fill of foreign bonds. Amortization and repayments exceeded the few new private issues. Some private loans within the Commonwealth were floated in London in 1936 and 1937, and a substantial Australian loan was raised in that market in 1938. For the most part, the British authorities kept restrictions on long-term lending, and after serious weakness in sterling in 1938, gradually limited all outflow of British funds, closing down forward facilities in December 1938 and purchases of foreign outstanding securities in April 1939. Government lending to replace the private capital market found a beginning, but for expanding exports and employment rather than to ease national adjustments to changing circumstances. The Export Credit Guarantees Department in Britain and the Export-Import Bank in the United States, both started before the 1937 recession, were expanded. In Britain a primary motive was to provide economic assistance to potential allies,

5. League of Nations, *Review of World Trade, 1938*, pp. 34, 35.

and loans to the Turkish, Greek, Romanian, Chinese, and Polish governments were undertaken, together with commercial credits to New Zealand importers. The Export-Import Bank expanded lending to Latin American countries, Poland, and China to encourage the purchase of U.S. products. An Export-Import Bank loan of $20 million to Brazil to unfreeze commercial debts represented less a capital movement than a change from private to government ownership of foreign assets within the United States. An additional $50 million was made available to purchase additional goods. Of more enduring interest was a $50 million U.S. Treasury advance in March 1939 to the Brazilian government to establish a foreign exchange fund and to assist in starting a central bank. This may be interpreted as merely a loan to sell U.S. exports to assist employment. Alternatively, it may be viewed as an early step in replacing the shattered private market for international lending on a governmental basis.

Rearmament

If the world economy was in dire straits, its polity was in worse. The Ethiopian War of 1935 had been followed by Japan's renewed attack on China in 1937, the Spanish Civil War, not to mention German military movement into the Rhineland in 1936, the *Anschluss* and Munich in 1938, and the occupation of Czechoslovakia in 1939. Britain started seriously to rearm. In 1937 it announced a five-year program of expenditure for armaments of £1.5 billion, of which £400 million was to be financed by borrowing. Taxes were raised in the budget for the year ending March 31, 1938, and again in the following year. In February 1939 the limit for borrowing in the program was raised from £400 to £800 million. By July 1939 the pressure was increased still further. The armament outlays for the fiscal year ending March 31, 1940, were lifted from £630 million to £750 million, of which £500 million was to be borrowed. Actual defense expenditure rose from £46 million in the second quarter of 1937 to £124 million two years later. These disbursements converted the economy from one of idle resources to scarcity, from falling prices to inflation, and gradually from resource allocation by competitive markets to the disequilibrium system of price controls, consumer rationing, and supply allocations. Bottlenecks were attacked in a number of industries—not only armaments, but such ancillary lines as ship construction. A start was made to bring new land under cultivation and accumulate seed, farm machinery, and fertilizer as well as stocks of food. A stockpile of cotton was obtained by a government swap of cotton against rubber with the United States.[6]

The delays in getting defense spending under way in France were discussed in Chapter 11. No real progress was made until after Munich, when Paul Reynaud took over the Ministry of Finance under the Daladier government, won powers to govern by decree, reversed the policies of the Blum government and of Daladier's first minister of finance, and initiated a sharp upturn in French spending and production. National defense industries, which had been nationalized in August 1936 but had been slow to expand production, were galvanized into rapid action. In March 1939 a production service was begun in the Ministry of National Defense. In April, controls were imposed on transfers of labor, and limits to profits were set in the armament industry. In May the military was given power to requisition transport, redundant employees were reassigned from the railways, and war risk insurance was established. Production rose rapidly, and with it hours of work.

Japan reached full employment by the middle of 1938. Three hundred million yen were transferred by the Bank of Japan to a revolving fund to finance raw material imports for the export industries and to disguise gold losses. A disequilibrium system of foreign exchange controls, price controls, and resource allocations followed.

A Supreme Autarky Commission was established in Italy in October 1937 to emphasize withdrawal of another Axis member from the world economy.

Contemporary sources were vastly impressed by the German armament effort as displayed by volunteers with regular equipment in Spain, and by the Wehrmacht's marches into the Rhineland, Austria, and Czechoslovakia. Intelligence sources and public information both suggested that German military preparations had been under way since 1933 and that, as Hitler boasted, Rm 90 billion had been spent on armaments. The last statement was an exaggeration. As to the first, up until the occupation of the Rhineland in the

6. Economists are confounded that history is replete with examples of errors of economic policy, as seen by contemporary analysts, that turned out to be useful. Among them was the U.S. farm policy that produced large supplies of redundant cotton and wheat during the depression, which proved highly useful in war.

spring of 1936, German rearmament was still small. In the three years through the end of March 1936, only Rm 8 billion had been spent, half of it in the last year. In the three following years, Rm 32 billion were spent (18 billion in the last year), making Rm 40 billion in the six years to March 31, 1939. An accelerating rate of spending brought the total at outbreak of war to Rm 50 billion.[7] These figures include capital expenditures for armament plants and stockpiling of commodities as well as material.

The move to intensive rearmament came in the summer of 1936, when Hermann Göring was appointed plenipotentiary of the Second Four-Year Plan with instructions to get ready for war in four years. No specific plan of military reequipment has been found, nor was the overall four-year plan or its constituent elements, such as raw material production, worked out well as a highly rational coordinated program. Successes were achieved in a number of areas, such as agriculture, rubber (Buna-S), and aluminium, but output fell far short of targets in oil and iron ore, in which Germany remained heavily dependent on imports in 1939.

The German armament program was held back by a blitzkrieg strategy, by the resistance of financiers and industrialists, and by an unwillingness to depart substantially from peacetime standards. German successes in the Rhineland, Austria, Czechoslovakia, and Poland made the strategy of blitzkrieg credible and rendered preparation for a drawn-out conflict unnecessary. The resistance of industrialists was economic, not political, and was expressed as an opposition to the substantial diversion of steel from existing uses to such roundabout purposes as iron ore development. Not understanding that a nation can finance anything it can produce, Schacht fought armament expansion on financial grounds. By 1936 he had fallen into disfavor over his cautious approach to raw material development. Relieved as minister of economics in August 1937, he remained president of the Reichsbank until January 1939. A Rm 3 billion credit demanded of the Reichsbank was granted with great reluctance in 1937. He refused further credits after March 1938, which led to his dismissal.

But the basic reason for the limited character of the armament program, given the aggressive intentions of the Nazi leadership, was its inability, even unwillingness, to depart from peacetime norms.

7. Burton H. Klein, *Germany's Economic Preparations for War*, 1959, pp. 16ff.

Consumption, investment in consumption industries, and government nonwar expenditure passed previous peaks at the end of the decade.[8] There was no real mobilization of manpower or drastic extension of hours of work. Hitler was partly unwilling, partly unable, to achieve the mobilization required to back up his boasts.

Despite the discrepancy between talk and performance in armament, sufficient pressure was applied to the German economy to require it to develop a disequilibrium system. Hourly wages were frozen at the level of October 1933, prices at that of October 1936. The clearing system was extended from creditor countries and southeast Europe to Latin America. German relations with the world economy, like those of Japan and Italy, no longer responded to changes in money, prices, or capital flows, but were highly controlled. Three of the leading ten industrial countries had largely withdrawn from the world economy.

Efforts to rebuild the world economy

Recovery had gone far enough in 1937 to lead governments outside the Axis and communist countries to explore the means of rebuilding the world economy and ensuring against any renewed depression. This effort had at least three aspects. In April 1937 the British and French governments invited Paul Van Zeeland, former prime minister of Belgium and a distinguished economist, to prepare a report on the possibility of removing obstacles to trade. This appeared in January 1938. In September 1937 the League of Nations Committee for the Study of the Problems of Raw Materials submitted its report to the Economic Committee of the League, which in turn reported to the League Council in December of that year. Somewhat earlier, in June 1937, an International Labor Conference passed a resolution on international cooperation in the provision of information on public works, under which, and in collaboration with the Economic, Financial, and Transit Department of the League of Nations, which had been asked by the assembly to examine measures for the prevention or mitigation of economic depressions, it convened an international conference on public works in June 1938.

As we saw earlier, the coordination of national expenditures for public works had been proposed from many sources, including the

8. Ibid., p. 76.

German heretical economists and the International Labor Office, for discussion at the World Economic Conference of 1933. The flowering of Keynesian thought made the subject more timely. The spread of rearmament, on the other hand, made it impossible to accomplish anything. The twenty-five governments represented at the preparatory meeting of the International Public Works Committee in June 1938 limited themselves to recommending exchange of information on the planning, timing, and finance of state expenditure on capital projects. Given the burgeoning expenditure for armament, this was the best that could be done. But it was highly academic. Only after the Second World War was it found that the long lags in moving among the planning, design, and execution stages made national countercyclical spending difficult to the point of impossibility, much less international coordination of national countercyclical spending. Later the International Bank for Reconstruction and Development was to insist that it could not carry out the provision of its charter which required it, inter alia, to time its development expenditures in anticyclical fashion.[9]

The report of the league's Committee for the Study of the Problems of Raw Materials[10] is hardly distinguishable from the long line of official studies and reports on the raw material problem that preceded and followed it[11] (eliminating, however, esoteric proposals for international compensation for terms-of-trade changes or tying the issuance of money to stocks of primary products). The problems for primary products were found in inelasticities of supply and demand, their solution in schemes that restricted production or exports or provided for stockpiling. Equal access was to be preserved and consumer representation established on administrative bodies. In 1938 part of the difficulty in demand was lack of foreign exchange, while inelasticity of supply was partly the result of a need for foreign exchange on the part of producing countries, combined with a lack of availability of foreign loans. Like all such studies, that of

9. See International Bank for Reconstruction and Development submission to the Economic and Employment Commission of the United Nations, press release no. 134, May 11, 1949. The question of anticyclical lending is nowhere discussed in *The International Bank for Reconstruction and Development, 1946–1953*, 1954.

10. League document A.27.1937.II.B.

11. See, for example, United Nations, *Commodity Trade and Economic Development*, Report by a Committee of Experts, 1952; and Contracting Parties for the General Agreement on Tariffs and Trade, *Trends in International Trade*, Report by a Panel of Experts, 1958.

the league committee achieved no useful result, and for the same principal reason. At a given point in time producing and consuming countries find it difficult, if not impossible, to agree on prices they are persuaded will be at a market-clearing level for an extended period. A period of rapid price decline, like that from September to December 1937, was particularly inappropriate as a moment to agree on a long-run equilibrium price. Where commodity schemes were in operation, export quotas were being reduced rapidly, but not sufficiently to prevent price declines. After the middle of 1938 the position was equally inauspicious for the opposite reason, that raw material prices were rising. Very quickly, however, as with the international coordination of public works, world rearmament and eventually war pushed the problem into the background.

The Van Zeeland report on trade was equally academic, and partly for the same reason—rearmament. Van Zeeland argued that tariffs should be reduced reciprocally, with concessions extended widely through the most-favored nation clause; that quotas should be replaced by tariffs or at least tariff quotas; and that the open door was needed in access to raw materials. He urged the gradual dismantling of clearing agreements, the removal of foreign exchange controls by creditor countries to permit capital movements and by debtor countries to the extent of financing foreign trade, even though control over other capital movements might need to be retained. The Bank for International Settlements might provide for the financing of trade by establishing a multilateral clearing arrangement or a common fund used to finance international trade while exchange controls were in process of dismantlement. The ultimate means of control of hot money was the reestablishment of the gold standard. Means to that end would be to extend agreements under the Tripartite Monetary Agreement. Instead of guaranteeing exchange rates for twenty-four hours at a time, this should be done for six months. But the reestablishment of the gold standard was the final step in the restoration of the world economy, not the first.

Like the reports on public works and raw materials, the Van Zeeland report received little attention, partly, as indicated, for the same reason: the rapidly approaching war and the need to prepare for it. In addition, the sponsorship of France and Britain and the intellectual leadership of a distinguished Belgian were not sufficient. Action could come only from enlisting the forceful commitment of the United States. The United States was prepared to push ahead in lowering its own tariffs on a reciprocal basis and to chip away at empire preference. It had made a feeble beginning of international monetary cooperation in the Tripartite Monetary Agreement, but with little real understanding of what was implied.[12]

Whether U.S. leadership in rebuilding the world economy would have been forthcoming without the war is a question that cannot be answered.[13] A start had been made, but there was little follow-up. The world was far from the powerful leadership felt during and after the war in the provisions for rebuilding the world economy embodied in the Atlantic Charter, Article 7 of Lend-Lease, Dumbarton Oaks, Bretton Woods, Hot Springs, the Anglo-American Financial Agreement, the International Trade Organization and General Agreement on Tariffs and Trade, the Marshall Plan, and Point 4. Not only was American initiative feeble and hesitant, there was no alternative to it. Even without the war, the exercise embodied in the league Committee on Raw Materials, the International Labor Office on coordination of public works, and the Van Zeeland report for reducing barriers to trade was doomed to remain academic.

12. As an illustration of how little he understood the international monetary system, take Morgenthau's suggestion that the Soviet Union should be invited to join the Tripartite Monetary Agreement (see Blum, *From the Morgenthau Diaries*, vol. 1, p. 460).

13. That the initiative came from the United States, though with a quick response from Britain, is the theme of the opening chapters of Richard N. Gardner, *Sterling-Dollar Diplomacy*, 1969. For an account of negotiations in London, see E. F. Penrose, *Economic Planning for the Peace*, 1953.

14

An Explanation
of the 1929
Depression

We return to the original questions: What produced the world depression of 1929 and why was it so widespread, so deep, so long? Was it caused by real or monetary factors? Did it originate in the United States, in Europe, in the primary-producing countries of the periphery, in the relations among them? Was the fatal weakness the nature of the international capitalist system or the way it was operated, that is, the policies pursued by governments? Were such policies, to the extent they were important, the consequence of ignorance, short-sightedness, or ill will? Were the depth and length of the depression a reflection of the strength of the shock to a relatively stable system, or were they a measure of the system's instability in the presence of a blow or series of blows of normal force (however measured)? Or—to bring the issue back among Paul Samuelson, Milton and Rose Friedman, and me—was the depression a fortuitous event, the consequence of deliberate and misguided monetary policy on the part of the U.S. Federal Reserve Board, or were its origins complex and international, involving both financial and real factors? Inevitably in drawing the threads together there will be a considerable amount of confirmation of preconceptions. I am open to the accusation of having selected statistics, facts, and incidents from the history of the decade which support a position chosen a priori. But I would claim that I have not knowingly suppressed any facts that do not fit the explanation that follows, nor ignored other explanations, such as U.S. monetary policy (Friedman), misuse of the gold standard (Robbins), mistaken deflation (Keynes), secular stagnation (Hansen), structural disequilibrium (Svennilson), and the like. The chapter is entitled "An Explanation," not "The Explanation."

The explanation of this book is that the 1929 depression was so wide, so deep, and so long because the international economic system was rendered unstable by British inability and U.S. unwillingness to assume responsibility for stabilizing it by discharging five functions:

(1) maintaining a relatively open market for distress goods;
(2) providing countercyclical, or at least stable, long-term lending;
(3) policing a relatively stable system of exchange rates;
(4) ensuring the coordination of macroeconomic policies;
(5) acting as a lender of last resort by discounting or otherwise providing liquidity in financial crisis.

These functions, I believe, must be organized and carried out by a single country that assumes responsibility for the system.[1] If this is done, and especially if the country serves as a lender of last resort in financial crisis, the economic system is ordinarily capable, in my opinion though not in that of others, of making adjustments to fairly serious dislocations by means of the market mechanism. There will be times when the structural dislocation is so far-reaching that more thoroughgoing measures are called for, such as the Marshall Plan and the British loan after the Second World War. D. E. Moggridge believes that the dislocation was so deepseated in 1929 through 1931 that no rescue loans from France and the United States to Austria, Germany, and England would have served to halt the spiraling

---

1. Political scientists refer to the leadership position of a single country as "hegemony." I prefer to think of it as responsibility. Hegemony may, however, be more realistic as well as more cynical. It should be noted that political scientists debate whether hegemony is needed for the maintenance of peace and of world economic stability. See Robert O. Keohane, *After Hegemony: Cooperation and Discord in the World Political Economy*, 1984. Keohane thinks that international regimes can substitute for hegemony. Regimes are institutionalized habits of cooperation. They are more precisely defined as "principles, norms, rules and decision-making procedures around which actor expectations converge in a given issue-area" (Stephen D. Krasner, "Structural Causes and Regime Consequences: Regimes as Intervening Variables," 1983, p. 1).

collapse of currencies.[2] The question is whether the shocks to the system—overproduction in primary products, French insistence on collecting reparations from Germany, U.S. demands for payment of war debts, overvaluation of the pound and undervaluation of the French franc, the halting of foreign lending by New York, the stock market crash, and the like—were so great that they would overwhelm any set of defenses; or whether, in the absence of some country willing and able to act as a stabilizer, any random shock to the system above some minimum level could set the unstable system off toward depression.

My contention is that the difficulty lay in considerable latent instability in the system and the absence of a stabilizer. Before the First World War, Britain stabilized the world by the discharge of the functions listed, more or less, and with the enormous help of gold standard mythology, which internalized both stable exchange rates and coordinated macroeconomic policies. There were occasions when Britain was either not involved or stood aside, as in 1873 when Central Europe and the United States shared a long depression.[3] In 1890, after five years of accelerated foreign lending, the London capital market suddenly stopped. The system was saved, after depression lasting from 1890 to 1895, by a deus ex machina in the form of a substantial flow of gold from the Rand mines of the Transvaal, discovered in 1886.[4] In 1929, 1930, and 1931 Britain could not act as a stabilizer, and the United States would not. When

2. See his "Policy in the Crises of 1920 and 1929." Haberler agrees with the position taken here, that the aftermaths of the First and Second world wars called for different therapies because of differences in the extent of physical, economic, and political devastation and dislocation. See his "Die Weltwirtschaft und das internationale Währungssystem in der Zeit zwischen den beiden Weltkriegen," pp. 288–89. It may be remarked, however, that some years ago Haberler sided with those such as Roy Harrod, Friederich Lutz, Jacob Viner, and Senator Joseph Ball who opposed the notion of "dollar shortage," and in some instances the Marshall Plan, maintaining that stability and growth could be reestablished in Europe right after the war if countries would "halt the inflation and adjust the exchange rate." See the discussion in my *Dollar Shortage*, 1950, pp. 2–6.

For a largely political view that the two postwar eras are of the same piece, together with dissents, see Charles S. Maier, "The Two Postwar Eras and the Conditions for Stability in Twentieth-Century Europe," 1981, with comments by Stephen A. Schuker and me, and a reply by Maier.

3. See my *Manias, Panics, and Crashes*, p. 211.

4. See my "International Propagation of Financial Crises."

every country turned to protect its national private interest, the world public interest went down the drain, and with it the private interests of all.

Maintaining a market for distress goods

Maintaining a market for distress goods can be regarded as another form of financing. Free trade has two dimensions: (1) to adapt domestic resources to changes in productive capacities abroad and (2) to keep the import market open in periods of stress. The first is more readily done by a rapidly growing country which needs to transfer resources out of less productive occupations and is willing to embrace the competition of imports. By holding firm to free trade during depression at some short-run cost to resources in import-competing lines, the second provides a market for surpluses accumulated abroad. Britain clung to free trade from 1846 (or some year thereafter, such as 1860, when all tariffs but those for revenue had been dismantled) until 1916. After 1873, although not growing rapidly, it continued to adhere to free trade since its declining industries were exporters rather than import-competers. Britain's tenacity in adhering to free trade in depression may have been born of cultural lag and the free trade tradition of Adam Smith rather than of conscious service to the world economy.

The contrast is with the Smoot-Hawley Tariff Act of 1930. At the first hint of trouble in agriculture, Hoover reached for the Republican household remedy, as Schumpeter characterized it, in the face of a recommendation of the World Economic Conference of 1927 that nations of the world should adopt a tariff truce. The action was important less for its impact on the U.S. balance of payments, or as conduct unbecoming a creditor nation, than for its irresponsibility. The congressional rabble enlarged protection from agriculture to primary products and manufactures of all kinds, and Hoover, despite more than thirty formal protests from other countries and the advice of 1,000 economists, signed the bill into law. This gave rise to (or at least did nothing to stop) a headlong stampede to protection and restriction on imports, each country trying to ward off deflationary pressure of imports, and all together ensuring such pressure through mutual restriction of exports. As with exchange depreciation to raise domestic prices, the gain for one country was a loss for all. With tariff retaliation and competitive depreciation, mutual losses were certain. The formula of tariff truce and exchange stabilization proposed for the World Economic Conference of 1933 offered no positive means of raising prices or expanding employment. It would nonetheless have been significant as a means of slowing further decline. With no major country providing a market for distress goods or willing to tolerate appreciation, much less offering to furnish long-term capital or discounting facilities to countries suffering from payment difficulties, the fallacy of composition with the whole less than the sum of its parts ensured that deflation would roll on.

Countercyclical lending

In the nineteenth century Great Britain tended to lend abroad on a countercyclical basis, with some exceptions such as the 1890 episode already referred to.[5] But by and large, and especially after mid-century, foreign and domestic lending were maintained in counterpoint. Domestic recession stimulated foreign lending, while a boom at home caused both lending to be cut back and imports to be expanded, providing an export stimulus abroad in place of domestic investment with borrowed funds. Countercyclical lending stabilized the system.

In the 1920s, U.S. foreign lending was positively correlated with domestic investment, not counterpoised. The boom of the 1920s was accompanied by foreign lending; the depression of the 1930s saw the capital flow reversed. In *The United States and the World Economy*, written in 1943, Hal Lary recorded the fundamental fact that the United States cut down on imports and lending at the same time. The cut in lending actually preceded the stock market crash as investors were diverted from the boom in foreign bonds that followed the Dawes loan to the boom in domestic stocks dating from the spring of 1928. The deflationary pressure on Germany may be debated; the pressure on the less developed countries at the periphery is clear-cut.[6] As Table 1 shows, moreover, Britain joined the United States in reducing its lending in 1929 over 1928.

5. See my "The Cyclical Pattern of Long-Term Lending."
6. Fleisig, "The United States and the World Periphery in the Early Years of the Great Depression."

Stable exchange rates

Exchange rates were stable in the nineteenth century because of the gold standard. The price of gold was fixed in Britain in 1717 and in France in 1726 and maintained, with interruptions for war and crisis, until 1931 and 1928, respectively. Most economists believe that the gold standard was managed by the Bank of England, with occasional help from the Bank of France, the Bank of Hamburg, and the State Bank of Russia. The system was accepted as an objective fact, hardly subject to alteration. It was internalized and thus legitimate.

When after the inflations of the First World War, exchange rates were either restored or adjusted, it was important to get them fixed at equilibrium levels. Attention was devoted to the problem. In most countries, economists worked at calculating purchasing power parities, without, however, always making adequate allowance for structural changes, such as the loss of overseas assets by Britain or the large volume of French capital that in 1926 was waiting abroad for the opportune moment to return to its normal habitat. Italy chose an exchange rate based almost entirely on prestige. The resulting pattern of rates put stress on the system.

Then came the depression and the response of many countries on the periphery, cut off from borrowing and facing sharply declining export prices and values, to depreciate their currencies. A certain amount of competitive exchange depreciation took place. Britain did not care how far the pound sank, but it created the Exchange Equalization Account to keep it from rising. The response of monetary authorities to the chaotic behavior of exchange rates in the 1930s was to adopt fixed rates at Bretton Woods in 1944 as a standard to prevent beggar-thy-neighbor tactics. When the set of rates came under stress as countries pursued independent macroeconomic policies, many economists came out in favor of floating. It was originally thought by many, and is still widely maintained by monetarists, that freely flexible exchange rates provide insulation from world conditions of instability for a given country. Experience both in the 1930s and in the 1970s, however, seems to indicate otherwise. In a world of deflation, as in the 1930s, flexible exchange rates with overshooting are deflationary. Depreciation leaves domestic prices unchanged and reduces prices in countries where exchange rates have appreciated. In a world of inflation, on the other hand, as in the 1970s, the ratchet works in the opposite sense: depreciation raises domestic prices; appreciation leaves foreign prices unchanged.

Economists have yet to agree on how best to achieve the optimal degree of exchange rate stability, steady in the short run, adjusted in the long as structural changes are called for and macroeconomic policies diverge. Nor is it clear how leadership would provide it today, though the United States dominated the Bretton Woods institutions until the early 1970s.

Coordination of macroeconomic policies

Like exchange rates, macroeconomic policies were coordinated more or less automatically in the nineteenth century under the gold standard. The Bank of England had gradually developed techniques for management of the London money and capital markets, which communicated monetary policy to the rest of the country and the world. Fiscal policy scarcely existed in a world of balanced peacetime budgets, except as the shape of taxes changed. Such changes were designed for resource allocation and income redistribution, not for maintaining stability of national income.

The gold standard basically broke down in the interwar period when the United States and France, accumulating gold, sterilized it. Monetary policy was conducted largely for domestic purposes, except for the episode of 1927, which was later regarded as a mistake. German inflation in 1923 rendered that country paranoid about inflation. Positive fiscal policy was followed practically nowhere, not even in Sweden. And monetary policies went uncoordinated: it was "devil take the hindmost" or *sauve qui peut.*

Lender of last resort

The lender of last resort function has two dimensions, one domestic, one international. On the domestic front, it received timely attention. Montagu Norman of the Bank of England rescued the William Deacons Bank in January 1929. In October of that year, George Harrison of the Federal Reserve Bank of New York rushed into the breach with open market operations well in excess of the limits assigned him by the Federal Reserve Board in Washington in an effort to shore up the liquidity of the New York market. In Italy a variety of banks were saved secretly in 1930, well before the first bank panic in the United States in November and December of that year. The German record was less positive. A Social Democratic memorandum in July 1931 argued that the Reichsbank should undertake a new issue of banknotes without regard to the legal limits imposed by its gold and foreign exchange reserves, avoiding the danger of inflation by raising the discount rate. It undertook the latter, but not the former.[7] And the Danatbank was allowed to fail, a sin of omission regarded as incomprehensible from today's perspective.[8]

It was, however, in the international dimension that the lender of last resort was most conspicuously missing. The task is a difficult one at best, but Britain tried, up to the last 50 million schillings for Austria in June 1931, when the rest of the world had backed out. After that setback, Britain stood aside from a loan to Germany, while the French and Americans undertook one—"too little and too late," not to mention the stringent French political conditions. When it came England's turn to seek help, the United States and France proceeded with one loan at a time—salami tactics, when the Bagehot prescription was to lend freely—and attached economic conditions to the second loan so severe that they brought the Labour government down. Conditionality in rescue loans raised in Third World negotiations with the IMF today is not a new problem.

British leadership

Not until 1931 was it clear that Britain could not provide the leadership. In the early 1920s there were League of Nations programs for the stabilization of the currencies of Austria and Hungary. These were to a considerable extent British in spirit, with help of experts from Scandinavia, the Low Countries, and the dominions such as staffed the League of Nations Economic, Financial, and Transit Department. Later the Dawes and Young plans to settle German reparations were dominated by British experts, with Americans serving as front men to foster the British hope of tying reparations to war debts. By 1931 British capacity for leadership had gone. In small

7. Holtfrerich, "Alternativen zu Brünings Wirtschaftspolitik in der Weltwirtschaftskrise," p. 6.

8. Irmler, "Bankenkrise und Vollbeschäftigungspolitik," p. 287.

part it had been dissipated in puerile central bank quarrels between Norman and Moreau, although much of the competition for domination over the smaller central banks of Europe was the product of Moreau's imagination. (Benjamin Strong tried hard to arbitrate these quarrels, and his death in 1928 was a loss for the stability of the system.) More significant was the burden of French sterling balances, which inhibited Britain as a lender of last resort. At the World Economic Conference in 1933 it was clear that Britain had turned away from a leading world role, cultivating the Commonwealth and freedom to manage sterling, and largely leaving it to the United States to devise a world program.

Lack of U.S. leadership

Revisionist historians, such as William A. Williams, insist that the United States undertook a leading world role, under Charles E. Hughes, as early as the Disarmament Conference of 1922.[9] It is difficult or impossible to find support for this position in the field of international economics, which holds with the conventional wisdom of such historians as E. H. Carr, that "in 1918, world leadership was offered, by almost universal consent, to the United States . . . [and] was declined."[10] There was interest in the affairs of Europe in New York, in the Federal Reserve Bank of New York under Strong and Harrison, and in the financial community represented by such people as Dwight Morrow, Thomas Lamont, and Norman Davis. A few non–New Yorkers, such as Charles G. Dawes and Andrew Mellon, were brought into international finance and diplomacy. On the whole, however, the isolationism expressed by Henry Cabot Lodge in leading the rejection of the Versailles Treaty and U.S. adherence

9. See, for example, William Appleman Williams, *The Tragedy of American Diplomacy*, 1959, esp. ch. 4, "The Legend of Isolationism." Mr. Williams, a Marxist revisionist historian, states: "Hoover did not grasp the fact that the depression was a sign of stagnation in a corporate economy which was born during the civil war and came to maturity in the decade from 1895 to 1905" (p. 123); and: "From the fall of 1932 Roosevelt and Hull stressed the importance of foreign trade for domestic revival and expansion and for world wide relief of conditions which caused war and revolution" (p. 128). It is difficult to see how a historian could ignore such evidence as the First Inaugural Address, cited earlier, to be able to make such a statement about Roosevelt.

10. Edward Hallett Carr, *The Twenty Years' Crisis, 1919–1939: An Introduction to the Study of International Relations*, 1946, p. 234.

to the League of Nations typified the dominant sentiment. The United States was uncertain in its international role. It felt that the British were shrewder, more sophisticated, more devious in their negotiating tactics, so that the United States came out of international conferences losers. Stimson would have been willing to undertake a major discounting operation to rescue the Reichsmark in July 1931; Hoover, Mellon, and (though from New York) Mills were opposed to sending good money after bad, as discounting calls for. In 1933 James Warburg, Moley, and presumably Woodin and Roosevelt still resisted sending good money after bad. Proposals for embryonic international monetary funds were legion, and even Britain presented one officially. They were uniformly turned down with a lecture on how much the United States had already lost in unpaid war debts and the Standstill Agreement.[11] It was not until 1942 that Harry D. White began preparing a world plan for discussion at Bretton Woods—together with the plan of Lord Keynes—a world plan for limited discounting.

Cooperation

Clarke's conclusion that central bank cooperation was maintained up to mid-1928 but failed thereafter has already been dealt with in some detail. In summary, such cooperation as there was on matters such as hegemony over small central banks or the choice of an equilibrium exchange rate was inadequate before 1926, and the Bank of France supported the pound loyally (and expensively) in the late summer of 1931. A deeper question is whether cooperation as such would have been sufficient. In *America's Role in the World Economy*,[12] Alvin Hansen prescribed for the United States policies of maintenance of full employment at home and cooperation with international efforts at freer trade, restoring capital movements, improvement of the world monetary system, and so on. With the ad-

11. Pedersen blames the liquidity crisis of 1931 on the United States for its failure to support the German mark and, when that had been forced to suspend gold payments, for its failure to underwrite sterling. See "Some Notes on the Economic Policy of the United States During the Period 1919–1932," in his *Essays in Monetary Theory and Related Subjects*, pp. 208–9. This would be agreed today, and Professor Pedersen put it forward himself, as noted earlier, in 1933. As he himself points out, however (p. 210), the United States was acting with "the normal prejudices of the period."

12. Alvin Hansen, *America's Role in the World Economy*, 1945.

vantage of hindsight, it appears that more than cooperation was provided—namely, leadership—and that mere cooperation would not have built the institutions and policies of the Organization for Economic Cooperation and Development, Group of Ten, Bank for International Settlements, International Monetary Fund, International Bank, General Agreement on Tariffs and Trade, and so on. As an acquaintance on the International Monetary Fund staff put it (admittedly to an American), if the United States did not take the leadership, nothing happened. Leadership may lack followership, and foolish or even sensible proposals may be defeated through lack of support. But the most sensible proposals emanating from small countries are valueless if they lack the capacity to carry them out and fail to enlist the countries that do. The World Economic Conference of 1933 did not lack ideas, as that of 1927 seems to have done. But the one country capable of leadership was bemused by domestic concerns and stood aside.

One special form of cooperation would have been joint Anglo-American leadership in the economic affairs of the world. The 1980s equivalent is the frequently proposed troika of Germany, Japan, and the United States, which could furnish the world leadership needed today now that American capacity or will to provide it alone has been dissipated. However, economists and political scientists usually agree that such arrangements, whether duopoly or bilateral monopoly, are unstable. Carr states explicitly that the hope for Pax Anglo-Saxonica was romantic and that Pax Americana "would be an easier contingency."[13] Vansittart, referring to the Standstill agreements and the German occupation of the Rhineland, wrote apropos of the World Economic Conference: "When action was required two years earlier, the two governments [British and American] sheltered behind each other like the British and French governments three years later."[14] With a duumvirate, a troika, or slightly wider forms of collective responsibility such as the Summit of Seven or the Group of Ten, the buck has no place to stop.

Changing leaders

Friedman and Schwartz make a great deal of the role in the great depression of the shift of monetary leadership in the United States

13. Carr, *The Twenty Years' Crisis, 1919–39*, pp. 233–34.
14. Vansittart, *The Mist Procession*, p. 466.

from New York to Washington.[15] They suggest that this sounds far-fetched, since it is a "sound general principle that great events have great origins," but note that small events at times have large consequences through chain reactions and cumulative force. The universality of the asserted principle seems dubious to this observer;[16] the observation that shifts of the locus of leadership give rise to instability does not. Had they not focused so exclusively on monetary conditions in the United States, Friedman and Schwartz might have noted the accentuation of the depression that came with the transfer of the presidency from Hoover to Roosevelt (occurring after the money supply had been greatly enlarged) and the still more significant (in my judgment) transfer of leadership in the world economy from Whitehall to the White House.

This notion of the instability of a financial system with two centers, or of one where leadership is in the process of being dropped by one and picked up by another, is cited by Edward Nevin as crucial to the collapse of the gold standard in 1931. He quotes Sir Ernest Harvey's testimony before the Macmillan Committee: "such leadership as we possess has been affected by the position which America has gained," making a change in the ancient system as set out in the Macmillan Report, under which the bank rate regulated the reserve position of the United Kingdom, and other countries adjusted their positions to that of Britain. He then went on to say, "Better that a motorcar should be in charge of a poor driver than of two quite excellent drivers who are perpetually fighting to gain control of the vehicle."[17] The analogy of two excellent drivers fighting for control of the wheel may be more graphic than apposite. The instability seems rather to have come from the growing weakness of one driver and the lack of sufficient interest in the other. William Adams Brown, Jr., describes the gold standard of the period as "without a focal point," meaning that it had two, but the conclu-

15. Friedman and Schwartz, *A Monetary History of the United States, 1867–1960*, p. 419.

16. Cf. Benjamin Franklin, *Maxims Prefixed to Poor Richard's Almanac*, 1757: "Little strokes fell great oaks" and "A little neglect may breed mischief: for want of a nail the shoe was lost; for want of a shoe the horse was lost; for want of a horse the rider was lost." The exception for cumulative feedback embraces the second quotation, but not the first.

17. Nevin, *The Mechanism of Cheap Money*, pp. 9n., 12, 14.

sions of his monumental work do not dwell on this critical aspect of the world economy.[18]

Role of the small countries and France

One passenger in the vehicle which did not lack interest was France. And one group which lacked responsibility—to discontinue the metaphor, or perhaps they should be regarded as passengers in the back seat—consisted of the smaller countries: Belgium, the Netherlands, Switzerland, and Scandinavia. The smaller countries can be disposed of first. They are sometimes blamed, as in Born's analysis, for having acted irresponsibly in, say, converting sterling into gold in the summer of 1931 or raising tariffs with alacrity after 1930. There is, however, no universally accepted standard of behavior for small countries. On one showing, they lack power to affect the outcome of great events and are therefore privileged to look after the private national interest rather than concern themselves with the public good of stability in the world economy as a whole. On a somewhat higher ethical level, the small countries may be held to the Kantian categorical imperative, which enjoins them to act only in ways that can be generalized. In such circumstances, of course, they would not have withdrawn credits from Austria in the spring of 1931, nor from Germany and Britain in the summer, nor from the United States in the autumn. The economist chooses between these standards perhaps on the basis of comparative cost. If the Netherlands had known the cost of leaving its sterling unconverted into gold, it seems unlikely that it would have done so, even at the risk of accelerating the collapse of the pound and deepening the world depression. It may be that such countries as Sweden, Canada, and New Zealand that set high standards of international conduct—in foreign aid, contributions to United Nations peacekeeping missions, etc.—do so solely for ethical reasons; or they may choose among occasions to take largely the opportunities that are relatively

18. W. A. Brown, *The International Gold Standard Reinterpreted, 1914–34*, vol. 2, p. 781: "The essential difference between the international gold standard of 1928–29 and that of 1914 was that when the world returned to gold after the war it built its international financial system around a nucleus of London and New York, and not a single center." The title of his ch. 20 is "The Experiment of a Gold Exchange Standard without a Focal Point."

cheap. One may thus note that the small countries contributed substantially to the deflation by the speed with which they cut imports, depreciated, or converted sterling and dollars into gold, but find it hard to blame them for it.[19]

There is another aspect to the role of small countries: they could offer programs for recovery because they knew that the major cost of programs adopted would fall on other countries. Proposals for an embryonic international monetary fund in the Washington discussions preceding the World Economic Conference of 1933 were put forward by Poland, Turkey, Belgium, the ILO, and one was made by Britain, though this latter was quickly withdrawn when the United States frowned on it. Lacking resources to make these schemes effective, small countries were reduced to advisory roles without conviction, even when the proposals were sound. An essential ingredient of followership is to convince the leader that he is the author of the ideas that require the use of his resources.

The case of France is different. France sought power in its own national interest, without adequately taking into account the repercussions of its positions on world economic or political stability. Its intransigence in the matter of reparations or the attempt to attach political conditions to the second Austrian credit of June 1931 or the contemplated German loan of July of that year illustrate the position. Hurt in the depreciation of sterling in September, the Bank of France, under strong political pressure at home, converted its dollars into gold in the private national interest during 1931–32, all the while protesting its cooperation and concern for the interest of the United States. The rivalry between the Bank of France and the Bank of England over which should take over the leadership in restoring independence to central banks and stabilization of currencies in Eastern Europe would be pathetic, had it not run risks of instability for the system as a whole when the French threatened to withdraw balances from London.

Not quite big enough to have responsibility forced on it, nor small enough to afford the luxury of irresponsibility, the French po-

19. For an interesting political model of countries that are free-riders behind the leadership of others, see Norman Froelich and Joe A. Oppenheimer, "I Get Along with a Little Help from My Friends," 1970. But note (p. 119) that leadership is rewarded in this model rather than made to pay for the privilege, as implied where the responsibilities of leadership are maintaining an open market for goods, a countercyclical export of capital and a mechanism for rediscounting in crisis.

sition in the interwar period was unenviable. It had the power to act as a destabilizer, but it was insufficiently powerful to stabilize.[20] "Great Britain and the United States together were the active nucleus that replaced the single centre of prewar days, but the position and policy of France actively affected their mutual as well as their joint relations to the outlying countries."[21] In these circumstances France could be (and was) blamed for upsetting the system when she had no capacity to take it over and run it in the presence of two larger powers, one feeble, the other irresponsible.

Public versus private interest

Cynicism suggests that leadership is fully rewarded for its pains in prestige and that no matter how much it protests its commitment to the public welfare, its fundamental concern is private. Bismarck insisted that free trade was the weapon of the dominant economy anxious to prevent others from following in its path. "The white man's burden" is an expression used today only in mockery. A country like France deliberately setting out to achieve prestige suggests that those with a concern for problem solving are either perfidious or self-deceiving. Nevertheless, there is a difference between accepting and declining responsibility for the way the system is run. The British accepted responsibility, although, as the 50 million schilling loan emphasizes, they were unable to discharge it. The French and the United States were unwilling to underwrite stability. Under Coolidge and Hoover, the United States refused to commit itself to any program of foreign reconstruction or currency stabilization, leaving these questions to the Federal Reserve System.[22] There was hardly any improvement in Roosevelt's commitment to the world economy until timidly in 1936, at the time of the Tripartite Monetary Pact, and ultimately during the Second World War. Inside France, as between France and the other leading powers, "all groups thought their opponents more united and dedicated than they were, and a concern for the general interest was virtually absent."[23]

20. See my "International Monetary Politics of a Near-Great Power: Two French Episodes, 1926–36 and 1960–70," 1972.

21. W. A. Brown, *The International Gold Standard Reinterpreted, 1914–34*, p. 785.

22. Chandler, *Benjamin Strong*, p. 255.

23. Sauvy, *Histoire économique de la France entre les deux guerres*, vol. 1., p. 73.

Unable to cope with the public good, the British more and more turned their energy to the private. Keynes's advocacy of a tariff and the refusal to contemplate stabilization after 1931 are examples. One may find a hint or two in the documents that the initiative came from the dominions rather than Britain.[24] For a time, until well after the war, the British economics profession and public almost drew the lesson that each country should take care of itself without regard to external effects.

The point is illustrated in the memorandum written by Hubert Henderson at the British Treasury in 1943, entitled "International Economic History of the Interwar Period."[25] This summarizes the crude view that the depression resulted from nationalism and tariffs, the collapse of world trade, bilateralism and preferences, and disregard of the advice of the League of Nations, leading to the conclusion that after the war there is need for the world to be more resolute in avoiding economic nationalism and attempting to construct a freely working economic system with international credits, the reduction of trade barriers, and the outlawry of qualitative regulation.[26] Henderson states that the history of the interwar period provides no support for this view. He opposes exchange depreciation: "There can be little doubt that the depreciation of the pound was in part responsible for the sharper fall in gold prices, and disillusionment is general in the United Kingdom and still more in the United States on the power of exchange depreciation to promote national recovery."[27]

But the conventional view is false in all essential respects. The old international order has broken down for good. Nothing but

24. See *Documents diplomatiques français, 1932–39*, 1967, vol. 3, no. 470, Bonnet to Paul-Boncour, July 9, 1933, p. 871: "One fact is evident: it is that Britain is not free. Its dominions and in particular Canada whose Prime Minister Bennett is a man of extraordinary violence have a predominant influence on her, to the point of modifying totally her opinion in the space of a few seconds." This is doubtless hyperbole. For an up-to-date account of the origins of imperial preference written by a Canadian, see Drummond, *Imperial Economic Policy, 1917–39*.

25. See Hubert D. Henderson, *The Interwar Years and Other Papers*, 1955, pp. 236–95.

26. Ibid., pp. 236, 290.

27. Ibid., pp. 260, 262; see also p. 291: "Of the various expedients which different governments employed in the 1930s, none produced more unfortunate results than deliberate exchange depreciation. It was the least helpful to the countries which tried it, and the most harmful to other countries."

futility and frustration can come from the attempt to set it up again. Individual countries must be free to regulate their external economies effectively, using control of capital movements, quantitative regulation, preferences, autonomous credit policies, etc.[28]

This foot-dragging, which Keynes shared during the 1930s and until late in the war, is understandable. It misses the main lesson of the interwar years, however: that for the world economy to be stabilized, there has to be a stabilizer—one stabilizer.

Relevance to the 1980s and 1990s

Leadership is a word with negative connotations in the 1980s, when participation in decision making is regarded as more aesthetic. Much of the overtones of *der Führer* and *il Duce* remain. But if leadership is thought of as the provision of the public good of responsibility, rather than exploitation of followers or the private good of prestige, it remains a positive idea. It may one day be possible to pool sovereignties to limit the capacity of separate countries to work against the general interest; such pooling is virtually attained today in some of the functions needed to stabilize the world economic system, such as the Basel arrangements for swaps and short-term credits, which, pending a world central bank, serve as a world rediscounting mechanism in crisis. In this area, and in the world agencies for maintaining freer trade and a liberal flow of capital and aid, however, leadership is necessary in the absence of delegated authority. That of the United States is slipping. It is not yet clear that the rising strength of Europe in an enlarged European Economic Community or of Japan will be accompanied by an assertion of leadership in providing a market for distress or aggressive goods, in stabilizing the international flow of capital, or in providing a discount mechanism for crisis. Presumably the Basel arrangements for the last will endure. There are indications that the European market for goods will remain ample, except in agriculture, which is an important exception from a world viewpoint. There is still some distance to go to stabilize the flow of capital countercyclically.

As the U.S. economic leadership in the world economy falters and Europe and Japan gather strength, three outcomes are politically stable, three unstable. Among the stable outcomes are contin-

28. Ibid., p. 293.

ued or revived U.S. leadership, after the exchange controls of 1963 to 1968 and the recent wave of protectionism have been reversed; an assertion of leadership and assumption of responsibility for the stability of the world system by Europe, Japan, or some unsuspected third country such as Brazil; or an effective cession of economic sovereignty to international institutions: a world central bank, a world capital market, and an effective General Agreement on Tariffs and Trade. The last is the most attractive, but perhaps, because difficult, the least likely. As between the first two alternatives, the responsible citizen should be content with either, flipping a coin to decide, if the third alternative proves unavailable, simply to avoid the undesirable alternatives.

The three outcomes to be avoided because of their instability are: (1) the United States, Japan, and the EEC vying for leadership of the world economy, (2) one unable to lead and the others unwilling, as in 1929 to 1933, and (3) each retaining a veto over programs of stability or strengthening of the system without seeking to secure positive programs of its own. The articles of agreement of the International Monetary Fund (IMF) were set up to provide the United States with a veto over action it opposed. In the 1969 reform that legislated the addition of Special Drawing Rignts (SDRs) to the monetary system, quotas of the IMF were adjusted to provide a veto to the EEC as well. This leaves open the possibility of stalemate, as in the United Nations Security Council, when two major powers are unable to agree. In the circumstances of the Security Council there is a danger of regressive spiral into war; the analogue in the economic field is stalemate—and depression.

The third positive alternative of international institutions with real authority and sovereignty remains pressing.

Bibliography

Aldcroft, D. See Richardson, H. W., and D. Aldcroft.

Aliber, Robert Z. "Speculation in the Foreign Exchanges: The European Experience, 1919–1926." *Yale Economic Essays* 2, no. 1 (Spring 1962): 170–245.

American Bureau of Metal Statistics. *Yearbook of the American Bureau of Metal Statistics, 11th Annual Issue, 1930*. New York: American Bureau of Metal Statistics, 1931.

Angell, James W. *The Recovery of Germany*. New Haven: Yale University Press, 1929; enlarged and revised edition, 1932.

———. *The Program for the World Economic Conference: The Experts' Agenda and the Document*. Boston: World Peace Foundation, 1933.

Armstrong, Hamilton Fish. "France and the Hoover Plan." *Foreign Affairs* 10, no. 1 (October 1931): 23–33.

Arndt, H. W. *The Economic Lessons of the 1930s*. London: Oxford University Press, 1944.

Artaud, Denise. *La question des dettes interalliées et la reconstruction de l'Europe (1917–1929)*. 2 vols. Paris: Librairie Honoré Champion, 1978.

Auriol, Vincent. *Hier et aujourd'hui*. Paris: Charlot, 1945.

Baade, Fritz. "Fighting Depression in Germany." In *So Much*

Alive: The Life and Work of W. S. Woytinsky, edited by Emma S. Woytinsky, 61–69. New York: Vanguard Press, 1962.

Backhaus, Juergens. "Economic Theories and Political Interests: Scholarly Economics in Pre-Hitler Germany." *Journal of European Economic History* 12, no. 3 (Winter 1983): 661–67.

Bagehot, Walter. *Lombard Street*. London: John Murray, 1917.

Balderston, T. "The Origins of Economic Instability in Germany, 1924–30: Investment and the Capital Market." *Economic History Review*, 2d ser. 36, no. 3 (August 1983): 395–415.

Banco di Roma. *Banca e industrie fra le due guerre*. Vol. 1: *Atti del convegne conclusivo della ricerca promossa dal Banco di Roma in occasione del suo primo centario*. Vol. 2: *Le riforme istituzionale e il pensiero giuridico*. Bologna: Il Mulino, 1981.

———. *Le istituzioni finanziarie degli anni Trenta nell' Europa continentale*. Bologna: Il Mulino, 1982.

Bank for International Settlements. Annual reports. Various years.

Banks and Industry in the Interwar Period. A special issue of *Journal of European Economic History* 13 (Fall 1984).

Barber, Clarence. "On the Origins of the Great Depression." *Southern Economic Journal* 44 (1978): 432–56.

Bassett, R. *Nineteen Thirty-One: Political Crisis*. London: Macmillan, 1958.

Baudhuin, Fernand. *Histoire économique de la Belgique, 1914–1938*. 2 vols. Brussels: Etablissements Emile Bruyles, 1946.

Bauer, P. T. *The Rubber Industry: A Study in Competition and Monopoly*. Cambridge, Mass.: Harvard University Press; London: Longmans, Green, 1948.

Beenstock, Michael, Forrest Capie, and Brian Griffiths. "The Economic Recovery in the United Kingdom in the 1930s." *Bulletin*. Center for Economic Policy Research, no. 2 (April 1984): 1.

Belli, Franco. "La legge bancarie del 1926 e del 1936–38." In Banco di Roma, *Banca e industrie fra le due guerre*, vol. 2: *Le riforme istituzionale e il pensiero giuridico*, 203–68. Bologna: Il Mulino, 1981.

Bellman, Harold. "The Building Trades." In *Britain in Recovery*. London: Pitman, 1938.

Bennett, Edward W. *Germany and the Diplomacy of the Financial Crisis, 1931*. Cambridge, Mass.: Harvard University Press, 1962.

Bernanke, Ben S. "Non-monetary Effects of the Financial Crisis in the Propagation of the Great Depression." *American Economic Review* 73, no. 3 (June 1983): 257–76.

Bernstein, E. M. See Review Committee for Balance of Payments Statistics.

Bernstein, Michael A. "A Reassessment of Investment Failure in the Interwar American Economy." *Journal of Economic History* 44, no. 4 (June 1984): 479–88.

Beyen, J. W. *Money in a Maelstrom*. New York: Macmillan, 1949.

Blum, John Morton. *From the Morgenthau Diaries*. Vol. 1: *Years of Crisis, 1928–1938*. Boston: Houghton Mifflin, 1959.

Booth, Alan. See Glynn, Sean, and Alan Booth.

Borchardt, Knut. "Zwangslagen und Handlungsspielräume in der grossen Wirtschaftskrise der frühen dreissiger Jahre: Zur Revision des überlieferten Geschichtsbildes." In Bayerische Akademie der Wissenschaften, *Jahrbuch, 1979*, 1–47. Munich: C. H. Beck, 1979.

———. "Zur Frage der währungspolitischen Optionen Deutschlands in der Weltwirtschaftskrise." In *Theorie und Politik der internationalen Wirtschaftsbeziehungen*, edited by K. Borchardt and Franz Holtheu, 165–81. Stuttgart: Gustav Fischer Verlag, 1980.

———. "Zur Aufarbeitung der Vor- und Frühgeschichte der Keynesianismus in Deutschland." In *Jahrbücher für Nationalökonomie und Statistik* 197, no. 4 (1982): 359–70.

———. "Could and Should Germany Have Followed Great Britain in Leaving the Gold Standard?" *Journal of European Economic History* 13 (Winter 1984): 471–97.

———. "Inflationsgefahren in Weltwirtschaftskrise: Zu den Spielräumen der Brüningschen Wirtschaftspolitik, 1930–32." In *International Capital Movements, Debt, and Monetary System*, edited by Wolfram Engels, Armin Gutkowski, and Henry Wallich, 21–42. Mainz: Hase & Koehler, 1984.

Born, Karl Erich. *Die deutsche Bankenkrise, 1931: Finanzen und Politik*. Munich: R. Piper, 1967.

Bouvier, Jean. "Le banche francesi, l'inflazione e la crisi economica, 1919–1939." In Banco di Roma, *Le istituzioni finanziarie degli anni Trenta nell' Europa continentale*, 11–64. Bologna: Il Mulino, 1982.

Boyle, Andrew. *Montagu Norman*. London: Cassell, 1967.

Brand, R. H. "Gold: A World Problem." *International Conciliation*, no. 333 (October 1937): 663–77.

Brown, E. C. "Fiscal Policy in the Thirties, a Reappraisal." *American Economic Review* 46, no. 5 (December 1956): 857–79.

Brown, William Adams, Jr. *The International Gold Standard Reinterpreted, 1914–1934*. 2 vols. New York: National Bureau of Economic Research, 1940.

Brüning, Heinrich. *Reden und Aufsätze eines deutschen Staatsmannes*. Edited by Wilhelm Vernekohl. Münster: Regensburg, 1968.

———. *Memoiren, 1918–1934*. Stuttgart: Deutsche Verlags-Anstalt, 1970.

Brunner, Karl. "Epilogue: Understanding the Great Depression." In *The Great Depression Revisited*, edited by Karl Brunner, 316–58. The Hague: Martinus Nijhoff, 1981.

———, ed. *The Great Depression Revisited*. The Hague: Martinus Nijhoff, 1981.

Bulmer-Thomas, Victor. "The Central American Economies in the Interwar Period." In *Latin America in the 1930s: The Periphery in World Crisis*, edited by Rosemary Thorp, 279–314. London: Macmillan, 1984.

Bundy, McGeorge. See Stimson, Henry L., and McGeorge Bundy.

Burck, Gilbert, and Charles Silberman. "Why the Depression Lasted So Long." In *American Economic History: Essays in Interpretation*, edited by Stanley Coben and F. G. Hill, 496–512. Philadelphia: J. B. Lippincott, 1966; reprinted from *Fortune* 51, no. 3 (March 1955): 84ff.

Burtle, James L. See Rolfe, Sidney E. and James L. Burtle.

Butler, William F. "Is Another Great Depression Possible?" Unpublished memorandum. Chase Manhattan Bank, April 28, 1969.

Cagan, Phillip. "Comments on 'Some Macroeconomic Impacts of the National Recovery Act, 1933–35.'" In *The Great Depression Revisited*, edited by Karl Brunner, 282–85. The Hague: Martinus Nijhoff, 1981.

Cairncross, Alec, and Barry Eichengreen. *Sterling in Decline*. Oxford: Blackwell, 1983.

Cairncross, Alex K. *Home and Foreign Investment, 1880–1913*. Cambridge: Cambridge University Press, 1953.

Cameron, Rondo E. *France and the Economic Development of Europe, 1800–1914*. Princeton: Princeton University Press, 1961.

Capie, Forrest. *Depression and Protectionism: Britain Between the Wars*. London: Allen & Unwin, 1983.

———. See also Beenstock, Michael, Forrest Capie, and Brian Griffiths.

Carr, Edward Hallett. *The Twenty Years' Crisis, 1919–1939: An Introduction to the Study of International Relations*. London: Macmillan, 1939; 2d ed., 1946.

Cassese, Sabino. "Introduzione al dibattio." In Banco di Roma, *Banca e industrie fra le due guerre*, vol. 1: *Atti del convegne conclusivo della ricerca promossa dal Banco di Roma in occasione del suo primo centario*, 99–103. Bologna: Il Mulino, 1981.

Chandler, Lester V. *Benjamin Strong, Central Banker*. Washington, D.C.: Brookings Institution, 1958.

Clark, Carolyn. See Shearer, Ronald A., and Carolyn Clark.

Clarke, Stephen V. O. *Central Bank Cooperation, 1924–31*. New York: Federal Reserve Bank of New York, 1967.

———. "The Reconstruction of the International Monetary System: The Attempts of 1922 and 1933." *Studies in International Finance*. International Finance Section, Princeton University, no. 33 (1973).

———. "The Influence of Economists on the Tripartite Agreement of September 1936." *European Economic Review* 10 (1975): 375–89.

———. "Exchange-Rate Stabilization in the Mid-1930s: Negotiating the Tripartite Agreement." *Studies in International Finance*. International Finance Section, Princeton University, no. 41 (1977).

Clay, Henry. *Lord Norman*. London: Macmillan, 1957.

Clough, Shepard B. *The Economic History of Modern Italy*. New York: Columbia University Press, 1964.

Commercial and Financial Chronicle. Various issues, 1933.

Commission of Inquiry into National Policy in International Economic Relations. *International Economic Relations*. Minneapolis: University of Minnesota Press, 1934.

Commodity Yearbook, 1939. New York: Commodity Research Bureau, 1939.

Copland, Douglas. *Australia in the World Crisis, 1929–1933*.

Alfred Marshall Lectures delivered in the University of Cambridge, October and November 1933. Cambridge: Cambridge University Press; New York: Macmillan, 1934.

Cox, James M. *Journey Through My Years*. New York: Simon & Schuster, 1946.

Curtius, Julius. *Sechs Jahre Minister der Deutschen Republik*. Heidelberg: Carl Winter-Universitätsverlag, 1948.

Davis, Joseph S. *The World Between the Wars, 1919–1939: An Economist's View*. Baltimore: Johns Hopkins University Press, 1975.

Dean, Vera Micheles. "Austria: The Paralysis of a Nation." *Foreign Policy Reports* 3, no. 22 (January 4, 1933): 256–66.

Debeir, Jean-Claude. "La crise du franc de 1924: Un exemple de spéculation 'internationale.'" *Relations internationales*, no. 13 (1978): 29–49.

de Paiva Abreu, Marcelo. "Argentina and Brazil During the 1930s: The Impact of British and American International Economic Policies." In *Latin America in the 1930s: The Periphery in World Crisis*, edited by Rosemary Thorp, 144–62. London: Macmillan, 1984.

Despres, Emile. *International Economic Reform: The Collected Papers of Emile Despres*. Edited by Gerald M. Meier. New York: Oxford University Press, 1973.

Deutsche Bundesbank. *Währung und Wirtschaft in Deutschland, 1876–1975*. Frankfurt-am-Main: Knapp, 1976.

Díaz Alejandro, Carlos F. *Essays on the Economic History of the Argentine Republic*. New Haven: Yale University Press, 1970.

———. "Latin America in the Depression, 1929–39." In *The Theory and Experience of Economic Development: Essays in Honour of Sir W. Arthur Lewis*, edited by Mark Gersovitz et al., 334–55. London: Allen & Unwin, 1982.

———. "Latin America in the 1930s." In *Latin America in the 1930s: The Periphery in World Crisis*, edited by Rosemary Thorp, 17–49. London: Macmillan, 1984.

di Marco, Luis Eugenio, ed. *International Economics and Development: Essays in Honor of Raul Prebisch*. New York: Academic Press, 1972.

Divine, David. *Indictment of Incompetence: Mutiny at Invergordon*. London: MacDonald, 1970.

Documents diplomatiques français, 1932–1939. 1st ser., 1932–35, vols. 1–3. Paris: Imprimerie Nationale, 1966. 2d ser., 1936–39, vols. 1–4. Paris: Imprimerie Nationale, 1967.

Dohan, Michael R. "Soviet Foreign Trade: The NEP Economy and Soviet Industrialization Strategy." Ph.D. diss., Massachusetts Institute of Technology, 1969.

Dowie, J. A. "1919–20 Is in Need of Attention." *Economic History Review* 28, no. 3 (August 1975): 429–50.

Drummond, Ian M. *Imperial Economic Policy, 1917–39: Studies in Expansion and Protection*. Toronto: University of Toronto Press, 1974.

———. "London, Washington, and the Management of the Franc, 1936–39." *Studies in International Finance*. International Finance Section, Princeton University, no. 45 (1979).

DuPlessis, J. C. *Economic Fluctuations in South Africa, 1910–1949*. Stellenbosch: Bureau of Economic Research, n.d. (1950 or 1951).

Duroselle, J.-B. *De Wilson à Roosevelt*. Paris: Colin, 1960.

Eccles, Marriner S. *Beckoning Frontiers: Public and Personal Recollections*. New York: Alfred A. Knopf, 1951.

The Economist. Various issues.

Eichengreen, Barry J. "Sterling and the Tariff, 1929–32." *Studies in International Finance*. International Finance Section, Princeton University, no. 48 (1981).

———. "Keynes and Protection." *Journal of Economic History* 44, no. 2 (June 1984): 363–74.

———. See also Cairncross, Alec, and Barry Eichengreen.

Einzig, Paul. *International Gold Movements*. 2d ed. London: Macmillan, 1932.

———. *The Comedy of the Pound*. London: Kegan Paul, 1933.

———. *Bankers, Statesmen, and Economists*. London: Macmillan, 1935.

———. *World Finance Since 1914*. London: Kegan Paul; New York: Macmillan, 1935.

Falkus, M. E. "The German Business Cycle in the 1920s." *Economic History Review*, 2d ser. 28, no. 3 (August 1975): 451–65.

Federal Reserve Bank of New York files.

Federal Reserve Bulletin. Various issues.

Federal Reserve System. *Banking and Monetary Statistics*. Washington, D.C.: Federal Reserve Board, 1943.

Federn, Walter. "Der Zusammenbruch der Österreichischen Kreditanstalt." *Archiv für Sozialwissenschaft und Sozialpolitik* 67, no. 4 (June 1932): 403–35.

Feis, Herbert. *Seen from E.A.: Three International Episodes*. New York: Alfred A. Knopf, 1947.

———. *The Diplomacy of the Dollar 1919–1939*. New York: W. W. Norton, 1950.

———. *1933: Characters in Crisis*. Boston: Little, Brown, 1966.

Feldman, Gerald D. *Iron and Steel in the German Inflation, 1916–23*. Princeton: Princeton University Press, 1977.

Ferrell, Robert H. *American Diplomacy in the Great Depression: Hoover-Stimson Foreign Policy, 1929–1933*. New Haven: Yale University Press, 1957.

Field, Alexander J. "Asset Exchanges and the Transactions Demand for Money, 1919–29." *American Economic Review* 74, no. 1 (March 1984): 43–59.

———. "A New Interpretation of the Onset of the Great Depression." *Journal of Economic History* 44, no. 2 (June 1984): 489–98.

Fishlow, Albert. "Origins and Consequences of Import Substitution in Brazil." In *International Economics and Development: Essays in Honor of Raul Prebisch*, edited by Luis Eugenio di Marco, 311–65. New York: Academic Press, 1972.

Fitzgerald, E. V. K. "Restructuring in a Crisis: The Mexican Economy and the Great Depression." In *Latin America in the 1930s: The Periphery in World Crisis*, edited by Rosemary Thorp, 272–78. London: Macmillan, 1984.

Fleisig, Heywood W. "Long-Term Capital Flows and the Great Depression: The Role of the United States, 1927–1933." Ph.D. diss., Yale University, 1969.

———. "The United States and the World Periphery During the Early Years of the Great Depression." In *The Great Depression Revisited: Essays on the Economies of the Thirties*, edited by Herman van der Wee, 145–81. The Hague: Martinus Nijhoff, 1972.

Fohlen, Claude. *Une affaire de famille au XIXe siècle: Méquillet Noblot*. Paris: Colin, 1955.

Franklin, Benjamin. *Maxims Prefixed to Poor Richard's Almanac*. Philadelphia, 1757.

Friedman, Milton. *The Balance of Payments: Free Versus Fixed Exchange Rates*. Washington, D.C.: American Enterprise Institute for Public Policy Research, 1967.

————. *Newsweek* (May 25, 1970): 78.

Friedman, Milton, and Rose D. Friedman. "The Anatomy of Crisis . . . and the Failure of Policy." *Journal of Portfolio Management* 6, no. 1 (Fall 1979): 15–21.

Friedman, Milton, and Anna Jacobson Schwartz. *A Monetary History of the United States, 1867–1960*. Princeton: Princeton University Press, 1963.

————. *The Great Contraction*. Princeton: Princeton University Press, 1966; reprinted from ch. 7 of Friedman and Schwartz, *A Monetary History of the United States, 1867–1960*. Princeton: Princeton University Press, 1963.

Froelich, Norman, and Joe A. Oppenheimer. "I Get Along with a Little Help from My Friends." *World Politics* 23, no. 1 (October 1970): 104–20.

Fukai, Eigo. "The Recent Monetary Policy of Japan." In *The Lessons of Monetary Experience: Essays in Honor of Irving Fisher*, edited by A. D. Gayer, 379–95. New York: Farrar & Rinehart; London: Allen & Unwin, 1937.

Furnivall, J. S. *Netherlands India: A Study of Plural Economy*. Cambridge: Cambridge University Press, 1939.

Galbraith, J. Kenneth. *The Great Crash, 1929*. Boston: Houghton Mifflin, 1955.

Gardner, Richard N. *Sterling-Dollar Diplomacy*. Rev. ed. New York: McGraw-Hill, 1969.

Garvey, George. "Keynes and the Economic Activities of Pre-Hitler Germany." *Journal of Political Economy* 83, no. 2 (April 1975): 391–404.

[Contracting Parties for the] General Agreement on Tariffs and Trade. *Trends in International Trade*. Report by a Panel of Experts. Geneva, 1958.

Gilbert, Martin. *Winston S. Churchill*. Vol. 5: *1922–1939: The Prophet of Truth*. Boston: Houghton Mifflin, 1977.

Gilbert, Milton. *Currency Depreciation*. Philadelphia: University of Pennsylvania Press, 1939.

Glynn, Sean, and Alan Booth. "Unemployment in Interwar Britain: A Case for Relearning the Lessons of the 1930s?" *Economic History Review*, 2d ser. 36, no. 3 (August 1983): 329–48.

Gordon, Robert A. *Business Fluctuations*. 2d ed. New York: Harper & Row, 1952.

Gordon, Robert J., and James A. Wilcox. "Monetarist Interpretations of the Great Depression: An Evaluation and Critique." In *The Great Depression Revisited*, edited by Karl Brunner, 49–107. The Hague: Martinus Nijhoff, 1981.

Graham, Frank D., and Charles R. Whittlesey. *Golden Avalanche*. Princeton: Princeton University Press, 1939.

Great Britain, Committee on Finance and Industry. *Report* (Macmillan Report) Cmd. 3897. London: H.M. Stationery Office, 1931.

Green's Commodity Market Comments. October 21, 1970.

Griffiths, Brian. See Beenstock, Michael, Forrest Capie, and Brian Griffiths.

Grigg, P. J. *Prejudice and Judgement*. London: Jonathan Cape, 1948.

Grotkopp, Wilhelm. *Die grosse Krise: Lehren aus der Überwindung der Wirtschaftskrise, 1929–32*. Düsseldorf: Econ-Verlag, 1954.

Guthrie, John A. *The Newsprint Industry: An Economic Analysis*. Cambridge, Mass.: Harvard University Press, 1941.

Haberler, Gottfried. *Prosperity and Depression*. Geneva: League of Nations, 1937.

———. "Die Weltwirtschaft und das internationale Währungssystem in der Zeit zwischen den beiden Weltkriegen." In Deutsche Bundesbank, *Währung und Wirtschaft in Deutschland, 1876–1975*, 205–48. Frankfurt-am-Main: Knapp, 1976.

———. *Selected Essays of Gottfried Haberler*, edited by Anthony Y. C. Koo. Cambridge, Mass.: MIT Press, forthcoming, 1986.

Hahn, L. Albert. *Fünfzig Jahre zwischen Inflation und Deflation*. Tübingen: J. C. B. Mohr (Paul Siebeck), 1963.

Hansen, Alvin H. *Full Recovery or Stagnation*. New York: W. W. Norton, 1938.

———. *America's Role in the World Economy*. New York: W. W. Norton, 1945.

Harris, C. R. S. *Germany's Foreign Indebtedness*. London: Oxford University Press, 1935.

Harris, Seymour E. *Exchange Depreciation: Its Theory and History, 1931–35, with Some Consideration of Related Domestic Policies*. Cambridge, Mass.: Harvard University Press, 1936.

Harrison, Joseph. "The Interwar Depression and the Spanish Economy." *Journal of European Economic History* 12, no. 2 (Fall 1983): 295–321.

Hasib, Abdul. *Monetary Negotiations in the World Economic Conference*. Publications of the Faculty of Arts, Muslim University, Alijar, Egypt, 1958.

Hawtrey, Ralph G. *The Art of Central Banking*. London: Longmans, Green, 1932.

Henderson, Hubert D. *The Interwar Years and Other Papers*. Oxford: Clarendon Press, 1955.

————. See also Keynes, J. M., and H. D. Henderson.

Hilgerdt, F. See League of Nations. (F. Hilgerdt).

Hobsbawm, E. J. *Industry and Empire: An Economic History of Britain Since 1750*. London: Weidenfeld & Nicolson; New York: Pantheon, 1968.

Hodson, H. V. *Slump and Recovery, 1929–37*. London: Oxford University Press, 1938.

Holtfrerich, Carl-Ludwig. *Die deutsche Inflation, 1914–1923*. Berlin: Walther de Gruyter, 1980.

————. "Alternativen zu Brünings Wirtschaftspolitik in der Weltwirtschaftskrise." *Frankfurter Historische Vorträge*, no. 9. Wiesbaden: Franz Steiner, 1982.

Homze, Edward L. *Foreign Labor in Nazi Germany*. Princeton: Princeton University Press, 1967.

Hoover, Herbert. *The Memoirs of Herbert Hoover*. Vol. 3: *The Great Depression, 1929–1941*. New York: Macmillan; London: Hollis & Carter, 1952.

House, E. M., and Charles Seymour. *What Really Happened in Paris: The Story of the Peace Conference, 1918–1919*. New York: Charles Scribner's Sons, 1921.

Howson, Susan K. *Domestic Monetary Management in Britain, 1919–38*. Cambridge: Cambridge University Press, 1975.

————. "The Management of Sterling, 1932–39." *Journal of Economic History* 40, no. 1 (March 1980): 53–60.

————. "Sterling's Managed Float: The Operations of the Exchange Equalization Account, 1932–1949." *Studies in International Finance*. International Finance Section, Princeton University, no. 46 (1980).

Howson, Susan K., and Donald Winch. *The Economic Advisory Council, 1930–1939: A Study in Economic Advice During Depression and Recovery*. Cambridge: Cambridge University Press, 1977.

Hughes, Helen. Draft manuscript on economic history of Australia.

Hull, Cordell. *The Memoirs of Cordell Hull.* 2 vols. New York: Macmillan; London: Hodder & Stoughton, 1948.

Hunter, Helen Manning. "The Role of Business Liquidity During the Great Depression and Afterwards: Differences Between Large and Small Firms." *Journal of Economic History* 42, no. 4 (December 1982): 883–902.

Hurst, Willard. "Holland, Switzerland, and Belgium and the English Gold Crisis of 1931." *Journal of Political Economy* 40, no. 5 (October 1932): 638–60.

International Bank for Reconstruction and Development. Press Release no. 134, May 11, 1949.

The International Bank for Reconstruction and Development, 1946–1953. Baltimore: Johns Hopkins University Press, 1954.

Irmler, Heinrich. "Bankenkrise und Vollbeschäftigungspolitik (1931–1936)." In Deutsche Bundesbank, *Währung und Wirtschaft in Deutschland, 1876–1975,* 283–329. Frankfurt-am-Main: Knapp, 1976.

Iversen, C. "The Importance of the International Margin." In *Explorations in International Economics: Notes and Essays in Honor of F. W. Taussig,* 68–83. New York: McGraw-Hill, 1936.

Jacobsson, Per. *Some Monetary Problems, International and National.* London: Oxford University Press, 1958.

Jeanneney, Jean-Noël. *François de Wendel en république: L'argent et le pouvoir, 1914–1940.* Paris: Seuil, 1976.

———. *Leçon d'histoire pour une gauche au pouvoir: La faillite du Cartel (1924–26).* Paris: Seuil, 1977.

———. "De la spéculation financière comme arme diplomatique: A propos de la première bataille du franc (novembre 1923–mars 1924)." *Relations internationales,* no. 13 (1978): 5–27.

Johnson, G. Griffith, Jr. *The Treasury and Monetary Policy, 1933–1938.* Cambridge, Mass.: Harvard University Press, 1939.

Johnson, Paul. *Modern Times: The World from the Twenties to the Eighties.* New York: Harper & Row, 1983.

Jones, Joseph M., Jr. *Tariff Retaliation: Repercussions of the Hawley-Smoot Bill.* Philadelphia: University of Pennsylvania Press, 1934.

Jonung, Lars. "The Depression in Sweden and the United States: A Comparison of Causes and Policies." In *The Great Depression*

Revisited, edited by Karl Brunner, 286–315. The Hague: Martinus Nijhoff, 1981.

Kahn, A. E. *Great Britain in the World Economy*. New York: Columbia University Press; London: Pitman, 1946.

Kahn, R. F. "The Relation of Home Investment to Unemployment." *Economic Journal* 41, no. 2 (June 1931): 193–98.

———. *The Making of Keynes' General Theory*. Cambridge: Cambridge University Press, 1984.

Keese, Dietmar. "Die volkswirtschaftlichen Gesamtgrössen für das Deutsche Reich in den Jahren 1925–36." In *Die Staats- und Wirtschaftskrise des Deutschen Reiches, 1929–1933*, edited by Werner Conze and Hans Rospach, 35–81. Stuttgart: Ernst Klett, 1967.

Keohane, Robert O. *After Hegemony: Cooperation and Discord in the World Political Economy*. Princeton: Princeton University Press, 1984.

Keynes, J. M. *The Economic Consequences of the Peace*. London: Macmillan, 1919; New York: Harcourt Brace, 1920.

———. *Treatise on Money*. 2 vols. London: Macmillan; New York: Harcourt Brace, 1930.

———. "The Great Slump of 1930." *The Nation and Athenaeum* (December 1930). Reprinted in *Essays in Persuasion*, 135–49. New York: Harcourt Brace, 1932.

———. "The Consequences to the Banks of the Collapse of Money Values." *Vanity Fair*, August 1931. Reprinted in *The Collected Writings of John Maynard Keynes*, vol. 9: *Essays in Persuasion*, 150–58. Cambridge: Royal Economic Society, 1972.

———. "An Economic Analysis of Unemployment." In *Unemployment as a World Problem*, edited by Q. Wright, 3–42. Norman Wait Harris Lectures for 1931. Chicago: University of Chicago Press, 1931.

———. *Essays in Persuasion*. London: Macmillan, 1931; New York: Harcourt Brace, 1932.

———. *The Means to Prosperity*. London: Macmillan; New York: Harcourt Brace, 1933.

———. "National Self-Sufficiency." *Yale Review* 22, no. 4 (June 1933): 755–69.

———. *The General Theory of Employment, Interest, and Money*. London: Macmillan; New York: Harcourt Brace, 1936.

Keynes, J. M., and H. D. Henderson. *Can Lloyd George Do It?* London: The Nation and Athenaeum, 1929.

Kindleberger, Charles P. "Competitive Currency Depreciation Between Denmark and New Zealand." *Harvard Business Review* 12, no. 4 (July 1934): 416–27.

―――. *The Dollar Shortage.* Cambridge, Mass.: Technology Press, 1950.

―――. *The Terms of Trade: A European Case Study.* New York: The Technology Press of Massachusetts Institute of Technology and John Wiley & Sons, 1956.

―――. "International Monetary Politics of a Near-Great Power: Two French Episodes, 1926–36 and 1960–70." *Economic Notes* (Monte dei Paschi di Siena) 1, nos. 2–3 (1972): 30–44.

―――. *Manias, Panics, and Crashes: A History of Financial Crises.* New York: Basic Books, 1978.

―――. "The International Causes and Consequences of the Great Crash." *Journal of Portfolio Management* 6, no. 1 (Fall 1979): 11–14.

―――. "The Cyclical Pattern of Long-Term Lending." In *The Theory and Experience of Economic Development: Essays in Honour of Sir W. Arthur Lewis,* edited by Mark Gersovitz et al., 300–312. London: Allen & Unwin, 1982.

―――. *A Financial History of Western Europe.* London: Allen & Unwin, 1984.

―――. "International Propagation of Financial Crises: The Experience of 1888–93." In *International Capital Movements, Debt, and Monetary System,* edited by Wolfram Engels, Armin Gutowski, and Henry Wallich, 217–34. Mainz: Hase & Koehler, 1984.

Kindleberger, Charles P., and Jean-Pierre Laffargue, eds. *Financial Crises: Theory, History, and Policy.* Cambridge: Cambridge University Press, 1982.

Klein, Burton H. *Germany's Economic Preparations for War.* Cambridge, Mass.: Harvard University Press, 1959.

Krasner, Stephen D. "Structural Causes and Regime Consequences: Regimes as Intervening Variables." In *International Regimes,* edited by Stephen D. Krasner, 1–21. Ithaca, N.Y.: Cornell University Press, 1983.

Kreider, Carl. *The Anglo-American Trade Agreement: A Study of*

British and American Commercial Policies, 1934–39. Princeton: Princeton University Press, 1943.

Krohn, Claus Dieter. "Wirtschaftstheorie als politische Interessen: Die akademische Nationalökonomie in Deutschland, 1918–1933." *Campus Forschung* 226 (1981).

Kroll, Gerhard. "Die deutsche Wirtschaftspolitik in der Weltwirtschaftskrise." In *Moderne deutsche Wirtschaftsgeschichte*, edited by Karl Erich Born, 398–409. Cologne: Kiepenheuer & Witsch, 1966.

Laffargue, Jean-Pierre. See Kindleberger, Charles P., and Jean-Pierre Laffargue.

Lalumière, Pierre. *L'inspection des finances.* Paris: Presses Universitaires de France, 1959.

Lary, Hal B. *The United States in the World Economy: The International Transactions of the United States During the Interwar Period.* Washington, D.C.: U.S. Government Printing Office, 1943.

Latham, A. J. H. *The Depression and the Developing World, 1914–1939.* Totowa, N.J.: Barnes & Noble, 1981.

Lautenbach, Wilhelm. *Zins, Kredit und Produktion,* edited by Wolfgang Stützel. Tübingen: J. C. B. Mohr (Paul Siebeck), 1952.

League of Nations. (Bertil Ohlin). *The Course and Phases of the World Economic Depression.* Geneva: League of Nations, 1931.

———. *Balance of Payments, 1930.* Geneva: League of Nations, 1932.

———. *Review of World Trade, 1934.* Geneva: League of Nations, 1934.

———. Sixth International Studies Conference. A record of a second study conference on "The State and Economic Life," held in London, May 29–June 2, 1933. Paris: International Institute of Intellectual Cooperation, 1934.

———. (James E. Meade). *World Economic Survey, 1937–38.* Geneva: League of Nations, 1938.

———. (James E. Meade). *World Economic Survey, 1938–39.* Geneva: League of Nations, 1939.

———. *Review of World Trade, 1938.* Geneva: League of Nations, 1939.

———. (F. Hilgerdt). *The Network of World Trade.* Geneva: League of Nations, 1942.

———. (Ragnar Nurkse). *International Currency Experience: Les-*

sons of the Interwar Period. Princeton, N.J.: League of Nations, 1944.

—. *Economic Stability in the Postwar World: Report of the Delegation on Economic Depression.* Geneva: League of Nations, 1945.

—. *Statistical Yearbook.* Various issues.

—. *Monthly Bulletin of Statistics.* Various issues.

Leith-Ross, Frederick. *Money Talks: Fifty Years of International Finance.* London: Hutchinson, 1968.

Lewis, William Arthur. *Economic Survey, 1919–1939.* London: Allen & Unwin, 1949; Philadelphia: Blakiston, 1950.

—. Review of C. P. Kindleberger, *The World in Depression, 1929–1939.* In *Journal of Interdisciplinary History* 6 (1975): 172–74.

Lindert, Peter H. "Key Currencies and Gold, 1900–1913." *Studies in International Finance.* International Finance Section, Princeton University, no. 24 (August 1969).

Londoño, Carlos. See Thorp, Rosemary, and Carlos Londoño.

Lüke, Rolf E. *Von der Stabilisierung zur Krise.* Zürich: Polygraphischer, 1958.

Lundberg, Erik. *Business Cycles and Economic Policy.* Translated by J. Potter. London: Allen & Unwin, 1957.

—. *Instability and Economic Growth.* New Haven: Yale University Press, 1968.

Luther, Hans. *Vor dem Abgrund, 1930–1933: Reichsbankpräsident in Krisenzeiten.* Berlin: Propyläen, 1964.

McFerrin, John Berry. *Caldwell and Company: A Southern Financial Empire.* Chapel Hill: University of North Carolina Press, 1939. Reissued, Nashville, Tenn.: Vanderbilt University Press, 1969.

Maier, Charles S. "The Two Postwar Eras and the Conditions for Stability in Twentieth-Century Western Europe." *American Historical Review* 86, no. 1 (April 1981): 327–52.

Malach, Vernon W. *International Cycles and Canada's Balance of Payments, 1921–33.* Toronto: University of Toronto Press, 1954.

Malenbaum, Wilfred. *The World Wheat Economy, 1885–1939.* Cambridge, Mass.: Harvard University Press, 1953.

Mantoux, Etienne. *The Carthaginian Peace, or the Economic Consequences of Mr. Keynes.* New York: Charles Scribner's Sons, 1952.

Marcus, Edward. *Canada and the International Business Cycle, 1927–39*. New York: Bookman Associates, 1954.

März, Edouard. Comment on "Policy in the Crises of 1920 and 1929," by D. E. Moggridge. In *Financial Crises: Theory, History, and Policy*, edited by Charles P. Kindleberger and Jean-Pierre Laffargue, 187–94. Cambridge: Cambridge University Press, 1982.

Matthews, R. C. O. *A Study in Trade-Cycle History: Economic Fluctuations in Great Britain, 1832–1842*. Cambridge: Cambridge University Press, 1954.

Meade, James E. See League of Nations. (James E. Meade).

Meltzer, Allan H. "Monetary and Other Explanations of the Start of the Great Depression." *Journal of Monetary Economics* 2 (1976): 455–72.

———. "Comments on 'Monetarist Interpretations of the Great Depression.'" In *The Great Depression Revisited*, edited by Karl Brunner, 148–64. The Hague: Martinus Nijhoff, 1981.

Menne, Bernhard. *The Case of Dr. Brüning*. London: Hutchinson, 1943.

Meyer, Richard H. *Banker's Diplomacy: Monetary Stabilization in the Twenties*. New York: Columbia University Press, 1970.

Migone, Gian Giacomo. *Gli Stati Uniti e il fascismo: Alle origini dell' egemonia Americana in Italia*. Milan: Feltrinelli, 1980.

Ministère des Finances et Ministère de l'Agriculture, du Commerce et des Travaux Publics. *Enquête sur les principes et les faits généraux qui régissent la circulation monétaire et fiduciaire*. 6 vols. Paris: Imprimerie Impériale, 1867.

Mintz, Ilse. *Deterioration in the Quality of Foreign Bonds Issued in the United States, 1920–1930*. New York: National Bureau of Economic Research, 1951.

Mishkin, Frederic S. "The Household Balance Sheet and the Great Depression." *Journal of Economic History* 38, no. 4 (December 1978): 918–37.

Mitchell, Broadus. *Depression Decade: From New Era Through New Deal, 1929–1941*. New York: Rinehart & Winston, 1947; New York: Harper & Row, 1969.

Modigliani, Franco. See Neisser, Hans, and Franco Modigliani.

Moggridge, D. E. *The Return to Gold, 1925: The Formulation of Economic Policy and Its Critics*. Cambridge: Cambridge University Press, 1969.

————. *British Monetary Policy, 1924–31: The Norman Conquest of $4.86*. Cambridge: Cambridge University Press, 1972.

————. "Policy in the Crises of 1920 and 1929." In *Financial Crises: Theory, History, and Policy*, edited by Charles P. Kindleberger and Jean-Pierre Laffargue, 171–87. Cambridge: Cambridge University Press, 1982.

Moley, Raymond. With the assistance of Elliott Rosen. *The First New Deal*. New York: Harcourt, Brace & World, 1966.

Moll, J. Th. See Neytzell de Wilde, A., and J. Th. Moll.

Montgomery, Arthur. *How Sweden Overcame the Depression, 1930–1933*. Stockholm: A. Bonniers, 1938.

Moreau, Emile. *Souvenirs d'un gouverneur de la Banque de France: Histoire de la stabilisation du franc (1926–1928)*. Paris: Génin, 1954.

Morgenstern, Oskar. *International Financial Transactions and Business Cycles*. Princeton: Princeton University Press, 1959.

Morgenthau, Henry. See Blum, John Morton.

Morison, Elting E. *Turmoil and Tradition: A Study of the Life and Times of Henry L. Stimson*. Boston: Houghton Mifflin, 1960.

Moulton, Harold G., and Leo Pasvolsky. *War Debts and World Prosperity*. Washington, D.C.: Brookings Institution, 1932.

Nanto, Dick K., and Shinji Takagi. "Korekiyo Takahashi and Japan's Recovery from the Great Depression." *American Economic Review* 75 (May 1985): 369–74.

Neal, Larry. "The Economics and Finance of Bilateral Clearing Agreements: Germany, 1934–38." *Economic History Review*, 2d ser. 32, no. 3 (August 1979): 391–404.

Neisser, Hans. *Some International Aspects of the Business Cycle*. Philadelphia: University of Pennsylvania Press, 1936.

Neisser, Hans, and Franco Modigliani. *National Incomes and International Trade: A Quantitative Analysis*. Urbana: University of Illinois Press, 1953.

Néré, J. *La crise de 1929*. Paris: Colin, 1968.

Nevin, Edward. *The Mechanism of Cheap Money: A Study in British Monetary Policy, 1931–1939*. Cardiff: University of Wales Press, 1955.

Newbold, J. T. W. "The Beginnings of the World Crisis, 1873–1896." *Economic History* 2, no. 7 (January 1932): 425–551.

New York Times. Various issues.

Neytzell de Wilde, A., and J. Th. Moll. With the assistance of A. J. Gooszen. *The Netherlands Indies During the Depression: A Brief Economic Survey*. Amsterdam: J. M. Meulenhoff, 1936.

Nichols, Jeannette P. "Roosevelt's Monetary Diplomacy, 1933." *American Historical Review* 56, no. 2 (January 1951): 295–317.

Niveau, Maurice. *Histoire des faits économiques contemporains*. 2d ed. Paris: Presses Universitaires de France, 1969.

Nötel, Rudolf. "Money, Banking and Industry in Interwar Austria and Hungary." *Journal of European Economic History* 13 (1984): 137–202.

Noyes, Alexander Dana. *The Market Place: Reminiscences of a Financial Editor*. Boston: Little, Brown, 1938.

Nurkse, Ragnar. "International Monetary Equilibrium." *Essays in International Finance*. International Finance Section, Princeton University, no. 4 (April 1945). Reprinted in American Economic Association, *Readings in the Theory of International Trade*. Philadelphia: Blakiston, 1949.

————. See also League of Nations. (Ragnar Nurkse).

O'Connell, Arturo. "Argentina into the Depression: The Problems of an Open Economy." In *Latin America in the 1930s: The Periphery in World Crisis*, edited by Rosemary Thorp, 188–221. London: Macmillan, 1984.

Ohlin, Bertil. See League of Nations. (Bertil Ohlin).

Oppenheimer, Joe A. See Froelich, Norman, and Joe A. Oppenheimer.

Pasvolsky, Leo. See Moulton, Harold G., and Leo Pasvolsky.

Patrick, Hugh T. "The Economic Muddle of the 1920s." In *Dilemmas of Growth in Prewar Japan*, edited by James William Morley, 211–66. Princeton: Princeton University Press, 1971.

Pedersen, Jørgen. *Essays in Monetary Theory and Related Subjects*. Copenhagen: Samfundsvidenskabeligt Forlag, 1975.

Penrose, E. F. *Economic Planning for the Peace*. Princeton: Princeton University Press, 1953.

Pentzlin, Heinz. *Hjalmar Schacht: Leben und Wirken einer umstrittenen Persönlichkeit*. Berlin: Ullstein, 1980.

Perrot, M. *La Monnaie et l'opinion en France et en Angleterre, 1924–36*. Paris: Colin, 1955.

Pigou, A. C. *Aspects of British Economic History, 1918–1925*. London: Macmillan, 1948.

Platt, D. C. M. *Foreign Finance in Continental Europe and the United States, 1815–1870: Quantities, Origins, Functions, and Distribution.* London: Allen & Unwin, 1984.

Pohl, Manfred. *Hermann J. Abs: A Biography in Text and Pictures.* Mainz: Hase & Koehler, 1983.

Pressburger, Fritz Georg. "Die Krise der Österreichischen Creditanstalt." *Revue internationale de l'histoire de la banque* 2 (1969): 83–118.

Rabelo Versiani, Flavio. "Brazilian Industrial Growth: The 1920s and the Depression." In *Latin America in the 1930s: The Periphery in World Crisis,* edited by Rosemary Thorp, 163–87. London: Macmillan, 1984.

Reddaway, W. B. "Was $4.86 Inevitable in 1925?" *Lloyds Bank Review,* no. 96 (April 1970): 15–28.

Reuss, Frederick G. *Fiscal Policy for Growth Without Inflation: The German Experiment.* Baltimore: Johns Hopkins University Press, 1963.

Review Committee for Balance of Payments Statistics. Report to the Budget Bureau. *The Balance of Payments Statistics of the United States: A Review and Appraisal* (E. M. Bernstein Report). Washington, D.C.: U.S. Government Printing Office, 1965.

Richardson, H. W. *Economic Recovery in Britain, 1932–39.* London: Weidenfeld & Nicolson, 1967.

Richardson, H. W., and D. Aldcroft. *Building in the British Economy Between the Wars.* London: Allen & Unwin, 1969.

Rist, Charles. "L'expérience de 1926 et la franc d'aujourd'hui." In *Monnaie d'hier et de demain,* edited by J. Lacour-Gayet et al. Paris: Editions SPID, 1952.

Robbins, Lionel. *The Great Depression.* London: Macmillan, 1934.
———. *Autobiography of an Economist.* London: Macmillan, 1971.

Rolfe, Sidney E., and James L. Burtle. *The Great Wheel: The World Monetary System.* New York: Quadrangle Books, 1973.

Roose, Kenneth D. *The Economics of Recession and Revival: An Interpretation of 1937–38.* New Haven: Yale University Press, 1954.

Roosevelt, Franklin D. *The Papers and Addresses of Franklin Delano Roosevelt.* Vol. 2: *The Years of Crisis.* New York: Random House, 1938. Vol. 7: *The Continuing Struggle for Liberalism.* New York: Macmillan, 1941.

Röpke, Wilhelm. *Crises and Cycles*. London: William Hodge, n.d. (1936?).

———. *International Economic Disintegration*. New York: Macmillan, 1942.

Rosen, Elliott. See Moley, Raymond.

Rostow, W. W. "The Strategic Role of Theory: A Comment." *Journal of Economic History* 31, no. 1 (March 1971): 76–86.

———. *The World Economy: Theory and Prospect*. Austin: University of Texas Press, 1978.

Rothbard, Murray. *America's Great Depression*. 3d ed. Kansas City, Kan.: Sheed & Ward, 1975.

Rothschild, K. W. *Austria's Economic Development Between the Wars*. London: Muller, 1947.

Rueff, Jacques. Preface to *Souvenirs d'un gouverneur de la Banque de France*, by Emile Moreau. Paris: Génin, 1954.

———. "Sur un point d'histoire: Le niveau de la stabilisation Poincaré." *Revue d'économie politique* 69 (March–April 1959): 169–78.

Sachs, Jeffrey. "LDC Debt in the 1980s, Risk and Reforms." In *Crises in the Economic and Financial Structure*, edited by Paul Wachtel, 197–243. Lexington, Mass.: D. C. Heath, 1982.

Safarian, A. E. *The Canadian Economy in the Great Depression*. Toronto: University of Toronto Press, 1959.

Salter, Arthur. *Recovery: The Second Effort*. London: Bell; New York: Century, 1932.

———. *Memoirs of a Public Servant*. London: Faber & Faber, 1961.

———. *Slave of the Lamp*. London: Weidenfeld & Nicolson, 1967.

Samuelson, Paul A. "Myths and Realities about the Crash and Depression." *Journal of Portfolio Management* 6, no. 1 (Fall 1979): 7–10.

Sauvy, Alfred. *Histoire économique de la France entre les deux guerres*. Vol. 1: *1918–1931*. Paris: Fayard, 1965. Vol. 2: *1931–1939*. Paris: Fayard, 1967.

Sayers, R. S. "The Springs of Technical Progress in Britain, 1919–1939." *Economic Journal* 60, no. 238 (June 1950): 275–91.

———. *The Bank of England, 1891–1944*. 3 vols. Cambridge: Cambridge University Press, 1976.

Schacht, Hjalmar H. G. *The Stabilization of the Mark*. London: Allen & Unwin, 1927.

————. *The End of Reparations.* London: Jonathan Cape; New York: Jonathan Cape & Harrison Smith, 1931.

————. "Germany's Colonial Demands." *Foreign Affairs* 15, no. 2 (January 1937): 223–34.

————. *Confessions of the "Old Wizard."* Boston: Houghton Mifflin, 1956. Published in England under the title *My First Seventy-Six Years.* London: Allan Wingate, 1955.

Schattschneider, E. E. *Politics, Pressures and Tariffs: A Study of Free Private Enterprise in Pressure Politics as Shown by the 1929–30 Revision of the Tariff.* New York: Prentice-Hall, 1935.

Schlesinger, Arthur M., Jr. *The Age of Roosevelt.* Vol. 2: *The Coming of the New Deal.* Boston: Houghton Mifflin, 1959; London: Heinemann, 1960.

Schliemann, Jürgen. *Die deutsche Währung in der Weltwirtschaftskrise, 1929–33: Währungspolitik und Abwertungskontroverse unter den Bedingungen der Reparationen.* Berne: Paul Haupt, 1980.

Schmidt, Carl T. *German Business Cycles, 1924–1933.* New York: National Bureau of Economic Research, 1934.

Schmidt, Paul. *Statist auf diplomatischen Bühne, 1923–45.* Bonn: Athenäum-Verlag, 1949.

Schrecker, Ellen. *The Hired Money: The French Debt to the United States.* New York: Arno Press, 1978.

Schuker, Stephen A. *The End of French Predominance in Europe: The Financial Crisis of 1924 and the Adoption of the Dawes Plan.* Chapel Hill: University of North Carolina Press, 1976.

————. Review of *The Collected Writings of John Maynard Keynes,* vol. 17: *Activities 1922–1932: Treaty Revision and Reconstruction*; vol. 18: *Activities 1922–1932: The End of Reparations,* edited by Elizabeth Johnson. *Journal of Economic Literature* 18, no. 1 (March 1980): 124–26.

Schumpeter, Joseph A. *Business Cycles: A Theoretical, Historical and Statistical Analysis of the Capitalist Process.* 2 vols. New York: McGraw-Hill, 1939.

Schwartz, Anna J. "Understanding 1929–1933." In *The Great Depression Revisited,* edited by Karl Brunner, 5–48. The Hague: Martinus Nijhoff.

————. See also Friedman, Milton, and Anna Jacobson Schwartz.

Schwartz, Jordan. *1933: Roosevelt's Decision: The United States Leaves the Gold Standard.* New York: Chelsea House, 1969.

Seymour, Charles. See House, E. M., and Charles Seymour.

Shaplen, Robert. *Kreuger, Genius and Swindler.* New York: Alfred A. Knopf, 1960; London: André Deutsch, 1961.

Shearer, Ronald A., and Carolyn Clark. "Canada and the Interwar Gold Standard, 1920–35: Monetary Policy Without a Central Bank." In *A Retrospective on the Classical Gold Standard, 1821–1931,* edited by Michael D. Bordo and Anna J. Schwartz, 277–309. Chicago: University of Chicago Press, 1984.

Silberman, Charles. See Burch, Gilbert, and Charles Silberman.

Simpson, Amos E. *Hjalmar Schacht in Perspective.* The Hague: Mouton, 1969.

Skidelsky, Robert. *Politicians and the Slump: The Labour Government of 1929–1931.* London: Macmillan, 1967.

Sobel, Robert. *The Great Bull Market: Wall Street in the 1920s.* New York: W. W. Norton, 1968.

Stimson, Henry L., and McGeorge Bundy. *On Active Service in Peace and War.* New York: Harper & Bros., 1947.

Stolper, Gustav. *German Economy, 1870–1940: Issues and Trends.* New York: Reynal & Hitchcock; London: Allen & Unwin, 1940.

Stuart, G. M. Verrijn. "The Netherlands During the Recent Depression." In *The Lessons of Monetary Experience: Essays in Honor of Irving Fisher,* edited by A. D. Gayer, 237–58. New York: Farrar & Rinehart; London: Allen & Unwin, 1937.

Stucken, Rudolf. *Deutsche Geld- und Kreditpolitik, 1914 bis 1963.* Tübingen: J. C. B. Mohr (Paul Siebeck), 1964.

Sturmthal, Adolf. *The Tragedy of European Labor, 1918–1939.* New York: Columbia University Press, 1943; London: Gollancz, 1944.

Svennilson, Ingvar. *Growth and Stagnation in the European Economy.* Economic Commission for Europe. Geneva: United Nations, 1954.

Swerling, Boris C. See Timoshenko, Vladimir P., and Boris C. Swerling.

Takagi, Shinji. See Nanto, Dick K., and Shinji Takagi.

Tavernier, K. See Wee, Herman van der, and K. Tavernier.

Taylor, Henry C., and Anne Dewess Taylor. *World Trade in Agricultural Products.* New York: Macmillan, 1943.

Temin, Peter. "Three Problems in Economic History." *Journal of Economic History* 31, no. 1 (March 1971): 58–75.

———. "The Beginning of the Depression in Germany." *Economic History Review* 24, no. 2 (May 1971): 240–48.

————. *Did Monetary Forces Cause the Great Depression?* New York: W. W. Norton, 1976.

Thomas, Brinley. *Monetary Policy and Crisis: A Study of Swedish Experience.* London: Routledge, 1936.

Thomas, Mark. Discussion of "Keynes and Protection," by Barry Eichengreen. *Journal of Economic History* 44, no. 2 (June 1984): 375–79.

Thorp, Rosemary. Introduction to *Latin America in the 1930s: The Periphery in World Crisis*, edited by Rosemary Thorp, 1–16. London: Macmillan, 1984.

————, ed. *Latin America in the 1930s: The Periphery in World Crisis.* London: Macmillan, 1984.

Thorp, Rosemary, and Carlos Londoño. "The Effect of the Great Depression on the Economies of Peru and Colombia." In *Latin America in the 1930s: The Periphery in World Crisis*, edited by Rosemary Thorp, 81–110. London: Macmillan, 1984.

Timoshenko, Vladimir P. *World Agriculture and the Depression.* Ann Arbor: University of Michigan Press, 1953.

Timoshenko, Vladimir P., and Boris C. Swerling. *The World's Sugar: Progress and Policy.* Stanford: Stanford University Press, 1957.

Toniolo, Gianni. "Crisi economica e smobilizzo pubblico delle banche miste (1930–1934)." In *Industria e banca nella grande crisi 1929–1934*, edited by Gianni Toniolo, 284–352. Milan: Etas Libri, 1978.

————. *L'economia dell' Italia fascista.* Rome: Laterza, 1980.

————. "Per un' analisi comparata delle cause delle crisi bancarie nell' Europa dei primi anni Trenta." In Banco di Roma, *Le istituzioni finanziarie degli anni Trenta nell' Europa continentale*, 219–35. Bologna: Il Mulino, 1982.

Tortella Casares, Gabriel, and Jordi Palafox. "Banche e industria in Spagna, 1918–1936." In Banco di Roma, *Le istituzioni finanziarie degli anni Trenta nell' Europa continentale*, 161–96. Bologna: Il Mulino, 1982.

Treviranus, Gottfried Reinhold. *Das Ende von Weimar: Heinrich Brüning und seine Zeit.* Düsseldorf: Econ-Verlag, 1968.

Triantis, Stephen G. *Cyclical Changes in Trade Balances of Countries Exporting Primary Products, 1927–1933.* Toronto: University of Toronto Press, 1967.

Triffin, Robert. "La théorie de la surévaluation monétaire et la dévaluation belge." *Bulletin de l'Institut des Recherches Economiques de l'Université de Louvain* 9, no. 1 (November 1937): 3–36.

Tugwell, Rexford G. *The Brains Trust*. New York: Viking Press, 1968.

United Nations. *Commodity Trade and Economic Development*. Report by a Committee of Experts. New York, 1952.

U.S. Bureau of the Census. *Historical Statistics of the United States, 1789–1945*. Washington, D.C.: U.S. Government Printing Office, 1949.

U.S. Department of State. *Foreign Relations of the United States*. Washington, D.C.: U.S. Government Printing Office. Various issues.

van der Wee, Herman. See Wee, Herman van der.

Vansittart, Lord. *The Mist Procession: The Autobiography of Lord Vansittart*. London: Hutchinson, 1958.

Vaubel, Roland. "International Debt, Bank Failures and the Money Supply: The Thirties and the Eighties." *Cato Journal* 4, no. 1 (Summer 1984): 249–67.

Wachtel, Paul, ed. *Crisis in the Economic and Financial Structure*. Lexington, Mass.: D. C. Heath, 1982.

Walker, E. Ronald. *Australia in the World Depression*. London: P. S. King, 1933.

Wanniski, Jude. *The Way the World Works*. New York: Basic Books, 1977.

Warburg, James P. *The Long Road Home: The Autobiography of a Maverick*. Garden City, N.Y.: Doubleday, 1964.

Warren, George F., and Frank A. Pearson. *Prices*. New York: Wiley, 1933.

Webb, Steven B. "The Supply of Money and Reichsbank Financing of Government and Corporate Debt in Germany, 1919–1923." *Journal of Economic History* 44, no. 2 (June 1984): 499–507.

Wee, Herman van der, ed. *The Great Depression Revisited: Essays on the Economies of the Thirties*. The Hague: Martinus Nijhoff, 1972.

Wee, Herman van der, and K. Tavernier. *Le Banque Nationale de Belgique et l'histoire monétaire entre les deux guerres mondiales*. Brussels: National Bank of Belgium, 1975.

Weinstein, Michael M. "Some Macroeconomic Impacts of the National Industrial Recovery Act, 1933–1935." In *The Great*

Depression Revisited, edited by Karl Brunner, 262–81. The Hague: Martinus Nijhoff, 1981.

White, Eugene Nelson. "A Reinterpretation of the Banking Crisis of 1930." *Journal of Economic History* 44, no. 1 (March 1984): 119–38.

Whittlesey, Charles R. See Graham, Frank D., and Charles R. Whittlesey.

Wicker, Elmus R. *Federal Reserve Monetary Policy, 1917–1933*. New York: Random House, 1966.

———. "A Reconsideration of the Causes of the Banking Panic of 1930." *Journal of Economic History* 40, no. 3 (September 1980): 571–84.

Wilcox, James A. See Gordon, Robert J., and James A. Wilcox.

Williams, David. "London and the 1931 Financial Crisis." *Economic History Review*, 2d ser. 15, no. 3 (April 1963): 513–28.

Williams, John H. *Postwar Monetary Plans and Other Essays*. New York: Alfred A. Knopf, 1947.

Williams, William Appleman. *The Tragedy of American Diplomacy*. Cleveland: World Publishing, 1959.

Williamson, John, ed. *IMF Conditionality*. Washington, D.C.: Institute for International Economics, 1983.

Winch, Donald. See Howson, Susan K., and Donald Winch.

Woytinsky, Emma S., ed. *So Much Alive: The Life and Work of W. S. Woytinsky*. New York: Vanguard Press, 1962.

Woytinsky, W. S. *Internationale Hebung der Preise als Ausweg der Krise*. Leipzig, 1931.

———. "International Measures to Create Employment: A Remedy for the Depression." *International Labor Review* 25, no. 1 (January 1932): 1–22.

———. *Stormy Passage: A Personal History Through Two Russian Revolutions to Democracy and Freedom, 1905–1960*. New York: Vanguard Press, 1961.

Wright, H. R. C. "Fears of Inflation in 1919: Wage Push and Conspiracy Theories." Paper presented on "Topics in Economic History" at the Canadian Economic Association meeting, Dalhousie University, Halifax, Nova Scotia, May 25, 1981.

Youngson, A. J. *The British Economy, 1920–57*. London: Allen & Unwin, 1960.

Index

Karstedt Company, 149
Keese, Dietmar, 131n
Kemmerer, Edwin J., 182
Keohane, Robert O., 289n
Kettner, 144
Key countries, 203n
Key currency, 203n
Keynes, John Maynard, 7, 154, 177,
  226, 259–60, 289, 297, 304; and
  pound stabilization, 29, 30, 31,
  176n, 258n, 303; on price behavior, 29, 139, 168–69, 225n; and
  public works spending, 172n,
  210; on reparations, 18, 23, 250;
  sterling depreciation urged by,
  159–60; on tariffs, 126, 303; and
  war debts, 25; and World Eco-
  nomic Conference, 31, 209, 210,
  216, 259
Keynesians/Keynesianism, xv, 71–
  72, 250, 271n, 272, 273–75;
  Depression analysis of, xiii, 4–5,
  181, 289; Japanese familiar with,
  163; Nazis and, 175n; and public
  works spending, 172n, 273, 285.
  See also Keynes, John Maynard
Keynes-Kahn multiplier, 163, 172n
Kiel, 175n
Kindersley, Robert, 143, 155, 204,
  207n
Kitchin short cycle, 3
Klingenhagen, Barbara, xxii
Kolmar & Co., 144
Komiya, Ryutaro, xxii, 164n
Kondratieff long cycle, 3
Korea, 280
Kraft durch Freude ("Strength
  through Joy"), 237
Krämer, Carl, 160
Kreuger, Ivar, 179, 181
Kreuger & Toll, 118, 179n
Kroll, Gerhard, 161n
Krona, 180, 181n
Kuznets cycle, 3
Kwantung, 280

Labor, 14, 16; British, 42; French,
  6, 16, 251–55; German, 16, 19,

237–38; U.S., 231–32. See also
  Employment rates; Wages
Labour government: Australian, 80;
  British, 28–29, 30, 31, 64, 101,
  126, 156, 295
Lamont, Thomas, 21, 296
Land speculation, 14, 53
Land tenure, 72, 84
Lard, 83
Lary, Hal B., 100n, 292
Latin America, 243–44; and agri-
  culture, 73–84 passim, 139, 189–
  90, 243, 277; debts in, 90n, 243;
  German clearing arrangements
  with, 238; gold losses in, 88; in-
  vestment in, 122; lending to, 22,
  39, 41, 54–55, 118, 122, 281; Re-
  ciprocal Trade Agreement Act
  and, 235. See also individual
  countries
Latin Monetary Union, 246
Lausanne Conference, 18, 172, 174,
  175–76, 192, 202
Lautenbach, Wilhelm, xxii, 7, 171
Laval, Pierre, 6, 142, 150, 175, 202,
  249, 251
Layton, Walter, 153, 209
Leadership, 11, 65, 286–87, 294–
  305 passim; Britain and, 11, 127,
  289, 290–91, 295–96, 298, 299,
  301, 302; British-French central
  bank, 38, 52–53, 147, 296, 301;
  U.S. and, 11, 125–26, 286–87,
  289, 294–305 passim
League of Nations, 46–47, 74, 202,
  258, 284, 285–86, 295, 303; and
  Austrian loans, 144, 146–47;
  Roosevelt and, 197; sanctions on
  Italy sought by, 239–40; and tariff
  truce, 64; U.S. and, 21, 296–97
"Leave-it-alone liquidationists,"
  119n
Lederer, Emil, 175n
Lee, Higginson & Co., 118, 133
Leffingwell, Rufus, 25n
Lehman, H. H., 196
Leith-Ross, Frederick, 66, 68–69,
  157, 203, 205, 223

Designer: Rick Chafian
Compositor: Wilsted & Taylor
Text: 10/12 Times Roman
Display: Times Roman
Printer: Murray Printing Company
Binder: Murray Printing Company